SSSP

Springer
Series in
Social
Psychology

SSSP

Daniel Bar-Tal   Carl F. Graumann
Arie W. Kruglanski   Wolfgang Stroebe
Editors

Stereotyping and Prejudice
Changing Conceptions

Springer-Verlag New York Berlin Heidelberg
London Paris Tokyo

Daniel Bar-Tal
School of Education
Tel-Aviv University
Tel-Aviv 69978
Israel

Carl F. Graumann
Psychologisches Institut
Universität Heidelberg
D-6900 Heidelberg 1
Federal Republic of Germany

Arie W. Kruglanski
Department of Psychology
University of Maryland
College Park, MD 20742
USA

Wolfgang Stroebe
Psychologisches Institut
Universität Tübingen
7400 Tübingen
Federal Republic of Germany

Library of Congress Cataloging-in-Publication Data
Stereotyping and prejudice : changing conceptions / Daniel Bar-Tal . . .
   [et al.].
     p.   cm. — (Springer series in social psychology)
     ISBN 0-387-96883-0 (alk. paper)
     1. Stereotype (Psychology) 2. Prejudices. I. Bar-Tal, Daniel.
   II. Series.
   BF323.S63S74   1989
   305—dc19   88-38198

Printed on acid-free paper.

Typeset by Publishers Service, Bozeman, Montana.
Printed and bound by R.R. Donnelly & Sons, Harrisonburg, Virginia.
Printed in the United States of America.

9 8 7 6 5 4 3 2 1

ISBN 0-387-96883-0 Springer-Verlag New York Berlin Heidelberg
ISBN 3-540-96883-0 Springer-Verlag Berlin Heidelberg New York

Preface

The study of stereotyping and prejudice is a study of human nature, group membership, and intergroup relationships. It sheds light on each of these aspects of social psychology. With respect to the first two, it has been observed that since groups provide the best framework for satisfying various human needs, individuals continuously organize themselves in collectives. They belong to a variety of groups—many of which they voluntarily select and some to which they are ascribed. Group membership, therefore, is one of the most salient and important of an individual's characteristics.

The implication of this characteristic is that human beings not only constantly classify other people into group categories, either by identifying membership or constructing their own categories, but also judge and evaluate them on this basis. The stereotypes and prejudice are outcomes of this process. They are the beliefs and attitudes toward members of another group.

In addition, the study of stereotyping and prejudice reflects an interest in intergroup relationships. While we recognize that a discussion of intergroup relationships may focus on behaviors describing actions such as confrontations, violence, wars, cooperation, alliance, negotiation, or coordination, we also believe that each of these intergroup behaviors is mediated by perceptions, beliefs, and attitudes. In the case of intergroup behaviors, the listed actions are not performed instinctively or mindlessly, but are preceded by cognitive processes which, among other outputs, involve the formation of stereotypes and prejudice toward the other group. It is on their basis that a group decides on a course of action.

In view of the noted importance of stereotyping and prejudice as social constructs, it is not surprising that social psychology from its emergence as a discipline has devoted considerable attention to the study of these problems. Through the years different approaches and theories have been offered to explain the origin of these phenomena. Some of them had their life within the particular *zeitgeist* and later were moved into oblivion as new "fashionable" approaches appeared. Thus, for example, while in the 1940s the psychoanalytic influences directed the focus to the psychodynamic foundations of stereotyping and prejudice, in the 1950s and 1960s the attention shifted to the "realistic" conflict-based causes and in the 1970s, there was a preoccupation with group identity and its effects on intergroup relations, especially among Europeans. Presently, as the cognitive revolution successfully spreads its message, social psychologists mostly investigate the cognitive basis of stereotypes and prejudice formation. In this continuous development, each approach and theory provides a new perspective and adds another layer to the understanding.

It is obvious that the study of stereotyping and prejudice has important implications for the "real world" which is plagued by intergroup animosity, conflicts, and confrontations. It can be noted, to the credit of social psychology, that the study of stereotyping and prejudice is one of the few areas that has had an impact on the "real world." The results of studies as well as various conceptions served as a basis for different public policies in different countries. For example, policies of desegregation in the U.S. or integration in Israel were at least partially based on the accumulated knowledge in social psychology.

The present volume brings a collection of new contributions about stereotyping and prejudice to advance further our knowledge on these issues. Although they provide an array of views, they do reflect the present mainstream of social psychology, which is mainly cognitive. But, even within the cognitive framework, the different chapters discuss divergent emphases.

The idea to advance the knowledge about stereotyping and prejudice by publishing a book of original contributions emerged in Bad Homburg, Federal Republic of Germany. There, under the hospitality of the Werner-Reimers Foundation, a group of Europeans and Israelis met to discuss various aspects of stereotyping and prejudice. The editors decided to form a group of contributors which would cover the wide scope of present interests in this phenomenon. The final product reflects this objective. The volume presents 12 chapters which together shed complementary lights on the issues which have preoccupied human minds. We hope that the book will stimulate further interest and concern with the problem of stereotyping and prejudice.

Daniel Bar-Tal
Carl F. Graumann
Arie W. Kruglanski
Wolfgang Stroebe

Contents

Part III   Structure and Meaning of Stereotypes and Prejudice

Part IV   Change of Stereotypes and Prejudice

Contributors

Yehuda Amir, Department of Psychology, Bar-Ilan University, Ramat-Gan 52100, Israel.

Daniel Bar-Tal, School of Education, Tel-Aviv University, Tel-Aviv 69978, Israel.

Yoram Bar-Tal, School of Medicine, Tel-Aviv University, Tel-Aviv 69978, Israel.

Rachel Ben-Ari, Department of Psychology, Bar-Ilan University, Ramat-Gan 52100, Israel.

Susan T. Fiske, Department of Psychology, University of Massachusetts, Amherst, Massachusetts 01003, USA.

Carl F. Graumann, Psychologisches Institut, Universität Heidelberg, D-6900 Heidelberg 1, Federal Republic of Germany.

David L. Hamilton, Department of Psychology, University of California, Santa Barbara, California 93106, USA.

Miles Hewstone, Department of Psychology, University of Bristol, Bristol BS8 1HH, England.

Murray Horwitz, Department of Psychology, Boston College, Chestnut Hill, Massachusetts 02167, USA.

Arie W. Kruglanski, Department of Psychology, University of Maryland, College Park, MD 20742, USA.

Chester A. Insko, Department of Psychology, University of North Carolina, Chapel Hill, North Carolina 27514, USA.

Steven L. Neuberg, Department of Psychology, Arizona State University, Tempe, Arizona 85287, USA.

Jacob M. Rabbie, Instituut vor Sociale Psychologie, Rijksuniversiteit te Utrecht, 3508 TC Utrecht, The Netherlands.

Shalom H. Schwartz, Department of Psychology, The Hebrew University, Jerusalem 91905, Israel.

Steven J. Sherman, Department of Psychology, Indiana University, Bloomington, Indiana 47405, USA.

Walter G. Stephan, Department of Psychology, New Mexico State University, Las Cruces, New Mexico 88003, USA.

Wolfgang Stroebe, Psychologisches Institut, Universität Tübingen, 7400 Tübingen, Federal Republic of Germany.

Naomi Struch, Department of Psychology, The Hebrew University, Jerusalem 91905, Israel.

Yaacov Trope, Department of Psychology, The Hebrew University, Jersualem 91905, Israel.

Margret Wintermantel, Psychologisches Institut, Universität Heidelberg, D-6900 Heidelberg 1, Federal Republic of Germany.

Part I
Introduction

Chapter 1

Stereotype, Prejudice, and Discrimination: Changing Conceptions in Theory and Research

Wolfgang Stroebe and Chester A. Insko

Readers of the chapters on prejudice and discrimination in the three editions of the *Handbook of Social Psychology* (Harding, Kutner, Proshansky, & Chein, 1954; Harding, Proshansky, Kutner, & Chein, 1969; Stephan, 1985) will be impressed by the reduction in theoretical perspectives which this area seems to have experienced within the space of less than two decades. While the earlier chapters (Harding et al., 1954, 1969) approached prejudice and stereotypes from multiple theoretical perspectives, covering psychoanalytic, sociological, developmental, and personality-oriented explanations, Stephan's (1985) chapter focuses only on one perspective, the cognitive approach.

Obviously, there is nothing unusual if, in the course of scientific development, one theoretical approach is replaced by another. According to the "falsification-ist" position (Popper, 1963), science should develop from an interplay of conjectures and refutations, where theories are developed, severely tested, and then, typically after an accumulation of theory-divergent facts, replaced by new ones of higher empirical content (i.e., theories that explain all the facts accounted for by the old theories as well as those facts that were inconsistent with the old approach).

On closer inspection, however, it becomes apparent that the "falsificationist" model does not give a very accurate description of the development of theory and research in the area of prejudice and discrimination. Psychoanalytical and drive theoretical explanations of prejudice were not refuted empirically; they simply went out of fashion. Thus, Stephan (1985) does not even attempt to confront empirically the cognitive approach with these earlier theories. He justifies the exclusive concern with a cognitive analysis by arguing that "in the interval since the publication of the last *Handbook*, this area is the one in which the greatest advances in our knowledge have occurred" (p. 600).

Stephan's assessment is as true today as it was then. The emphasis on cognitive processes in most chapters of this volume demonstrates that the cognitive analysis is still dominant and empirically fruitful. However, the cognitive approach focuses on the organization of knowledge about groups into higher-level cognitive structures such as schemata, scripts, and prototypes, and thus offers a limited view of stereotype and prejudice. Even further, Stephan ignored much of the work on Social Identity Theory, which has also been very important in recent years (e.g., Tajfel, 1981, 1982; Turner, 1987). It would, therefore, seem timely to broaden our perspective once again and to examine whether some of the other approaches to the area of intergroup relations such as the "Realistic Conflict Theory" (Campbell, 1965; Sherif, 1967) the "Authoritarian Personality," (Adorno, Frenkel-Brunswick, Levinson, & Sanford, 1950), or the social learning theory (e.g., Eagly, 1987; Eagly & Kite, 1987; Eagly & Steffen, 1984) can add to our understanding of stereotypes and prejudice. So instead of staying within the confines of a social cognitive analysis, this chapter will attempt to present a more comprehensive treatment of theories and research on prejudice.

The chapter consists of two parts. The first part will be concerned with the conceptualization and measurement of social stereotypes and with the dynamic relationship between "stereotype" and the related concepts of "prejudice" and "discrimination." The focus of the chapter will be on outgroup stereotypes. It will be argued that the concepts of "stereotype" and "prejudice" are closely related and that prejudice as a negative attitude towards an outgroup or the members of that group is usually based on a negative stereotype, that is, on beliefs that associate that group with predominantly negative attributes. The second part of this chapter will review and evaluate the major theoretical approaches to stereotyping and prejudice. Since it will become obvious that each of these theoretical approaches offers only a partial explanation, we will end our theoretical discussion by outlining an integrative perspective on stereotypes and prejudice.

Social Stereotypes: Concept and Measurement

The Concept of "Stereotype"

There have been three distinct phases in the social psychological conceptualization of the term "stereotype," and it is quite instructive to review this development before we suggest our own definition. The word *stereotype* was originally coined in 1798 to describe a printing process involving the use of fixed casts of the pages of type (Ashmore & Del Boca, 1981). In the context of social and political ideas, the term was introduced by an American journalist, Walter Lippman, in 1922 to refer to the "pictures in our heads" of various social groups. As applied to cognitive representations of social groups, the stereotype metaphor seemingly implies undesirable rigidity, permanence, and lack of variability from application to application. Although Lippman himself was somewhat ambivalent in his evaluation of stereotypes, many social psychologists have regarded them as incorrect generalizations that are rigid, oversimplified, and biased (e.g., Allport, 1954; English & English, 1958; Katz and Braly, 1933; Klineberg, 1951). Typical of this position is the definition of English and English (1958) who conceive of stereotype as "a relatively rigid and oversimplified or biased perception or conception of an aspect of reality, especially of persons or social groups, ..." (p. 253).

After decades of vilification, Brown (1958, 1965) initiated the redemption of the stereotype concept with his attack on the "mistaken lines of objections" (1965, p. 176) expressed by the social psychologist who has "perverted his science to achieve a moral purpose (1965, p. 366). Brown summarized his general position in the following statement:

> Stereotypes are not objectionable because they are generalizations about categories; such generalizations are valuable when they are true. Stereotypes are not objectionable because they are generalizations that have been proven false; for the most part we do not know whether they are true or false – in their probabilistic forms. Stereotypes are not objectionable because they are generalizations acquired by hearsay rather than by direct experience; many generalizations acquired by hearsay are true and useful. What is objectionable about them? I think it is their ethnocentrism and the implication that important traits are inborn for large groups (1965, p. 181).

Whereas Brown still maintained that stereotypes differed in important ways from other categories, the watershed came with Tajfel's (1969) paper, "Cognitive Aspects of Prejudice," in which he formulated what were to become the basic postulates of the "cognitive approach" to stereotypes and prejudice. The role of motivational biases was minimized, and stereotypes were conceived of as categories that bring coherence and order to our social environment. The biases and exaggerations characteristic of stereotypes were seen as the result of limitations of the human capacity for processing information.

There is one important difference, however, between stereotypes and other categories: Stereotypes of outgroups are typically less positive than those of ingroups. Such ethnocentrism (i.e., ingroup favoritism and outgroup devaluation) has been observed in a wide variety of cultures (LeVine & Campbell, 1972). In a modification of his 1969 position, Tajfel (1981), therefore, argued that one of the questions that cannot be answered, if we confine our interest to cognitive functions, concerns the analysis of the functions that stereotypes serve for a social group within which they are widely diffused. Stereotypes help to preserve or create positively valued differentiations of a group from other social groups and contribute, therefore, to the creation and maintenance of group ideologies explaining or justifying a variety of social actions against the outgroup. Thus, theorists in this area seem to have come full circle in their view about the role of motivational factors in stereotyping.

Although definitions of scientific concepts are never completely atheoretical, the presence or absence of motivational biases in stereotyping is open to empirical research and should not be preempted by a definition of the stereotype concept. Thus, in line with other workers in this field (e.g., Ashmore & Del Boca, 1981; Brigham, 1971) we will define *stereotype* as *a set of beliefs about the personal attributes of a group of people*. Given the disagreement regarding whether or not stereotypes are rigid or accurate, such a general definition is a reasonable beginning point for the investigation of the topic.

The Measurement of Ethnic or National Stereotypes

For many decades, research on stereotypes focused exclusively on national or racial stereotypes. Thus, most of the methods of measurement have been developed in studies measuring racial or national stereotypes. This section will describe some of the landmark studies on this issue to illustrate the major methods of stereotype measurement.

The method of Katz and Braly. The first study to deal specifically with ethnic or national stereotypes is the widely-referenced investigation by Katz and Braly (1933). Katz and Braly asked a sample of Princeton University students to select from a list of 84 traits those that they regarded as typical of each of ten national or ethnic groups. After making their initial selections, subjects were asked to go back through the ten lists of traits and mark the five traits that were "most typical" of each group. Using only the data for these five most-typical traits, Katz and Braly calculated the 12 most frequently assigned traits for each group. By only reporting the 12 most typical traits, Katz and Braly were implicitly adopting a consensus criterion in their operational definition of stereotypes. The Katz and Braly study was replicated in 1950 by Gilbert (1951) and in 1967 by Karlins, Coffman, and Walters (1969).

The method of Brigham. Brigham (1971) had subjects indicate the percentage of individuals in a given group who were characterized by a given trait. Ratings of frequency distributions of traits across different social groups are closely related to the perceived probability with which these traits are associated with a given social group and thus allow an interpretation of the relationship between stereotypes and prejudice in terms of expectancy-value models (e.g., Anderson, 1965; Fishbein & Ajzen, 1975). Thus, Jonas and Hewstone (1986) found high rank-order correlations (.78–.89) between percentage and probability ratings.

A further advantage of the percentage procedure may be its implicit assumption that any given group consists of an aggregate of individuals. Thus, any subject who is reluctant to give an overall characterization of a group as, for example, "scientifically minded" is still able to think and respond in terms of the individuals within the group who are "scientifically minded." After all, both Gilbert (1951) and Karlins and colleagues (1969) reported that some of their subjects were reluctant to make the typical and most typical selection. Perhaps the problem would have been to some extent alleviated if subjects had been able to respond in terms of percentages.

It is somewhat unclear whether the two procedures lead to comparable results. In one study in which subjects first followed the Katz and Braly procedure and then the percentage procedure, Brigham reported that the percentages for the five most typical traits ranged from 10 to 100 and averaged 55. Furthermore, "in many cases" the percentages for all five most-typical traits were less than 50. In contrast, Stapf, Stroebe, and Jonas (1986) concluded from their study of the stereotypes of a large sample of American students that results based on percentage ratings were very similar to those of the Princeton studies that used the Katz and Braly procedure (Gilbert, 1951; Karlins et al., 1969; Katz & Braly, 1933). Furthermore, when "typicality" is rated directly (rather than being inferred from the consensus of trait ascriptions), results are quite similar to those based on "percentage" ratings. Thus, Jonas and Hewstone (1986) found correlations of .70 to .90 between the two methods. Similarly, Eagly and Steffen (in press) concluded from a comparison of the two procedures that the two methods can be used interchangeably.

The diagnostic ratio of McCauley and Stitt. While ratings in terms of the percentage of people in a given group who are characterized by a given trait seem to be straightforward, closer examination suggests a potential problem: Many traits that would produce ratings at or near 100% are not obviously included in the stereotype. Consider, for example, the percentage of Germans who are mortal or who are two-legged. Since being either mortal or two-legged is not distinctive of Germans, such traits are not included in the stereotype. McCauley and Stitt (1978; see also McCauley, Stitt, & Segal, 1980) have suggested an adjustment in Brigham's percentage measure to address such problems. McCauley and Stitt's adjustment involves the division of Brigham's percentage by the percentage of "all the world's people" who have the same trait, for example, the division of the percentage of all the world's people who are judged scientifically minded. As McCauley and Stitt note, such division produces an index that, in the context of Bayes' rule and the psychology of prediction, is often referred to as a "diagnostic ratio." In the context of stereotypes, diagnostic ratios greater than 1.00 indicate that a given trait is more characteristic of a given group than of people in general, and diagnostic ratios less than 1.00 indicate that a given trait is less characteristic of a given group than of people in general. Note that such an index will be 1.00 for judgments of traits, such as mortality, that are seen as characteristic of all groups and people and not distinctive for any group.

McCauley and Stitt (1978) argued that the diagnostic ratio makes sense for their own data. For example, 43.1% of Germans were perceived as scientifically minded; but since an even smaller number — 32.1% — of all the world's people were perceived as scientifically minded, the resulting diagnostic ratio of 1.34 (43.1/32.1 = 1.34) indicates that scientific mindedness is, in fact, part of the American stereotype of Germans.

Although not mentioned by McCauley and Stitt (1978), it is of interest to note that the linking of trait attributions to distinctive as opposed to generally shared characteristics is consistent with Jones and Davis's (1965) theory of correspondent inference. A correspondent inference is a tendency to describe an act and a trait similarly, for example, to attribute a competitive act to a competitive trait. Jones and Davis argue that correspondent inferences are more likely to occur if the act is distinctive, rare, or unusual. Thus, a competitive act in the context of a competitive game would not result in a correspondent inference, while a competitive act in the context of a social occasion would. McCauley and Stitt and Jones and Davis thus agree on the importance of distinctiveness for trait attributions.

Conclusions. While it is arguable whether the Brigham or the Katz and Braly method is psychologically more plausible, indicating the percentage of all the world's people who possess a given trait is exceedingly difficult, probably because people lack stereotypes about such global groupings. One also wonders whether these ratings are even necessary. Recall that we previously criticized the use of simple or absolute percentage ratings for nondistinctive traits such as mortality. But is this critique fair? Since investigators rarely, if ever, ask for ratings of nondistinctive traits, perhaps not. Katz and Braly report that they constructed their list largely from the attributions made by a separate group of subjects who were simply asked to list the most typical traits for the ten national or ethnic groups of concern. It is apparent that these traits are to some degree distinctive. Certainly totally nondistinctive traits like mortality do not appear in the Katz and Braly list. But why is this the case? The answer relates to the way concepts are formed. According to Bourne (1966), "A concept exists whenever two or more distinguishable objects or events have been grouped or classified together and sit apart from other objects on the basis of some common feature" (p. 1). Thus, when asked to list the "most typical" traits, subjects thought in terms of distinctive, as opposed to nondistinctive characteristics. Brigham's percentage, as it has been previously used, does therefore give a meaningful result. The rating reflects the absolute percentage of a given group possessing a *distinctive* trait. The percentage ratings also reflect most closely our own definition of social stereotype in terms of the perceived probability with which a given attribute is associated with a social group.

Stereotypes and Prejudice

The concept of prejudice. The distinction between stereotype and prejudice parallels the distinction commonly made between beliefs or opinions and attitudes. Stereotypes are beliefs or opinions about the attributes of a social group or its members, whereas prejudice is usually conceptualized as a negative intergroup attitude (e.g., Harding et al., 1954, 1969). An attitude is a tendency to evaluate an entity (attitude object) with some degree of favor or disfavor. A *prejudice is an attitude toward members of some outgroup and in which the evaluative tendencies are predominantly negative* (Harding et al., 1954, 1969). In line with the then predominant three-component view of attitude (e.g., Chein, 1951; Krech & Crutchfield, 1948), Harding and colleagues (1954, 1969) assume that the responses that express evaluation can be divided into three classes: cognition, affect, and behavior. According to this view, a prejudice is characterized by a cognitive component (e.g., a stereotype about the members of the outgroup), an affective component (e.g., dislike) and a conative component (e.g., discriminatory behavior toward the members of the outgroup). After having been virtually displaced by the one-component view of attitude proposed by Fishbein and Ajzen (1975), this type of three component definition has recently had a surprising comeback (e.g., Breckler, 1984; Zanna & Rempel, 1988).

Because in everyday language, the term "prejudice" carries the surplus meaning of a dislike based on irrational beliefs about members of an outgroup, we would like to emphasize that the concept of prejudice as defined above does not have such implications. While outgroup rejection may often seem unjustified, there are other instances when it is justifiable and legitimate (e.g., the rejection by American blacks of the KKK, and the rejection by Jews of the Nazi party). It should also be emphasized that even though the prevalent definition of prejudice as a *negative* attitude is followed in this chapter, this is not meant to imply that all intergroup attitudes are negative. For example, in a study of national stereotypes of American college students, Stapf and colleagues (1986) found that these students indicated that the Canadians and the Swiss were nearly as likeable as the Americans, while the Swedes received even more positive ratings.

The relationship between stereotypes and prejudice. How are stereotypes toward some group related to prejudice? Information processing approaches (e.g., Anderson, 1965; Fishbein & Ajzen, 1975) as well as consistency theories (e.g., Heider, 1958; Rosenberg, 1960) assume that the attitude toward an attitude object is related to the attributes perceived as associated with that object and the positive or negative evaluation of these attributes. For example, if an American perceives the Germans as "scientifically minded," "industrious" and "intelligent" (stereotype), *and* if he evaluates these traits positively, he is likely to hold a positive attitude towards the Germans. Thus, both types of theories assume that prejudice and stereotypes are closely related, but they differ in their assumptions about the direction of causality. While information-processing approaches postulate that a person's attitude towards a social group *results from* his salient beliefs about that group (Ajzen & Fishbein, 1980; Fishbein and Ajzen, 1975), consistency theories make the additional assumption that attitude change can lead to changes in a person's beliefs about a given group (e.g., Rosenberg, 1960).

Although the Katz and Braly (1933) study is primarily remembered as the first study to measure ethnic and national stereotypes, for Katz and Braly, the measurement of stereotypes was secondary to their main purpose of explaining the variation in attitudes toward, or evaluation of, various ethnic or national groups. Katz and Braly began their article by pointing out that the administration of Bogardus and Thurstone scales to different samples of U.S. citizens revealed remarkably similar results. The rank order of evaluation was always for Americans, English, and Scottish to be most highly esteemed and Hindus, Turks, and blacks to be least highly esteemed. As an explanation of this stable rank order, Katz and Braly proposed that evaluations of groups are a function of the traits that are ascribed to them, and thus such attributions reflect stereotypes that are absorbed from American culture.

To provide evidence for their explanation, Katz and Braly made three assessments — each on a different group of students. The first assessment was the previously described measurement of stereotypes. The second was a rating of each of the listed adjectives for their desirability as traits in friends and associates. And the third was a rank ordering of ten national or ethnic groups on the basis of preference for association with their members. The latter rank order was then compared with the rank of these groups based on a derived index. This index was obtained, first, by multiplying the average desirability rating of a trait by the frequency with which it was judged typical for a group, and, second, by averaging across these traits by desirability products within each group. Katz and Braly note that the two rank orders are markedly similar. Although they did not compute the rank–order correlation, it is, in fact, + .89. More recently, Eagly and Mladinic (1988) found significant positive correlations (.50–.60) between subjects' attitudes towards members of the Democratic and the Republican parties and summated Expectancy X Value products based on stereotypic trait ascriptions and the evaluation of these traits on a good–bad scale.

In contrast, Brigham (1971), in his influential review on ethnic stereotypes, reported some data that seemed to suggest that ethnic stereotypes are essentially unrelated to prejudice. Brigham (1971), like Katz and Braly (1933), collected data bearing on the consistency between trait ascription and group evaluation. However, he reported his results at the level of the individual trait, and thus discovered a some-what puzzling problem. Subjects were asked to judge American blacks in terms of 15 traits. The judgment followed the Katz and Braly "typical" paradigm and also the percentage-rating procedure. Brigham reported that the biserial correlations between evaluation of blacks and the Katz and Braly assessments were significant only for three of the 15 traits (intelligent, .29, spend money unwisely, − .47, irresponsible, − .48). Furthermore, the two traits with the highest percentage of ascription, athletic and musical, had correlations remarkably close to zero, .04 and − .08, respectively. However, since Brigham did not weight these attributes by either importance or evaluation, his findings do not contradict theoretical expecta-tions of a consistency between stereotypes and prejudice. According to so-called combinatorial theories such as Anderson's (1965), information-integration-through-averaging theory, and Rosenberg's (1960) and Fishbein's (1967) expectancy-value-summation theories, consistency can only be expected if beliefs are weighted by their importance or their evaluation and then combined.

In summary, despite the results reported by Brigham (1971), there are strong the-oretical reasons to assume a close relationship between prejudice and the relevant stereotypes (Anderson, 1965; Fishbein & Ajzen, 1975; Heider, 1958; Rosenberg, 1960). Thus, even though the existence of a prejudice toward some social group does not imply that all stereotypic beliefs about this group have to be negative, there should be a close relationship between a person's attitude towards some group and at least some of his or her beliefs about that group.

Stereotype, Prejudice, and Discrimination

The concept of discrimination. While the existence of negative opinions and mutual dislike between different social groups may be deplorable, stereotypes and prejudice become a social problem mainly when they result in hostile and discriminatory behavior towards members of an outgroup. Following Allport (1954), we define *dis-crimination* as *any behavior which denies "individuals or groups of people equality of treatment which they may wish"* (p. 50). This definition is elaborated in an official memorandum of the United Nations referred to by Allport (1954). This memoran-dum states: "Discrimination includes any conduct based on a distinction made on grounds of natural or social categories, which have no relation either to individual capacities or merits, or the concrete behavior of the individual person" (Allport, 1954, p. 51).

The relationship between stereotype, prejudice, and discrimination. That prejudice and discrimination are not always related was first reported by LaPiere (1934) who, in his travels with a young Chinese couple, found that innkeepers and restaurateurs admitted the couple even though they had stated on the phone that "members of the Chinese race" would not be welcome. This investigation served as a model for several of the early studies on the attitude–behavior relationship (e.g., Kutner, Wilkins, & Yarrow, 1952; Minard, 1952), which replicated the findings of the LaPiere study. Even though they demonstrated an inconsistency between different forms of discrimination rather than between prejudice and discrimination, these studies have a bearing on the issue of attitude–behavior consistency. Since different forms of discriminatory behavior against a given outgroup should be determined by the *same* attitude, the finding that members of a racial minority are discriminated against in one situation, but not in another, indicates an attitude–behavior inconsistency. These findings, as well as those of experimental studies which disclosed similar inconsistencies (e.g., DeFleur & Westie, 1958, Weitz, 1972) contributed to the disenchantment with the attitude concept (e.g., Wicker, 1969).

In their classic analysis of this research Ajzen and Fishbein (1977) provided a convincing explanation for these inconsistencies. They argued that such discrepancies are partially due to the fact that attitudes or prejudice are usually measured at a more global level than behavior. Thus, while a specific behavior (e.g., refusing admission) is directed towards a specific person (e.g., a Chinese couple) or object in a specific situation (e.g., the reception area of a restaurant or hotel) at a specific time, attitudes are normally measured at a much more general level (e.g., attitudes towards the members of the Chinese race). Thus, measures of racial attitudes often leave behavior and behavior-setting unspecified and even define the target of discrimination only in terms of racial or ethnic categories.

Why should such differences in the level of specificity of the measures of attitude and behavior result in an apparent inconsistency? Since the categorical information given on the outgroup target is likely to elicit images of the prototypical Chinese or the prototypical black, the well-dressed, middle-class individuals employed in some of the early studies did not correspond to the racial image elicited by the measure of prejudice at that time (e.g., Kutner et al., 1952, LaPiere, 1934).

A second reason why behavior and attitudes may differ is the fact that behavior is determined by subjective norms as well as by attitudes (Ajzen & Fishbein, 1973; Fishbein & Ajzen, 1975). Differences in the norms governing the different settings in which discrimination is being observed, or in the identifiability of different forms of discriminatory behavior, can result in discrepancies between different behavioral manifestations of prejudice. For example, the restaurateurs, in the study by Kutner and colleagues (1952), who refused to accept a booking for a racially mixed group but allowed a well-dressed black woman to join her white friends already sitting at a table may have feared the "scene" likely to result from a refusal to admit a black customer. Such fear of a public display of racism can even lead to "reverse racism." Thus, Dutton (1971) reported that restaurateurs refused admittance to inappropriately dressed black patrons less often than to inappropriately dressed white patrons.

The work of Ajzen and Fishbein (1973, 1977) has two implications for the relationship between measures of prejudice and discrimination: First, if specific acts of discrimination are to be predicted, one should assess individual attitudes towards the specific behavior and the subjective norms that apply to that situation. Second, even though global measures of prejudice are typically poor predictors of specific actions, such global scores correlate well with composite measures of behavior that reflect a fairly representative sample of discriminatory acts, directed towards a reasonably representative sample of members of the target group, in a wide variety of situations.

Summary and Conclusions

The first part of this chapter defined the terms *stereotype, prejudice* and *discrimination* and discussed the relationship between these concepts. Stereotype was defined as a set of beliefs about the personal attributes of a group of people, and prejudice, a tendency to evaluate unfavorably the members of an outgroup. It was argued on theoretical grounds that the attitudes of people towards the members of an outgroup should be closely related to their beliefs about the characteristics of this group. Due to this interrelationship between these two concepts, theories of stereotype should also account for prejudice and theories of prejudice for stereotypes.

Discrimination was defined as any conduct which denies individuals or groups of people equality of treatment which they may wish. After reviewing some of the early work on prejudice and discrimination, which seemed to imply that the two concepts are essentially unrelated, we discussed the classic analysis of Ajzen and Fishbein (1977), in which they specify the conditions under which attitude-behavior consistency (or inconsistency) can be expected.

The Origins of Stereotypes and Prejudice

A Framework for the Evaluation of Theories of Stereotypes and Prejudice

There are a great variety of theories that account for stereotypes and prejudice on different levels of analysis and in terms of widely differing psychological processes. It is, therefore, often unclear whether these approaches are contradictory or complementary. Researchers have proposed several ways to organize the different approaches to understanding stereotypes and prejudice. Thus, Allport (1954) and Ashmore (1970) categorized theories according to their "level of analysis." Theories differ in whether they explain stereotypes and prejudice in terms of sociocultural causes or in terms of individual processes. At one extreme, there are theories that conceive of stereotypes and prejudice as the result of social conflict (conflict theories) or socialization (the social learning theory). At the other extreme, there are approaches that account for stereotypes and prejudice in terms of individual motives and personality traits (scapegoat theory, authoritarian personality) or in terms of limitations of the information-processing capacity of the individual (cognitive approach).

Less attention has been paid to a second dimension that seems to be orthogonal to that of "level of analysis": Some theories assume a motive to derogate the targets of prejudice (conflict theories, scapegoating, authoritarian personality). Other theories (social learning theory, cognitive approach) do not make this assumption. It is interesting to note that those theories that assume a derogatory motive mainly focus on the development of prejudice and treat stereotypes as an epiphenomenon.

Although these criteria are useful as a framework for ordering the different approaches, they do not help one to evaluate their range of application. To develop criteria for an empirical evaluation of these theories, a set of questions, which should be answered by a comprehensive theory of stereotyping and prejudice, was compiled from the literature. There are four related issues which should be addressed: (1) the *existence of individual differences*; that is, how can individual differences in the intensity and in the targets of prejudice be explained? (2) the *existence of group or societal differences*; that is, how can differences between groups or between different societies in the intensity or the targets of prejudice be explained? (3) the *problem of content*; that is, how can one explain the content of specific stereotypes? and (4) the *problem of ethnocentrism*; that is, why are stereotypes of ingroups typically more positive than those of outgroups. The second part of this chapter will discuss the different theoretical approaches to stereotyping and prejudice in terms of the classification developed above and evaluate them according to the four criteria outlined. We begin with theories relating to sociocultural causes and subsequently consider theories relating to individual personality causes.

Sociocultural Causes of Stereotypes and Prejudice

At the societal level of analysis, the distinction between motivational and non-motivational approaches corresponds to two meta-theories in contemporary sociology which Dahrendorf (1959) termed coercion versus integration theories of society. Coercion theorists (e.g., Marx, Dahrendorf) conceive of societies as organizations held together by force and constraint exerted by a few members of a society who dominate and suppress the majority. According to this perspective, which assumes that societies are characterized by conflicts of interest, stereotypes, prejudice, and the ensuing devaluation of outgroups are only partial aspects of an ideology by which the powerful justify the suppression of the powerless. Integration theorists (e.g., Rousseau, Parsons), on the other hand, make the assumption that social cohesion and social order result from a general agreement of values that outweighs all possible or actual differences of opinion or interest. These values are transmitted to the members of a society through socialization processes and stereotypes and prejudice are part of this societal heritage. Conflict theories of stereotypes and prejudice could be subsumed under the first meta-theoretical perspective, and social learning theories under the second.

Conflict theories. There are two different conflict theories of prejudice, namely the *realistic conflict theory* (cf. Campbell, 1965; Sherif, 1967) and the *social identity theory* (cf. Tajfel, 1982). The realistic conflict theory conceives of prejudice as the outcome of intergroup competition for some scarce resource. Campbell (1965, pp. 287–291) formulated the basic assumptions of this approach in terms of a set of postulates or hypotheses: "Real conflict of interest, . . . and/or the presence of hostile, threatening, and competitive outgroup neighbors, which collectively may be called 'real threat,' cause the perception of threat" which then results in hostility towards the source of the threat.

Since intergroup conflict affects not only feelings toward members of the outgroup, but also the attitudes of group members towards each other, Campbell (1965) also addresses the impact of intergroup conflict on group processes. He argued that real threat increases ingroup solidarity, the awareness of own ingroup identity, and the tightness of group boundaries. Real threat further reduces the risk of defection from the group by increasing punishments and rejection of defectors and by creating punishment and rejection of deviants. In other words, real threat increases ethnocentrism, that is, a state that is characterized by heightened ingroup solidarity *and* a devaluation of outgroups. Because, on a psychological level, the process that mediates between intergroup conflict and ethnocentrism is the perception of a threat, Campbell emphasizes in his last postulate that ethnocentrism can also be caused by a false perception of threat from an outgroup.

The notion that intergroup conflict, whether real or perceived, is a necessary and sufficient cause of ethnocentrism and antagonism between groups was later challenged by Tajfel and his colleagues (Tajfel, 1982; Tajfel & Turner, 1979). Firstly, they argued that conflict of interest does not necessarily lead to ethnocentrism. For example, if differences in the distribution of resources have been institutionalized, legitimized, and justified through a consensually accepted status system, then they do not result in antagonism between groups. Secondly, Tajfel argued that conflict of interest is not even a necessary condition of ethnocentrism. Experiments using the minimal group paradigm (cf. Tajfel, 1970) have received results which Tajfel and his associates interpreted as indicating that the mere perception of belonging to two distinct groups is sufficient to trigger intergroup discrimination favoring the ingroup.

To account for such interpreted findings, Tajfel and Turner (1979, 1985) formulated the social identity theory, which assumes an individual motive to achieve or maintain a positive social identity. Because the status of the social groups to which people belong is an important determinant of their social identity, they will either leave groups of low status or they will try to raise the status of their groups. In terms of this theory, ingroup favoritism in the minimal group paradigm can be explained as an attempt to achieve a positive differentiation between ingroup and outgroup in a situation in which money is the only available dimension of comparison (see also Chapter 5 by Horwitz & Rabbie).

Social identity theory modifies the implications of the realistic conflict theory in two important respects. First, it restricts the assumption that every conflict over scarce resources will result in hostility. Second, it emphasizes that conflict will not only develop over scarce physical resources but can also occur over a scarce "social" resource. Stereotypes and prejudice are often weapons in a fight over a scarce social resource, namely prestige and status within a society. In order to account for the valence of such social resources, Tajfel and Turner (1979, 1985) assume a motive to achieve or maintain a positive self-esteem which does not really fit into a sociocultural theory of prejudice.

The conflict theoretical approach offers solutions to both the problems of individual differences and the issue of group or societal differences. According to social identity theory, individual differences in prejudice can be due to differences in the need for a positive self-concept or to differences in the competitiveness of the individual situation. For example, members of the working classes may be in a competition for jobs with members of minority groups, whereas this may not be true for the middle classes. Societal differences can be due to the fact that different societies are in conflict with different groups (see also Chapter 8 by D. Bar-Tal).

Conflict theories also offer a satisfactory explanation of ethnocentrism. Although outgroup derogation can already be triggered by the mere perception of belonging to two different groups, it also serves a useful function in the conduct of an intergroup conflict. Prejudice and stereotypes can be seen as part of an ideology of a group which, on one hand, buttresses group members' beliefs in their own superiority, and on the other hand, justifies aggression and violence toward members of the outgroup.

It is worth noting, however, that conflict theories set stereotypes and prejudice apart from other beliefs and attitudes. Whereas our beliefs about objects and animals are assumed to come from many different sources, our beliefs about the members of outgroups are supposed to be rooted in intergroup conflict, or at least in intergroup categorization. This restriction in the range of processes assumed to lead to stereotyping and prejudice was unproblematic when stereotypes and prejudice were still believed to be the result of deficient thought processes. These days, however, when stereotypes and prejudice are defined as subcategories of beliefs or attitudes, the implied assumption that other processes of belief and attitude formation do not apply to the development of prejudice is no longer tenable.

Social learning theory. In contrast to conflict theories, social learning theory does not assume a motive to derogate outgroups. According to the social learning perspective, stereotypes and prejudice are either the result of observations of "actual" differences between groups in a given society, or they are based on social influences deriving from sources such as mass media, schools, parents, and peer groups.

Eagly and her colleagues (Eagly, 1987; Eagly & Kite, 1987; Eagly & Steffen, 1984) have recently suggested that gender stereotypes as well as many ethnic stereotypes are shaped by the social roles that group members occupy when intergroup contacts occur. Social roles are important determinants of the behavior of group members, and observations of these behaviors are the basic data from which people form their images of groups of people. This role theoretical analysis does not presume that people are exposed to the "real" attributes of groups of people. Rather they are exposed to certain displays of attributes, and these displays are limited by the social contexts in terms of which the perceiver interacts with the target group.

If perceivers often observe a particular group of people engaging in a particular activity, they are likely to believe that the abilities and personality attributes required to carry out that activity are typical for that group of people. For example, the repeated observation of women caring for children may lead to the belief that characteristics thought to be necessary for child care, such as nurturance and warmth, are typical for women.

Many ethnic and racial stereotypes may also have originated from social structural differences. For example, in American society, racial groups are differentiated on the basis of social class, with blacks on average having a lower socioeconomic status than whites. Thus, interactions across racial lines are often characterized by differences in power and privilege. As a consequence, the content of beliefs about racial groups may confound class differences with racial stereotypes, reflecting the characteristic behavior ascribed to differing social classes (Smedley & Bayton, 1978; Stephan & Rosenfield, 1982; Triandis & Triandis, 1965).

Since stereotypes as probabilistic beliefs are difficult to falsify from informal observations, one could extend the thesis of Eagly and her colleagues (Eagly, 1987; Eagly & Steffen, 1984) by arguing that there would be quite a delay in the adjustment of stereotypes to changes in the situation of a target group. Thus, present day stereotypes may often reflect the social reality of the distant past. For example, Stephan and Rosenfield (1982) suggested that the stereotype of blacks as lazy, ignorant, and physically dirty, which was predominant in the U.S. until a few decades ago (cf. Katz & Braly, 1933), may have reflected the situation of the blacks during slavery. In those days, blacks had little access to institutions of higher education. Payment was in terms of board and lodging and thus did not reward actual performance. There was, therefore, little incentive to work hard. Finally, blacks were housed in primitive settings with minimal provisions for personal hygiene. Thus, at that particular time, the stereotype was probably a reflection of their actual situation.

This stereotype was then transmitted by processes of socialization, involving schooling, parents, peer groups, and mass media. Since racial, ethnic, and gender stereotypes have been found to develop fairly early in life (e.g., Tajfel & Jahoda, 1966; Koblinsky, Cruse, & Sugawara, 1978) parents are likely to be particularly instrumental in their transmission, not only by the information they give to their offspring, but also because their behavior toward members of outgroups may serve as a model. Thus, children do not only adopt stereotypes and prejudices from their parents but also typical forms of interaction with members of outgroups. An additional process by which parents transmit their own beliefs and feelings about members of outgroups to their children is through the regulation of the contacts of their children with other children. By forbidding their children to play with specific other children (e.g., children of different races or of lower socioeconomic status) they create the impression that these children are bad or nasty.

The influence of mass media like television or radio rests on the one-sidedness with which certain groups are portrayed. Thus, Plotkin (1964; cited in Dovidio & Gaertner, 1986) reported that at that time blacks were portrayed on TV only once every 2.5 hours and that they were almost always seen in positions of subordinate status to whites. The portrayal of blacks in the mass media has changed markedly during the last decades. Although, according to Greenberg and Mazingo (1976; cited in Dovidio & Gaertner, 1986), the first starring role for a black prime-time dramatic series did not occur until 1967 (Bill Cosby in "I Spy"), by 1967, 34% of all dramas included blacks and the percentage increased to 52% in 1968. Greenberg and Mazingo further note that giving and taking orders were equalized for blacks and whites by 1973. It will be difficult, however, to assess the impact of these changes on stereotypes and prejudice, since they were accompanied by (less dramatic) changes in the socioeconomic standing of blacks within the U.S.

The social learning approach has no problems in accounting for individual or group differences in intensity or content of prejudice. It would be more difficult, however, to account for the predominance of outgroup derogation in terms of a social learning theory. If stereotypes were merely a more or less realistic reflection of societal differences, positive outgroup attitudes should be as frequent as negative ones. Thus, while this theory can account for the fact that the powerful have negative stereotypes of the powerless, additional assumptions would have to be incorporated into social learning theory to account for the fact that such negative stereotypes are often mutual and that outgroup derogation is the predominant pattern (LeVine & Campbell, 1972).

By emphasizing education, communication, and direct observation as bases for the development of stereotypes and prejudice, the social learning approach provides an important extension to the perspective developed by conflict theorists. It would be overly simplistic, however, to describe the two approaches as mutually consistent and complementary. While the social learning perspective considers the processes involved in acquiring prejudice as in no way different from the processes involved in the acquisition of other kinds of knowledge, the conflict theoretical approach assumes a motivational bias operative in the formation of beliefs about outgroups.

Personal Causes of Stereotypes and Prejudice

Psychodynamic as well as cognitive approaches focus on the intrapersonal processes that give rise to outgroup rejection and devaluation. However, since the two approaches espouse to widely differing models of man, they arrive at very different interpretations of the psychological causes of stereotypes and prejudice.

Psychodynamic theories. Psychodynamic theories provide the prototypical example for individual-level explanations of stereotypes and prejudice. According to this approach, prejudice is the result of neither societal conflicts nor social learning processes, but instead a sign of some intrapersonal conflict or maladjustment. Since prejudice is, therefore, merely a symptom of a deeper personality conflict, Ashmore (1970) has dubbed the psychodynamic approach to prejudice "symptom theories."

According to the *scapegoat theory* (e.g., Allport & Kramer, 1946; Bettelheim & Janowitz, 1950, 1964; Epstein & Komorita, 1965, 1966; Miller & Bugelski, 1948; Stagner & Congdon, 1955) which is one of the better known symptom theories, prejudice or more exactly aggression toward members of the outgroup is the result of a displacement of aggression from a powerful frustrator to a powerless minority group. The scapegoat theory was derived from the frustration–aggression hypothesis of Dollard, Miller, Doob, Mowrer, & Sears (1939). Dollard et al. postulated that aggressive behavior is always a reaction to some frustration. If individuals are prevented from reaching some attractive goal, they react with aggression, which is normally directed toward the person causing the frustration. If this person is too powerful or cannot be identified, then the aggression will be directed toward some less powerful individual. The scapegoat hypothesis simply adds the assumption that members of minority groups frequently serve as targets of such displaced aggression, with the displacement being rationalized by blaming the minority for the frustration or by attributing negative attributes to the minority.

Although the scapegoat theory is quite plausible, it offers an incomplete explanation of the development of prejudice. While it may account for the origin of aggressive energy, it cannot account for the choice of targets. Thus, the theory does not explain why the prejudice of the South Africans is mainly directed toward blacks, while the Jews were the major target of prejudice among the Germans during the Hitler regime. It seems plausible, as Ashmore (1970) suggested, that minorities that are highly visible but at the same time powerless are particularly likely to be chosen as scapegoats; but the theory does not contain any principle which would allow one to define the characteristics of the group chosen as a target of aggression except for the provision that it must be powerless.

The explanation of prejudice provided by the theory of the *Authoritarian Personality* (Adorno, Frenkel-Brunswik, Levinson, & Sanford, 1950) suffers from a similar deficiency. The theory makes three assumptions: (1) Prejudice is part of a broader ideological framework and is thus correlated with other political, economic, and social beliefs; (2) this correlation is caused by more basic personality factors; and (3) this personality base of prejudice is primarily the result of the quality of parental control during the formative period of personality organization. To test these assumptions a study was conducted in the U.S. shortly after the end of World War II in which interviews and a number of different scales were used. The major scales were: the anti-Semitism scale (A-S), the Ethnocentrism scale (E), the Political and Economic Conservatism scale (PEC), and the Implicit Antidemocratic Trends or Fascism scale (F). The first two scales are direct and explicit measures of prejudice, with the A-S scale assessing anti-Semitism and the E scale measuring prejudice against Jews and other minority groups (e.g., blacks, Filipinos, foreigners). A high correlation between the two scales seemed to support the hypothesis that individuals who are anti-Semitic are also prejudiced against other outgroups. The PEC scale was developed because Adorno et al. (1950) assumed that individuals of politically and economically conservative persuasion would be particularly likely to be prejudiced. However, the weak relationship between the PEC scale and the A-S and the E scale raised doubts about this hypothesis. The F scale finally was constructed as a measure of the kind of antidemocratic and authoritarian personality structure which was assumed to cause and to support prejudice. The high correlations between scores on the F scale and on the measures of ethnocentrism and anti-Semitism seemed to support the hypothesis that prejudice is associated with antidemocratic and authoritarian tendencies.

The interviews of small groups of individuals who were selected on the basis of their extreme (low/high) scores on the F scale presented further evidence of the relationship between personality and prejudice. These data suggested a syndrome of affective and cognitive elements that together form the authoritarian personality. The typical authoritarian character is somebody whose upbringing had been strict and disciplined and who displaced all the resentment he might have felt for his parents toward outgroups. As Billig (1976) summarized,

> [the] general picture of the authoritarian painted by Adorno et al. is of a weakling, who copes with his own inadequacies by excessive reference to the powers that be and by venting his aggressiveness upon his social inferiors and upon "inferior" outgroups – particularly Jews and Negroes (p. 109).

Thus, the explanation of prejudice offered by Adorno et al. (1950) involves scapegoating, but a long-term scapegoating in which the aggression that the authoritarian person feels toward his or her father is projected onto outgroups.

As often with classic pieces of research, the study of Adorno et al. suffered from numerous methodological weaknesses which raise doubt about the validity of many of their main findings (cf. Ashmore, 1970; Hyman & Sheatsley, 1954; Kirscht & Dillehay, 1967). For example, all A-S-, E-, and F-scale items were scored in a positive direction so that the correlations between these scales may have been artificially boosted by an acquiescent response tendency. The F scale correlates highly with intelligence and educational status, both factors with a known relationship to prejudice. Finally, the interviewers knew the prejudice scores of their subjects at the time of the interview. This might have affected the type of questions asked.

On a more conceptual level, Rokeach (1960) argued that the theory of authoritarian personality is restricted to the authoritarianism of the right and disregards authoritarianism connected with other political belief systems. As Rokeach argued, "authoritarianism and intolerance are surely not a monopoly of the Fascists, anti-Semites, Ku Klux Klanners, and conservatives" (1960, p. 13). They can be observed with all political orientations and walks of life and what is needed is a scale of authoritarian belief systems which is free of ideological bias. Rokeach (1960) claims that his Dogmatism Scale measures the degree of dogmatism in a person's belief system independent of political content and biases.

In terms of the four criteria outlined at the beginning of our theoretical analysis, the theory of the *authoritarian personality* offers a very incomplete explanation of stereotypes and prejudice. Only the assumption that individual differences in prejudice are related to differential levels in F values has been supported empirically. F values have been found to correlate strongly and significantly with prejudice in studies conducted in several countries (cf. Pettigrew, 1958).

The assumption that differences in the level of prejudice of different societies or societal groups should be related to differences in the degree of authoritarianism prevalent in a given society has been less well supported. Thus, Pettigrew (1958) found that a sample of white South African students, who were highly prejudiced against blacks (e.g., 72% of the sample agreed with the statement that "there is something inherently primitive and uncivilized in the native, as shown in his music and extreme aggressiveness") had F values which were not higher than those of American college student populations. Furthermore, those South African students who were born on the African continent and were significantly more intolerant of black Africans than the remainder of the sample did not differ in their F values from those born elsewhere.

Pettigrew (1958) reported some additional findings that suggest that group or societal differences in prejudice are more likely to be due to differences in sociocultural norms than personality factors. Pettigrew found that anti-black prejudice among his South African sample correlated as highly with subjects' scores on a measure of social conformity as with their F values. Furthermore, those students who could be expected to be especially responsive to the norms of South African society (i.e., those who were born in Africa, those who identified with the Nationalist Party, those who were upwardly mobile, and those who had been molded by the conservative traditions of the Afrikaans-speaking people) tended to be intolerant of black Africans, regardless of their personality structure.

The importance of sociocultural norms as determinants of prejudice was further demonstrated in a study of two small samples of white adults who were randomly selected from several communities in the North and the South of the United States (Pettigrew, 1959). Again, there were marked differences in prejudice but not in F values between the Southerners and Northerners. Furthermore, a pattern of results pointing to the importance of conformity in accounting for the more anti-black attitudes of Southerners than Northerners among U.S. respondents emerged. For example, in the South, but not the North, there were more anti-black attitudes among church attenders, political party identifiers, and women. It was also found that experience outside of mainstream Southern culture reduced anti-black attitudes. For example, in the South, but not in the North, veterans were less anti-black than non-veterans. Although education and anti-black attitudes were negatively correlated for both Northerners and Southerners who responded, the correlation was more negative for Southerners. Such results are consistent with the postulated influence of sociocultural norms on prejudice.

A further weakness of the theory of the authoritarian personality relates to the issue of content of stereotypes. This is the attempt to account for an extensive belief system solely in terms of parental behavior. One can only agree with Billig (1976) who states this point forcefully when he writes:

> Such an ideological system of beliefs, although shot through with contradictions and inconsistencies, could not have been fortuitously created by each authoritarian solely as a result of his relations with his parents. Cultural and social influences must have inevitably shaped the ideologies of the post-war American authoritarian. The mass-media, schooling, beliefs of parents, etc., must have all gone some way to producing the final belief-system" (1967, p. 111).

In conclusion, symptom theories such as the scapegoat theory or the authoritarian personality theory offer at best a partial explanation of prejudice. While they may account for variations in prejudice within a given culture or region, they fail to explain differences in levels of prejudice between different cultures or regions. Furthermore, they cannot really explain why different groups become targets of prejudice or the specific content of the belief systems developed by prejudiced individuals.

The cognitive approach. The roots of the cognitive perspective on stereotyping are typically seen in a change in the "Zeitgeist" that led to a replacement of the irrational model of human beings reflected by psychoanalysis with a model of humans as rational processors of information. As Ashmore and Del Boca (1981) suggest, this historical interpretation is probably incorrect. It was really the psychodynamic theories of prejudice that subscribed to rationality. Because they conceived of human beings as eminently rational creatures, capable of objectively processing and evaluating information, when people seemed to fail in this respect (i.e, when they held stereotypes), such failure was explained by motivational factors (Ashmore & Del Boca, 1981). The cognitive theorists (e.g., Simon, 1955; Tajfel, 1969), on the other hand, accepted that the human capacity for information processing is limited and that these constraints of the cognitive system were responsible for many of the apparent breakdowns in perception and cognition. Thus, they felt no need to invoke motivational factors to account for the formation and maintenance of stereotypes.

This section will focus on belief congruence theory (Rockeach, Smith, & Evans, 1960) and accentuation theory (Eiser & Stroebe, 1972; Tajfel, 1957, 1959a, 1959b; Tajfel & Wilkes, 1963), two early cognitive theories of stereotype and prejudice, which derive from differing theoretical traditions. While belief congruence theory at least partially involves cognitive consistency notions, accentuation theory was probably the first approach that analyzed stereotyping purely from a judgmental or information-processing perspective. This latter perspective will then be extended, and we will briefly outline the more recent developments in cognitive research on stereotyping. A more extensive review of the cognitive program can be found in Chapters 2, 3, and 4 of this book.

According to *belief congruence theory* (Rokeach, Smith, & Evans, 1960) outgroup members are rejected not because of racial or physical characteristics; but rather because of their dissimilar or incongruent beliefs. According to Rokeach et al. (1960), "*insofar as psychological processes* are involved, belief is more important than ethnic or racial membership as a determinant of racial discrimination" (p. 135). In emphasizing psychological processes, Rokeach et al. explicitly exclude institutionalized manifestations of rejection, such as norms against marriage with an outgroup member, and thus focus exclusively on the basis for private (as opposed to public) rejection (see also Chapter 7 by Schwartz & Struch). Since it is apparent from the general context of the discussion that Rokeach et al. use the term "belief" to include beliefs, attitudes, and values, the theory in essence emphasizes the importance of attributed behavioral characteristics, as opposed to physical characteristics, as the root cause of private rejection. It is furthermore obvious that since stereotypes consist primarily of behavioral characteristics, the theory comes very close to asserting that stereotypes cause prejudice.

The publication of the theory of Rokeach et al. (1960) was followed by a large amount of research (cf. Insko, Nacoste, & Moe, 1983, for a review). Although much of this research was done with American subjects, studies were also conducted in Canada, South Africa, and the Philippines. Of the various research procedures, the most common (e.g., Stein, Hardyck, & Smith, 1965) was one in which bogus questionnaires were used to portray the other's beliefs as either similar to or different from each subject's own beliefs as measured on a previous questionnaire, and the race or ethnicity of the other who had purportedly filled out the questionnaire was indicated in the context of accompanying demographic information with a picture. Since the two-level belief and two-level race variables were usually manipulated within subjects, each subject examined four different questionnaires. The questionnaires were represented as having been filled out by other subjects of the same sex and age, and the subjects were typically eighth- or ninth-grade students. The results of many such studies generally indicated that the pattern of results depended very much on the nature of the dependent variable. For semantic differential ratings, or for simple ratings of liking–disliking, belief effects tended to be markedly larger than race effects; for ratings of moderate social distance, such as acceptance into the same club or neighborhood, belief effects were only somewhat larger than race effects; and for ratings of small social distance, such as "date my brother or sister," the race effects were markedly larger than the belief effects. Superficially the results for moderate and particularly small social distance would appear to indicate that belief congruence theory is simply wrong. However, recall that as formulated by Rokeach et al. the theory related exclusively to private evaluation. Thus, to the extent that large race effects for more "sensitive" behavioral associations are a result of normative pressures, the theory is not necessarily inconsistent with the obtained evidence.

Aside from the social norms problem, however, Robinson and Insko (1969) raised a question concerning whether or not the above studies even provide an appropriate test of the theory. According to belief congruence theory, racial or ethnic discrimination is a result of attributed differences in beliefs. It therefore follows that an appropriate test of this supposition should manipulate the beliefs that are assumed different, and, in addition, determine the discrepancies so that they correspond to the discrepancies that are actually attributed. This problem relates to the appropriate procedure for constructing the belief-dissimilar stimulus persons. What investigators like Stein et al. (1965) did was to create the belief–dissimilar stimulus persons by altering in some consistent but arbitrary way the subject's own prior belief responses. But such a dissimilar stimulus person may or may not correspond to each subject's stereotype of the racially or ethnically distinct other. Assuming that the belief content reflects known stereotypes, the belief discrepancy should be determined by the traits that each subject actually attributes to the racially or ethnically distinct other. Thus, what is required is that the subject initially respond to the items both in terms of own beliefs and in terms of the beliefs that are attributed to the typical racially distinct other. The second set of responses can then be used to construct the dissimilar stimulus persons (just as the first set of responses is used to construct the similar stimulus persons).

However, when Robinson and Insko (1969) and Moe, Nacoste, and Insko (1981) used this more appropriate procedure, they found results roughly comparable to those obtained by the previous investigators. The race effects were larger for the smaller social distance items and the belief effect larger for the larger social distance and general evaluative items. The two studies were conducted 12 years apart in the same junior high school in a small southern U.S. community. The race effects did significantly decline over the 12-year period, but the general pattern of the relative magnitude of the race and belief effects remained. Consistent with Rokeach et al.'s supposition that race effects are due to social pressure, Moe et al. found that their measure of social pressure (social approval–disapproval of cross race contact by parents and friends) correlated across items with the race effect .79 for white teenagers and .84 for black teenagers. Such evidence suggests that race effects may be due to social norms, and that a theory of private rejection need not to be embarrassed by such institutionalized manifestations of rejection. A general emphasis upon the importance of norms is, of course, consistent with the above described evidence of Pettigrew (1958, 1959).

Belief congruence theory offers only a partial explanation of the development of stereotypes and prejudice. Implicit in this theory is the assumption that the strength of the outgroup rejection depends on the discrepancy perceived between one's own attitudes and beliefs and those attributed to members of outgroups. In order to explain individual or group differences in stereotypes and prejudice, one has to go beyond the theory and develop hypotheses about the psychological causes of the origin of stereotypes. Two theoretical approaches have been suggested: balance theory and social learning theory.

According to cognitive balance theory (e.g., Heider, 1958), outgroup members should be perceived as holding different beliefs, because the perception of outgroup membership is balanced with the perception of belief-dissimilarity. There is one problem with this interpretation. Since the perception of outgroup membership (as a negative unit relation) would also be balanced with prejudice (as a negative sentiment relation), it seems unlikely that balance processes should take such an indirect route (via the perception of belief incongruence) rather than affecting prejudice directly. It would be more plausible to assume that prejudice and attributed belief-incongruence are the joint result of the perception of outgroup membership. This latter assumption would also be in line with the findings reported by Tajfel and Jahoda (1966) that children show clear signs of outgroup rejection with regard to national groups of whom they have no knowledge.

A more viable alternative interpretation can be derived from social learning theory. A social learning perspective would suggest that as children grow up they learn not only to distinguish between various social groups, but they also learn that members of outgroups hold attitudes and beliefs that differ from those of members of their own groups (Ashmore, 1970). This interpretation would also be more consistent than balance theory with the findings of Insko and his associates (e.g., Insko and Robinson, 1969; Moe et al., 1981), which establish the perception of belief incongruence as an independent cause of disliking over and above the effect of perceived racial differences.

The term *accentuation theory* was coined by Eiser and Stroebe (1972) as a label for the judgmental approach of Tajfel (e.g., Tajfel & Wilkes, 1963). Accentuation theory applies to any judgmental situation in which a series of stimuli vary along two (or more) dimensions. The dimensions along which the stimuli are being judged is referred to as the "focal" dimension and the additional dimension as the "peripheral" dimension (Eiser & Stroebe, 1972). If the two dimensions are correlated, there should be an overestimation of the judged differences between the stimuli on the focal dimension. This overestimation or accentuation is relative to a control condition in which the peripheral dimension is absent.

Accentuation theory is applicable both to situations in which focal and peripheral dimensions have the same number of levels and to situations in which peripheral dimensions have fewer levels than the focal dimension. Stereotypes can be conceived of as an assumed correlation between a discrete category such as race or gender (the peripheral dimension) and one or several continuous trait dimensions such as size, intelligence or emotionality (the focal dimensions). According to accentuation theory, differences between individuals falling into different categories are overestimated (accentuated) while differences within the same category are underestimated (assimilated). Accentuation effects have been demonstrated for physical (e.g., Lilli, 1970; Lilli & Lehner, 1971; Marchand, 1970; Tajfel & Wilkes, 1963) as well as social (e.g., Eiser, 1971; Eiser & Mower-White, 1975) stimulus material.

Tajfel and Wilkes (1963) had subjects estimate in centimeters the lengths of eight lines. In the experimental condition, the four shorter lines were labeled with an "A" and the four longer lines were labeled with a "B". In one control condition the "A-B" classification was omitted, and in another the classification was not correlated with, or predictive of, line length. The results indicated that, relative to either control condition, the differences between the fourth and the fifth lines were accentuated, but that there was no significant reduction in the differences among either the four shorter lines or the four longer lines. Stated differently, the results produced support for the first prediction, concerning an increase in interclass difference, but not for the second prediction, concerning a reduction in intraclass differences.

Subsequent experiments by Marchand (1970), Lilli (1970), and Lilli and Lehner (1971) produced similar results. However, only the Lilli and Lehner (1971) experiment, in which the focal dimension was the height of forehead on schematic drawings, produced evidence for intragroup assimilation as well as intergroup accentuation. Lilli and Lehner (1971) found a highly significant negative correlation between the two effects. Research by Eiser (1971) and by Eiser and Mower-White (1975) produced evidence for the generality of the accentuation effect in the context of social judgments (i.e., placements of Thurstone statements along an attitude dimension). Accentuation effects were also reported in several studies which predated the Tajfel and Wilkes (1963) experiment, and were thus developed independent of the Tajfel tradition (e.g., Campbell, 1956; Liberman, Harris, Howard, & Griffith, 1957; Secord, 1959; Secord, Bevan, & Katz, 1956).

There are two ways by which the expectation of an association between category membership and position on a trait dimension could be acquired: It could either be learned from parents, peers, mass media, and the like, or it could be inferred from observation. However, even if correlations exist in real life between categories and trait dimensions (i.e., if the Italians are smaller than the Norwegians or the Swiss less emotional than the Spaniards), these correlations are unlikely to be perfect as in the experimental studies of accentuation theory. It is, therefore, an intriguing question of what regularity in the stimulus-classification correspondence is necessary for accentuation effects to occur.

This issue was studied by Lilli and his associates (cf. 1970; Lilli & Rehm, 1988), who used the Tajfel and Wilkes paradigm to manipulate the relationship between classification and focal dimension. Numerically, these relationships can be described by their prospective probabilities, ranging from 1.0 (perfect correspondence) to .5 (random) with steps at .92 (nearly perfect), .83 (moderate correspondence), and .68 (nearly random). As in the study of Tajfel and Wilkes, the stimuli consisted of eight different lengths of lines, and the classification used the letters A and B. The five stimulus conditions were presented to different groups of subjects in a training phase, where subjects learned the stimulus–classification relationship assigned to them. In the subsequent test phase, subjects had to judge the length of the randomly presented lines in centimeters. The results showed that substantial interclass effects occur only under $p = 1.00$ and the $p = .92$ conditions, indicating that a nearly perfect relationship between stimuli and classification is necessary to produce inter- and intraclass effects. Since such perfect correlations are rare in real life, it seems likely that many of our stereotypes have either been acquired through social learning or are based on "illusory correlations."

The *theory of illusory correlation* (e.g., Hamilton & Gifford, 1976) describes the conditions which may lead an observer to perceive a correlation between two sets of variables, when in fact no such correlation exists. The concept of illusory correlation was originally suggested by Chapman (1967) and Chapman and Chapman (1967). These authors found, for example, that both clinicians and naive interpreters of the draw-a-person test tended to overestimate the correlation between the paranoia of a patient and the occurrence of atypical eye drawings—presumably because of the assumed association between suspiciousness and the eyes. This general idea was applied to stereotypes by David Hamilton and his associates (cf. Hamilton, 1981; Hamilton & Gifford, 1976; Hamilton & Sherman, Chapter 3) who reasoned that the attribution of undesirable behavioral tendencies to American blacks by American whites could be a form of illusory correlation. In this case, however, the illusory correlation would be based on the relatively fewer number of blacks than whites and of undesirable than desirable behaviors. Even though there was no actual correlation between race and desirability of behavior, the conjunction of distinctive race with distinctive behavior would lead to the perception of a correlation between race and behavior or the assumption that blacks are more likely to engage in undesirable behavior.

To test these assumptions, Hamilton and Gifford (1976) presented subjects with slides, each of which contained a sentence stating that some person, who was either a member of "Group A" or "Group B," had performed a particular act which was either desirable or undesirable. Even though Group A had more members than Group B (and thus twice as many statements described members of Group A as Group B), the ratio of desirable to undesirable behaviors was 9 to 4 in both groups.

Thus, Group B was smaller than Group A, undesirable behavior was less frequent than desirable behavior, and there was no correlation between group membership and desirability of behavior. After exposure to the slides, subjects had to recall the group membership of the person who had enacted each of the behaviors. The results indicated that there was no effect for the desirable behavior, but that the undesirable behaviors were attributed to Group B to a greater extent than was the case in the original statements. Group B was also evaluated less positively than Group A. In a second experiment, Hamilton and Gifford found that the negative impression of the minority group could be reversed if desirable behaviors were less frequent than undesirable behaviors.

Hamilton and Gifford argued that the overall pattern of results for both experiments was consistent with the position that an illusory correlation may arise from "the *co-occurrence* of two distinctive events" (p. 405), and that the "perception of a relationship" (p. 405) provides the basis for the obtained results. One might interpret this position as implying that the underlying mechanism is attention-produced learning, but Hamilton and Gifford did not use exactly these words. They did observe that the results more generally indicate "that not all stereotyping originates in the learning and motivation processes emphasized in the stereotype literature: cognitive factors alone can be sufficient to produce differential perceptions of social groups" (p. 405).

There have been a great number of studies replicating the Hamilton and Gifford findings (cf. Hamilton and Sherman, Chapter 3), and it is now well established that in the context of groups for which subjects have no prior information the illusory-correlation effect is a reliable effect. However, for most groups encountered in everyday life, people are known to hold previously developed stereotypes and prejudices. To assess the impact of distinctiveness-based illusory correlations in everyday life, it would, therefore, be important to examine the interaction between distinctiveness effects and preexisting associative or evaluative bonds.

McArthur and Friedman (1980) were probably the first to study this issue. They conducted three experiments in which subjects possessed prior information about certain groups. In one experiment the groups were young or old, in a second black or white, and in a third male or female. The subjects were white, male and female undergraduates. A further variable in all three experiments was the desirability of the ascribed behavior. Desirable behavior was always more frequent than undesirable, and was, of course, uncorrelated with the group classification.

McArthur and Friedman expected to replicate Hamilton and Gifford's results only when the group was old, black, or female. This prediction was based on the assumption that "young white college students would share the societal prejudice of associating undesirable traits with people who are old, black, or female" (p. 616) and that this associative bond would weaken or eliminate the distinctiveness based illusory correlation. In the first experiment in which the group was young or old, the results did indeed replicate Hamilton and Gifford only when the group was old. In fact, when the group was young, the pattern was reversed. This is true for both the evaluative ratings and for the group membership attributions. When the younger group appeared infrequently, its members were evaluated more (not less) favorably than when the younger group appeared frequently. Also, when the younger group appeared infrequently, its members were associated less (not more) frequently with the undesirable behavior. Somewhat similar, though less consistent, results were obtained for the other two studies. In the case of the third experiment involving male and female groups, the data were best understood by using sex of subject as a variable. The overall pattern indicated that the Hamilton and Gifford effect tended to occur only when the group was of opposite sex to the subjects.

Thus, the findings of this study are complex and difficult to interpret. Since undesirable behavior was always associated with minority status, the design of the study does not allow one to decide whether the effect of the illusory correlation was counteracted by the presence of contrary associations or of contrary affective bonds (i.e., when the minority group was the subject's own group). Furthermore, it is unclear why the pattern of results should have been reversed when the minority group was the subject's own group (or a group for which there were positive associa- tions). Under such circumstances, it makes sense that the illusory-correlation tendency for the minority group to appear undesirable would not have occurred. However, what happened was a complete reversal of this tendency; that is, when the subject's group was the minority group, it was evaluated more favorably than when it was the majority group. The reasons for such a result are not clear, but possibly the minority status made the subject's group membership and the implicit evaluative bonds more salient.

A study by Schaller and Maas (1987: described in Hamilton and Sherman, Chapter 3) demonstrates more clearly that the effect of distinctiveness-based illusory correlations can be weakened or eliminated by the existence of inconsistent affective bonds. Using the Hamilton and Gifford paradigm, Schaller and Maas observed the typical illusory correlation effect for subjects in a control condition for whom there was no mention of group membership. However, when subjects believed they belonged to one or the other of the stimulus groups, the illusory correlation effect was significantly weakened if the shared infrequency effect would lead to a devaluation of their own group.

The findings of McArthur and Friedman (1980) and Schaller and Maas (1987) limit the generalizability of the distinctiveness-based frequency illusory correlation. They suggest that illusory correlations due to the co-occurrence of infrequent or otherwise distinctive stimuli may not develop when such correlations would be inconsistent with expectations based on preexisting associative or affective bonds (e.g., when the correlation contradicts an established stereotype or would lead to a devaluation of one's own group).

In summary, it is the assumption of a correlation between categories and traits that, according to the cognitive approach, is responsible for most of the apparent biases in stereotyping. Due to the superimposition of a classification on a set of trait dimensions with which it is correlated, differences between stimuli falling into different categories are overestimated and differences between stimuli within the same category are underestimated. This has been demonstrated for physical as well as social stimulus material. Correlative expectations also affect the interpretation of social actions and the encoding of information about social groups (cf. Hewstone, Chapter 10).

Since this approach assumes that the correlative expectations underlying stereotypes are either acquired through observations or through socialization processes, the model has no difficulty in addressing three of the four issues central to stereotyping. However, by rejecting motivational explanations, the approach has problems in accounting for the predominance of ethnocentrism, even though a potential solution has been suggested by Linville (1982).

Points of Integration

It should have become evident from our review of theories of stereotype and prejudice that there is no single approach that satisfactorily addresses the four issues that have been used as criteria for the evaluation of the different theoretical positions discussed in this chapter. This view is now widely accepted by stereotype researchers. Thus, the late Henri Tajfel, whose classic paper (Tajfel, 1969) was very instrumental in bringing about the cognitive revolution in stereotype research, at a later time (Tajfel, 1981) modified the position taken in his 1969 paper. Tajfel (1981) argued that in addition to the individual function of stereotypes as an aid in the cognitive structuring of an individual's social environment, stereotypes also serve social functions for the group. They help group members to preserve or create positively valued differentiations of a group from other social groups, and they contribute to the creation and maintenance of group ideologies, explaining or justifying a variety of social actions against outgroups.

Even Hamilton, one of the main proponents of the cognitive approach, has rejected the notion that stereotypes and prejudice could be explained as solely due to biases in cognitive functioning. Hamilton and Trolier (1986) state:

> Any particular form of stereotyping or prejudice, such as racism, is in all likelihood multiply determined by cognitive, motivational, and social learning processes, whose effects combine in a given social context to produce specific judgmental and behavioral manifestations. Therefore, any attempt to understand such phenomena as a product of one process alone is probably misguided (p. 153).

Hamilton and Trolier do not detail how motivational determinants interact with cognitive ones to produce specific judgmental and behavior manifestations. This last section will, therefore, be used to sketch such an integrative perspective on stereotype and prejudice.

As a starting point for this analysis, we would like to use the observation that, despite individual differences, many stereotypes seem to be widely shared within a given society or culture. For example, studies of ethnic or national stereotypes show impressive consensus and stability in the beliefs about the attributes of ethnic or national groups (Katz & Braly, 1933; Gilbert, 1951; Karlins et al., 1969). In a recent study of the national stereotypes of more than 1400 American college students, Stapf et al. (1986) found that the five traits with the highest percentage ratings corresponded closely to those of the earlier studies. There is only one theoretical perspective that can satisfactorily account for the historic and cultural stability in stereotypes (and prejudice), namely, social learning theory.

Ethnic and national stereotypes can thus be conceived of as culturally shared categories that transcend the individual. Even though they may be modified by experience, they are mostly acquired through channels of socialization such as parents, schools, and mass media. Since many stereotypes such as gender and national stereotypes stabilize already at the early age of 6 or 7 (Koblinksky et al., 1978; Tajfel & Jahoda, 1966), parents are likely to play an important role in their socialization. Further, Pettigrew (1958, 1959) and Moe et al. (1981) have reported evidence for the influence of societal norms.

The acceptance of such culturally shared categories, which imply an association between category membership and position on some trait dimensions, will then lead directly to ingroup favoritism and/or outgroup rejection, as well as to many of the judgmental biases studied and described by the cognitive approach. Cognitive research on the learning of correlations between categories and trait dimensions, as well as on the conditions that lead to the formation of illusory correlations, also contributes to our understanding of the development of stereotypes. As a further product of socialization, children may also acquire the notion that members of certain outgroups hold values and beliefs that differ dramatically from those shared within their own group. This perceived belief incongruence may cause, or contribute to, outgroup rejection.

By emphasizing processes of self-categorization and the need for a positive differentiation of membership groups from outgroups, the social identity theory of Tajfel and Turner (1979, 1985; Turner, 1987) offers an interpretation of the processes involved in ingroup favoritism and outgroup derogation that is both cognitive and motivational. The theory assumes that people are motivated to evaluate themselves positively and that, if they define themselves in terms of some group membership, they will be motivated to evaluate that group positively. Furthermore, since groups are evaluated in relation to other groups, a positive social identity requires that one's own group be favorably different from relevant comparison groups. Such processes of self-categorization and positive differentiation operate within a social environment that provides us with a rich matrix of culturally shared categorizations, as well as many dimensions on which to compare membership groups to outgroups. Thus, outgroup derogation is only one of the potential consequences of an individual's attempt to establish positively valued distinctiveness for relevant membership groups.

Since intergroup conflicts typically arise between groups in contact, conflict theory is probably less relevant as an explanation of the formation of stereotypes than as a theory of change. Intergroup conflict seems to be the one major factor that can lead to dramatic changes in established stereotypes. This has been demonstrated in Seago's (1947) study of the change in American stereotypes toward Germans and Japanese during the period between 1941 and 1945. Even after the invasion of Norway, Denmark, Holland, and France, the U.S. stereotype of the German in 1941 was practically identical to that reported by Katz and Braly in 1933 (scientifically minded, industrious, extremely nationalistic, stolid, and efficient). With the declaration of war and thus the open outbreak of conflict between the two countries, American attitudes toward the Germans deteriorated rapidly. In 1942 "aggressive" and "cruel" were added to the list, as was "arrogant" in 1943. However, at no time was the American stereotype of the Germans as negative as that toward the Japanese after Pearl Harbor. This is partly due to the fact that the initial attitude toward Germans was more positive than that toward the Japanese. However, the main reason could be that the Japanese attacked American territory, while the Germans did not.

The acceptance of this type of multiprocess theory of stereotyping and prejudice also has implications for the methodology of future research on prejudice. Instead of conducting studies aimed at demonstrating the validity of one of the processes, future research on stereotyping should attempt to assess the differential impact of cognitive and motivational processes on the development, maintenance, and change of stereotypes.

Acknowledgments. The authors would like to thank Alice Eagly and Miles Hewstone for their helpful comments on an earlier draft of this chapter.

References

Adorno, T.W., Frenkel-Brunswik, E., Levinson, D.J., & Sanford, R.N. (1950). *The authoritarian personality.* New York: Harper.

Ajzen, I., & Fishbein, M. (1973). Attitudinal and normative variables as predictors of specific behaviors. *Journal of Personality and Social Psychology, 27,* 41–57.

Ajzen, I., & Fishbein, M. (1977). Attitude–behavior relations: A theoretical analysis and review of empirical research. *Psychological Bulletin, 84,* 888–918.

Ajzen, I., & Fishbein, M. (1980). Understanding attitudes and predicting behavior. Englewood Cliffs, NJ: Prentice Hall.

Allport, G.W. (1954). *The nature of prejudice.* Reading, MA: Addison-Wesley.

Allport, G.W., & Kramer, B.M. (1946). Some roots of prejudice. *Journal of Psychology, 22,* 9–39.

Anderson, N.H. (1965). Averaging versus adding as a stimulus-combination rule in impression formation. *Journal of Experimental Psychology, 70,* 394–400.

Ashmore, R.D. (1970). The problem of intergroup prejudice. In: B.E. Collins, *Social psychology* (pp. 246–296). Reading, MA: Addison-Wesley.

Ashmore, R.D., & Del Boca, F.K. (1981). Conceptual approaches to stereotypes and stereotyping. In D. Hamilton (Ed.), *Cognitive processes in stereotyping and intergroup behavior* (pp. 1–35). Hillsdale, NJ: Erlbaum.

Bettelheim, B., & Janowitz, M. (1950). *Dynamics of prejudice.* New York: Harper.

Bettelheim, B., & Janowitz, M. (1964). *Social change and prejudice: Dynamics of prejudice.* London: The Free Press of Glencoe.

Billig, M. (1976). *Social psychology and intergroup relations.* London: Academic Press.

Bourne, L.E. (1966). *Human conceptual behavior.* Boston: Allyn & Bacon.

Breckler, S.J. (1984). Empirical validation of affect, behavior, and cognition as distinct components of attitude. *Journal of Personality and Social Psychology, 47,* 1191–1205.

Brigham, J.C. (1971). Ethnic stereotypes. *Psychological Bulletin, 76,* 15–38.

Brown, R. (1958). *Words and things.* Glencoe, IL: Free Press.

Brown, R. (1965). *Social Psychology.* New York: Free Press.

Campbell, D.T. (1956). Enhancement of contrast as composite habit. *Journal of Abnormal and Social Psychology, 53,* 350–355.

Campbell, D.T. (1965). Ethnocentric and other altruistic motives. In D. Levine (Ed.), *Symposium on motivation* (pp. 283–311). Lincoln, NE: University of Nebraska Press.

Chapman, L.J. (1967). Illusory correlation in observational report. *Journal of Verbal Learning and Verbal Behavior, 6,* 151–155.

Chapman, L.J., & Chapman, J.P. (1967). Genesis of popular but erroneous psycho-diagnostic observations. *Journal of Abnormal Psychology, 72,* 193–204.

Chein, I. (1951). Notes on a framework for the measurement of discrimination and prejudice. In M. Jahoda, M. Deutsch, & S.W. Cook (Eds.), *Research methods in social relations* (pp. 382–390). New York: Dryden.

Dahrendorf, R. (1959). *Class and class conflict in industrial society.* Stanford, CA: Stanford University Press.

DeFleur, M.L., & Westie, F.R. (1958). Verbal attitudes and overt acts: An experiment on the salience of attitudes. *American Sociological Review, 23,* 667–673.

Dollard, J., Miller, N.E., Doob, L.W., Mowrer, O.H., & Sears, R.R. (1939). *Frustration and aggression.* New Haven: Yale University Press.

Dovidio, J.F., & Gaertner, S.L. (1986). Prejudice, discrimination, and racism: Historical trends and contemporary approaches. In J.F. Dovidio & S.L. Gaertner (Eds.), *Prejudice, discrimination, and racism* (pp. 1–34). San Diego, CA: Academic Press.

Dutton, D.G. (1971). Reactions of restaurateurs to blacks and whites violating restaurant dress regulations. *Canadian Journal of Behavioural Science, 5,* 34–45.

Eagly, A.H. (1987). *Sex differences in social behavior: A social-role interpretation.* Hillsdale, NJ: Erlbaum.

Eagly, A.H., & Kite, M.E. (1987). Are stereotypes of nationalities applied to both women and men? *Journal of Personality and Social Psychology, 53,* 451–462.

Eagly, A.H., & Mladinic, A. (1988). *Gender stereotypes and attitudes towards women and men.* Unpublished manuscript.

Eagly, A.H., & Steffen, V.J. (1984). Gender stereotypes stem from the distribution of women and men into social roles. *Journal of Personality and Social Psychology, 46,* 735–754.

Eagly, A.H., & Steffen, V.J. (in press). A note on assessing stereotypes. *Personality and Social Psychology Bulletin.*

Eiser, J.R. (1971). Enhancement of contrast in the absolute judgment of attitude statements. *Journal of Personality and Social Psychology, 17,* 1–10.

Eiser, J.R., & Mower-White, C.J. (1975). Evaluative consistency and social judgment. *Journal of Personality and Social Psychology, 4,* 769–775.

Eiser, J.R., & Stroebe, W. (1972). *Categorization and Social Judgment.* London: Academic Press.

English, H., & English, A. (1958). *A comprehensive dictionary of psychological and psychoanalytical terms.* New York: Langmons, Green and Co.

Epstein, R., & Komorita, S.S. (1965). Parental discipline, stimulus characteristics of outgroups, and social distance in children. *Journal of Personality and Social Psychology, 2,* 416–420.

Epstein, R., & Komorita, S.S. (1966). Childhood prejudice as a function of parental ethnocentrism, punitiveness, and outgroup characteristics. *Journal of Personality and Social Psychology, 3,* 259–264.

Fishbein, M. (1967). A behavior theory approach to the relations between beliefs about an object and the attitude toward the object. In N. Fishbein (Ed.), *Readings in attitude theory and measurement* (pp. 389–400). New York: Wiley.

Fishbein, M., & Ajzen, I. (1975). *Belief, attitude, intention, and behavior: An introduction to theory and research.* Reading, MA: Addison-Wesley.

Gilbert, G.M. (1951). Stereotype persistence and change among college students. *Journal of Abnormal and Social Psychology, 46,* 245–252.

Greenberg, B.S., & Mazingo, S.L. (1976). Racial issues in the mass media. In P.A. Katz (Ed.), *Towards the elimination of racism* (pp. 309–339). New York: Pergamon.

Hamilton, D.L. (1981). Illusory correlation as a basis for stereotyping. In D.L. Hamilton (Ed.), *Cognitive processes in stereotyping and intergroup behavior.* (pp. 115–144). Hillsdale, NJ: Erlbaum.

Hamilton, D.L., & Gifford, R.K. (1976). Illusory correlation in interpersonal perception: A cognitive basis of stereotypic judgments. *Journal of Experimental Social Psychology, 12,* 392–407.

Hamilton, D.L., & Trolier, T.K. (1986). Stereotypes and stereotyping: An overview of the cognitive approach. In J.F. Dovidio & S.L. Gaertner (Eds.), *Prejudice, discrimination, and racism* (pp. 127–158). Orlando, FL: Academic Press.

Harding, J., Kutner, B., Proshansky, H., & Chein, I. (1954). Prejudice and ethnic relations. In G. Lindzey (Ed.), *Handbook of social psychology* (Vol. 2) (pp. 1021–1061). Cambridge, MA: Addison-Wesley.

Harding, J., Proshansky, H., Kutner, B., & Chein, I. (1969). Prejudice and ethnic relations. In G. Lindzey & E. Aronson (Eds.), *The handbook of social psychology* (Vol. 5) (pp. 1–76). Reading, MA: Addison-Wesley.

Heider, F. (1958). *The psychology of interpersonal relations.* New York: Wiley.

Hyman, H.H., & Sheatsley, P.B. (1954). The authoritarian personality: A methodological critique. In R. Christie & M. Jahoda (Eds.), *Studies in the scope and method of the authoritarian personality* (pp. 50–122). Glencoe, IL: The Free Press.

Insko, C.A., Nacoste, R.W., & Moe, J.L. (1983). Belief congruence and racial discrimination: Review of the evidence and critical evaluation. *European Journal of Social Psychology, 13,* 153–174.

Jonas, K., & Hewstone, M. (1986). The assessment of national stereotypes: A methodological study. *Journal of Social Psychology, 126,* 745–754.

Jones, E.E., & Davis, K.E. (1965). From acts to dispositions. In L. Berkowitz (Ed.), *Advances in experimental social psychology* (Vol. 2) (pp. 219–266). New York: Academic Press.

Karlins, M., Coffman, T.L., & Walters, G. (1969). On the fading of social stereotypes: Studies in three generations of college students. *Journal of Personality and Social Psychology, 13,* 1–16.

Katz, D., & Braly, K.W. (1933). Racial stereotypes of 100 college students. *Journal of Abnormal and Social Psychology, 28,* 280–290.

Kirscht, J.P., & Dillehay, R.C. (1967). *Dimensions of authoritarianism: A review of research and theory.* Lexington, KY: University of Kentucky Press.

Klineberg, O. (1951). The scientific study of national stereotypes. *International Social Science Bulletin, 3,* 505–515.

Koblinsky, S.G., Cruse, D.F., & Sugawara, A.I. (1978). Sex role stereotypes and children's memory of story content. *Child Development, 49,* 452–458.

Krech, D., & Crutchfield, R.S. (1948). *Theory and problems of social psychology.* New York: McGraw-Hill.

Kutner, B., Wilkins, C., & Yarrow, P.R. (1952). Verbal attitudes and overt behavior involving racial prejudice. *Journal of Abnormal and Social Psychology, 47,* 649–652.

LaPiere, R.T. (1934). Attitudes versus actions. *Social Forces, 13,* 230–237.

LeVine, R.A., & Campbell, D.T. (1972). *Ethnocentrism: Theories of conflict, ethnic attitudes, and group behavior.* New York: Wiley.

Liberman, A.M., Harris, K.S., Howard, S.H., & Griffith, B.C. (1957). The discrimination of speech sounds within and across phoneme boundaries. *Journal of Experimental Psychology, 54,* 358–368.

Lilli, W. (1970). Das Zustandekommen von Stereotypen über einfache und komplexe Sachverhalte: Experimente zum klassifizierenden Urteil. *Zeitschrift für Sozialpsychologie, 1,* 57–79.

Lilli, W., & Lehner, F. (1971). Stereotype Wahrnehmung: Eine Weiterentwicklung der Theorie Tajfel's. *Zeitschrift fur Sozialpsychologie, 2,* 285–294.

Lilli, W., & Rehm, J. (1988). Judgmental bases of intergroup conflict. In W. Stroebe, A.W. Kruglanski, D. Bar-Tal, & M. Hewstone (Eds.), *The social psychology of intergroup conflict* (pp. 29–45). New York: Springer.

Linville, P.W. (1982). The complexity–extremity effect and age-based stereotyping. *Journal of Personality and Social Psychology, 42*, 193–211.

Lippman, W. (1922). *Public opinion.* New York: Harcourt & Brace.

Marchand, B. (1970). Auswirkung einer emotional wertvollen und einer emotional neutralen Klassifikation auf die Schätzung einer Stimulusserie. *Zeitschrift für Sozialpsychologie, 1*, 370–376.

McArthur, L.Z., & Friedman, S.A. (1980). Illusory correlation in impression formation: Variations in the shared distinctiveness effect as a function of the distinctive person's age, race, and sex. *Journal of Personality and Social Psychology, 39*, 615–624.

McCauley, C., & Stitt, C.L. (1978). An individual and quantitative measure of stereotypes. *Journal of Personality and Social Psychology, 39*, 929–940.

McCauley, C., & Stitt, C.L., & Segal, M. (1980). Stereotyping: From prejudice to prediction. *Psychological Bulletin, 87*, 195–208.

Miller, N.E., & Bugelski, R. (1948). Minor studies in aggression: The influence of frustrations imposed by the in-group on attitudes expressed toward out-groups. *Journal of Psychology, 25*, 437–442.

Minard, R.D. (1952). Race relationships in the Pocahontas coal field. *Journal of Social Issues, 8*, 29–44.

Moe, J.L., Nacoste, R.W., & Insko, C.A. (1981). Belief versus race as determinants of discrimination: A study of southern adolescents in 1966 and 1979. *Journal of Personality and Social Psychology, 41*, 1031–1050.

Pettigrew, T.F. (1958). Personality and sociocultural factors in intergroup attitudes: A cross-national comparison. *Journal of Conflict Resolution, 2*, 29–42.

Pettigrew, T.F. (1959). Regional differences in an anti-Negro prejudice. *Journal of Abnormal and Social Psychology, 59*, 28–36.

Plotkin, L. (1964). *The frequency of appearance of Negroes on television.* New York: The Committee on Integration, New York Society for Ethical Culture.

Popper, K.R. (1963). *Conjectures and refutations.* London: Routledge & Kegan Paul.

Robinson, J.E., & Insko, C.A. (1969). Attributed belief similarity–dissimilarity versus race as determinants of prejudice: A further test of Rokeach's theory. *Journal of Experimental Research in Personality, 4*, 72–77.

Rokeach, M. (1960). *The open and closed mind.* New York: Basic Books.

Rokeach, M., Smith, P.W., & Evans, R.I. (1960). Two kinds of prejudice or one? In M. Rokeach (Ed.), *The open and closed mind* (pp. 132–168). New York: Basic Books.

Rosenberg, M.J. (1960). An analysis of affective–cognitive consistency. In C.I. Hovland & M.J. Rosenberg (Eds.), *Attitude organization and change* (pp. 15–64). New Haven: Yale University Press.

Schaller, M., & Maas, A. (1987). *Illusory correlations and social categorization.* Unpublished manuscript, University of Padova, Italy.

Seago, D.W. (1947). Stereotypes: Before Pearl Harbor and after. *Journal of Psychology, 23*, 55–63.

Secord, P.F. (1959). Stereotyping and favorableness in the perception of Negro faces. *Journal of Abnormal and Social Psychology, 59*, 309–314.

Secord, P.F., Bevan, W., & Katz, B. (1956). The Negro stereotype and perceptual accentuation. *Journal of Abnormal and Social Psychology, 53*, 78–83.

Sherif, M. (1967). *Group conflict and cooperation.* London: Routledge & Kegan Paul.

Simon, H.A. (1955). A behavior model of rational choice. *Quarterly Journal of Economics, 69*, 99–118.

Smedley, J.W., & Bayton, J.A. (1978). Evaluation of race–class stereotypes by race and perceived class of subjects. *Journal of Personality and Social Psychology, 36*, 530–535.

Stagner, R., & Congdon, C.S. (1955). Another failure to demonstrate displacement of aggression. *Journal of Abnormal and Social Psychology, 51*, 695–696.

Stapf, K.H., Stroebe, W., & Jonas, K. (1986). *Amerikaner über Deutschland und die Deutschen: Urteile und Vorurteile*. Köln: Westdeutscher Verlag.

Stein, D.D., Hardyck, J.A., & Smith, M.B. (1965). Race and belief: An open and shut case. *Journal of Personality and Social Psychology, 1*, 281–289.

Stephan, W.G. (1985). Intergroup relations. In G. Lindzey & E. Aronson (Eds.), *The handbook of social psychology* (Vol. 2) (pp. 599–658). New York: Random House.

Stephan, W.G., & Rosenfield, D. (1982). Racial and ethnic attitudes. In A.G. Miller (Ed.), *In the eye of the beholder: Contemporary issues in stereotyping* (pp. 92–136). New York: Praeger.

Tajfel, H. (1957). Value and the perceptual judgment of magnitude. *Psychological Review, 64*, 192–204.

Tajfel, H. (1959a). The anchoring effects of value in a scale of judgments. *British Journal of Psychology, 50*, 294–304.

Tajfel, H. (1959b). Quantitative judgment in social perception. *British Journal of Psychology, 50*, 192–204.

Tajfel, H. (1969). Cognitive aspects of prejudice. *Journal of Social Issues, 25*, 79–97.

Tajfel, H. (1970). Experiments in intergroup discrimination. *Scientific American, 223*(5) pp.96–102.

Tajfel, H. (1981). *Human groups and social categories*. Cambridge: Cambridge University Press.

Tajfel, H. (1982). Social psychology of intergroup relations. In M.R. Rosenzweig & L.R. Porter (Eds.), *Annual review of psychology* (pp. 1–39). Palo Alto, CA: Annual Reviews.

Tajfel, H., & Jahoda, G. (1966). Development in children of concepts and attitudes about their own and other countries. *Proceedings of the 18th International Congress of Psychology, 36*, 17–33. Moscow Symposium.

Tajfel, H., & Turner, J. (1979). An integrative theory of intergroup conflict. In W.G. Austin & S. Worchel (Eds.), *The social psychology of intergroup relations* (pp. 33–47). Belmont, CA: Wadsworth.

Tajfel, H., & Turner, J. (1985). The social identity theory of intergroup behavior. In S. Worchel & W.G. Austin (Eds.), *Psychology of intergroup relations* (pp. 7–24). Chicago, IL: Nelson-Hall.

Tajfel, H., & Wilkes, A.L. (1963). Classification and quantitative judgment. *British Journal of Psychology, 54*, 101–114.

Triandis, H.C., & Triandis, L.M. (1965). Some studies of social distance. In I.D. Steiner & M. Fishbein (Eds.), *Recent studies of social psychology* (pp. 207–217). New York: Holt.

Turner, C. (1987). *Rediscovering the social group*. Oxford: Blackwell.

Weitz, S. (1972). Attitude, voice, and behavior: A repressed affect model of interracial interaction. *Journal of Personality and Social Psychology, 24*, 14–21.

Wicker, A.W. (1969). Attitude versus actions: The relationship of verbal and overt behavioral responses to attitude objects. *Journal of Social Issues, 25*, 41–78.

Zanna, M.P., & Rempel, J.K. (1988). Attitudes: A new look at an old concept. In D. Bar-Tal & A. Kruglanski (Eds.), *The social psychology of knowledge* (pp. 315–334). New York: Cambridge University Press.

Part II

Formation of Stereotypes and Prejudice

Chapter 2

A Cognitive Approach to Stereotyping

Walter G. Stephan

Over the course of the last two decades, no paradigm in social psychology has had such a profound impact as social cognition. In the area of intergroup relationships, its impact has been to provide a theoretical underpinning for our understanding of prejudice, stereotyping, discrimination, and intergroup contact (Stephan, 1985). While the cognitive approach cannot replace the earlier emphases on the motivational, affective, and moral aspects of intergroup relationships, it can provide new insights into the ways in which prejudice, discrimination, and especially stereotypes develop and change.

Stereotypes are most susceptible to the cognitive approach precisely because they consist entirely of cognitions concerning groups. Previous analyses of stereotypes were primarily concerned with their historical origins and the socialization and contact experiences that fostered them (Stephan & Rosenfield, 1982). Relatively little attention was paid to their structure or the cognitive processes that strengthened or weakened them. They were regarded as invalid overgeneralizations that were morally wrong (Brigham, 1971). Although this description aptly characterizes most pejorative stereotypes, it tended to draw researchers away from an examination of the normal cognitive processes that supported the existence of both pejorative and non-pejorative stereotypes. This chapter is concerned with the role of such normal cognitive processes in sustaining stereotypes.

I begin by introducing a general model that addresses the structuring and processing of cognitive information. I then apply the model to the stereotyping process, focusing on automatic encoding, controlled encoding, and retrieval. I conclude by drawing implications from the model and the data for attempts to change stereotypes.

A Model of Cognitive Information Processing

Models of cognition deal with the structuring and processing of information in the mind. Although there are many models to choose from, I will focus on one developed by Anderson (1983), because it is particularly useful in discussing stereotypes.

In the model there are three memory systems. Two of these systems, declarative and production memory, are relatively permanent. The third type of memory, working memory, is temporary. Declarative memory contains structured information that is largely factual, while production memory contains procedural information (i.e., how to do things). Working memory contains the information that is currently being processed or has been recently processed. Declarative memory is roughly analogous to the data in a computer (e.g., this manuscript and other manuscripts on this diskette), production memory is analogous to the program that is run on the data (e.g., the word processing program I am using), and working memory is analogous to the information about the data or the program that is currently on the viewing screen of the computer (e.g., this paragraph).

Working memory consists of the information to which the system has access at any given time. The information in working memory exists in varying degrees of activation. The most activated information is that which has been most recently or frequently processed. The activation of information in working memory may occur as a result of processing environmental stimuli through the sense organs, the retrieval of information from declarative memory, the execution of procedures from production memory, or through consciously focusing attention on system-relevant goals. For instance, an individual may see, hear, touch, and smell another person, recall the personality traits of that person, perform the procedures required to categorize this person as an outgroup member, and then plan how to behave toward this person. Only a limited amount of information can be present in working memory at any given time.

Information in declarative memory is structured through a network of nodes and connecting links. Both nodes and links can vary in strength, depending on such factors as the frequency and recency with which they have been activated. Activation of factual information in declarative memory spreads through the network formed by the nodes and the links connecting them. Activation of information in declarative memory may be under conscious control (controlled activation), or it can occur automatically (automatic activation). The amount of information that can be consciously activated at one point in time is quite limited, whereas the amount of information that can be automatically processed is almost unlimited. Controlled processing is thought to be performed serially, but automatic information processing can be parallel or simultaneous. For example, an individual may consciously retrieve the traits of an outgroup and then, one at a time, think through the degree to which they apply to a given outgroup member. At the same time the node associated with the outgroup is activated, activation will automatically and simultaneously spread to related information about this group that is associated with the group node.

The meaning of a given node of abstract information is defined by its relationship with other nodes in declarative memory. For instance, the node for a social group such as men may be associated with other nodes denoting the traits ascribed to men. Large networks of interrelated nodes of abstract information are referred to as schemata. Schemata contain all the information an individual possesses within a given domain. The information in schemata is thought to be organized hierarchically with

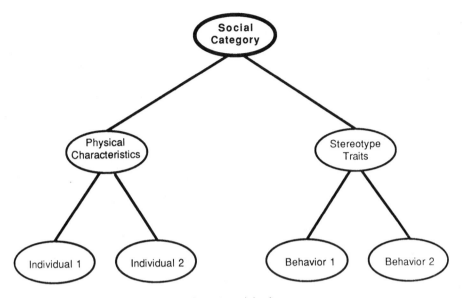

Figure 2-1. A social schemata.

the most concrete information at the lowest levels and the most abstract information at the highest levels. The schemata for a social group might include a group node at the highest level, with nodes for stereotype traits and distinguishing physical characteristics at an intermediate level, and nodes for specific group members and expected behaviors at a lower level (Figure 2-1).

Declarative memory and working memory are closely intertwined. Information that is in working memory may be permanently stored in declarative memory, from which it can be subsequently retrieved as needed. The probability that information in working memory will be stored in declarative memory depends on the frequency with which this information has been activated, and to a lesser extent, on the duration of activation of the information. The ease with which information may be retrieved from declarative memory depends on the strength of the memory trace, the degree of activation of the information, and the number and strength of the links between this node of information and other nodes. The strength of the memory trace depends on the frequency with which the information has been activated from declarative memory. Thus, the strength and complexity of an individual's schema of an outgroup will depend primarily on the frequency with which information about the outgroup is processed and the number of different types of information that are processed. The ease with which information about this group can be retrieved will depend on the frequency with which the individual thinks of others in terms of this group, how salient or important group membership is in the present context, and the complexity of the network of information associated with this group.

Production memory contains the procedures that can be performed on information in working memory. These procedures may be as simple as categorizing an individual as a member of a social group or as complex as those required to make attributions about the causes of behavior (Smith, 1984). In either case, a matching process is performed in which the information in working memory is compared to the information required to elicit a given procedure from production memory. For instance, if an individual is trying to determine the nationality of another person, the available information on this person (e.g., his/her physical appearance and dress) will be compared to the characteristics of various nationality groups. When a match is sufficiently close, the procedure will be executed and result in the performance of the relevant behavior—if the behavior is in accordance with the goals the system is attempting to achieve. For instance, if an individual's characteristics match those of an Italian, then this individual may be addressed in Italian.

The Model Applied to Stereotypes

In this section, I discuss the structure of stereotype information and its processing. The structural elements of stereotypes include their location within schemata, their defining and characteristic features, and their relationship to prototypes. In considering the processing of stereotype information, I will focus on encoding and retrieval. My concern will be with normal processing, especially the biases that normally occur during the processing of social category information.

The Structure of Social Category Information

Schemata. The stereotyped traits associated with social categories may be viewed as one level of information within schemata of social groups (see Figure 2-1). For social shcemata, it has frequently been argued that information is processed from the top down, meaning that information processing starts at the more abstract levels of knowledge structures and proceeds downward through the hierarchy to the lower levels. However, in order to place an individual in a social category, information may initially be processed at an intermediate level in the hierarchy (e.g., the physical features associated with the group) to categorize the person into the appropriate group (Rumelhart, 1984). Thus, information processing concerning a stranger may begin with encoding the person's features into working memory and proceed to matching these features with those stored in production memory in order to categorize the person. After categorizing the person, the traits of the category may be retrieved from declarative memory followed by the generation from production memory of possible behaviors based on these traits.

For many categories, there appears to be a level within hierarchical schemata that leads to optimal information processing. Such basic levels of categorization are generally at an intermediate position in the hierarchy. At the basic levels, instances are more quickly categorized than at higher or lower levels. Also, basic levels of categories are learned at a younger age and they are preferred to other levels when sorting stimuli (Rosch, Mervis, Gray, Johnson, & Boyes-Braem, 1976). Social categories such as sex and race appear to be relatively basic (McCann, Ostrom, Tyner, & Mitchell, 1985; Pliske & Smith, 1979; Smith & Branscombe, 1986) and may be used so frequently that their application becomes automatic. When Bem (Bem & Bem, 1977) refers to sexism as a nonconscious ideology, it appears that she is referring to the automatic use of sex as a social category that has the effect of subordinating and objectifying women (cf. Schur, 1984).

Category features. Stereotypes may be regarded as sets of features associated with basic level categories (cf. Smith, Shoben, & Rips, 1974). For some categories there are certain features, known as defining features, that are necessary and sufficient to define membership in the category (cf. identifying attributes, Ashmore & Del Boca, 1981). Basic level categories, like sex and race, probably have a small number of defining features (Rosch, Mervis, Gray, Johnson, & Boyes-Braem, 1976). The defining features of basic categories tend to be discrete or discontinuous (e.g., male or female).

In contrast, many social categories, such as social class, have a large number of defining features, and no one feature is necessary or sufficient to define membership. The defining features of such categories are often continuous (e.g., income). Such social categories are "fuzzy" precisely because they have numerous continuous defining features that are neither necessary nor sufficient for categorical identification.

In addition to defining features, most social categories have characteristic features associated with them (cf. ascribed attributes, Ashmore & Del Boca, 1981). These features are not used to define category membership, but they are perceived as being possessed by many members of the category. For stereotypes, one set of characteristic features consists of the traits associated with a particular group. Characteristic features vary in how strongly they are associated with the category and with one another.

Prototypes. Another concept that has proven useful in understanding the processing of stereotype information is prototypes. Prototypes, consisting of the attributes of the typical category member, exist for many categories. In processing social information, the incoming information may be compared to the prototypes of the categories to which the individual might belong (Rosch, 1978). Such comparisons may be used to determine if an individual is a member of a given social group. For instance, information on the appearance of a young male might be compared to the prototype of "man" to decide if he is a "boy" or a "man." It is likely that prototypes are used more frequently to identify members of "fuzzy" categories than for basic categories (cf. Mayer & Bower, 1986).

If an individual is judged to be high on prototypicality, expectancies derived from the prototype may be elicited (Cantor & Mischel, 1977). Individuals high on prototypicality are likely to be used to predict the traits and behaviors of the outgroup as a whole (Wilder, 1984). Also, when individuals are judged to be high on prototypicality, the affect associated with members of the group may be evoked (Fiske & Pavelchak, 1982).

Processing Social Category Information

Social category information is frequently encoded automatically. Since automatic processing can occur simultaneously and demands relatively little processing capacity, it is likely that the social categories of salient others are frequently activated without our being aware of it. But we can also encode social categories through the use of controlled processing in which we consciously process information in working memory about members of specific social groups. Thus, in many instances we may be encoding the sex, race, and age of the people with whom we are interacting, even though we are unaware of it, while in some instances we consciously chose to attend to these social categories. In the next two sections the consequences of automatic and controlled encoding will be discussed.

Automatic encoding. Social categories may be automatically activated when social stimuli are made salient by virtue of their being distinctive, deviant, unexpected, or negative. For instance, being a member of a statistical minority may make a person's social category salient (Taylor & Fiske, 1978). Thus, a single black in a group of whites is salient and will disproportionately influence observers' perceptions (Taylor, Fiske, Close, Anderson, & Ruderman, 1975).

When a social category has been activated, related material in declarative memory becomes more accessible for subsequent processing because the activation spreads through the associated network (Meyer & Schvaneveldt, 1971). Priming a category, by briefly causing it to be attended to, appears to make it more probable that people who are ambiguous with respect to category membership will be categorized as members of the primed category (Higgins, Rholes, & Jones, 1977, Srull & Wyer, 1979). Priming the category facilitates the processing of stereotype-related traits (Dovidio, Evans, & Tyler, 1986; Smith & Branscombe, 1986), and physical features (Klatzky, Martin, & Kane 1982) in working memory.

In one study it was found that briefly presenting the group labels "black" or "white" decreased subsequent reaction times for traits associated with these two groups (Dovidio, et al., 1986). In another study, a lone male or female in a group of members of the opposite sex recalled more stereotype-related information for the opposite sex than their own sex, presumably because interacting with a group of out-group members repeatedly primed the category and traits of the opposite sex (Higgins & King, 1981). The priming of traits has been found to lead to extreme judgments of others on trait-related dimensions (Bargh, Bond, Lombardi, & Tota, 1986; Bargh & Pietromonaco, 1982; Srull & Wyer, 1980). It also appears that processing stereotype-consistent information on one trait may strengthen the links to other extreme traits that are a part of that stereotype.

Other studies indicate that the affect associated with social categories may be automatically primed when the social categories are activated (Srull & Wyer, 1979). General support for this idea comes from the finding that when strong affective reactions to attitude objects are primed, they facilitate access to affectively congruent adjectives (Fazio, Sanbonmatsu, Powell, & Kardes, 1986). In the case of stereotypes, support may be found in the Dovidio et al. study cited above. Using

white subjects they found that the reaction times were shorter for identifying negative traits as applicable to the group after the word "black" was used as a prime than
in a control condition. Likewise, the reaction times decreased for positive traits,
after "white" was presented as a prime (Dovidio et al., 1986).

These findings concerning priming suggest that when a social category is activated, other people in the social context may be similarly categorized and the traits
associated with that category will be accessible to working memory with the result
that more extreme evaluations may occur. When category-related affect is primed,
traits that are affectively consistent with the evaluation of the category will be more
accessible than affectively inconsistent traits. For disliked groups, this means that
negative traits will be more available to be used as attributions for behavior than
positive ones. A study by Greenberg and Pyszczynski (1985) illustrates this process.
White students regarded a black debater who lost a debate as less competent than a
losing white debater if another white referred to blacks by using a pejorative label.
The black debater was not negatively evaluated if no remark was made or if he had
won. The pejorative label apparently primed negative affect and associated negative
traits that were then used as attributions for the black's behavior, but only if the
behavior was consistent with the affect that was primed.

Controlled encoding. Actively processing social category information can set in
motion a sequence of related events that confirms the existence of stereotyped traits
associated with the category. This expectancy–confirmation sequence has three
stages beginning with procedures elicited from production memory leading to the
collection of expectancy-confirming information, proceeding to the biased processing of expectancy-confirming and disconfirming information, and ultimately leading to behavior that will elicit self-fulfilling prophecies. These three stages describe
a temporal sequence, but they do not constitute an invariant sequence, and any one
of them may occur without being accompanied by the others. After discussing each
of the three stages, the effects of actively encoding information through the use of
sets will be presented.

Stage I concerns situations in which people are acquiring information about
another person or group. In such situations, there is a tendency for people to seek
out and prefer information about others that will confirm preconceptions concerning their traits (Bodenhausen & Wyer, 1985; Duncan, 1976; Skov & Sherman,
1986; Snyder & Swann, 1978; Wilder & Allen, 1978). The reason appears to be
that seeking expectancy-confirming evidence is cognitively more efficient than
seeking information that disconfirms expectancies (Skov & Sherman, 1986). The
tendency to seek expectancy-confirming evidence creates an initial barrier that
must be overcome in any attempt to change stereotypes by modifying the associated
expectancies.

Stage II is concerned with the effects of expectancies on cognitive processing. The
activation from declarative memory of traits associated with social categories can
create behavioral expectancies (Deaux & Lewis, 1984; Jackson & Cash, 1985).
Under most conditions, these expectancies contribute to the likelihood that the existence of the traits will be perceived to have been confirmed. The reason is that

expectancy-confirming information is readily encoded and used as a basis for subsequent judgments (Higgins, et al., 1977; Rothbart, Evans, & Fulero, 1979). In its most extreme form, this bias leads to the perception that the expectancy has been confirmed, even when no expectancy-confirming evidence has been presented.

There appear to be two factors that contribute to the differential encoding of expectancy-confirming evidence. The first factor is that stereotype-based expectancies tend to be weak. For example, in a recent study of racial stereotypes, the traits associated with whites and blacks were rarely selected as applying to these groups by more than 25% of the respondents (Dovidio & Geartner, 1986). Because these weak expectancies apply to groups, rather than specific individuals, some "exceptions to the rule" are anticipated and are not necessarily taken as disconfirmations of the group stereotype (Srull, Lichtenstein, & Rothbart, 1985; Stern, Mars, Millar, & Cole, 1984). The second factor is that stereotype-based expectations often concern ambiguous traits (Rothbart & John, 1985). For instance, if members of a given group are expected to be suspicious, their behavior is unlikely to be perceived as disconfirming the expectancy. For ambiguous traits, such as suspiciousness, it is difficult to determine what behaviors would disconfirm them, so disconfirmations may not be encoded as such.

One study found that when whites observed a black behaving in a menacing manner they judged the person to be more aggressive than when a white was seen behaving in the same way (Duncan, 1976; see also Sager & Schofield, 1980). In this case the expectation that blacks would behave aggressively was probably weak and the behavior did not disconfirm it, so the expectation was perceived as having been confirmed. For the white stimulus person, there may have been a weak expectation of friendliness or civility, and the potentially disconfirming information was not interpreted as aggression. If the behavior has been salient and clearly aggressive, it probably would have been encoded as aggression in both groups. A study by Locksley, Borgida, Brekke, and Hepburn (1980) is consistent with this line of reasoning. In that study, stereotype-consistent trait judgments were made for the assertiveness of males and females, but these sex differences disappeared when very explicit contradictory information was presented.

In addition, when processing demands are complex, expectations based on stereotypes may serve as simplifying mechanisms (heuristics) that bias information processing in working memory. Under these conditions, expectancy-confirming evidence appears to be selectively attended to and forms the basis for subsequent judgments of the categorized person (Bodenhausen & Wyer, 1985). Also, if people are given instructions to think about the information they have received about the other person, confirming evidence is more likely to be encoded than disconfirming evidence, and subsequent impressions will be congruent with the confirming evidence (Wyer & Martin, 1986). The latter effect apparently occurs because thinking about the information strengthens the links between the social category node and the confirming evidence, leading the confirming evidence to be more accessible in memory. The bias to selectively encode expectancy-confirming evidence poses a major barrier to changing stereotypes that consist of weak or ambiguous traits.

Under some conditions, there is a tendency to attend to information that is disconfirming (Hastie & Kumar, 1979). Srull, Lichtenstein, and Rothbart (1985) argue that disconfirming evidence is most likely to be encoded when the expectancy is strong and unambiguous. Such expectancies more frequently characterize beliefs about individuals rather than stereotypes of groups. When expectancies are strong it appears that the unexpected information is encoded more elaborately (at a deeper level) than expected information (Hemsley & Marmurek, 1982; Srull et al. 1985; Stern, et al., 1984). The deeper encoding appears to involve creating more complex links in working memory between the items of disconfirming evidence and other items of information previously associated with the social category node. Curiously, expectancy-disconfirming information on one trait may enhance the memory of evidence on other traits that are consistent with the stereotype (O'Sullivan & Durso, 1984; Srull et al., 1985). This finding suggests that even as information that might counteract a stereotype is being encoded, other aspects of the stereotype are being strengthened.

Despite the more elaborate encoding of expectancy-disconfirming evidence, behavior that disconfirms expectancies tends to be attributed to situational, rather than internal, factors (Crocker, Hannah, & Weber, 1983; Kulik, 1983). Also, even in those studies indicating that expectancy-disconfirming evidence is better encoded than confirming evidence (e.g., Hastie & Kumar, 1979; Hemsley & Marmurek, 1982), the impressions of the other person remained congruent with the initial impression and the confirming evidence. An explanation for the latter finding is that a trait linked to a group node in declarative memory will be weakened only if the attributional inference process elicited in production memory produces an internal attribution to account for the expectancy-disconfirming evidence that is being processed in working memory. To the extent that these attributional processes are operating, people whose expectations are disconfirmed will not change their future expectations or impressions of the individual or the group to which he/she belongs. Taken together, the studies on expectancies reflect a general tendency to respond in ways that support pre-existing stereotypes, even when stereotype-inconsistent information has been encoded (Stangor, 1986; Wilder & Shapiro, 1984).

In addition, it has been found that when people's behaviors are inconsistent with stereotype-based expectancies, they are liked less than when their behavior confirms the stereotype (Costrich, Feinstein, Kidder, Maracek, & Pascale, 1975; Jackson & Cash, 1985). These findings indicate that even when a stereotyped group is successful in counteracting a stereotype, they may create or reinforce prejudice against the group.

Most of the preceding studies of expectancies have examined the effects of unexpected information on subsequent judgments of the same person about whom information was provided. A small number of studies have also examined the effects of stereotype-disconfirming information on judgments of the prevalence of the trait in the stereotyped group. Although some studies suggest that providing stereotype-disconfirming individuating information may change the original stereotype (e.g., Hamill, Wilson, & Nisbett, 1980), people seem to be very conservative in allowing stereotype-inconsistent information to influence judgments of stereotyped groups (Grant & Holmes, 1981; Rasinski, Crocker, & Hastie, 1985).

Stage III in the expectancy-confirmation sequence concerns the relationship between expectancies and behavior. Expectancies frequently lead to self-fulfilling prophecies (Snyder, Tanke, & Berscheid, 1977). For example, an individual who expects another person to be friendly may act in such an outgoing and receptive manner that the other person responds by being friendly (cf. Fazio, Effrein, & Falender, 1981; Snyder & Swann, 1978). In one study white interviewers sat at a greater distance from black interviewees, made more speech errors, and terminated the interview more quickly than with white interviewees, and these behaviors were found to lead to lower performances by interviewees (Word, Zanna, & Cooper, 1974). In the case of self-fulfilling prophecies also, the original expectancy will be perceived as having been confirmed.

In some situations when the expectancy is negative, the person holding the expectancy will act in ways that are inconsistent with the expectancy (Ickes, Patterson, Rajecki, & Tanford, 1982). In one study it was found that subjects with an expectation that the person they were interacting with was unfriendly were more friendly toward this person than subjects in a control condition (Ickes, et al., 1982). However, in this study the subjects with the negative expectation nonetheless judged the other person to be less friendly than did subjects who expected this person to be friendly. Thus, the negative expectation was perceived to have been fulfilled, even though the subjects did not act in ways that would have led to its fulfillment. The conclusion that can be drawn from these studies of self-fulfilling prophecies is that there is a pervasive tendency to perceive that expectancies have been fulfilled, regardless of whether the people holding the expectancies act in accordance with, or contrary to, the expectations they hold.

Controlled processing can also be initiated by "sets" to process information in accord with specific goals. In intergroup interaction, sets may occur in situations where members of different groups explicitly attempt to "size one another up" or form impressions of one another. When an individual has an explicit set to form an overall impression of a group, expectancy-disconfirming information is more likely to be encoded than confirming information (Srull et al., 1985). A set to form an impression also appears to increase the likelihood that trait inferences will be made from observed behavior (Bassili & Smith, 1986). Additionally, an impression formation set appears to reduce some types of biased information processing. In one study, when subjects were asked to form an impression of two groups, they were less likely to fall prey to illusory correlation (the perception that a trait is associated with a group when the available information indicates otherwise) or produce biased evaluations based on illusory correlations than if they were asked to memorize the incoming information (Pryor, 1986).

It appears that when an impression-formation set is activated from production memory, it causes people to attempt to integrate the information they are processing in working memory, and it may create strong beliefs that such an integration is possible. These strong beliefs may lead to the deeper encoding of expectancy-disconfirming evidence, thus increasing its impact on procedures performed in working memory. Thus, if one wishes people to attend to expectancy-disconfirming evidence in order to change their stereotypes, asking them to form impressions may facilitate this process.

A set to expect that information processing demands will be great leads to a reliance on category-based expectancies as a way of simplifying later decisions (Bodenhausen & Lichtenstein, in press). When processing demands actually are high, there is a tendency to recall less expectancy-disconfirming information than when processing demands are low (Srull, et al., 1985). Thus, when attempting to alter stereotypes through the provision of stereotype-disconfirming evidence it may be important for processing demands to be low or at least to be perceived as being low.

Retrieval. The retrieval of information associated with social categories is also subject to a number of normal processing biases that constrain the information retrieved. In general, it is the meaning of information in working memory or inferences derived from this information that are stored in declarative memory, rather than the exact details of the information (Anderson, 1980; Smith & Miller, 1979). To verify this statement, close your eyes and try to recall the exact words that were used to communicate the idea presented in the preceding sentence.

In a series of studies it has been shown that after people have made categorical judgments on the basis of factual information, the social categories they used are often more influential in making subsequent judgments than the original factual information (Lingle, Geva, Ostrom, Lieppe, & Baumgardner, 1979; Lingle & Ostrom, 1979). Another set of studies indicates that information relevant to making categorical judgments is more likely to be subsequently recalled than information irrelevant to these judgments (Ostrom, Lingle, Pryor, & Geva, 1980). In both sets of studies, information that was closely associated with the category node activated in working memory during encoding was most easily recalled. Both expectancy-consistent and expectancy-inconsistent information appear to be more easily recalled than expectancy-irrelevant information (Brewer, Dull, & Lui, 1981). The tendency not to recall expectancy-irrelevant information makes it difficult to add new dimensions to schemata of outgroups because the current schemata are likely to guide encoding and storage in declarative memory.

Another bias occurs for recall of the *frequency* of presentation of expected and unexpected information. People often recall that expectancy-confirming information has been more frequently presented than it actually has been, a type of illusory correlation (Hamilton & Rose, 1980; Rothbart, Evans, & Fulero, 1979). When the link between a category node and an associated trait is strong, people have a tendency to believe that the link has been frequently activated. Illusory correlation contributes to stereotyping because it leads people to believe that information confirming the existence of stereotype-associated traits has been more frequently observed than it actually has been.

Distinctive pairings of groups with traits may also be highly memorable (Hamilton, Dugan, & Trolier, 1985). When a distinctive outgroup engages in unexpected or negative behavior, this association is likely to be recalled as having occurred frequently (Rothbart, Fulero, Jenson, Howard, & Birrell, 1978). For instance, it has been found that the frequency with which negative behaviors are presented as having been performed by a minority group is overestimated (Hamilton & Gifford, 1976; McArthur & Friedman, 1980). Evaluations of the distinctive group were found to be correspondingly negative in the Hamilton and Gifford (1976) study. Such overestimates can impede changes in stereotypes to the extent that distinctive outgroup members engage in negative behaviors, but they can facilitate change if distinctive outgroup members engage in highly positive behaviors (Hamilton & Gifford, 1976; Sanbonmatsu, Sherman, & Hamilton, in press).

Factual information provided about ingroups is more extensively recalled than similar information about outgroups (Park & Rothbart, 1982). The reason is that people tend to encode information about ingroups using specific, highly differentiated categories, whereas they encode outgroup information by using global categories. This finding is consistent with studies of eyewitness identification showing that blacks and whites have more difficulty identifying outgroup members they have previously seen than they do identifying ingroup members (for a review, see Brigham & Malpass, 1985). Thus, one problem in creating more differentiation in the perception of outgroup members is the propensity not to recall information that would lead one to differentiate among them.

The context in which information is retrieved from declarative memory can also affect what is remembered. One study found that a positive mood at recall led to better memory of positive traits than did a negative mood (Isen, Shalker, Clark, & Karp, 1978). When the mood at recall matches the mode at encoding, recall is better than when the moods do not match (Isen, 1984). Other studies indicate that prior evaluations of social groups influence recall. Also, negative traits of disliked outgroups and positive traits of the ingroup are most likely to be remembered (Dutta, Kanungo, & Freibergs, 1972). One study found that ethnocentric whites made more negative than positive trait distortions (false recall of traits that had not been presented) for a black stimulus person than for a white stimulus person, and this effect increased over time (Higgins & King, 1981). The tendency to recall trait information that is consistent with affect at the time of encoding may make it difficult to change stereotypes toward negatively evaluated groups or in situations that create negative moods.

Taken together, the studies of retrieval indicate that the maintenance of stereotypes is facilitated by a tendency not to recall expectancy-irrelevant information or other factual information about outgroups—especially positive information about disliked groups, the tendency to overestimate the frequency with which stereotype-confirming information has been observed, and the tendency to overestimate the frequency with which minority groups have behaved in negative ways.

Changing Stereotypes

The studies employing the cognitive approach that have just been reviewed clearly indicate why stereotypes are so resistant to change. Nonetheless, these studies also provide a rich source of ideas concerning techniques of changing stereotypes.

Changes in the Structure of Stereotypes

Stereotypes consist of hierarchically structured information linking groups, traits, and behaviors. The links vary in strength, and the traits vary in number and interconnectedness. Groups may be subdivided into a number of subtypes, each of which may have a stereotype associated with it.

To change stereotypes one may focus on each of the different aspects of the structured information that comprises them (cf. Crocker, Fiske, & Taylor, 1984). In order to create more favorable stereotypes, links between a group node and a positive trait or links between a positive trait and a positive behavior can be strengthened or created. Similarly, to reduce the impact of a negative stereotype, links between a group node and a negative trait or between a negative trait and a negative behavior can be weakened. Likewise, interconnections between traits and between behaviors can be similarly modified. Finally, new subtypes can be created or people can be encouraged to use alternate categories with less pejorative associated traits.

Figure 2-2 illustrates the nodes and links in a hypothetical stereotype. The figure shows that the group node is connected to the traits associated with it by links that vary in strength (indicated in the figure by the thickness of the connecting lines). Some of the traits are more central than others, as indicated by the number of links they have to one another. In the figure, the connections of one of the traits to the expected behaviors and the interconnections among these behaviors are also shown.

Strengthening or creating positive links. Because there is no reason to expect that the processes affecting group/trait links and trait/behavior links differ, I will concentrate on group/trait links, since they are the basic elements of stereotypes. Links between the group node and positive traits can be strengthened by the processing of confirming instances in working memory. The automatic activation in declarative memory of related positive traits may also strengthen group/trait links.

To add new positive traits, it is necessary for the behavior of group members to be encoded, for internal attributions to be made, and for the trait to be linked to the group node. The behavior is most likely to be encoded if it is salient in the situation (distinctive or vivid) or if it has been primed. Internal attributions are a product of inference processes activated from production memory (Smith, 1984). Attributional inferences depend on such factors as consensus, distinctiveness, and consistency information (Kelley, 1967). Specifically, an internal trait attribution to a group (i.e., stereotyping) is most probable when many, if not all, outgroup members consistently behave in ways that are low on consensus (i.e., ways that differ from other people such as being kind when others would not be). Linking the trait to the group node is most likely if the group node has been activated either through priming or controlled processing. The group/trait link must also be activated frequently for the link to acquire strength.

Weakening negative links. The process of weakening links between the group node and negative traits is more complex than strengthening positive group/trait links. To weaken group/trait links the tendency in Stage I to seek out and prefer expectancy-

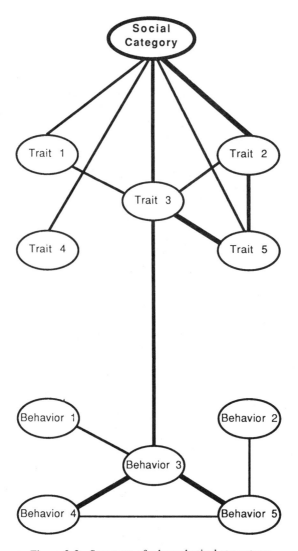

Figure 2-2. Structure of a hypothetical stereotype.

conforming evidence must be overcome. One technique that has been found to be effective is leading people to consciously consider traits opposite to those that are expected (Lord, Lepper, & Preston, 1984). Also, situations in which the ingroup members are dependent on the outgroup members increase both the effort that goes into processing information about the outgroup (Borgida & Omoto, 1986; Erber & Fisske, 1984) and the chances that expectancy-disconfirming evidence will be encoded (Darley, Fleming, Hilton & Swann, 1986).

In Stage II, if the expectancy-disconfirming information is encoded, it may not have an impact on the group/trait link unless the disconfirming evidence is attributed internally (Crocker et al., 1983). Rothbart and John (1985) have argued that expectancy-disconfirming behavior is most likely to lead to weakening stereo-types if it clearly disconfirms the stereotype, occurs frequently in a variety of settings, the outgroup members who engage in the disconfirming behavior are perceived as otherwise prototypical, and if the disconfirmations are strongly associated with the group label. To this list Weber and Crocker (1983) would add that the disconfirmations should be dispersed across a number of group members. In addition, other factors that increase the probability of controlled processing of stereotype-disconfirming information, such as having people actively consider the response options open to the other person (Langer, Bashner, & Chanowitz, 1985), asking them to form impressions (Srull, et al., 1985), or creating low processing loads (Srull, 1981), should increase the chances of weakening group/trait links.

In Stage III, the problem is the tendency to create self-fulfilling prophecies. For-tunately, self-fulfilling prophecies are not inevitable, as indicated in a study by Hil-ton and Darley (1985). If the people about whom the expectancy is held are aware of the other person's expectations, they can successfully counteract the expectancy. They are particularly likely to counteract the expectancy if they are certain that they do not possess the expected trait (Swann & Ely, 1984). Also, people can be success-fully trained to explicitly behave in disconfirming ways (Cohen & Roper, 1972). Thus, to change stereotypes it may be valuable for people who are stereotyped to be aware of the associated expectations so they can counteract them.

Interconnections among traits. Interconnections among traits are strengthened through the spread of activation process whenever the specific traits are individually activated. In addition to this passive strengthening of trait/trait links, these links can be actively strengthened whenever information specifically linking the traits is acti-vated in working memory. For these processes to have a favorable effect on stereo-types, positive trait/trait links must be activated, while the activation of negative trait/trait links must be avoided. One study suggests that the complexity and strength of the trait/trait links influences how controlled processing of new information will influence the affect associated with the category. For simple schemata, controlled processing of new information will have a greater impact in evaluations of the category when the dimensions are uncorrelated rather than correlated (Millar & Tessor, 1986). This finding underscores the importance of trying to change stereo-types in their formative stages, when they are still simple and the traits have not become correlated.

Subtyping and alternate categories. In addition to modifying the internal links within the stereotypes themselves, it is also possible to reduce the use of stereotypes by adding new subtypes or by substituting different social categories. Subtyping is promoted by the presentation of information that is inconsistent with current stereo-types and that is concentrated within a relatively small number of individuals (Weber & Crocker, 1983). Subtyping is also facilitated if stereotype-disconfirming behavior occurs among group members who are not representative of the group in other ways (e.g., are atypical in terms of demographic characteristics, Weber & Crocker, 1983). Subtyping may be particularly likely if members of a disliked group engage in expectancy-disconfirming behavior that is unusually positive. They may then become "exceptions to the rule" (Pettigrew, 1979). While subtyping has the advantage of increasing the perceived differentiation among subsets of outgroup members, it may not be beneficial if the subtypes that are created have stereotypes that are no more positive than the previously existing stereotypes.

Substituting alternative social categories may occur when alternative categories are readily available and stereotype-disconfirming evidence is powerful. For instance, social role information has been found to be more influential than group labels in making trait judgments (Deaux & Lewis, 1984). Thus, it may be useful to provide alternative categories, such as roles, in an attempt to reduce the impact of social group categories that have negative stereotypes. Increasing the salience of social roles could be especially useful in decreasing reliance on stereotypes that are heavily influenced by role-related traits, such as the stereotypes of blacks and whites and women and men (Eagly & Steffen, 1984; Stephan & Rosenfield, 1982). The goal would be to encourage people to use role categories to encode behavior when the use of another social category (e.g., race) would confirm negative stereotypes associated with that category.

As a final caveat it should be noted that changing stereotypes is only one aspect of the greater issue of improving intergroup relationships. In many instances, it may be more important to improve other aspects of intergroup relationships than to change stereotypes. In particular, it is often more important to change prejudice or discrimination toward outgroups than to change stereotypes. While changes in stereotypes, prejudice, and discrimination may be brought about by some of the same techniques, it appears that these three aspects of intergroup relationships are not especially closely connected, perhaps because cognition, affect, and behavior operate in accordance with different processes.

Acknowledgments. The author wishes to thank Arie Kruglanski and Cookie Stephan for their helpful comments on an earlier version of this chapter.

References

Anderson, J.R. (1980). *Cognitive psychology and its implications.* San Francisco: Freeman.

Anderson, J.R. (1983). *The architecture of cognition.* Cambridge, MA: Harvard University Press.

Ashmore, R., & Del Boca, F.K. (1981). Conceptual approaches to stereotypes and stereotyping. In D. Hamilton (Ed.), *Cognitive processes in stereotyping and intergroup behavior* (pp. 1–36). Hillsdale, NJ: Erlbaum.

Bargh. J.A., Bond, R.N., Lombardi, W.J., & Tota, M.E. (1986). The additive nature of chronic and temporary sources of construct accessibility. *Journal of Personality and Social Psychology, 50,* 869–878.

Bargh, J.A., & Pietromonaco, P. (1982). Automatic information processing and social perception: The influence of trait information presented outside of conscious awareness on impression formation. *Journal of Personality and Social Psychology, 43,* 437–449.

Bassili, J.N., & Smith, M.C. (1986). On the spontaneity of trait attributions: Converging evidence for the role of cognitive strategy. *Journal of Personality and Social Psychology, 50,* 239–245.

Bem, S.L. & Bem, D.J. (1977). Homogenizing the American woman: The power of an unconscious ideology. In J.C. Brigham & L.S. Wrightsman (Eds.), *Contemporary issues in social psychology* (3rd ed.) (pp. 172–185). Monterey, CA: Brooks/Cole.

Bodenhausen, G.V., & Lichtenstein, M. (in press). Social stereotypes and information processing strategies: The impact of task complexity. *Journal of Personality and Social Psychology.*

Bodenhausen, G.V., & Wyer, R.S., Jr. (1985). Effects of stereotypes on decision making and information-processing strategies. *Journal of Personality and Social Psychology, 48,* 267–282.

Borgida, E., & Omoto, A.M. (1986, August). *Racial stereotyping and prejudice: The role of personal involvement.* Paper presented at the meeting of the American Psychological Association, Washington D.C.

Brewer, M.B., Dull, V., & Lui, L. (1981). Perceptions of the elderly: Stereotypes as prototypes. *Journal of Personality and Social Psychology, 46,* 646–670.

Brigham, J.C. (1971). Ethnic stereotypes. *Psychological Bulletin, 76,* 15–38.

Brigham, J.C., & Malpass, R.S. (1985). The role of experience and contact in the recognition of faces of own- and other-race faces. *Journal of Social Issues, 41*(3), 139–156.

Cantor N., & Mischel, W. (1977). Traits as prototypes: Effects on recognition memory. *Journal of Personality and Social Psychology, 35,* 38–48.

Cohen, E.G., & Roper, S. (1972). Modification of interracial interaction disability: An application of status characteristics theory. *American Sociological Review, 37,* 643–657.

Costrich, N.J., Feinstein, L. Kidder, L., Marachek, J., & Pascale, L. (1975). When stereotypes hurt: Three studies of penalties for sex-role reversal. *Journal of Experimental Social Psychology, 11,* 520–530.

Crocker, J., Fiske, S.T., & Taylor, S.E. (1984). Schematic bases of belief change. In R. Eiser (Ed.), *Attitude judgment* (pp. 197–226). New York: Springer.

Crocker, J., Hannah, D.B., & Weber, R. (1983). Person memory and causal attributions. *Journal of Personality and Social Psychology, 44,* 55–66.

Darley, J.M., Fleming, J.H., Hilton, J.L., & Swann, W.B., Jr. (1986). *Dispelling negative expectancies: The impact of interaction goals and target characteristics on the expectation confirmation process.* Unpublished manuscript, Princeton University, Princeton.

Deaux, K., & Lewis, L.L. (1984). Structure of gender stereotypes: Interrelationships among components and gender labels. *Journal of Personality and Social Psychology, 46,* 991–1004.

Dovidio, J.F., Evans, N., & Tyler, R.B. (1986). Racial stereotypes: The contents and their cognitive representation. *Journal of Experimental Social Psychology, 22,* 22–37.

Dovidio, J.F., & Geartner, S.L. (1986). Prejudice, discrimination and racism: Historical and contemporary approaches. In J.F. Dovidio and S.L. Geartner (Eds.), *Prejudice, discrimination, and racism* (p. 34). New York: Academic Press.

Duncan, B. (1976). Differential social perception and attribution of intergroup violence: Testing the lower limits of stereotyping Blacks. *Journal of Personality and Social Psychology, 34,* 590–598.

Dutta, S., Kanungo, R.N., & Freibergs, V. (1972). Retention of affective material: Effects of intensity of affect on retrieval. *Journal of Personality and Social Psychology, 23,* 64–80.

Eagly, A.H., & Steffen, V.J. (1984). Gender stereotypes stem from the distribution of women and men into social roles. *Journal of Personality and Social Psychology, 20,* 235–254.

Erber, R., & Fiske, S.T. (1984). Outcome dependency and attention to inconsistent information. *Journal of Personality and Social Psychology, 47,* 709–726.

Fazio, R.H., Effrien, E.A., & Falender, V.J., (1981). Self-perception following social interaction. *Journal of Personality and Social Psychology, 41,* 232–342.

Fazio, R.H., Sanbonmatsu, D.M., Powell, M.C., & Kardes, F.R. (1986). *Journal of Personality and Social Psychology, 50,* 229–238.

Fiske, S.T., & Pavelchak, M.A. (1982). Category-based versus piecemeal-based affective responses. In R.M. Sorrentino & E.T. Higgins (Eds.), *Handbook of motivation and cognition* (pp. 167–203). New York: Guilford.

Grant, P.R., & Holmes, J.G. (1981). The integration of implicit personality theory, schemas and stereotype images. *Social Psychology Quarterly, 44,* 107–115.

Greenberg, J., & Pyszczynski, T. (1985). The effect of an overheard ethnic slur on evaluations of the target: How to spread a social disease. *Journal of Experimental Social Psychology, 21,* 61–72.

Hamill, R., Wilson, T.D., & Nisbett, R.E. (1980). Insensitivity to sample bias: Generalizing from atypical cases. *Journal of Personality and Social Psychology, 39,* 478–589.

Hamilton, D.L., Dugan, P., & Troiler, T. (1985). The formation of stereotype beliefs: Further evidence for distinctiveness-based illusory correlations. *Journal of Personality and Social Psychology, 48,* 5–17.

Hamilton, D.L., & Gifford, R.K. (1976). Illusory correlations in interpersonal perception: A cognitive basis for stereotype judgments. *Journal of Experimental Social Psychology, 12,* 392–407.

Hamilton, D.L., & Rose, T. (1980). Illusory correlation and the maintenance of stereotype beliefs. *Journal of Personality and Social Psychology, 39,* 832–845.

Hastie, R., & Kumar, A.P. (1979). Person memory: Personality traits as organizing principles in memory for behaviors. *Journal of Personality and Social Psychology, 37,* 25–38.

Hemsley, G.D., & Marmurek, H.V.C. (1982). Person memory: The processing of consistent and inconsistent person information. *Personality and Social Psychology Bulletin, 8,* 433–438.

Higgins, E.T., & King, G. (1981). Accessibility of social constructs: Information processing consequences of individual and contextual variables. In N. Cantor & J.F. Kihlstrom (Eds.), *Personality, cognition, and social interaction* (pp. 69–122). Hillsdale, NJ: Erlbaum.

Higgins, E.T., Rholes, W.S., & Jones, C.R. (1977). Category accessibility and impression formation. *Journal of Experimental Social Psychology, 13,* 141–154.

Hilton, J.L., & Darley, J.M. (1985). Constructing other persons: A limit of the effect. *Journal of Experimental Social Psychology, 21,* 1–18.

Ickes, W.J., Patterson, M.L., Rajecki, D.W., & Tanford, S. (1982). Behavioral and cognitive consequences of reciprocal versus compensatory responses to preinteraction strategies. *Social Cognition, 1,* 160–190.

Isen, A.M. (1984). Toward understanding the role of affect in cognition. In R.S. Wyer & T.K. Srull (Eds.), *Handbook of Social Cognition* (Vol. 2) (pp. 179–236). Hillsdale, NJ: Erlbaum.

Isen, A.M., Shalker, T.W., Clark, M., & Karp, L. (1978). Affect, accessibility of material in memory, and behavior: A cognitive loop? *Journal of Personality and Social Psychology, 36,* 1–12.

Jackson, L.A., & Cash, T.F. (1985). Components of gender stereotypes: Their implications for inferences on stereotypic and nonstereotypic dimensions. *Personality and Social Psychology Bulletin, 11,* 326–344.

Kelley, H.H. (1967). Attribution theory in social psychology. In D. Levine (Ed.), *Nebraska symposium on motivation* (Vol. 15). (pp. 192–240). Lincoln, NE: University of Nebraska Press.

Klatzky, R.L, Martin, G.L., & Kane, R.A. (1982). Influence of social-category activation on processing of visual information. *Social Cognition, 1,* 95–109.

Kulik, J. (1983). Confirmatory attribution and the perpetuation of social beliefs. *Journal of Personality and Social Psychology, 44,* 1171–1181.

Langer, E.J., Bashner, R.S., & Chanowitz, B. (1985). Decreasing prejudice by increasing discrimination. *Journal of Personality and Social Psychology, 49,* 113–120.

Lingle, J.H., Geva, N., Ostrom, T.M., Lieppe, M.P., & Baumgardner, M.H., (1979). Thematic effects of person judgments on impression formation. *Journal of Personality and Social Psychology, 37,* 674–687.

Lingle, J.H., & Ostrom, T.M. (1979). Retrieval selectivity in memory-based impression judgments. *Journal of Personality and Social Psychology, 37,* 180–194.

Locksley, A., Borgida, E., Brekke, N., & Hepburn, C. (1980). Sex stereotypes and social judgment. *Journal of Personality and Social Psychology, 39,* 821–831.

Lord, C.G., Lepper, M.R., & Preston, E. (1984). Considering the opposite: A corrective strategy for social judgment. *Journal of Personality and Social Psychology, 47*, 1231–1243.

Mayer, J.D., & Bower, G.H. (1986). Learning and memory for personality prototypes. *Journal of Personality and Social Psychology, 51*, 473–492.

McArthur, L.Z. & Friedman, S. (1980). Illusory correlation in impression formation: Variations in the shared distinctiveness effect as a function of the distinctive person's age, race, and sex. *Journal of Personality and Social Psychology, 39*, 615–624.

McCann, C.D., Ostrom, T.M., Tyner, L.K., & Mitchell, M.L. (1985). Person perception in heterogeneous groups. *Journal of Personality and Social Psychology, 49*, 1449–1459.

Meyer, D.E., & Schvaneveldt, R.W. (1971). Facilitation in recognizing pairs of words: Evidence of a dependence between retreival operations. *Journal of Experimental Psychology, 90*, 227–234.

Millar, M.G., & Tessor, A. (1986). Thought-induced attitude change: The effects of schema structure and commitment. *Journal of Personality and Social Psychology, 51*, 259–269.

Ostrom, T.M., Lingle, J.H., Pryor, J.B., Geva, N. (1980). Cognitive organization of person impressions. In R. Hastie, T. Ostrom, E. Ebbesen, R. Wyer, D. Hamilton, & D. Carlston (Eds.), *Person memory: The cognitive basis of person perception* (pp. 55–88). Hillsdale, NJ: Erlbaum.

O'Sullivan, C.S., & Durso, F.T. (1984). The effect of schema incongruent information on memory for stereotype attributes. *Journal of Personality and Social Psychology, 47*, 55–70.

Park, B., & Rothbart, M. (1982). Perception of outgroup homogeneity and levels of social categorization: Memory for the subordinate attributes of ingroup and outgroup members. *Journal of Personality and Social Psychology, 42*, 1050–1068.

Pettigrew, T.F. (1979). The ultimate attribution effort: Extending Allport's cognitive analysis of prejudice. *Personality and Social Psychology Bulletin, 5*, 461–476.

Pliske, R., & Smith, K. (1979). Semantic categorization in a linear order problem. *Memory and Cognition, 4*, 297–302.

Pryor, J.B. (1986). The influence of different encoding sets upon the formation of illusory correlations and group impressions. *Personality and Social Psychology Bulletin, 12*, 216–226.

Rasinski, K.A., Crocker, J., & Hastie, R. (1985). Another look at sex stereotypes and social judgments: An analysis of the social perceiver's use of subjective probabilities. *Journal of Personality and Social Psychology, 49*, 327–337.

Rosch, E. (1978). Principles of categorization. In E. Rosch & B.B. Loyd (Eds.), *Cognition and categorization* (pp. 87–116). Hillsdale, NJ: Erlbaum.

Rosch, E., Mervis, C.B., Gray, W.D., Johnson, D.M., & Boyes-Braem, P. (1976). Basic objects in natural categories. *Cognitive Psychology, 8*, 382–439.

Rothbart, M., Evans, M., & Fulero, S. (1979). Recall of confirming events: Memory processes and the maintenance of social stereotypes. *Journal of Experimental Social Psychology, 15*, 343–355.

Rothbart, M., Fulero, S., Jenson, C., Howard, J., & Birrell, (1978). From individual to group impressions: Availability heuristics in stereotype formation. *Journal of Experimental Social Psychology, 14*, 237–255.

Rothbart, M., & John, O.P. (1985). Social categorization and behavioral episodes: A cognitive analysis and the effects of intergroup contact. *Journal of Social Issues, 41*(3), 81–104.

Rumelhart, D.E., (1984). Schemata and the cognitive system. In R.S. Wyer & T.K. Srull (Eds.), *Handbook of Social Cognition* (Vol. 1) (pp. 161–188). Hillsdale, NJ: Erlbaum.

Sagar, H.A., & Schofield, J.W. (1980). Racial and behavioral cues in black and white children's perceptions of ambiguously aggressive acts. *Journal of Personality and Social Psychology, 39*, 590–598.

Sanbonmatsu, D.M., Sherman, S.J., & Hamilton, D.L. (in press). Illusory correlation in the perception of individuals and groups. *Social Cognition*.

Schur, E.M. (1984). *Labeling women as deviant*. New York: Random House.

Skov, R.B., & Sherman, S.J. (1986). Information-gathering processes: Diagnosticity, hypothesis-confirmatory strategies, and perceived hypothesis confirmation. *Journal of Experimental Social Psychology, 22*, 93–121.

Smith, E. (1984). Models of social inference. *Psychological Review, 91*, 392–413.

Smith, E.R., & Branscombe, N.R. (1986). *Stereotype traits can be processed automatically.* Unpublished manuscript, Purdue University, Lafayette, IN.

Smith, E., & Miller, F.D., (1979). Salience and the cognitive mediation of attribution. *Journal of Personality and Social Psychology, 37*, 2240–2252.

Smith, E.E., Shoben, E.J., & Rips, L.J. (1974). Structure and process in semantic memory. *Psychological Review, 81*, 214–241.

Snyder, M., & Swann, W.B. (1978). Hypothesis-testing in social interaction. *Journal of Personality and Social Psychology, 36*, 1202–1212.

Snyder, M., & Tanke, E.D., & Berscheid, E. (1977). Social perception and interpersonal behavior: On the self-fulfilling nature of social stereotypes. *Journal of Personality and Social Psychology, 35*, 656–666.

Srull, T.K. (1981). Person memory: Some tests of associative storage and retrieval models. *Journal of Experimental Psychology: Human Learning and Memory, 7*, 440–463.

Srull, T.K., Lichtenstein, M., & Rothbart, M. (1985). Associative storage and retrieval processes in person memory. *Journal of Experimental Psychology: Learning, Memory, and Cognition, 11*, 316–345.

Srull, T.K., & Wyer, R.S., Jr. (1979). The role of category accessibility in the interpretation of information about persons: Some determinants and implications. *Journal of Personality and Social Psychology, 37*, 1660–1672.

Srull, T.K., & Wyer, R.S., Jr. (1980). Category accessibility and social perception: Some implications for the study of person memory and interpersonal judgments. *Journal of Personality and Social Psychology, 38*, 841–856.

Stangor, C. (1986). *Response biases and individual construct accessibility: Alternative measures of gender stereotypes.* Unpublished manuscript, New York University.

Stephan, W.G. (1985). Intergroup relations. In G. Lindzey and E. Aronson (Eds.), *The handbook of social psychology*, (pp. 599–638). New York: Random House.

Stephan, W.G., & Rosenfield, D. (1982). Racial and ethnic stereotypes. In A.G. Miller (Ed.), *In the eye of the beholder* (pp. 92–126). New York: Praeger.

Stern, L.D., Mars, S., Cole, E., & Millar, M.G. (1984). Processing time and recall of inconsistent and consistent behaviors of individuals and groups. *Journal of Personality and Social Psychology, 47*, 253–262.

Swann, W.B., Jr., & Ely, R.J. (1984). A battle of wills: Self-verification versus behavioral confirmation. *Journal of Personality and Social Psychology, 46*, 1287–1302.

Taylor, S.E., & Fiske, S.T. (1978). Salience, attention, and attribution. In L. Berkowitz (Ed.), *Advances in experimental social psychology* (Vol. 11) (pp. 250–289). New York: Academic Press.

Taylor, S.E. Fiske, S.T., Close, M., Anderson, C., & Ruderman, A. (1975). Solo status as a psychological variable. Cited in S.E. Taylor & S.T. Fiske (1978). Salience, attention, and attribution. In L.Berkowitz (Ed.), *Advances in experimental social psychology* (Vol. 11) (pp. 250–289). New York: Academic Press.

Weber, R., & Crocker, J. (1983). Cognitive processing in the revision of stereotypic beliefs. *Journal of Personality and Social Psychology, 45*, 961–977.

Wilder, D.A. (1984). Intergroup contact: The typical member and the exception to the rule. *Journal of Experimental Social Psychology, 20*, 177–194.

Wilder, D.A., & Allen, V.L. (1978). Group membership and preference for information about others. *Personality and Social Psychology Bulletin, 4*, 106–110.

Wilder, D.A., & Shapiro, P.N. (1984). Role of outgroup cues in determining social identity. *Journal of Personality and Social Psychology, 47*, 342–348.

Word, C., Zanna, M.P., & Cooper, J. (1974). The nonverbal mediation of self-fulfilling prophecies in interracial interaction. *Journal of Experimental Social Psychology, 10,* 109–120.

Wyer, R.S., Jr., & Martin, L.L. (1986). Person memory: The role of traits, group stereotypes, and specific behaviors in the cognitive representation of persons. *Journal of Personality and Social Psychology, 50,* 661–675.

Chapter 3

Illusory Correlations: Implications for Stereotype Theory and Research

David L. Hamilton and Steven J. Sherman

Within the last 15 years a considerable amount of research on stereotyping has been guided by a social-cognitive approach to this topic. This approach, which has a long and rich tradition in the stereotyping literature (cf. Allport, 1954; Ashmore & Del Boca, 1981; Tajfel, 1969), views stereotypes as mental representations of social groups and seeks to understand how these cognitive structures influence informa- tion processing, social perception, and interpersonal and intergroup behavior. Several recent reviews and discussions of this literature, which is now quite exten- sive, are available elsewhere (e.g., Hamilton, 1981a; Hamilton & Trolier, 1986; Jones, 1982; Stephan, 1985). Research within this tradition has also investigated how these cognitive structures develop through information processing mechan- isms. The purpose of this chapter is to examine in some detail the research evidence pertaining to one such mechanism that has generated interest among researchers representing this cognitive orientation.

Several years ago Hamilton and Gifford (1976) published an article demonstrating that a cognitive bias in the way information is processed can result in the differential perception of two social groups. Because stereotyping is based on the perception of differences between groups, they argued that this cognitive bias could constitute the basis for the formation of stereotypes.

This cognitive bias, called an illusory correlation, refers to an erroneous judg- ment of the relationship between two variables (Chapman & Chapman, 1967). As a general concept, the notion of an illusory correlation pertains to *any* mis- perception of degree of association between variables. Thus, illusory correlations may reflect the unwarranted perception of positive or negative relationships (San- bonmatsu, Sherman, & Hamilton, 1987), and may reflect either an overestima- tion or an underestimation of an actual association (Chapman & Chapman, 1967, 1969; Hamilton & Rose, 1980; Trolier & Hamilton, 1986). Moreover, such illusory correlations can arise as a result of a variety of factors and processes, such as the influence of expectancies based on preexisting beliefs, the salience of certain kinds of information, the differential weighting of information, and use of the availability heuristic in making judgments (Chapman & Chapman, 1967, 1969; Hamilton,

1981b; Hamilton & Rose, 1980; Sanbonmatsu et al., 1987; Trolier & Hamilton, 1986; Tversky & Kahneman, 1973).

In this chapter we will focus primarily on one particular type of illusory correlation – illusory correlation based on the co-occurrence of distinctive stimulus events – and their implications for the development of stereotypic beliefs. The original demonstration of distinctiveness-based illusory correlations was reported by Chapman (1967), and its initial application to the realm of stereotype formation was presented in the Hamilton and Gifford (1976) paper. In recent years a considerable amount of research has been reported based on these early demonstrations. The purpose of this chapter is to summarize and review this research literature and to assess what we have learned from this work about the processes underlying group perceptions and stereotype formation.[1]

The chapter is organized into several sections. First, the original experiment reported by Hamilton and Gifford (1976) will be summarized in some detail. This is necessary because much of the subsequent work not only is based on their findings but also employed the same procedures and measures used in their experiment. The second section is concerned with the interpretation of Hamilton and Gifford's (1976) results and reviews several subsequent studies that tested the viability of alternative explanations for their findings. Third, we will summarize several recent extensions of this line of work in new directions, including applications to related topics and indications of some boundary conditions on the original findings. Finally, we will try to assess our current state of knowledge about distinctiveness-based illusory correlations and consider future directions of research on this topic.

Illusory Correlation and Group Perceptions: The Original Evidence

Hamilton and Gifford's (1976) study was based on the findings reported by Chapman (1967) that showed that subjects overestimated the frequency of co-occurrence of distinctive stimuli. In Chapman's (1967) study the notion of distinctiveness had a rather minimal meaning. His stimuli consisted of a series of word pairs that were presented to subjects multiple times in random sequence. Most of these words were short in length, but two of them were about twice as long as the others. Within the context of these word lists, then, the long words were distinctive

---

[1]A second literature on illusory correlations, also derived from Chapman's (1967) work, concerns the effect of preexisting associative beliefs on erroneous judgments of the relation between two variables. These associatively-based illusory correlations also have important implications for stereotyping (Hamilton & Rose, 1980; Kim & Baron, 1988; McArthur & Friedman, 1980; Slusher & Anderson, 1987), as well as other social judgment contexts (Berman & Kenny, 1976; Casas, Brady, & Ponterotto, 1983; Chapman & Chapman, 1967, 1969; Golding & Rorer, 1972; Kurtz & Garfield, 1978; Starr & Katkin, 1969; Wampold, Casas, & Atkinson, 1981). In the present chapter, however, we are concerned only with the literature on distinctiveness-based illusory correlations.

and, Chapman suggested, their-co-occurrence was particularly distinctive. The subject's task was to estimate the relative frequency with which each pair of words had been presented. Although each word pair had been shown the same number of times, subjects consistently overestimated the frequency of occurrence of the pair of longer words. Thus, in Chapman's study, distinctiveness was defined simply as an infrequently occurring stimulus category.

Hamilton and Gifford (1976, Experiment 1) reasoned that this overestimation of the frequency of co-occurrence of distinctive stimuli could influence the perceptions of groups. For a perceiver who interacts with members of one group much more often than with members of another group, the latter group is an infrequently occurring event and hence, by Chapman's (1967) definition, distinctive. Similarly, some kinds of behaviors are more common and normative than others, and hence infrequently occurring behaviors might also be distinctive. Based on Chapman's findings, Hamilton and Gifford (1976) predicted that perceivers would overestimate the frequency with which members of a smaller (and thus distinctive) group had engaged in less frequent kinds of behaviors. This, in turn, was predicted to influence subjects' evaluative perceptions of the group.

To test these ideas, subjects in the experiment were presented a series of 39 behavior-descriptive sentences. Each stimulus item identified a person by first name and membership in one of two groups identified simply as Group A and Group B, and described a behavior performed by that person (e.g., "Paul, a member of Group A, cleaned up the house before company came"; "Bruce, a member of Group B, did volunteer work for a political candidate"; "Joe, a member of Group A, made the other person very uncomfortable by his sarcastic remark"). The sentences described relatively common, everyday behaviors that ranged in desirability from mildly positive to mildly negative. Within the set of sentences, two-thirds described members of Group A, and desirable behaviors were more frequent than undesirable behaviors. Specifically, the behavior descriptions were distributed as follows:

Group A, desirable: 18
Group A, undesirable: 8
Group B, desirable: 9
Group B, undesirable: 4

The frequencies of desirable and undesirable behaviors for Group A were exactly double those values for Group B. Because of this property, there was no relationship between group membership and desirability. However, due to their relative infrequency, both Group B members and undesirable behaviors were distinctive, in the sense used by Chapman (1967). Their co-occurrence—that is, instances of a Group B person performing an undesirable behavior—would be particularly distinctive and, based on Chapman's findings, would be overestimated in subjects' judgments. If so, then subjects would perceive an "illusory correlation" between group membership and behavior desirability, even though no such relationship existed in the information presented to them. If such an illusory correlation existed, it could be the basis for the differential evaluative perception of the two groups.

To test this hypothesis, subjects were asked to complete several dependent measures. First, subjects were given a list of all of the stimulus sentences, with group membership omitted, and were asked to identify the group membership of the person who performed each behavior. From these group assignments, a 2 × 2 (Group A vs. Group B, desirable vs. undesirable behavior) frequency table was constructed for each subject, and a phi coefficient (a measure of association between two dichotomous variables) was calculated for each subject. This phi coefficient is an index of the subject's perceived relationship between group membership and behavior desirability. Second, subjects were asked to estimate how many desirable and undesirable behaviors were performed by members of each group. These estimates comprised a 2 × 2 table of frequency estimates for each subject and again a phi coefficient was calculated from each subject's judgments. This coefficient provides a second index of the subject's perceived association between group membership and behavior desirability. Third, subjects rated their impressions of the two groups on a series of trait rating scales.

The results of this experiment provided strong support for the hypotheses. For both the group assignment task and the frequency estimate task, the means of the subjects' phi coefficients were significantly greater than zero, indicating the presence of bias in subjects' judgments. Moreover, closer examination of the data supported the argument that this bias was due to the overestimation of the frequency of co-occurrence of distinctive stimulus events. On the group assignment task subjects responded to the individual behavior items and indicated, for each one, the group membership of the person who performed that behavior. One-third of both the desirable and undesirable behaviors had described members of Group B. Although subjects quite accurately assigned 35% of the desirable behaviors to Group B, 52% of the undesirable behaviors were attributed to members of this group. Similarly, on the frequency estimation task subjects were told how many people there had been in each group and were asked to estimate how many had performed undesirable behaviors. Although subjects were accurate (34%) in their estimate for Group A, they substantially overestimated the frequency of undesirable acts by members of Group B (44%). These findings substantiate that subjects did in fact form an illusory correlation between group membership and behavior desirability in processing this information.

Given that our interest was in stereotyping, the key question was whether this illusory correlation influenced subjects' perceptions of the two stimulus groups. Subjects' ratings of the two groups provided strong evidence of differential perceptions. As predicted, subjects rated Group A significantly more favorably than Group B on a variety of trait scales.

These findings, then, demonstrate that a cognitive bias in the way we process information can lead to the unwarranted differential perception of two social groups. Specifically, the subjects' sensitivity to stimulus distinctiveness, such as the co-occurrence of infrequent stimulus events, resulted in subjects overestimating the frequency with which members of the smaller group (Group B) performed the infrequently occurring (undesirable) category of behavior. The consequence was that, even though the proportion of desirable and undesirable acts was the same for both groups, the smaller group was evaluated less favorably than the larger group.

As Hamilton and Gifford (1976) indicated, the information conditions presented to subjects in their study correspond to those that are present in many real-world contexts. For example, most white Americans have much more exposure to and interaction with whites than with blacks. Black Americans, then, are an infrequently occurring stimulus category for the typical white perceiver (apart from any other stimulus value they may have). Similarly, undesirable behaviors occur less frequently than desirable behaviors. The implication of Hamilton and Gifford's (1976) findings is that, even if whites and blacks commit undesirable behaviors the same proportion of the time, the white perceiver may come to believe that blacks commit them more frequently and hence may evaluate that group less favorably.

This finding has important implications for the development of stereotypes. All stereotyping begins with and rests upon the differential perception of groups (Allport, 1954; Hamilton, 1976, 1979; Tajfel, 1969). Stereotypes then develop as specific beliefs become associated with those group differentiations. Thus, Hamilton and Gifford's (1976) results showed that a cognitive, information-processing bias can lay the foundation for stereotype development by creating differential evaluative perceptions of groups, even though the information available about the two groups was evaluatively equivalent.

Distinctiveness-Based Illusory Correlations and Group Perceptions: Alternative Interpretations

Although the results of Hamilton and Gifford's (1976, Experiment 1) experiment were consistent with their hypotheses, several alternative interpretations of their findings remained viable, and these alternatives rested on mechanisms other than the salience of infrequently occurring stimulus classes. In this section, we summarize several subsequent experiments that tested these alternative interpretations.

Evaluations Based on Group Size?

One class of alternative explanations derives from the simple fact that the two groups occurred with unequal frequency in Hamilton and Gifford's (1976) stimulus information. Thus, for example, it is possible that subjects perceived Group B to be a minority group, and if they had a priori beliefs that minority groups are generally less favorable than a majority group, this expectation could lead them to evaluate Group B in a less favorable light. Similarly, any assumption that "more is better" might lead subjects to perceive Group A, the larger group, more favorably. Another variant on this theme stems from the well-established "mere exposure" effect (Zajonc, 1968), in which greater frequency of exposure to a stimulus has been shown to produce enhancements in evaluative responses. Because there were twice as many members of Group A as of Group B, the more favorable evaluations of Group A could derive simply from this difference in frequency of exposure.

All of these possible explanations rest on the association of evaluation with group size. The appropriate strategy for testing these alternative accounts against the distinctiveness-based explanation is to create a condition in which an illusory correlation bias would produce more favorable evaluations of the smaller group. Hamilton and Gifford (1976, Experiment 2) conducted such a test by modifying the paradigm they used in their first study. Subjects again read a series of statements, each of which described a member of one of two groups (A or B) as having performed a behavior that was either desirable or undesirable. As in the previous study, there were twice as many statements about Group A members than Group B members. In this case, however, desirable (rather than undesirable) behaviors were infrequent, occurring only half as often as undesirable behaviors. Again, the ratio of desirable to undesirable behaviors was the same for both groups, so there was no association between group membership and behavior desirability in the information provided. An illusory correlation based on the co-occurrence of distinctive (infrequent) stimuli was again predicted. Now, however, because desirable behaviors were infrequent, the hypothesis was that subjects would overestimate Group B's performance of desirable behaviors, and this would lead them to evaluate the smaller group more, rather than less, favorably.

The same dependent measures were assessed in this experiment as in Hamilton and Gifford's (1976) first study. For both the group assignment and the frequency estimate tasks, the mean phi coefficients were again significantly different from zero, providing evidence that subjects had formed illusory correlations. In this case, however, these illusory correlations were in the opposite direction, in that they were based on subjects' overestimation of the frequency of Group B members performing *desirable* behaviors. On the trait rating scales, subjects again produced differential evaluations of the two groups, but now Group B was rated significantly more favorably than Group A.

In sum, the results of this experiment were directly and completely the opposite of those from the first study. This difference was produced simply by changing which category of behavior occurred frequently and which occurred infrequently, a change that altered which type of behavior was distinctive. The results, therefore, are consistent with predictions based on a distinctiveness-based illusory correlation. On the other hand, because Group A was twice as large as Group B in both experiments, any explanation of the results of the first study in terms of differential evaluations based on group size cannot account for this reversal of findings obtained in the second study. Hamilton and Gifford's (1976) second experiment, then, effectively eliminates any explanation based on a direct association between frequency and evaluation.

An Encoding or Retrieval Bias?

According to Hamilton and Gifford's (1976) account, subjects in their study formed illusory correlations as they read the sequentially presented series of stimulus sentences. In other words, the bias was presumed to have its roots in the initial encoding of the information. An alternative possibility, however, is that the stimulus information is properly encoded, such that all four categories of information are represented in memory with at least proportional accuracy, but that errors occur when subjects attempt to combine the various categories of information for purposes of making an evaluative response. For example, at the time of judgment the relevant information for making accurate judgments may be available, but subjects may differentially weight that information. If the frequency with which Group B performed undesirable behaviors were given more weight than other kinds of information, such a process would produce the lower evaluations of that group. Another possibility is that subjects use a simple but inappropriate combinatory rule in making these judgments that results in the differential group evaluations. For example, although the proportion of desirable and undesirable behaviors was the same for both groups, the absolute difference between desirable and undesirable behaviors was much greater for Group A than Group B. If this absolute difference were the basis for subjects' judgments, the differential evaluations of the groups would occur.

To test these alternative possibilities, Hamilton, Dugan, and Trolier (1985, Experiment 1) presented comparable information in two different forms and compared subjects' judgments of the two groups. One condition was a replication of Hamilton and Gifford's (1976) procedure in which behavior-descriptive sentences were presented sequentially and constituted the basis for subjects' judgments. In another condition, subjects did not read the individual sentences but instead were shown a 2 × 2 summary table that presented the frequency of desirable and undesirable behaviors performed by each group. If the differential group evaluations observed by Hamilton and Gifford (1976) were due to biases in combinatory processes when information is integrated at the time of making judgments, then similar differences in group perceptions should occur when the stimulus information in presented in tabular form. However, if the bias occurs during the encoding of sequentially presented items of information, resulting in overrepresentation of certain categories of that information, then the differential perceptions should occur in the sequential presentation condition but not when the information was presented in the summary table.

The results supported the latter interpretation. Subjects who read the series of behavior-descriptive items rated Group A significantly more favorably than Group B, replicating the earlier findings. In contrast, subjects who based their judgments on the table of frequencies did not differentially evaluate the two groups. These findings support the view that the perceived association between group membership and behavior desirability develops during the serial processing of sequentially presented information. Moreover, another condition included in this experiment showed that this illusory correlation, once formed, is not easily erased. Subjects in this third condition read the series of stimulus sentences and then, before completing the dependent measures, were shown the 2 × 2 summary table indicating the frequencies of desirable and undesirable statements about each group. These subjects also rated Group A more favorably than Group B, to a degree approaching that of subjects who saw only the stimulus sentences. Thus, in this case the summary table, which by itself had not led to biased group perceptions, was ineffective in overcoming the bias developed during sequential processing.

An Effect Due to Distinctiveness or Frequency of Occurrence?

Although the evidence summarized thus far argued persuasively that subjects did indeed form illusory correlations as they read the stimulus sentences, the precise basis for this bias had not been convincingly demonstrated. Hamilton and Gifford (1976) interpreted their results in terms of the differential impact of distinctive information, in particular the co-occurrence of two stimuli that occur with relative infrequency. There are, however, other possibilities. On quite plausible explanation was suggested by Rothbart (1981), who proposed that the illusory correlation, rather than being based on stimulus distinctiveness, may have been due to subjects' overestimation of the degree to which members of the statistically frequent group (Group A) had performed the statistically frequent (e.g., desirable) behaviors. As he stated (Rothbart, 1981, p. 174):

> If we ask which pairs of instances are going to be most available to memory, we can reasonably assert that it would be the cell containing positive behaviors associated with members of the A group. In fact, inasmuch as fully 46% of all pairings occur in this category, it is not unreasonable to assume that these instances are most available and that subjects would judge A to be comparatively more favorable than B − exactly the findings obtained by Hamilton and Gifford.

In other words, rather than forming an association between the minority group and the minority behavior category, subjects may have formed an association between the majority group and the majority type of behavior. In terms of the 2 × 2 classification of stimulus sentences presented to subjects, Hamilton and Gifford's explanation focused on the importance of one cell (Group B, infrequent behaviors) while Rothbart's reinterpretation emphasized the importance of another cell (Group A, frequent behaviors). Because overestimation of instances in either of these cells would produce the same biased correlation, the obtained results could be due to either of these possibilities.

Some of Hamilton and Gifford's (1976) results were at least suggestive on this issue. On the group assignment task, for example, subjects overattributed undesirable behaviors to Group B, but did not disproportionately assign desirable behaviors to Group A. Similarly, on the frequency estimation task, subjects overestimated the number of undesirable behaviors performed by Group B, but not the number of desirable behaviors describing members of Group A. More recent experiments have investigated this question more directly.

Regan and Crawley (1984) attempted to determine whether the evaluative difference in group perceptions was due primarily to subjects' association of undesirable behaviors with Group B or to the association of favorable information with Group A. Three conditions were created in their experiment. One condition was a replication of the Hamilton and Gifford (1976) procedure. Subjects in the other two conditions were presented with either (a) only those sentences that described Group A or (b) only those sentences that described Group B. The subjects then made evaluative ratings of the group or groups described in the sentences they had read. Regan and Crawley's (1984) reasoning was that these latter two conditions would provide baseline evaluations of Groups A and B against which the evaluations of the two groups in the replication condition could be compared. If Hamilton and Gifford's (1976) results reflect the differential impact of unfavorable information about Group B, then ratings of Group B should be lower in the replication condition than in the Group B Only condition. On the other hand, if the earlier findings were due to the greater availability of information about Group A members doing desirable behaviors, then ratings of Group A should be higher than those of Group B both in the replication condition and in a comparison of the conditions in which subjects read about only one of the groups.

In fact, Regan and Crawley's (1984) results supported only the first hypothesis, as evidenced in three aspects of their findings. First, those subjects who read the complete set of stimulus sentences, describing both groups, made significantly different ratings of the two groups, replicating Hamilton and Gifford's results. Second, ratings of Group A by subjects who read only about that group did not differ significantly from ratings of Group B by subjects who read only the Group B sentences, and neither of these differed from ratings of Group A by subjects in the replication conditions. Third, and most importantly, Group B was rated significantly less favorably by subjects who had read the complete set of behavior sentences (describing members of both groups) than by subjects who had read only those sentences pertaining to Group B. These results, then, indicate that the differential judgments of groups produced by an illusory correlation are due to a *devaluation* of the *minority* group rather than to an enhanced evaluation of the majority group.

The same issue was investigated in a different way by Hamilton et al. (1985, Experiment 2). They noted that both the original explanation and Rothbart's (1981) alternative account of Hamilton and Gifford's (1976) findings relied on the same processing mechanism—the differential availability in memory of a particular type of information from the stimulus set. That is, the distinctiveness-based explanation proposes that the co-occurrence of infrequent stimuli is salient and noticeable as it is encoded, and hence this information is particularly available for retrieval at a later time when judgments of the groups are called for. The alternative view emphasizes the actual relative frequency of the co-occurrence of majority group and majority behavior, such that this type of information should be particularly available for retrieval from memory. Both explanations, then, view the divergent evaluations of groups as having been biased by the differential availability of one type of information. The difference between explanations concerns which kind of information is particularly available.

Hamilton et al. (1985, Experiment 2) tested these explanations directly by assessing subjects' memory for the four different categories of information provided to subjects in an illusory correlation paradigm. The procedure was identical to that of Hamilton and Gifford (1976) except that, following the presentation of stimulus information, subjects were asked to recall as many of the sentences as they could. The typical frequency estimate and trait rating measures were assessed following the recall task.

Several aspects of Hamilton et al.'s (1985) results supported the distinctiveness-based interpretation of illusory correlation effects. First, subjects recalled a significantly higher proportion of sentences describing undesirable behaviors performed by Group B members than any of the other three types of sentences. This result supports Hamilton and Gifford's (1976) interpretation in terms of the greater relative availability of items representing the co-occurrence of infrequently represented categories. Second, phi coefficients based on subjects' frequency estimates, which are indicators of the extent to which an illusory correlation was formed, were positively and significantly correlated with the number of Group B/undesirable sentences subjects recalled, but uncorrelated with their recall of any of the other categories of items. This findings suggests that the differential availability of this type of information was most influential in biasing subjects' frequency estimates. And third, phi coefficients (based on either subjects' frequency estimates or the number of sentences of each type they recalled) were uncorrelated with subjects' ratings of Group A, but were significantly and negatively correlated with evaluations of Group B. These results indicate that the extent to which subjects formed an illusory correlation had no bearing on their ratings of the majority group, but it did lead to *lowered* ratings of the minority group. Therefore, these findings are consistent with the results of Regan and Crawley's (1984) research.

Differential Group Evaluations: Generalized Halo or Content Specific?

In Hamilton and Gifford's (1976) experiments subjects read statements that described a variety of everyday behaviors and rated the two groups on a series of trait attributes. The behaviors were diverse, including both social, interpersonal activities and intellectual, task-related behaviors. Correspondingly, the trait scales included attributes reflecting both the social/interpersonal and intellectual domains. Differential group evaluations were obtained on both trait dimensions.

One issue not addressed in Hamilton and Gifford's (1976) research concerns the nature of the evaluative bias that occurs as a result of an illusory correlation. One possibility is that the difference in subjects' impressions of the two groups is limited to the specific content implicated in the information on which the illusory correlation is based. Alternatively, these differential impressions may become more generalized through evaluative halo effects or due to inferences to other qualities based on one's implicit personality theory. The difference between these two possibilities is important because it pertains to the pervasiveness of the evaluative consequences that emanate from this cognitive bias.

Acorn, Hamilton, and Sherman (1988) have recently reported evidence bearing on this issue. Using the standard illusory correlation paradigm, they presented stimulus sets in which there were twice as many sentences describing members of Group A than of Group B, and twice as many desirable as undesirable behaviors. Thus, a distinctiveness-based illusory correlation would produce lower evaluations of Group B. The three conditions of the experiment differed in the content domain(s) represented in the stimulus behaviors. One stimulus set included statements describing behaviors reflecting both the social and intellectual domains, similar to Hamilton and Gifford's (1976) materials. A second set consisted only of social behaviors, while the third set contained only intellectual or task-related behaviors. In all three conditions, subjects then rated their impressions of the two groups on a series of trait scales that included both social and intellectual dimension attributes.

If illusory correlations have domain-specific effects on judgments of the groups, then subjects who received the social-only or intellectual-only stimulus sets would differentially evaluate the two groups only on those traits corresponding to the information provided. In contrast, Acorn et al. (1988) found that subjects rated Group A more favorably than Group B on *both* social and intellectual dimension traits in *all three* conditions. In other words, in the two key conditions of this experiment, subjects differentially evaluated the groups even on traits for which no relevant information had been presented. Thus, the evaluative impact of the illusory correlation bias is not limited to the dimensions contained in the information on which it is based, but generalizes to new domains of content as well. These findings suggest that when illusory correlations are formed they can contribute to the pervasive character commonly observed in stereotypic belief systems.

Summary

The research summarized in this section provides the basis for several important conclusions. First, the results of the original experiment by Hamilton and Gifford (1976, Experiment 1) are highly replicable. The basic aspects of Hamilton and Gifford's findings have now been reproduced in numerous other studies carried out by several investigators (Acorn et al., 1988; Hamilton et al., 1985; Jones, Scott, Solernou, Noble, Fiala, & Miller 1977; Pryor, 1986; Regan & Crawley, 1984; Sanbonmatsu, Sherman, & Hamilton, 1987; Schaller & Maass, in press; Spears, van der Pligt, & Eiser, 1985, 1986). This is not to say that the informational preconditions associated with the formation of illusory correlations in group perception will always produce the same outcome; they do not, as we shall see in the next section of this chapter. However, the literature that has accumulated on this topic in the last decade has clearly established that illusory correlation in group perception is a quite reliable phenomenon.

Second, as a result of the research discussed above, we now have a better understanding of the cognitive processes on which the illusory correlation bias is based. In particular, we now have much more confidence in Hamilton and Gifford's (1976) original interpretation that these effects derive from the distinctiveness of the co-occurrence of infrequent stimulus events. Alternative explanations based on an association between group size and favorability of evaluations and on the association of majority group and the majority behavior category have been tested and found not to provide adequate accounts for the data. Instead, the results summarized in this section have consistently supported implications of the distinctiveness-based explanation.

Extensions of the Original Work: Boundary Conditions and Related Processes

Both the original Hamilton and Gifford (1976) study and subsequent studies designed to clarify the process underlying the illusory correlation effect (Hamilton et al., 1985; Regan & Crawley, 1984) employed the same basic paradigm. Hypothetical groups were used as targets, and distinctiveness of both the groups and the type of behavior were manipulated by relative infrequency. More recent work, in the hopes of extending the original findings, has introduced modifications in this paradigm. In so doing, these recent studies have demonstrated illusory correlation effects that are more widespread and general than those originally reported, have outlined some of the boundary conditions for these effects, and have further eluci-dated some of the processes involved in social perception and stereotyping. In this section, we shall review some of these extensions and indicate the gains in knowledge that have been made by them.

The Operationalization of Distinctiveness

The Hamilton and Gifford (1976) experiments manipulated distinctiveness by rela-tive infrequency. Group B was the minority group based on frequency of occur-rence, and one category of behavior (e.g., undesirable) occurred infrequently. Hence, the pairing of Group B members with infrequent behaviors would constitute the co-occurrence of distinctive stimuli. Such stimuli would attract extra attention, be encoded more effectively, and be more available for subsequent judgments; and this would constitute the basis for the illusory correlation effect. However, infre-quency is not the only way in which stimuli can be made distinctive.

Spears, van der Pligt, and Eiser (1985) had subjects with pro- or anti-attitudes to nuclear power view opinion statements presumably made by the residents of two towns. One town was large, and many statements were read about the opinions of its residents. The other town was small, and statements from its residents were infre-quent. The statements expressed views either supporting or opposing the building of a nuclear power station, and one type of statement was considerably more fre-quent, although the proportion or pro-and anti-statements was the same for both towns. Thus, distinctiveness of both the attitude position and the town was achieved in the usual way, by relative infrequency. In addition, Spears et al. conjectured that statements congruent with the subject's own attitude position would be more distinc-tive because of their self-relevance and would attract extra attention.

The findings indicated that when the minority attitudes were attitude con-gruent, an enhanced perceived association was observed between the small town and congruent attitudes. However, when the two kinds of distinctiveness were pitted against each other (i.e., when the minority attitudes were incongruent with the subjects' position), the illusory correlation effect disappeared. In addition, the illusory correlation effects based on self-relevance of the congruent attitudes were much stronger for subjects who held extreme positions on the nuclear power issue. For these subjects, the congruent attitude statements should have been especially salient and distinctive. Spears, van der Pligt, and Eiser (1986) replicated these results and showed that the self-relevance of the information (i.e., attitude con-gruence) could serve as the basis for illusory correlation effects independently of the infrequency manipulation.

The Spears et al. (1985, 1986) studies were the first to report illusory correlation effects in which stimulus distinctiveness was defined by means other than relative infrequency. In addition to extending the conceptualization of distinctiveness in the illusory correlation paradigm, these studies are important in showing that illusory correlations could form not only between groups and types of behaviors but also between groups and attitude positions.

Sanbonmatsu, Sherman, and Hamilton (1987) also demonstrated that factors other than infrequency can increase the attention given to a target and can increase the likelihood of the target being falsely associated with distinctive behaviors. In their study, five groups (identified by letters A through E) were employed as targets, and each group engaged in the same number of desirable and undesirable behaviors (either 7 desirable and 3 undesirable behaviors or 3 desirable and 7 undesirable behaviors). Group C was made distinctive by virtue of the instructions presented by the experimenter. That is, subjects were told to pay special attention to Group C and were told that there was special interest in their impressions of Group C. As expected, illusory correlations formed such that subjects overestimated the extent to which Group C members engaged in the minority behaviors (whether desirable or undesirable), and trait ratings of the groups reflected these illusory correlations.

The findings from several studies, then, indicate that any factor that draws attention to a stimulus (infrequency, self-relevance, etc.) can serve as the basis for a perceived association between that stimulus and some other distinctive stimulus. This meaningfully broadens the definition of distinctiveness-based illusory correlation such that it is no longer specified in terms of a particular operationalization (i.e., infrequency). In this more general view, the illusory correlation is defined as being based on overestimation of the frequency of co-occurrence of *distinctive* events, where that distinctiveness can derive from any of several properties or processes.

The Target of Perception

In the studies cited thus far, the targets of perception have been groups. Although this is clearly most relevant for the understanding of stereotyping, it is interesting to consider whether similar kinds of illusory correlations are observed when the targets are individuals. To this end, Sanbonmatsu, Sherman, and Hamilton (1987) employed individuals as well as groups to serve as targets in their study. In certain conditions of the experiment, subjects read about five individual male targets, each of whom engaged in either 7 desirable and 3 undesirable behaviors or in 7 undesirable and 3 desirable behaviors. One of the individuals was made distinctive by instructing subjects to pay special attention to him. As described in the previous section, with this paradigm and with *group* targets, subjects formed illusory correlations based on a perceived association between the distinctive group and the minority (distinctive) behavior. However, in the case of *individual* targets, illusory correlations formed such that distinctive individuals were inappropriately perceived as being more associated with the majority behavior than were the other four nondistinctive individuals. In other words, subjects formed an illusory correlation that is opposite in nature to that usually observed when group targets are employed (see also Fiedler, Hemmeter, & Hofmann, 1984).

This illusory correlation effect for individual targets was replicated with a somewhat different paradigm by Sanbonmatsu, Shavitt, Sherman, and Roskos-Ewoldsen (1987). In this study, subjects observed five individual targets perform a knowledge task. In one condition, each target succeeded on 7 of 10 trials. In another condition, each target failed on 7 of the 10 trials. One target was made distinctive by asking subjects to pay special attention to him. Again, the distinctive target was perceived as having experienced the frequent outcome (either success or failure) significantly more often than the other four (nondistinctive) targets.

The differing results obtained with group versus individual targets led Sanbon-matsu, Sherman, and Hamilton (1987) to propose that different processes are involved in the formation of impressions of individuals and of groups. They suggested that impressions of individuals are made "on-line" as behavioral information about these individuals is received. Such on-line impression formation leads to a focus on typical and usual behaviors emitted by a distinctive individual so that a clear and consistent impression of this individual may be formed. This focus will result in a perceived association between distinctive individual targets and majority behaviors. On the other hand, impressions of groups are assumed not to form on-line because no consistent "group personality" is expected by subjects. Individual items of information about group members are stored, however, and the most distinctive kind of information (i.e., the co-occurrence of minority members and infrequent behaviors) is represented most strongly and becomes most available in memory. When impressions of groups are subsequently requested, the most available information comes to mind first and carries the most weight in impressions. Thus, judgments of groups are memory-based (rather than on-line). Such a process will lead to a perceived association between distinctive groups and infrequent or distinctive behaviors because of the greater availability in memory of such pairings.

An understanding of these processes in the formation of impressions of individuals and groups suggests that group impressions need not always be memory-based and that if perceivers are induced to form on-line impressions of groups, the usual type of illusory correlation seen in Hamilton and Gifford (1976) will not occur. In fact, a recent study by Pryor (1986) provides evidence for this point. This experiment followed the standard illusory correlation procedure, except that the instructions given to subjects were varied. Some subjects were instructed to try to remember all the behavioral information about the group members. Other subjects were given impression set instructions indicating that they should try to form general and global evaluations of the groups. Only with the memory set instructions did the typical illusory correlation occur. With impression set instructions, subjects presumably formed well-developed impressions of the groups as they read the behavioral information, including on-line inferences about the groups, and no association between the infrequent group and the infrequent behaviors was observed.

These findings indicate that the existence and the form of illusory correlations in the perception of targets depends heavily on how subjects process information about those targets. Different kinds of biased perceptions can be expected depending upon the processing goals of the subjects. Any manipulation that would encourage the on-line processing of groups should eliminate the classic illusory correlation effect.

Sanbonmatsu, Shavitt et al. (1987) also investigated judgments when one of the targets was the self rather than a distinctive other individual target. It was assumed that the self would be a naturally distinctive target and that on-line processing of the performance of the self would occur. Based on the results obtained for distinctive individual targets, one would expect an illusory correlation based on the relatively strong association perceived between the self and the frequent outcome. This pattern of illusory correlation was obtained with one exception— when the predominant outcome was failure and the task was important. This one exception to the illusory correlation effect resulting from on-line processing for individual targets or the self was interpreted in terms of motivational processes. Such processes will now be discussed.

Motivational Factors

The discovery of illusory correlations in social perception was important in part because it suggested a purely cognitive information-processing basis for biases in these perceptions. Unwarranted differential beliefs and feelings about groups or individuals could develop because certain information was more distinctive, was processed differently, and was more available in memory. Unlike more motivational theories of stereotyping, illusory correlation effects suggested a simple information-processing mechanism. However, it is clear that motivational factors also play a role in the impressions we form of group targets. A goal of some recent research has thus been to investigate the combined roles of cognitive and motivational factors in group perceptions and to understand the limits that motivation might place on the development of illusory correlations.

Some of the results of the previously cited Spears et al. (1985) research may be taken as evidence for the role of motivational factors in the illusory correlation effect. Recall that in their experiments the strength of the illusory correlation depended upon the extremity of the subject's attitude on the issue used, nuclear power. Extreme subjects greatly overrepresented the frequency of minority position attitudes in the small town when the minority position was congruent with their attitude position (showing a large illusory correlation). When the minority position was incongruent with the attitudes of extreme subjects, they did not perceive an association between the small town and the minority position and thus showed no illusory correlation.

Spears et al. (1985) interpreted these results in terms of the motivation associated with commitment and involvement. The ego involvement of subjects with extreme attitudes should be high, and they should thus be more motivated to see their own position as relatively prevalent. Thus, overestimations of the frequency of minority congruent attitudes in the small town indicates that motivational tendencies can serve to simplify the cognitive bias when the two processes are in concert. On the other hand, the effects of the cognitive bias can be diminished when the two processes are in opposition.

Sanbonmatsu, Shavitt et al. (1987) proposed that motivational factors would be especially prevalent when the target was the self. They employed the paradigm described earlier (five different targets, one of whom was made salient with each target succeeding or each failing on 7 of 10 occasions) with the self replacing the distinctive other target. It was assumed that the self would be a naturally distinctive target and, therefore, that illusory correlations would form such that the self was seen as more associated with the majority behaviors (because of on-line processing) than would the other four targets. However, motivational concerns about self-protection should modify this effect under certain conditions—when the task was presented as important and when the majority behavior was failure. In this case, the illusory correlation effect would lead the subject to perceive himself as less able than others on an important task. Findings indicated that, as predicted, biased perceptions of the association between the self and the majority outcome occurred in all cases—except when the majority outcome was failure and the task was important. Thus, motivational concerns can set limits on the cognitively based illusory correlation process.

Schaller and Maass (in press) have recently applied similar thinking to perceptions of groups. They proposed that if subjects believed they were members of one of the groups, this group membership would place motivational constraints on the formation of any illusory correlation that would cause one's own group to appear undesirable relative to another group. Using the Hamilton and Gifford paradigm, Schaller and Maass (in press) reported typical illusory correlation effects by subjects in a control condition for whom there was no mention of group membership—a shared infrequency effect based on overestimating the minority group and the infrequent behavior. However, when subjects believed they belonged to one or the other of the stimulus groups, they showed significantly weaker illusory correlations when the shared infrequency effect would lead to a disparagement of their own group. Once again, it appears that motivational concerns can set limits on the biases due to information processing mechanisms that underlie the illusory correlation effect.

A Perspective on Illusory Correlations and Stereotyping

The research literature on distinctiveness-based illusory correlations as a mechanism underlying stereotype formation is barely more than a decade old. Nevertheless, the accumulated findings that we have reviewed in the preceding sections of this chapter indicate that this research has been highly informative. The results from these experiments now provide substantial documentation that the phenomena originally demonstrated by Hamilton and Gifford (1976) are quite reliable, and this research has effectively bolstered the interpretation of these findings in terms of the effects of co-occurring distinctive stimulus categories. Moreover, recent evidence has shown that the processes on which these results are based can also have implications for judgments of individuals and of the self.

At the same time, this research has begun to identify some of the boundary conditions on the formation of distinctiveness-based illusory correlations, and in identifying some of the limits of the phenomenon, we have enhanced our understanding of the nature of the cognitive mechanisms that contribute to this bias. To be sure, questions remain and there are issues yet to be resolved. Nevertheless, the literature has now established distinctiveness-based illusory correlation as an important cognitive bias with serious ramifications for stereotype development. Our purpose in this final section is to step back from the specifics of individual experiments and to view this work in some broader perspectives concerning the place of illusory correlation research in the study of stereotypes.

Distinctiveness-based illusory correlations, as originally defined, arise from a situation in which the perceiver processes information about two variables (a) that are uncorrelated and (b) whose levels occur with unequal frequency. In terms of the 2×2 frequency table referred to earlier, the marginal values for both variables are skewed such that one level of the first variable co-occurs with one level of the other variable with relative infrequency, making their co-occurrence particularly distinctive. Recent findings indicate that the same outcomes occur when variables other than infrequency serve to make a particular kind of co-occurrence distinctive. Either way, this situation is a special case of the co-occurrence relationship between two variables. A considerable literature indicates that perceivers encounter a number of difficulties in judging correlational relations under a variety of conditions (cf. Alloy & Tabachnik, 1984; Arkes & Harkness, 1983; Arkes & Rothbart, 1985; Crocker, 1981; Hamilton, 1981b; Trolier & Hamilton, 1986). Viewed in this context, illusory correlation research focuses on particular information processing biases that occur in this "special case" in which a certain combination of two variables becomes highly distinctive.

Although the informational preconditions for distinctiveness-based illusory correlations represent a special case of the more general covariation judgment problem, those preconditions certainly do not reflect an unusual or atypical circumstance in everyday life. Many classes of information (variables) that we encounter in the social world have skewed distributions of occurrence or are distinctive for other reasons, and they would be uncorrelated with other variables that have distinctive properties. Whenever information of this kind is available, the conditions necessary (but not necessarily sufficient) for an illusory correlation to develop are present.

The circumstance of particular interest in this chapter, of course, is that in which one of those variables identifies membership in one of two groups. Certainly it is not uncommon for persons to have differing degrees of exposure to and/or interaction with members of various groups (e.g., whites and blacks, Arabs and Israelis, old people and young people, professionals and laborers, etc.). And different types of behavior occur with differential frequency in everyday life. Thus, given the varieties of information to which perceivers are routinely exposed and the results of the experiments reviewed in the preceding sections, it seems quite plausible that the mechanisms of illusory correlation may contribute to the perception of intergroup differences in many circumstances.

In this regard, it is important to point out again exactly how distinctiveness-based illusory correlations are relevant to the question of stereotyping. That is, this cognitive bias has its effect on the *development* of stereotypes by contributing to the *initial* perception of intergroup differences. More specifically, the illusory correlation bias results in the differential perception of groups that have been described by evaluatively equivalent information. Once this differentiation has been made, these groups become meaningful social categories in the perceiver's head, and these

cognitive categories can then be the basis for further biases in information processing about these groups in the future (cf. Hamilton & Trolier, 1986; Stephan, 1985;
Taylor, 1981; Wilder, 1981). Thus, illusory correlation is a process that has its bearing on the very early stages of stereotype formation.

Recognition of this point helps us to understand what are the most important, as
well as what are essentially meaningless, questions to raise about the role of illusory
correlations in stereotyping. As an example of the latter, one of us was once asked
to "name a currently-important stereotype that is based on an illusory correlation."
Like raising the nature –nurture issue for a particular behavior, the question is virtually unanswerable. It assumes, for example, that a particular stereotype can be identified as having been based on this process *or* that process, whereas any actual
stereotype is almost certainly multiply determined by several processes. We cannot
state that a particular stereotype is solely (or even primarily) *based on* cognitive
biases, any more than we can say that it is solely (or even primarily) *based on* media
portrayals of the group. Pursuing such issues at this point does not appear to us to
be fruitful.

Unexplored Empirical Issues

There are, however, more important and useful avenues of research. In particular,
it seems to us that there are three important issues concerning distinctiveness-based
illusory correlations that call for empirical investigation.

The first issue concerns the *development* of illusory correlations in children.
Questions of how and when cognitive biases function in children at various stages
of development seem particularly important for understanding the emergence of
stereotypic belief systems. As we have stressed earlier, a distinctiveness-based illusory correlation produces the unwarranted perception of differences between
groups, and as such, lays the foundation for stereotype formation. Presumably the
initial differentiation established through illusory correlation is, in many cases, a
relatively crude, perhaps largely evaluative differentiation between groups. A
stereotypic belief system develops as specific beliefs become associated with these
group conceptions. Although these associations may reflect the content of the information on which the illusory correlation is based, in many cases the content of the
stereotype evolves as new information becomes associated with these differential
group concepts. We know that children begin to make intergroup differentiations at
a fairly young age and that stereotypes develop gradually over the course of development (Katz, 1976; Martin & Halverson, 1981; Ruble & Stangor, 1986). We know of
no research investigating the role of illusory correlation processes in the initial
establishment of those intergroup differentiations in children, and we feel that this
question needs to be investigated.

A second issue that needs to be explored in future research concerns the *consequences* of this cognitive bias by which different intergroup perceptions are created
on the basis of equivalent information. In one sense, the consequences of
distinctiveness-based illusory correlations were evident from the beginning of this
line of research. That is, if an illusory correlation is an erroneous perception of an

association between group membership and behavior desirability, then the fact that this perceived association results in differential evaluations of groups is itself a consequence. In this context, however, we want to draw attention to consequences that extend beyond the initially created effect. That is, given differential group perceptions based on an illusory correlation, how do those differences influence subsequent processing of information about group members? Would these differences have an influence on a person's social behavior in interaction with a member of one of these groups? We know that well-established concepts of groups influence information processing and social behavior in a variety of ways (cf. Hamilton & Trolier, 1986; Stephan, 1985). The question of whether differential group concepts based on illusory correlation function in similar ways and with similar consequences is, we believe, an important item on the agenda for future investigation.

The final issue concerns strategies for *preventing* or *changing* stereotypes based on our understanding of illusory correlation as a mechanism of stereotype formation. In addressing this issue, it is important to distinguish between two different aspects of the nature and functioning of stereotypes. First, there is the initial development of stereotypes — the processes through which stereotypes are acquired. Second, and subsequent to the acquisition of stereotypes, there is the expression and maintenance of these stereotypes. The point to recognize here is that the processes that are important in the development of biased perceptions of groups may not be the same as the processes involved in the maintenance of these perceptions.

Distinctiveness-based illusory correlation is clearly a process that is primarily relevant to the development rather than the maintenance of stereotypes. The work on illusory correlation indicates one mechanism through which unwarranted differential perceptions of groups might arise. Once these stereotypes develop, their maintenance may be due to processes unrelated to the manner in which they were formed.

Thus, any implications of work on the illusory correlation phenomenon for altering stereotypes would pertain to the stage of stereotype development. Illusory correlation processes might help us understand how stereotypes develop and thus suggest ways to prevent the initiation of stereotype formation. However, it is less clear how an understanding of illusory correlation processes would be relevant for changing stereotypes once they have developed. This distinction between prevention and change subsequent to development is an important one, for different factors and processes may well be important for understanding these two different phases.

A second general point to make about the role of illusory correlation in understanding strategies for preventing or changing stereotypes is that this is but one process involved in the development of stereotypes. Other cognitive processes as well as processes based on learning and motivation clearly play important roles in the development and maintenance of stereotypes. For any actual ethnic stereotype it is not useful to think of stereotype acquisition or expression as being based on a single, pure process. Thus, any strategies for preventing or changing stereotypes would have to consider the implications of these other processes. We shall be concerned here only with some of the implications of illusory correlation, but this focus should not be viewed as a failure to recognize the relevance of other processes as well.

Any implications of illusory correlation processes for the prevention of stereotypes would obviously involve those factors that are important in the development of illusory correlations. In other words, prevention of illusory correlations depends upon interfering with the conditions necessary for the development of these biases in perception. What are these specific factors and conditions? In the first place, the formation of illusory correlations in group perception depends upon the distinctiveness of one of the groups. This distinctiveness can be achieved simply through differences in frequency (as many studies have shown), but any feature that calls attention to one of the groups (unusual physical appearance, manner of speaking, etc.) will add to the likelihood of forming an illusory correlation. The implications for prevention of stereotype development are that techniques that diminish the distinctiveness of the groups involved are likely to be effective. In the case of naturally occurring infrequent groups (e.g., racial minorities), this might mean that greater exposure to and contact with these groups would decrease their distinctiveness and thereby diminish the extent to which illusory correlations would form between these groups and distinctive characteristics or behaviors.

This argument has another interesting implication as well. Research on the contact hypothesis has found that mere contact with minority groups is not, in and of itself, effective in changing stereotypes or reducing prejudice, except under certain conditions (cf. Stephan, 1985). However, although increased contact might be ineffective in changing already developed stereotypes, it may well be useful in preventing the stereotypes from developing in the first place. Here, again, we see the importance of distinguishing stereotype acquisition from stereotype maintenance.

Another factor that is important in the development of illusory correlations is the distinctiveness of the behaviors with which the minority (or otherwise distinctive) group becomes associated. Hamilton and Gifford (1976) proposed that negative behaviors and characteristics are generally more distinctive than positive or neutral behaviors. Thus, through the processes involved in illusory correlation formation, distinctive groups will be mistakenly perceived as having negative attributes more than nondistinctive groups. It does seem true that negative acts are focused on by the media and are made salient by their presentation. Even without such attention to negative events, research has shown that negative information is more attention-grabbing and receives more weight in impression formation than does positive information (Fiske, 1980; Hamilton & Zanna, 1972; Hodges, 1974). It might thus be difficult to alter the distinctiveness of negative information. However, if distinctive positive acts (or even neutral acts) were given more attention by the media or by the educational system, the extreme distinctiveness of minority group members engaging in negative acts might be diminished.

A final possibility for preventing illusory correlations based on the co-occurrence of distinctive events would be to establish specific conditions that interfere with illusory correlation development. For example, we have seen how motivational factors can prevent the development of biased associations based on cognitive processes. Any motivational factors that would make it advantageous to acquire accurate group perceptions would thus interfere with the development of illusory correlations.

Making different groups dependent on one another, increasing the hedonic relevance of groups, or increasing the degree of normative or comparative functions of various groups would serve this purpose.

In addition to the introduction of motivational factors, the usual illusory correlation in group perception is based on the group impressions being recall-based rather than formed through on-line processing. These processes and the differences between them have already been discussed in some detail. Although we have argued that perceptions of groups typically reflect memory-based judgments, it is possible to induce the development of on-line impressions of groups. Once again, increasing the interdependence of groups might help to induce such processing. More generally, any condition that leads perceivers to form on-line impressions of a group based upon the behavior of its members should eliminate the type of illusory correlation that depends upon an increased memory for acts representing the co-occurrence of distinctive events.

Broader Contributions

Because the illusory correlation literature that we have discussed is concerned with stereotyping, much of this research has implications for practical or applied issues. Work on the illusory correlation helps us understand the development, maintenance, and nature of stereotypes, and hence has implications for dealing with or changing the negative aspects of stereotyping. Beyond that, however, research on illusory correlation has also led to more theoretical and process-oriented advances. In this regard, we have already discussed the contribution made to our understanding of the distinction between on-line and recall-based impression formation. We shall now discuss another generally important theoretical contribution made by work on the illusory correlation.

The history of research on social perception reveals a good deal of fragmentation. Work on the perception of groups (of which stereotyping is the major area), work on person perception and impression formation, and work on self-perception and the self-concept have proceeded rather separately and independently. These three areas can usually be found in different chapters of general social psychology texts, and seldom does work in one of these areas reference work in the other areas.

As research concerning the illusory correlation effect has proceeded from looking at groups as targets, to individuals, to the self, it has become clear that the processes involved in forming impressions of these three kinds of targets are different in some respects, but that they also share some important similarities. The work to date indicates that memory-based processes typically operate in the development of perceptions of groups and that on-line processing is more likely in the development of perceptions of individuals and the self. Yet this research also indicates that either of these two processes of impression formation (recall-based and on-line) is possible for the perception of any of the three kinds of targets. People can be induced to adopt on-line processing for groups, and there are times when on-line processing of information about the self is not possible (as when one's attention is used in deciding what to do or how to act in a situation, and no resources are available for on-line evaluation). Moreover, the outcome of impressions formed of groups, individuals, or the self can be understood in terms of the adoption of on-line or recall-based processing and in terms of the cognitively based illusory correlations that follow from these two kinds of processing.

As an example of the gains that can be made by taking into account the similarities in the processes involved in group, individual, and self-perception, consider that unwarranted differential perceptions of individuals or of the self can be just as harmful as are the perceptions of unwarranted differences among groups. Individuals who see themselves as less capable and less effective than others can come to feel helpless and depressed. Individuals, as well as groups, can be victims of discrimination. Consider an office setting where competent performance is the norm, and thus where incompetent behaviors are infrequent and distinctive. Imagine further that there is one individual on the staff who, by virtue of being the only female or the only member of a racial minority, is highly distinctive. Imagine that this individual performs at a level equal to that of his or her peers. Will a manager who oversees the operation accurately judge the performance level of the distinctive target? If the impressions of the individuals are recall-based, research indicates that the distinctive individual will be judged as less capable than the others—a distinctiveness-based illusory correlation that leads to the perception of association between the distinctive individual and the distinctive behavior. However, if the impressions of individual workers are made on-line, the distinctive individual might be perceived as performing more of the majority (competent) behaviors than the others. In either case, these differential perceptions might well lead to discriminatory behaviors and might serve as a basis for generating more general impressions of the group to which the distinctive individual belongs.

Recognition of the similarities of processes and consequences in the areas of stereotyping, person perception, and self-perception is important. Consideration of these similarities and their implications can help to advance our understanding of each of these different areas of social perception.

Acknowledgments. Preparation of this chapter was supported in part by NIMH Grant MH 40058. The authors are grateful to Phyllis Katz, Arie Kruglanski, and Wolfgang Stroebe for their comments on a preliminary version of this chapter.

References

Acorn, D.A., Hamilton, D.L., & Sherman, S.J. (1988). Generalization of biased perceptions of groups based on illusory correlations. *Social Cognition, 6,* 345–372.

Alloy, L.B., & Tabachnik, N. (1984). Assessment of covariation by humans and animals: The joint influence of prior expectations and current situational information. *Psychological Review, 91,* 112–149.

Allport, G.W. (1954). *The nature of prejudice.* Reading, MA: Addison-Wesley.

Arkes, H.R., & Harkness, A.R. (1983). Estimates of contingency between two dichotomous variables. *Journal of Experimental Psychology: General, 112,* 117–135.

Arkes, H.R., & Rothbart, M. (1985). Memory, retrieval, and contingency judgments. *Journal of Personality and Social Psychology, 49,* 598–606.

Ashmore, R.D., & Del Boca, F.K. (1981). Conceptual approaches to stereotypes and stereotyping. In D.L. Hamilton (Ed.), *Cognitive processes in stereotyping and intergroup behavior* (pp. 1–35). Hillsdale, NJ: Erlbaum.

Berman, J.S., & Kenny, D.A. (1976). Correlational bias in observer ratings. *Journal of Personality and Social Psychology, 34,* 263–273.

Casas, J.M., Brady, S., & Ponterotto, J.G. (1983). Sexual preference biases in counseling: An information processing approach. *Journal of Counseling Psychology, 30,* 139–145.

Chapman, L.J. (1967). Illusory correlation in observational report. *Journal of Verbal Learning and Verbal behavior, 6,* 151–155.

Chapman, J.L., & Chapman, J.P. (1967). Genesis of popular but erroneous psychodiagnostic observations. *Journal of Abnormal Psychology, 72,* 193–204.

Chapman, L.J., & Chapman, J.P. (1969). Illusory correlation as an obstacle to the use of valid psychodiagnostic signs. *Journal of Abnormal Psychology, 74,* 271–280.

Crocker, J. (1981). Judgment of covariation by social perceivers. *Psychological Bulletin, 90,* 272–292.

Fiedler, K., Hemmeter, U., & Hofmann, C. (1984). On the origin of illusory correlations. *European Journal of Social Psychology, 14,* 191–201.

Fiske, S.T. (1980). Attention and weight in person perception: The impact of negative and extreme behavior. *Journal of Personality and Social Psychology, 38,* 889–906.

Golding, S.L., & Rorer, L.G. (1972). Illusory correlation and subjective judgment. *Journal of Abnormal Psychology, 80,* 249–260.

Hamilton, D.L. (1976). Cognitive biases in the perception of social groups. In J.S. Carroll & J.W. Payne (Eds.), *Cognition and social behavior* (pp. 81–93). Hillsdale, NJ: Erlbaum.

Hamilton, D.L. (1979). A cognitive-attributional analysis of stereotyping. In L. Berkowitz (Ed.), *Advances in experimental social psychology* (Vol. 12) (pp. 53–84). New York: Academic Press.

Hamilton, D.L. (Ed.). (1981a). *Cognitive processes in stereotyping and intergroup behavior.* Hillsdale, NJ: Erlbaum.

Hamilton, D.L. (1981b). Illusory correlation as a basis for stereotyping. In D.L. Hamilton (Ed.), *Cognitive processes in stereotyping and intergroup behavior* (pp. 115–144). Hillsdale, NJ: Erlbaum.

Hamilton, D.L., Dugan, P.J., & Trolier, T.K. (1985). The formation of stereotypic beliefs: Further evidence for distinctiveness-based illusory correlation. *Journal of Personality and Social Psychology, 48,* 5–17.

Hamilton, D.L., & Gifford, R.K. (1976). Illusory correlation in interpersonal perception: A cognitive basis of stereotypic judgments. *Journal of Experimental Social Psychology, 12,* 392–407.

Hamilton, D.L., & Rose, T.L. (1980). Illusory correlation and the maintenance of stereotypic beliefs. *Journal of Personality and Social Psychology, 39,* 832–845.

Hamilton, D.L., & Trolier, T.K. (1986). Stereotypes and stereotyping: An overview of the cognitive approach. In J. Dovidio & S.L. Gaertner (Eds.), *Prejudice, discrimination, and racism* (pp. 127–163). New York: Academic Press.

Hamilton, D.L., & Zanna, M.P. (1972). Differential weighting of favorable and unfavorable attributes in impressions of personality. *Journal of Experimental Research in Personality, 6,* 204–212.

Hodges, B.H. (1974). Effect of valence on relative weighting in impression formation. *Journal of Personality and Social Psychology, 30,* 378–381.

Jones, R.A. (1982). Perceiving other people: Stereotyping as a process of social cognition. In A.G. Miller (Ed.), *In the eye of the beholder: Contemporary issues in stereotyping* (pp. 41–91). New York: Praeger.

Jones, R.A., Scott, J., Solernou, J., Noble, A., Fiala, J., & Miller, K. (1977). Availability and formation of stereotypes. *Perceptual and Motor Skills, 44,* 631–638.

Katz, P.A. (1976). The acquisition of racial attitudes in children. In P.A. Katz (Ed.), *Towards the elimination of racism* (pp. 125–156). New York: Pergamon.

Kim, H., & Baron, R.S. (1988). Exercise and the illusory correlation: Does arousal heighten stereotypic processing? *Journal of Experimental Social Psychology, 24*, 366–380.

Kurtz, R.M., & Garfield, S.L. (1978). Illusory correlation: A further exploration of Chapman's paradigm. *Journal of Consulting and Clinical Psychology, 46*, 1009–1015.

Martin, C.L., & Halverson, C.F. (1981). A schematic processing model of sex typing and stereotyping in children. *Child Development, 52*, 1119–1134.

McArthur, L.Z., & Friedman, S.A. (1980). Illusory correlation in impression formation: Variations in the shared distinctiveness effect as a function of the distinctive person's age, race, and sex. *Journal of Personality and Social Psychology, 39*, 615–624.

Pryor, J.B. (1986). The influence of different encoding sets upon the formation of illusory correlations and group impressions. *Personality and Social Psychology Bulletin, 12*, 216–226.

Regan, D.T., & Crawley, D.M. (1984, August). *Illusory correlation and stereotype formation: Replication and extension*. Paper presented at American Psychological Association Convention, Toronto, Canada.

Rothbart, M. (1981). Memory processes and social beliefs. In D.L. Hamilton (Ed.), *Cognitive processes in stereotyping and intergroup behavior* (pp. 145–181). Hillsdale, NJ: Erlbaum.

Ruble, D.N., & Stangor, C. (1986). Stalking the elusive schema: Insights from developmental and social-psychological analyses of gender schemas. *Social Cognition, 4*, 227–261.

Sanbonmatsu, D.M., Shavitt, S., Sherman, S.J., & Roskos-Ewoldsen, D.R. (1987). Illusory correlation in the perception of performance by self or a salient other. *Journal of Experimental Social Psychology, 23*, 518–543.

Sanbonmatsu, D.M., Sherman, S.J. & Hamilton, D.L. (1987). Illusory correlation in the perception of individuals and groups. *Social Cognition, 5*, 1–25.

Schaller, M., & Maass, A. (in press). Illusory correlation and social categorization: Toward an integration of motivational and cognitive factors in stereotype formation. *Journal of Personality and Social Psychology*.

Slusher, M.P., & Anderson, C.A. (1987). When reality monitoring fails: The role of imagination in stereotype maintenance. *Journal of Personality and Social Psychology, 52*, 653–662.

Spears, R., van der Pligt, J., & Eiser, J.R. (1985). Illusory correlation in the perception of group attitudes. *Journal of Personality and Social Psychology, 48*, 863–875.

Spears, R., van der Pligt, J., & Eiser, J.R. (1986). Generalizing the illusory correlation effect. *Journal of Personality and Social Psychology, 51*, 1127–1134.

Starr, B.J., & Katkin, E.S. (1969). The clinician as an aberrant actuary: Illusory correlation and the incomplete sentences black. *Journal of Abnormal Psychology, 74*, 670–675.

Stephan, W.G. (1985). Intergroup relations. In G. Lindzey & E. Aronson (Eds.), *The handbook of social psychology* (3rd ed., Vol. 2) (pp. 599–658). New York: Random House.

Tajfel, H. (1969). Cognitive aspects of prejudice. *Journal of Social Issues, 25*(4), 79–97.

Taylor, S.E. (1981). A categorization approach to stereotyping. In D.L. Hamilton (Ed.), *Cognitive processes in stereotyping and intergroup behavior* (pp. 83–114). Hillsdale, NJ: Erlbaum.

Trolier, T.K., & Hamilton, D.L. (1986). Variables influencing judgments of correlational relations. *Journal of Personality and Social Psychology, 50*, 879–888.

Tversky, A., & Kahneman, D. (1973). Availability: A heuristic for judging frequency and probability. *Cognitive Psychology, 5*, 207–232.

Wampold, B.E., Casas, J.M., & Atkinson, D.R. (1981). Ethnic bias in counseling: An information processing approach. *Journal of Counseling Psychology, 28*, 498–503.

Wilder, D.A. (1981). Perceiving persons as a group: Categorization and intergroup relations. In D.L. Hamilton (Ed.), *Cognitive processes in stereotyping and intergroup behavior* (pp. 213–257). Hillsdale, NJ: Erlbaum.

Zajonc, R.B. (1968). Attitudinal effects of mere exposure. *Journal of Personality and Social Psychology, 9*(2, Pt. 2).

Chapter 4

Category-Based and Individuating Processes as a Function of Information and Motivation: Evidence from Our Laboratory

Susan T. Fiske and Steven L. Neuberg

When do people form impressions of others based on the stereotypes and prejudices associated with the others' category memberships, and when instead do they form impressions based on the others' own particular individuating characteristics? Although people seem to think they should not respond to others on the basis of social group memberships, such category-based responses continue in subtle and not-so-subtle ways (e.g., Crosby, Bromley, & Saxe, 1980; Pettigrew & Martin, 1987). Moreover, while it is clear that people are also fully capable of individuating others, it appears that they do so only when certain conditions are met. Our intent in this chapter is to explicate these conditions and to address some of the factors that elicit them. In this manner, we hope to contribute to interventions aimed at reducing the incidence of impressions formed on the basis of stereotypes and prejudices.

Our own attempt to understand these issues builds on two major approaches toward impression formation (for reviews see Fiske & Taylor, 1984; Fiske & Pavel-chak, 1986; Schneider, Hastorf, & Ellsworth, 1979). These approaches can be traced back to Asch's (1946) statement of the competing holistic and elemental forms of impression formation. The first approach, a descendant of Asch's con-figural model, holds that people form impressions of others based on the social categories into which they place them (e.g., Allport, 1954; Cantor & Mischel, 1979; Taylor, 1981). We refer to these processes—those that heavily utilize social category information to the relative exclusion of an individual's other characteris-tics—as stereotype-oriented or *category-based processes*. Alternatively, the second approach proposes that people form impressions by simply combining (adding, aver-aging, or otherwise) the isolated characteristics of the individual other (e.g., Ander-son, 1974; Fishbein & Ajzen, 1975; Locksley, Borgida, Brekke, & Hepburn, 1980). We refer to these processes—those that heavily utilize an individual's characteristics to the relative exclusion of an individual's social category—as attribute-oriented or *individuating processes*. In the past, perhaps due to differing paradigmatic influ-ences and focuses, these two approaches have typically either ignored or rejected each other's insights. Our recent work synthesizes these two views, focusing on the conditions under which each of these processes may accurately represent people's attempts at impression formation (cf. Fiske & Pavelchak, 1986; Fiske & Neuberg, in press).

The Continuum Model

The Major Premises

We suggest that people can form impressions of others through a variety of processes that constitute a continuum ranging from primarily category-based to primarily individuating processes. Underlying this conceptualization are several important premises (see Fiske & Neuberg, in press, for a more complete presentation of the model and the assumptions upon which it is constructed). Because categorizing an individual as a member of a particular social group provides perceivers with useful information at relatively little cost in cognitive effort or time (e.g., Allport, 1954; Tajfel, 1981), we believe that category-based processes have priority over individuating processes. More specifically, we posit that people attempt processes at the category-based end of the continuum (and are frequently successful) before attempting more individuating impression formation processes. In that sense, category-based processes have priority over more individuating processes.

Moreover, relevant to the mechanisms by which a perceiver moves along this category-based/individuating continuum, we propose, first, that perceivers proceed along this continuum as a function of the ease with which they can "fit" a target's attributes to the target's initial category. As a perceiver becomes less able to interpret the target's attributes as validating the target's category, we posit that the perceiver is likely to attempt more individuating impression formation. Second, we propose that individuating processes require increased attention to, and use of, target attribute information (as opposed to a decreased use of social category information). We thus believe that successful individuation requires, or is mediated by, the conjunction of both increased *attention* to the target's attributes and *interpretation* of the target's attributes as not fitting the target's initial category assignment.

Finally, we propose that a perceiver's impression formation motives and goals greatly influence impression formation by altering the manner in which a perceiver attends to target information and interprets it. To the extent that a perceiver's motives increase attention to attribute information and encourage interpretation of that information as not fitting the target's category, then relatively individuating impression formation will be more likely.

An Overview of the Basic Model

We suggest that perceivers categorize others immediately upon encountering information that sufficiently cues a meaningful social category. This information may be a physical feature (e.g., skin color), a written or verbalized label ("Frank is a schizophrenic"), or a cluster of category-consistent features that rapidly cue a category in memory (e.g., secondary sex characteristics). Importantly, this *initial categorization* is rapid and essentially perceptual (cf. Bruner, 1957)—that is, it requires only cursory attention to the target's available features. Once a category is cued, category-based cognitions (e.g., stereotypes), affect (e.g., prejudices), and behavioral tendencies (e.g., discriminatory potential) become activated, although not necessarily acted upon.

If the perceiver determines that the target is of particular relevance or interest (cf. Brewer, 1988), the perceiver increases attention to the target in an attempt to determine whether the target's remaining features (i.e., attributes) fit the initial category label. If the attributes are interpreted as fitting the category label, the initial categorization is confirmed, and the perceiver's impression of the target will be based on the stereotypes and prejudices associated with this category.

If, however, this *confirmatory categorization* process is unsuccessful (i.e., the attributes are interpreted as not fitting the category label), the perceiver increases attention to the target's attributes and attempts to access a different category—one that can adequately encompass the bulk of the available target information. This *recategorization* process may consist of accessing a subcategory (e.g., a male nurse; see Brewer, Dull, & Lui, 1981; Deaux & Lewis, 1984; Taylor, 1981; Weber & Crocker, 1983), an exemplar (e.g., "this person reminds me of my fifth grade teacher;" see Brooks, 1978; Kahneman & Miller, 1986), a self-schema (e.g., "this person reminds me of the way I was when I was his age"; Markus, 1977; Markus, Smith, & Moreland, 1985), or an altogether new category that may seem more appropriate. If the perceiver can successfully access a category interpreted to fit better the available target information, the perceiver's cognitions, affect, and behavioral tendencies toward the target likely will be those appropriate to the newly selected category.[1]

If recategorization is unsuccessful, however, the perceiver must then integrate the available target information in some piecemeal, attribute-by-attribute manner (e.g., Anderson, 1974; Fishbein & Ajzen, 1975). This *piecemeal integration* process requires still more attention to attribute information. Ultimately, piecemeal-based processes will determine that perceiver's cognitions, affect, and behavioral tendencies toward the target. Note that this is the most individuating form of impression formation, in that the target's attributes are integrated with only minimal consideration of category information. In piecemeal integration, category membership merely plays the role of yet another target feature.

Regardless of whether the perceiver successfully implements confirmatory categorization, recategorization, or piecemeal integration processes, the perceiver determines whether further assessment of the target is needed. If further assessment does seem required (e.g., if the impression formed is incompatible with the

---

[1]Note that this recategorization process is relatively category based in that the impressions formed are determined by the nature of the newly selected category, but relatively individuating in that the new category is determined largely by the target's particular attributes. Thus, recategorization occupies the middle ground between purely category-based and purely individuating impression formation.

perceiver's goals), the perceiver will increase attention to the target's attributes and return to the confirmatory categorization stage of the model, this time assessing the fit of the target's attributes to the most recent conceptualization of the target. As before, if the validation process is successful, the perceiver's impressions will be based on this most recent conceptualization. And if unsuccessful, the perceiver will move on to the recategorization stage. This cycle of impression generation and further assessment decisions continues until the perceiver is satisfied with the impression, at which time impression formation stops.

Before moving on to present evidence from our laboratory that supports this model and its basic premises, we will first briefly define some concepts that are important to the remainder of our discussion.

What's a Category Label and What's an Attribute?

A perceiver may have access to a number of target features that can potentially provide information useful for impression formation. These features may be observed (e.g., age, skin color), inferred (e.g., extraversion, intelligence, honesty), communicated by others (e.g., "Ernest is an ex-con"), and the like. We call the target feature (or constellation of features) that a perceiver uses to understand and organize the remaining target features the *category-label*; we call the remaining target features *attributes*. The category-label need not organize the remaining features ideally. Rather, to serve the function of the category-label, a feature need only be construed by the perceiver as organizing the remaining features at least as well as any other available feature.

The category-label/attribute distinction is important because of the roles that each play in impression formation. As we mentioned above, the feature used as the category-label cues category-relevant information stored in memory. In our view, category information often has a disproportionate influence on impression formation, in that (1) it often becomes accessible before the perceiver can begin to use attribute information, (2) it influences how the target's actual attributes are interpreted and remembered, and (3) it often leads the perceiver to make category-consistent inferences about the target. Thus, this distinction is crucial in its implications for the processes and outcomes of impression formation.

For the distinction to be useful, however, one needs to be able to predict beforehand which feature will serve as the category-label and which features will serve as attributes. Previous research suggests that features possessing *temporal primacy* (Asch, 1946; Jones & Goethals, 1972), *physical manifestation* (Fiske & Cox, 1979; McArthur, 1982; Milord, 1978; Posner, Nissen, & Klein, 1976), *contextual novelty* (McArthur & Post, 1977; Taylor, 1981; Taylor et al., 1977), *cognitive accessibility within the perceiver* (Bargh et al., 1986; Higgins & King, 1981; Higgins, King & Mavin, 1982; Higgins, Rholes, & Jones, 1977; Srull & Wyer, 1979; Wyer & Srull, 1980; 1981), or *affective congruence with the perceiver's present mood* (Erber, 1985) are more likely to be used as category-labels than other available features (see Fiske & Neuberg, in press, for a review). Taking these factors into account, one can make reasonable assumptions about which of a target's available features will be used as the category-label in many differing situations. Accordingly, the assumptions we make in our research (described below) about which feature serves the role of category-label, and which features serve the roles of attributes, are consistent with this literature.

Our Laboratory's Evidence for the Model

We have claimed that impression formation becomes more individuating (1) when the perceiver is unable to validate an initial categorization of a target, that is, when the perceiver cannot interpret the target's attributes as fitting an initial category label, and (2) when the perceiver increases attention to, and use of, the target's attributes. We turn now to discuss several studies from our laboratory that investigate these premises by observing changes in impression formation resulting from differences in the configurations of category and attribute information.

Fiske, Neuberg, Beattie, and Milberg (1987) presented perceivers with information configurations that differed in the extent to which attribute information would be interpreted as validating a category label. Two conditions were created (based on pretesting) in which a perceiver would likely interpret the attributes as fitting a provided category label: (1) the "consistent" condition, in which the provided attribute information was judged to be consistent with the category label; and (2) the "label-focus" condition, in which the provided attribute information was judged as being neutral and nondiagnostic with respect to the category label. Because validating the category label was expected to be relatively easy in these two conditions, perceiver impressions were predicted to be relatively category-based.

Two other conditions were created in which a perceiver would likely interpret attribute information as *not* fitting the category label: (3) the "inconsistent" condition, in which the provided attribute information was judged to be inconsistent with the category label; and (4) the "attribute-focus" condition, in which no meaningful category label was provided and the attributes by themselves did not cue any particular category, thus making moot the process of category/attribute match. Because validating the category label was expected to be difficult in the inconsistent condition, and impossible in the attribute-focus condition, perceiver impressions were predicted to be relatively individuating—that is, based primarily on the target's attributes.

In the first study, subjects rated the likability of job-category labels and sets of relevant trait attributes in isolation from each other. Four weeks later, these same subjects rated individuals consisting of *both* a category label and a set of attributes;[2] each target's description was configured in one of the four manners just described— consistent, label-focus, inconsistent, and attribute-focus (see Table 4–1 for examples from each condition). These targets were evaluated with respect to how likeable and typical they were on 9-point scales.

---

[2]We are grateful to Mark Pavelchak (in press) for developing this method.

Table 4-1. Example Stimulus Set for Fiske, Neuberg, Beattie, & Milberg (1987), Experiment 1

Attribute-focus condition	Consistent condition	Inconsistent condition	Label-focus condition
Person	Loan shark	Doctor	Artist
Practical	Opportunistic	Bored	Adult
Educated	Shady	Obedient	Medium height
Scientific	Greedy	Unenterprising	Employed
Skilled	Shrewd	Uneducated	Television viewer
Observant	Heartless	Efficient	Brown-haired

As a manipulation check, we expected that targets in the consistent and label-focus conditions would be viewed as more typical of their category than would targets in the inconsistent condition. (In the other hypothesized individuating condition, attribute-focus, in which the "person" label was presented, the typicality judgment was not meaningful.) This was indeed the case, supporting our contention that these first two conditions allow perceivers more easily to interpret the attributed information as fitting the category label.

We expected that each subject's overall likability ratings of the targets would be positively correlated with that subject's earlier independent ratings of the category in the two conditions in which it was easier to fit the attributes to the category (i.e., consistent and label-focus), and with that subject's earlier independent ratings of the attribute sets in the two conditions in which it was difficult to fit the attributes to the category (i.e., inconsistent and attribute-focus). As Table 4–2 indicates, the results are largely consistent with predictions.[3] Moreover, regression analyses demonstrated that the categories account for a greater amount of the variance in the two "category-based" conditions, while the attribute sets account for a greater amount of variance in the two "individuating" conditions. These findings thus indicate that perceivers rely differentially on category and attribute information as a function of the ease with which they can interpret a target's attributes as confirming an available category label.

Note, however, that the expected category correlation in the label-focus condition, while substantial, is smaller than the category correlation in the consistent condition. This suggests that at least some of the subjects were moderating their use of the category information here, to take account of the neutral attributes (cf. Nisbett, Zukier, & Lemley, 1981). In light of this, it is interesting that the typicality ratings in the label-focus condition indicated slightly less typicality than in the consistent condition, suggesting that perhaps recategorization processes, inter-

---

[3]Note that in the consistent condition, the perceivers' likability ratings should be correlated with their earlier evaluations of *both* the category label and the attribute sets, as these attribute sets were designed to be consistent with the category label, evaluatively as well as descriptively.

Table 4-2. Correlation of Prior Category and Attribute Likeabilities with Combined Likeability Ratings by Condition (Fiske, Neuberg, Beattie, & Milberg, 1987, Experiments 1 & 2)

	Experiment 1 (n = 117)	Experiment 2 (n = 18)
Consistent condition:		
Category	.76***	.33
Attributes	.71***	.35
Label-focus condition:		
Category	.32**	.38
Attributes	.20*	−.12
Inconsistent condition		
Category	−.30**	−.31
Attributes	.67***	.70**
Attribute-focus condition:		
Category	.07	−.13
Attributes	.62***	.53*

*$p < .05$.
**$p < .01$.
***$p < .001$.

mediate between mostly category-based and mostly individuating processes, may have occurred here. We will return to this point below.

A second experiment was conducted to extend the results of Experiment 1. First, our conceptualization of impression formation assumes that assessing the fit of attributes to a category label occurs spontaneously. Experiment 1, however, does not demonstrate that subjects would have spontaneously evaluated category-attribute fit; it only shows that when they were asked to do so, their typicality ratings supported the manipulated ease of category confirmation, as intended. Second, we wanted to investigate further the existence of recategorization processes and the conditions that elicit them.

Experiment 2 replicated the first study, this time asking subjects to think aloud as they responded to the targets. As in Experiment 1, likability correlations indicated that subjects' impressions were based largely on the category in the consistent and label-focus conditions, and on the attributes in the inconsistent and attribute-focus conditions (see Table 4–2).[4] Moreover, as expected, subjects spontaneously

---

[4]Unlike Experiment 1, the same subjects had not provided prior ratings of the category and the attributes, but rather, the independent ratings were supplied by a separate group of judges selected from the same subject population. In order to minimize the influence of chance pairings, subjects and judges were randomly paired three separate times, and the reported correlations were averaged over the three pairings. Although this procedure introduces between-subject variance, and thus is clearly more conservative, we deemed it useful for diagnostic purposes.

commented on the fit of attributes to the category label in the three conditions in which a meaningful label was provided. On the average, subjects made 1.43 typicality comments per target person, in these conditions.

Furthermore, subjects often used impression formation processes intermediate to the extreme ends of the category-based/individuating continuum. That is, as proposed, subjects often recategorized the targets by accessing a subcategory of the initial category (e.g., not just a professor, but the "charismatic lecturer kind of professor"), by accessing an exemplar (e.g., "she reminds me of my roommate"), or by accessing a self-category (e.g., "his sense of humor reminds me of my own"). Impressions were then based on the contents of these new lower-level categories.

On the whole, then, the results of these two experiments are consistent with several of the premises outlined above. Impression formation does appear to consist of a continuum of various processes anchored on the two ends by category-based and individuating processes. Moreover, the ease with which a perceiver can confirm an initially available category label largely determines the type of process utilized. When a perceiver interprets a target's attributes as validating an available category (or as not *invalidating* it), category-based impression formation dominates; when a perceiver, however, finds it difficult to fit a target's attributes to an available category, relatively individuating impressing formation is likely to be successful.

Moving to address our third premise, recall that individuating processes are hypothesized to require increased attention to, or use of, attribute information. While this assumption seems reasonable, it could be the case that individuating processes require a *decrease* in use of category information, and that attribute use remains constant across different types of impression formation. Or as yet a third alternative, perhaps successful individuation requires both a decrease in category use and an increase in attribute use.

The protocol data discussed above, however, suggest that differential use of attribute information indeed does play the key role (Fiske, Neuberg, Beattie, & Milberg, 1987, Study 2). First, use of the category label did not significantly differ among the three conditions in which a label was provided (the consistent, label-focus, and inconsistent conditions). Hence, changes in category use do not seem to differentiate among the different impression formation processes. In contrast, use of the attribute information did vary as predicted, with the attributes being mentioned significantly more often in the two conditions that elicited relatively individuating processes than in the two conditions that elicited relatively category-based processes. This suggests that increased use of attribute information is required for successful individuating impression formation.

Other research also supports the idea that attention to attribute information differentiates among the processes along the continuum (Fiske, Neuberg, Pratto, & Allman, 1986). When perceivers engage in category-based impression formation, each additional attribute should not add appreciably to the amount of processing, once its fit to the category has been verified. However, when perceivers engage in individuating impression formation, each additional attribute should add incrementally to the amount of processing, for each attribute contributes independent information. Accordingly, as attribute set size increases under inconsistency—which

Table 4-3. Sample Stimulus Set for Fiske, Neuberg, Pratto, & Allman (1986), Experiment 1

Inconsistent/8	Consistent/4	Consistent/8
Schizophrenic	Alcoholic	Paranoid
Never confused	Obnoxious	Overcautious
Routine	Compulsive	Edgy
Ploddingly realistic	Weak-willed	Watchful
Overorganized	Blind to problem	Distrustful
Conformist		Jealous
Unimaginative		Suspicious
Mundane		Too sensitive
Too rational		Afraid

Inconsistent/4	Consistent/6	Inconsistent/6
Drug addict	Catatonic	Depressive
Fat	Withdrawn	Clownish
Overdressed	Listless	Busybody
Ambitious	Out-of-it	Vain
Puritanical	Stiff	Boastful
	Indifferent	Smug
	Inactive	Conceited

promotes individuated impression formation—processing time should increase steeply with each additional attribute. In contrast, as set size increases under consistency—which promotes category-based impression formation—processing time should increase only slightly with each additional attribute.

In three studies, stimulus people were described by mental patient category labels (e.g., schizophrenic, depressive, paranoid) and consistent or inconsistent trait attributes, as established by pretesting. Attribute set sizes in the first study included 4, 6, or 8 traits (see Table 4–3). As would be expected, category-inconsistent traits took longer to read and rate for likability than did category-consistent traits. More importantly, the slope of the increase, with each additional attribute, was significantly steeper for the inconsistent sets than for the consistent sets. These data suggest that perceived inconsistency, which promotes individuation, evokes greater use of attribute information to form impressions than does perceived consistency, which promotes category-based responses. A second study separated reading and rating times and demonstrated that the inconsistency set-size effect occurs early, upon initial attention to the attribute information. In a third study, subjects thought aloud as they formed impressions. The number of attribute mentions, but not the number of category mentions, showed the inconsistency set-size effect, as predicted (see Table 4–4). These results, then, indicate that it is differential attention to attribute information that mediates individuating impression formation processes, not differential attention to category information.

Table 4-4. Overall Rating Times, Reading Times, Likeability Decision Times, and Number of Attribute Mentions as a Function of Attribute Set Size and Category-Attribute Inconsistency (Fiske, Neuberg, Pratto, & Allman, 1986, Experiments 1, 2, & 3)

	Consistency	
	Consistent	Inconsistent
Rating time (sec) (Experiment 1)		
Set size		
4	10.472	11.039
6	11.019	12.751
8	12.238	15.080
Reading time (sec) (Experiment 2)		
Set size		
4	7.257	7.587
8	9.102	11.833
Decision time (sec) (Experiment 2)		
Set size		
4	8.721	9.707
8	8.702	10.252
Mentions of attributes (Experiment 3)		
Set size		
2	2.17	3.08
4	3.96	4.83
6	4.38	6.88

These results also suggest that the effects of perceived inconsistency increase with each additional piece of inconsistent information. There is thus no evidence, at least within the ranges of inconsistency presented here, that perceivers need a critical mass of perceived inconsistency to pass a threshold, after which they rely upon the attributes to form their impressions, but before which they do not. Nor is there any evidence here that perceivers' use of inconsistency levels off at an asymptote in individuating processing. Rather, the more perceived inconsistency, the more individuation. Changes from category-based to individuated impression formation thus appear to be encouraged by cumulative changes in the amounts of attribute use.

This is certainly not to say that category information is unimportant. On the contrary, in this study, the category label was typically mentioned 1.62 times for each target, but the average attribute was mentioned only 1.12 times. Similarly, in the Fiske, Neuberg, Beattie, and Milberg (1987) protocol data, the category label was typically mentioned 1.24 times for each meaningfully labeled target, but the average attribute was mentioned only .68 times. Thus, the category label is consistently important (cf. Rasinski, Crocker, & Hastie, 1985), but increases in use of attributes is required for individuating impression formation.

Summary

Up to now, we have presented data that provide support for our continuum model of impression formation. People can form impressions of others based largely on category membership information and the stereotypes and prejudices that those memberships elicit. People, however, can also form impressions of others that are based to a greater degree on the individual's own particular characteristics. To the extent that perceivers interpret a target's attributes as fitting the target's category, perceiver impressions of the target will be primarily category based. To the extent, however, that perceivers increase their attention to attribute information and interpret these attributes as not fitting the category, perceiver impressions of the target will be more individuating or attribute based. We move now to address our fourth premise, that a perceiver's impression formation motives importantly influence both the processes and outcomes of impression formation.

Motivational Influences on Impression Formation

We have proposed that the perceiver's progress through the category-based/ individuating continuum is determined by the manner in which the perceiver interprets category-attribute fit and by the amount of attention that the perceiver pays to target attribute information. We believe that a perceiver's impression formation goals influence both the interpretive process and the willingness to allocate attentional resources, and thus can have a critical impact on the outcomes of impression formation. We address this idea here, focusing primarily on the motivational construct of outcome dependency and the goal of impression accuracy.

For our purposes, motivation results when the environment impinges on the self in significant ways. When the environment presents desired or feared possibilities, a perceiver develops specific goals to facilitate the preferred outcome. With regard to impression formation, the perceiver can be considered motivated when the impression to be formed potentially has a significant impact on his or her own self.

The primary motivational construct in our work is outcome dependency – the state of relying upon another in order to satisfy a desired outcome. When outcome dependent on another, one may want to have an accurate understanding of the other person in order to be able to predict the other's behavior, may be to have greater control over one's own outcomes. The goal of impression accuracy would thus seem to encourage perceivers to attempt individuating impression formation. Of course, as discussed earlier, individuating processes require increased attention to attribute information in order to be successful. A series of studies from our laboratory indeed demonstrated that outcome dependency influences both the quantity and quality of attention to target information.

In one set of studies (Erber & Fiske, 1984), subjects were led to believe that they would be working on a joint task with a partner. Half of these subjects were told that they personally could win $20 based on their *joint* task performance; these subjects were thus outcome dependent on their partner. The remaining subjects were led to believe that they personally could win $20 based on their *individual* task perform- ance; these subjects were thus not outcome dependent on their partner (nor were they competing with their partner, who was eligible for a separate prize). Moreover, subjects were then led to believe either that their partner was likely to be competent at the task or that their partner was likely to be incompetent at the task.

Before the task began, subjects received information about their partner; half of this information was consistent with the initial competency expectation and half was inconsistent. The dependent measure of interest was subjects' attention to this attribute information. If outcome dependency indeed leads perceivers to try to understand targets better, one would predict that outcome dependency would most greatly influence perceivers' attention to inconsistent information, which is poten- tially more informative for increased prediction and control. As predicted, outcome dependency led subjects to attend longer to inconsistent attributes, but it did not influence subjects' attention to consistent attributes (see Table 4–5). In a second study, think-aloud data demonstrated that outcome dependent subjects concentrated specifically on the *dispositional* implications of the inconsistent information, fur- ther suggesting that outcome dependency increases attempts to accurately under- stand the individual.

It is thus apparent that outcome dependency can influence attention to target information, and importantly, to the kinds of information that might enable more accurate impressions. A second set of studies (Neuberg & Fiske, 1987) was designed to test directly the hypothesis that outcome dependency leads to more individuating impression formation of potentially stereotyped targets, and to investigate the atten- tional mechanisms through which this might occur.

In the first study, subjects expected to interact with a former long-term hospital patient as part of an alleged patient-reintegration program co-sponsored by the psy- chology department and a local hospital. As in the study just described, subjects expected to work with the former patient on a joint task. Half of the subjects believed that they could earn $20 based on their joint performance and thus were outcome dependent upon the ex-patient. The other subjects thought they would be rewarded based on their individual contribution to the task and thus were not out- come dependent upon the ex-patient. All subjects were then told that the former patient had entered the hospital as a schizophrenic – a category label pretested as affectively negative, as consistent with the traits nervous, edgy, inconsistent, suspi- cious, and obsessive, and as inconsistent with the traits outgoing, determined, and adaptable.

Subjects then read an introductory profile supposedly written by the former patient. Half of the subjects read a profile that was pretested as *neutral* with respect to the schizophrenic label. That is, the profile was neither consistent nor inconsis- tent with the affective valence and the stereotypic content of the label. As discussed earlier, neutral information in conjunction with a category label typically elicits relatively category-based processing. The remaining subjects read a profile that was pretested as *inconsistent* with the schizophrenic label. That is, this profile was positive and made the former patient appear outgoing, adaptable, determined,

Table 4-5. Attention and Dispositional Comments Regarding Consistent and Inconsistent Information as a Function of Outcome Dependency (Erber & Fiske, 1984, Studies 1 & 2)

	Outcome dependent	
	No	Yes
Attention to information (sec)		
(Study 1)		
Consistent	55.87	51.84
Inconsistent	53.64	60.67
Attention to information (sec)		
(Study 2)		
Consistent	130.22	138.40
Inconsistent	113.03	149.40
Dispositional comments about information		
(Study 2)		
Consistent	7.56	8.99
Inconsistent	4.38	9.05

and the like; such informational conditions typically elicit relatively individuated processing.

To determine whether subjects' impressions of the former patient were primarily category based or individuating, subjects rated the target's likability. When subjects were not outcome dependent, their responses were expected to be relatively category based in the neutral condition and relatively individuating in the inconsistent condition. Thus, their responses should be negative in the neutral condition (based on the negative schizophrenic label) and positive in the inconsistent condition (based on the positive profile information).

Outcome dependency was predicted to lead subjects to utilize individuating processes, regardless of information configuration. Thus, subjects' responses were predicted to be neutral in the neutral condition (based on the neutral profile information) and positive in the inconsistent condition (based on the positive profile information). In sum, subject evaluations of the former patient were expected to be lowest in the not-outcome-dependent/neutral-profile cell, medium in the outcome-dependent/neutral-profile cell, and highest and equal in the two inconsistent cells. In fact, these results were obtained (see Table 4–6). Thus, under circumstances in which category-based processes typically dominate (the neutral condition), individuating processes were instead elicited by making subjects outcome dependent on the negatively labeled target.

Moreover, the amount of time that subjects spent reading the patient profiles was measured as an indicator of attention to attribute information. As noted earlier, individuated processing was proposed to require an increase in attention to attribute information. If that is indeed the case, one would expect subjects in the three cells that demonstrated relatively individuating impression formation (the two outcome-dependent cells and the not-outcome-dependent/inconsistent cell) to pay more

Table 4-6. Effects of Outcome Dependency and Information Configuration on Affective Responses and Attention to Target Attribute Information (Neuberg & Fiske, 1987, Experiment 1)

	Not outcome dependent		Outcome dependent	
	Label-focus	Inconsistent	Label-focus	Inconsistent
Predicted liking	−3	+2	−1	+2
Obtained liking	10.08	12.04	11.27	11.83
Predicted attention	−3	+1	+1	+1
Obtained attention	74.83	94.58	91.62	96.83

Note. Liking was measured on a 15-point scale where 1 = not at all likeable (your worst enemy) and 15 = extremely likeable (your best friend). Attention was measured as seconds spent looking at attribute information. Predicted liking and attention scores indicate weights used in planned contrast analyses.

attention to the profiles than subjects in the one cell that demonstrated relatively category-based impression formation (not-outcome-dependent/neutral). This was indeed the case (see Table 4–6). Furthermore, increased attention and individuated processing were highly correlated, where variance ranges were not restricted. Thus, this first study demonstrated both that outcome dependency can lead to both relatively individuating impression formation and increased attention to attribute information.

A second study was designed to investigate further the importance of attention to attribute information in enabling individuating impression formation (Neuberg & Fiske, 1987, Experiment 2). Again, half of the subjects were made outcome dependent on the former patient, while the other half were not. In addition, half of the subjects were told that the target had entered the hospital as a schizophrenic; half were not provided with any label. All subjects then viewed a videotape, ostensibly of the former hospital patient. This videotape depicted behaviors pretested as being schizophrenic consistent (i.e., the actor appeared to be nervous, suspicious, not at all outgoing, etc.). Because the videotape was designed to be consistent with the schizophrenic label, we expected equal evaluations of the target in all four cells. That is, the impressions should be negative regardless of whether they are based on the negative category (in the not-outcome-dependent/schizophrenic cell) or the negative attributes (in the remaining three cells). This would indicate that outcome dependency does not merely lead perceivers to form more positive impressions of others, but rather, leads perceivers to attempt more accurate impressions of others.

The amount of attention used to arrive at these identical impressions therefore, was expected to differ. More specifically, in the not-outcome-dependent replication, attention to attribute information was expected to be less when the schizophrenic label was presented with the schizophrenic-consistent videotape (a condition that typically elicits category-based processing), than when no label was provided (a condition that requires individuated processing). In the outcome-dependent replication, attention to attribute information was expected to be relatively high regardless of the category label provided, as it was presumed that individuating impression

Table 4-7. Effects of Outcome Dependency and Information Configuration on Affective Responses and Memory-Based Attention (Neuberg & Fiske, 1987, Experiment 2)

	Not outcome dependent		Outcome dependent	
	Consistent	Attribute-focus	Consistent	Attribute-focus
Predicted liking	0	0	0	0
Obtained liking	6.70	7.20	6.70	6.60
Predicted attention	−3	+1	+1	+1
Obtained attention	7.71	12.00	13.55	12.05

Note. Liking was measured on a 9-point scale where 1 = not at all likeable and 9 = extremely likeable. Attention was measured as seconds to make a memory-based rating. Predicted liking and attention scores indicate weights used in planned contrast analyses.

formation would be attempted in both conditions here. The amount of time subjects took to form an evaluation of the patient was the measure of attention.

As expected, there were no differences in evaluations of the patient across the four cells. The attention results, however, replicated the results found in the previous study (see Table 4–7). Subjects in the not-outcome-dependent/no-label cell and the two outcome-dependent cells took significantly more time to evaluate the target than did subjects in the not-outcome-dependent/schizophrenic cell. Thus, although outcome dependency, in this case, did not alter the actual evaluations of the former patient—as the available information did not justify differential evaluation—it did alter the amount of attentional resources used to form these impressions.

Moreover, subjects were filmed as they were informed that the ex-patient had entered the hospital as a schizophrenic. Past research has indicated that nonverbal responses often reflect one's underlying affect for stereotyped others (e.g., Word, Zanna, & Cooper, 1974). As expected, subjects exposed to the schizophrenic label immediately showed greater changes in nonverbal behavior than did control subjects exposed to an affectively neutral "heart-patient" label. Interestingly, although outcome dependency inhibited category-based responses in the subsequent liking measure (discussed above) it did not do so here, before subjects were exposed to target attribute information. Thus, the fact that outcome dependency could diminish category-based responses only when attribute information was available suggests once again that outcome dependency encourages individuation by specifically increasing the use of attribute information.

Up to this point, then, we have presented evidence suggesting that outcome dependency elicits relatively individuating impression formation, and that these individuating processes are encouraged by an increase in attention to available attribute information. We do not propose, however, that just any increase in attention to attributes will necessarily lead to individuating impression formation. Recall that we earlier hypothesized that the manner in which perceivers interpret the category/attribute fit was also critical. If people attend longer to a target's attributes with the purpose of discounting apparent inconsistencies, validation of the initial category is likely and category-based impression formation will be the result.

Table 4-8. Effects of Accuracy-Driven Attention to Attribute Information on Affective Responses (Neuberg & Fiske, 1987, Experiment 3)

	No accuracy-driven attention		Accuracy-driven attention	
	Label-focus	Inconsistent	Label-focus	Inconsistent
Predicted liking	−3	+2	−1	+2
Obtained liking	10.13	11.67	11.27	11.64

Note. Liking was measured on a 15-point scale where 1 = not at all likeable (your worst enemy) and 15 = extremely likeable (your best friend). Predicted liking scores indicate weights used in contrast analyses.

Rather, we believe that the goal of impression accuracy makes such reinterpretation of "objectively" inconsistent attributes unlikely, thus encouraging individuating impression formation. Thus, increased attention, but only *in conjunction with* the goal of forming an accurate impression, should mediate outcome dependency's ability to elicit individuating impression formation.

To make a direct test of accuracy-driven attention as a mediator of outcome dependency's effects on impression formation, Neuberg and Fiske (1987) conducted a third experiment, essentially identical to Experiment 1, described earlier. All subjects expected to meet a schizophrenic and saw attribute information pretested as either inconsistent or neutral. Moreover, all subjects were provided with time sufficient to attend to individuating information, as determined by spontaneous attention to patient profiles in the first experiment's individuating conditions. Instead of manipulating outcome dependency, however, half the subjects were told to form an accurate impression of the patient while half were given no explicit goal. As expected, accuracy-driven attention mimicked outcome dependency's effects on impression formation (see Table 4–8). This supports the notion that outcome dependency increases individuation by increasing accuracy-driven attention to attributes. Importantly, increased time to attend by itself, without the explicit goal of forming an accurate impression, did not lead to individuated processing, as was expected.

Thus, across the three experiments just discussed, there is strong converging evidence that (1) outcome dependency, at least as manipulated here, can lead perceivers to form relatively individuating impressions, even under informational conditions that typically elicit more category-based processing and that (2) these influences of outcome dependency seem to be mediated by an increase in accuracy-driven attention to available target attributes. This latter point is especially important in that it stresses the influence of motivation on attentional and interpretive processes— exactly those processes that determine a perceiver's path along the category-based/individuating continuum.

Given that outcome dependency apparently elicits an impression accuracy goal, with clear effects on attention, interpretation, and impression formation, one would expect other situations eliciting this goal to have similar influences. For example, when perceivers are *accountable* to a third party for their impressions, and they believe that the third party wants an accurate impression, perceivers may also utilize relatively individuating processes (Tetlock, 1983b, 1985; for other situations that likely motivate individuating impression formation, see Kruglanski & Freund, 1983; Mayseless & Kruglanski, 1987; Snyder, Campbell, & Preston, 1982). Alternatively, other motivational circumstances may elicit impression formation goals that encourage category-based processing. For example, if a perceiver is accountable to a person who wants the perceiver to form a particular impression of a target (as opposed to an accurate impression), then the perceiver may be more likely to interpret the target's attributes as validating the particular conceptualization sought by the third party. This would likely result in a category-based impression, with the initial category being determined, in this case, by the third party (Tetlock, 1983a). Moreover, threats to self-esteem (Crocker & Gallo, 1985; Crocker, Thompson, McGraw, & Ingerman, 1987), publicly committed social outcome dependency (as opposed to the short-term, task-oriented outcome dependency discussed above; Berscheid, Graziano, Monson, & Dermer, 1976; Omoto & Borgida, 1988), the need to adopt *any* impression (i.e., the "need for structure"; Kruglanski, in press) and overt instructions to categorize (Pavelchak, in press), may encourage category-based impression formation by leading perceivers to interpret target attributes as validating an initial category or expectation.

Summary

Motivational factors can clearly have an important impact on impression formation. To the extent that a motivational factor increases a perceiver's attention to attribute information and leads the perceiver to interpret that information as not adequately fitting the target's category, relatively individuating impression formation is likely to be successful. Alternatively, to the extent that a motivational factor decreases a perceiver's attention to attribute information, or leads the perceiver to interpret the attribute information as fitting the target's category, category-based impression formation is more likely to be successful. It thus becomes clear that in order to understand the extent to which a perceiver may rely upon category-based stereotypes and prejudices when forming an impression of a target, one must be cognizant not only of the actual target information available, but also of the impression formation goals and motives that may be elicited by the perceiver's situational context.

Conclusion

Our aim here has been to summarize some of the conditions under which people form relatively category-based versus relatively individuating impressions of others (see Fiske & Neuberg, in press, for a more detailed literature review). When people are able to fit the attributes of a target to a social category they have applied to the target, impressions will be based on the stereotypes and prejudices the perceiver associates with that category. Category-based impression formation is thus likely to be successful when the target's attributes are consistent with an available category label, when the attributes are nondiagnostic and thus do not invalidate the category label, or when motivational circumstances such as accountability to a biased third-party or self-esteem threats make such impressions valuable to the perceiver.

In contrast, when people are unable to fit the attributes of a target to an assigned social category *and* allocate enough attention to a target's attributes, impressions will be based more on the target's individuating characteristics. Relatively individuating impression formation is thus more likely to be successful when the target's attributes are inconsistent with an available category label and when the perceiver is motivated to be accurate, perhaps by being outcome dependent on the target.

The two major themes of interpretation of category/attribute fit and of attention to attribute information have important implications for social intervention. First, because the perceiver must be able to interpret the target's traits as being incompatible with the assigned category, targets will have an opportunity to escape the encumbrance of their "negative" category membership only if they indeed present themselves as being category-inconsistent in significant ways. More importantly, however, the perceiver must be motivated to attend to this inconsistent information and interpret it in an unbiased manner. Interventions encouraging individuation must thus provide a perceiver with the goal of impression accuracy and provide a context in which attainment of this goal is possible (e.g., a context devoid of time pressure; Bechtold, Naccarato, Zanna, 1986; Kruglanski & Freund, 1983).

Note that intervention strategies based on our conceptualization would seem to differ significantly from those that attempt to reduce the incidence of stereotyping by changing the contents — that is, the stereotypes and prejudices — associated with people's social categories. We believe that it is easier to manipulate the temporary goals of perceivers — even the goals of those perceivers who may seem wedded to their bigotry — than it is to manipulate, either temporarily or more permanently, the stereotypes and prejudices of these same perceivers. Hence, we suggest, accepting for the time being that people possess detrimental stereotypes and prejudices, the implementation of more acute intervention strategies that aim to alter, through informational and motivational forces, the manner in which particular perceivers interact with and think about particular targets.

In conclusion, then, our work takes us beyond stereotyping research that mainly emphasizes category-based processes, and it takes us beyond impression formation research that mainly emphasizes individuating processes. By specifying how category-based and individuating processes operate, and the conditions under which each is likely to occur, we believe that our model provides a framework that potentially informs interventions on behalf of disadvantaged outgroups who suffer from stereotyping, prejudice, and discrimination.

Acknowledgments. The research reported here was supported by NSF Grants BNS 8406913, BNS 8596028, and NIMH Grant MH41801 to the first author.

References

Allport, G.W. (1954). *The nature of prejudice.* Reading, MA: Addison-Wesley.
Anderson, N.H. (1974). Information integration: A brief survey. In D.H. Krantz, R.C. Atkin-

son, R.D. Luce, & P. Suppes (Eds.), *Contemporary developments in mathematical psychology* (pp. 236–305). San Francisco: Freeman.

Asch, S.E. (1946). Forming impressions of personality. *Journal of Abnormal and Social Psychology, 41,* 258–290.

Bargh, J.A., Bond, R.N., Lombardi, W., & Tota, M. (1986). The additive nature of chronic and temporary sources of construct accessibility. *Journal of Personality and Social Psychology, 50,* 869–878.

Bechtold, A., Naccarato, M.E., & Zanna, M.P. (1986, September). *Need for structure and the prejudice-discrimination link.* Paper presented at the annual meeting of the Canadian Psychological Association, Toronto, Ontario.

Berscheid, R., Graziano, W., Monson, R., & Dermer, M. (1976). Outcome dependency, attention, attribution, and attraction. *Journal of Personality and Social Psychology, 34,* 978–989.

Brewer, M.B. (1988). A dual process model of impression formation. In T.K. Srull & R.S. Wyer, Jr. (Eds.), *Advances in social cognition* (Vol. 1) (pp. 1–36). Hillsdale, NJ: Erlbaum.

Brewer, M.B., Dull, V., & Lui, L. (1981). Perceptions of the elderly: Stereotypes as prototypes. *Journal of Personality and Social Psychology, 8,* 393–400.

Brooks, L. (1978). Nonanalytic concept formation and memory for instances. In E. Rosch & B.B. Lloyd (Eds.), *Cognition and categorization* (pp. 169–211). Hillsdale, NJ: Erlbaum.

Bruner, J.S. (1957). On perceptual readiness. *Psychological Review, 64,* 123–152.

Cantor, N., & Mischel, W. (1979). Prototypes in person perception. In L. Berkowitz (Ed.), *Advances in experimental social psychology* (Vol. 12) (pp. 3–52). New York: Academic Press.

Crocker, J., & Gallo, L. (1985, August). *The self-enhancing effect of downward comparison.* Paper presented at the meeting of the American Psychological Association, Los Angeles, CA.

Crocker, J., Thompson, L., McGraw, K.M., & Ingerman, C. (1987). Downward comparison, prejudice, and evaluations of others: Effects of self-esteem and threat. *Journal of Personality and Social Psychology, 52,* 907–916.

Crosby, F., Bromley, S., & Saxe, L. (1980). Recent unobtrusive studies of black and white discrimination and prejudice: A literature review. *Psychological Bulletin, 87,* 546–563.

Deaux, K., & Lewis, L. (1984). The structure of gender stereotypes: Interrelationships among components and gender label. *Journal of Personality and Social Psychology, 46,* 991–1004.

Erber, R. (1985). *Choosing among multiple categories: The effects of mood on category accessibility, inference, and interpersonal affect.* Unpublished doctoral dissertation, Carnegie-Mellon University, Pittsburgh, PA.

Erber, R., & Fiske, S.T. (1984). Outcome dependency and attention to inconsistent information. *Journal of Personality and Social Psychology, 47,* 709–726.

Fishbein, M., & Ajzen, I. (1975). *Belief, attitude, intention, and behavior: An introduction to theory and research.* Reading, MA: Addison-Wesley.

Fiske, S.T. & Cox, M.G. (1979). Person concepts: The effects of target familiarity and descriptive purpose on the process of describing others. *Journal of Personality, 47,* 136–161.

Fiske, S.T., & Neuberg, S.L. (in press). A continuum of impression formation, from category-based to individuating processes: Influences of information and motivation on attention and interpretation. To appear in M.P. Zanna (Ed.), *Advances in experimental social psychology* (Vol. 23). Academic Press: New York.

Fiske, S.T., Neuberg, S.L., Beattie, A.E., & Milberg, S.J. (1987). Category-based and attribute-based reactions to others: Some informational conditions of stereotyping and individuating processes. *Journal of Experimental Social Psychology, 23,* 399–427.

Fiske, S.T., Neuberg, S.L., Pratto, F., & Allman, C. (1986). *Stereotyping and individuating: The effects of information inconsistency and set size on attribute-oriented processing.* Unpublished manuscript, University of Massachusetts at Amherst.

Fiske, S.T., & Pavelchak, M.A. (1986). Category-based versus piecemeal-based affective responses: Developments in schema-triggered affect. In R.M. Sorrentino & E.T. Higgins (Eds.), *Handbook of motivation and cognition: Foundations of social behavior* (pp. 167–203). New York: Guilford Press.

Fiske, S.T., & Taylor, S.E. (1984). *Social cognition*. New York: Random House.

Higgins, E.T. & King, G.A. (1981). Accessibility of social constructs: Information-processing consequences of individual and contextual variability. In N. Cantor & J.R. Kihlstrom (Eds.), *Personality, cognition, and social interaction* (pp. 69–121). Hillsdale, NJ: Erlbaum.

Higgins, E.T., King, G.A., & Mavin, G. H. (1982). Individual construct accessibility and subjective impressions and recall. *Journal of Personality and Social Psychology, 43*, 35–47.

Higgins, E.T., Rholes, W.S., & Jones, C.R. (1977). Category accessibility and impression formation. *Journal of Experimental Social Psychology, 21*, 1–18.

Jones, E.E., & Goethals, G. (1972). Order effects in impression formation: Attribution context and the nature of the entity. In E.E. Jones, D.E. Kanouse, H.H. Kelley, R.E. Nisbett, S. Valins, & B. Weiner (Eds.), *Attribution: Perceiving the causes of behavior* (pp. 27–46). Morristown, NJ: General Learning Process.

Kahneman, D., & Miller, D.T. (1986). Norm theory: Comparing reality to its alternatives. *Psychological Review, 93*, 136–153.

Kruglanski, A.W. (in press). Motivations for judging and knowing: Implications for causal attribution. In E.T. Higgins & R.M. Sorrentino (Eds.), *Handbook of motivation and cognition: Foundations of social behavior* (Vol. 2). New York: Guilford Press.

Kruglanski, A.W., & Freund, T. (1983). The freezing and unfreezing of lay-inferences: Effects of impressional primacy, ethnic stereotyping, and numerical anchoring. *Journal of Experimental Social Psychology, 19*, 448–468.

Locksley, A., Borgida, E., Brekke, N., & Hepburn, C. (1980). Sex stereotypes and social judgment. *Journal of Personality and Social Psychology, 39*, 821–831.

Markus, H. (1977). Self-schemata and processing information about the self. *Journal of Personality and Social Psychology, 35*, 63–78.

Markus, H., Smith, J., & Moreland, R.L. (1985). Role of the self-concept in the perception of others. *Journal of Personality and Social Psychology, 49*, 1494–1512.

Mayseless, O., & Kruglanski, A.W. (1987). What makes you so sure?: Effects of epistemic motivations on judgmental confidence. *Organizational Behavior and Human Decision Processes, 39*, 162–183.

McArthur, L.Z. (1982). Judging a book by its cover: A cognitive analysis of the relationship between physical appearance and stereotyping. In A. Hastorf & A. Isen (Eds.), *Cognitive social psychology* (pp. 149–210). New York: Elsevier North-Holland.

McArthur, L.Z., & Post, D.L. (1977). Figural emphasis and person perception. *Journal of Experimental Social Psychology, 13*, 520–535.

Milford, J.T. (1978). Aesthetic aspects of faces: A (somewhat) phenomenological analysis using multidimensional scaling methods. *Journal of Personality and Social Psychology, 36*, 205–216.

Neuberg, S.L., & Fiske, S.T. (1987). Motivational influences on impression formation: Outcome dependency, accuracy-driven attention, and individuating processes. *Journal of Personality and Social Psychology, 53*, 431–444.

Nisbett, R.E., Zukier, H., & Lemley, R.E. (1981). The dilution effect: Non-diagnostic information weakens the implications of diagnostic information. *Cognitive Psychology, 13*, 248–277.

Omoto, A.M., Borgida, E. (1988). Guess who might be coming to dinner?: Personal involvement and racial stereotyping. *Journal of Experimental Social Psychology, 24*, 571–593.

Pavelchak, M. (in press). Forming impressions of others: A demonstration of two distinct processes using an idiographic measurement technique. *Journal of Personality and Social Psychology*.

Pettigrew, T.F., & Martin, J. (1987). Shaping the organizational context for black American inclusion. *Journal of Social Issues, 43*, 41–78.

Posner, M.I., Nissen, M.J., & Klein, R.M. (1976). Visual dominance: An information processing account of its origins and significance. *Psychological Review, 83*, 157–171.

Rasinski, K.S., Crocker, J., & Hastie, R. (1985). Another look at sex stereotypes and social judgments: An analysis of the social perceiver's use of subjective probabilities. *Journal of Personality and Social Psychology, 49*, 317–326.

Schneider, D.J., Hastorf, A.H., & Ellsworth, P.C. (1979). *Person perception*. Reading, MA: Addison-Wesley.

Snyder, M., Campbell, B.H., & Preston, E. (1982). Testing hypotheses about human nature: Assessing the accuracy of social stereotypes. *Social Cognition, 1*, 256–272.

Srull, T.K., & Wyer, R.S., Jr. (1979). The role of category accessibility in the interpretation of information about persons: Some determinants and implications. *Journal of Personality and Social Psychology, 37*, 1660–1672.

Tajfel, H. (1981). *Human groups and social categories*. New York: Cambridge University Press.

Taylor, S.E. (1981). A categorization approach to stereotyping. In D.L. Hamilton (Ed.), *Cognitive processes in stereotyping and intergroup behavior* (pp. 88–114). Hillsdale, NJ: Erlbaum.

Taylor, S.E., Fiske, S.T., Close, M., Anderson, C., & Ruderman, A. (1977). *Solo status as a psychological variable: The power of being distinctive*. Unpublished manuscript, Harvard University, Cambridge, MA.

Tetlock, P.E. (1983a). Accountability and complexity of thought. *Journal of Personality and Social Psychology, 45*, 74–83.

Tetlock, P.E. (1983b). Accountability and the perseverance of first impressions. *Social Psychology Quarterly, 46*, 285–292.

Tetlock, P.E. (1985). Accountability: A social check on the fundamental attribution error. *Social Psychology Quarterly, 48*, 227–236.

Weber, R., & Crocker, J. (1983). Cognitive processes in the revision of stereotypic beliefs. *Journal of Personality and Social Psychology, 45*, 961–977.

Word, C.O., Zanna, M.P., & Cooper, J. (1974). The nonverbal mediation of self-fulfilling prophecies in interracial interaction. *Journal of Experimental Social Psychology, 10*, 109–120.

Wyer, R.S., Jr., & Srull, T.K. (1980). The processing of social stimulus information: A conceptual integration. In R. Hastie, T.M. Ostrom, E.B. Ebbensen, R.S. Wyer, Jr., D. Hamilton, & D.E. Carlston (Eds.), *Person memory: The cognitive basis of social perception* (pp. 227–300). Hillsdale, NJ: Erlbaum.

Wyer, R.S., Jr., & Srull, T.K. (1981). Category accessibility: Some theoretical and empirical issues concerning the processing of social stimulus information. In E.T. Higgins, C.P. Herman, & M.P. Zanna (Eds.), *Social cognition: The Ontario symposium* (Vol. 1) (pp. 161–197). Hillsdale, NJ: Erlbaum.

Chapter 5

Stereotypes of Groups, Group Members, and Individuals in Categories: A Differential Analysis

Murray Horwitz and Jacob M. Rabbie

Introduction

A central thesis of this chapter is that the distinction between the concepts of "social groups" and "social categories" has been blurred in recent work on intergroup relationships. The conceptual distinction points to three different targets of stereotyping and prejudice: groups qua groups, individual members of groups, and individuals placed in social categories. Differentiating between these three domains will help clarify our understanding of what are distinctive phenomena involving distinctive psychological processes. More importantly, in dealing with stereotypes and prejudice, the differentiation should aid us in designing interventions that will be directed at the processes specific to each domain.

When persons perceive a "social category," what is being perceived is a number of individual entities who are similar to each other on one or more dimensions (van Leent, 1964) or in their resemblance to a prototype (Rosch, 1978). When persons perceive a "group," what is being perceived is a single entity (Campbell, 1958) that is capable of acting or reacting and of receiving good or bad outcomes; as parts of this entity, individual group members receive outcomes that are interdependent in varying degree with the group's outcomes (Horwitz & Rabbie, 1982). Groups may be perceived as entities of various size and clarity of boundaries, ranging from family units, teams, political parties, to national movements. The foregoing is a restatement of Lewin's (1948) conceptualization of the group as a system or "dynamic whole," ranging from a "compact unit" to a "loose mass," whose members are defined, not by their similarity to each other, but by their interdependence with each other and with the group as a whole.

The concept of a group with and within which members are interdependent appears to pose some difficulty for category-theorists. Billig (1976) refers to the idea of interdependence as "somewhat vacuous" (p. 332); Turner (1987) describes it as an "elastic term" that does "no more than redescribe the phenomena to the explained" (p. 29). The meaning and implications of the concept may be clarified by referring to the work of Kelley and Thibaut (1978), who have systematically spelled out the variety of ways that one party's positive or negative outcomes may be affected by the outcomes of another party. Deutsch (1982) has described how the different forms of perceived interdependence in a relationship affect the parties' cognitive, motivational, and moral orientations toward each other. Horwitz and Rabbie (1982, p. 262 et seq.) have discussed how a person's group membership affects the person's perception of the interdependence between own outcomes and those of ingroups and outgroups.

In the present chapter, we shall reserve the term "group" for the behaving system of which individuals are part members and the term "category" for the collection of individuals who are perceived to have similar traits. In a previous publication (Rabbie & Horwitz, 1988) we dealt briefly with the use of "groups" and "categories" as explanatory concepts in dealing with social identity and intergroup conflict. The present chapter restates and updates that discussion to include recent research findings. It aims especially to extend the analysis to the implications of distinguishing groups and categories for theory and research on stereotypes and prejudice.

Stephan (1985), in the *Handbook of Social Psychology*, defines stereotypes as "sets of traits ascribed to social groups . . . used to predict and explain behavior" (p. 600). He defines prejudice as "negative attitudes toward social groups" (p. 600). The referent of the term "social group" is ambiguous in these definitions. Are the trait ascriptions and negative attributes directed at individuals in a category, at a group as a unitary system, or at members who identify with group outcomes? Stephan's subsequent discussion indicates that "social group" in both definitions refers by and large to individuals in social categories. Indeed, his review indicates that the dominant thrust of current research in intergroup relationships is on the cognitive processes that cause persons to form categories, to place others into a category, to ascribe traits to them, and to evaluate and deal with them accordingly. Largely missing is the recognition that just as persons perceive active and reactive individuals in their social environments, so do they perceive active and reactive groups. The psychological situation with which they must cope thus includes not only individual-to-individual interaction, but individual-to-group and group-to-group interaction (Horwitz & Rabbie, 1982). The emphasis on the intrapsychic processes by which persons form categories has, as we shall show, diverted attention from the structure and dynamics of the psychological environment in which persons perceive interacting groups and individuals.

In current thinking about stereotypes and prejudice, the view proposed by Tajfel and his colleagues in their social-identity theory (Tajfel, 1978a; Tajfel & Turner, 1979) has been especially influential (Hewstone & Brown, 1986; Brewer & Miller, 1984; see also Chapter 1 by Stroebe & Insko, in this volume). The theory evolved from their interpretation—we would say, misinterpretation—of the results of experiments using the minimal intergroup paradigm (Doise, 1988). The early experiments showed that dividing subjects into two ad hoc groups will induce biases favoring the ingroup over the outgroup, whether in giving first-impression ratings to them (Rabbie & Horwitz, 1969) or in giving money to them (Tajfel, Flament, Billig, & Bundy, 1971). The controversy between Tajfel and his colleagues (Tajfel, 1982, Chapter 16; Turner, 1987) and ourselves (Horwitz & Rabbie, 1982; Rabbie & Horwitz, 1988) regarding the correct interpretation of these results centers on the issue about whether subjects are reacting to what they perceive as social categories or social groups. The first section of this chapter compares the rival interpretations offered by social-identity theory and what we would call a group-interdependence theory.[1] It reports the results of several recent experiments designed as critical tests of these alternative interpretations. The experiments bring to light the "hidden" interdependencies between group and member outcomes that subjects perceived in the minimal intergroup situation. The section concludes with a consideration of Tajfel's (1982, Chapter 16) own critique of the two theories.

The second section compares the different perceptual-cognitive processes that are involved in ascribing traits to groups and to individuals in categories. The contrast drawn is between the categorization processes by which traits ascribed to one or more individuals are generalized to others and the attributional processes by which a group's behaviors lead to the ascription of traits to the group itself. The analysis enables us to account for the predominance of negative attributions in intergroup encounters (Brewer, 1979a), for the high levels of emotional intensity associated with intergroup prejudice (Pettigrew, 1986), and for the failure to find that friendly attitudes toward individuals will generalize to friendly attitudes toward their disliked group (Cook, 1984). This section concludes with examples drawn from large-scale social conflicts that illustrate the importance of distinguishing between attributions about groups and attributions about individuals in social categories.

Section three extends the analysis to a consideration of how attributions about a group relate to attitudes about its individual members. We propose an alternative to Tajfel's (1978b) distinction between interindividual and intergroup behavior and contrast the implication of the two views for understanding the conditions under which ingroup members will depersonalize or, as in such cases as that of Nazi Germany, dehumanize outgroup members. The section concludes with a discussion of several principles that are applicable to promoting positive relationships between the individual members of opposing groups and indicates what we view as a promising direction of inquiry for promoting positive relationships between the groups themselves.

Interdependence Versus Categorization as Determinants of Bias in the Minimal Intergroup Situation

Origins of the Minimal Intergroup Paradigm

The roots of the minimal intergroup paradigm can be traced back to the well-known camp studies by Sherif et al. (1961). Based on this work, Sherif extended Lewin's ideas about interdependence within a group system to interdependence within an "intergroup system" (Sherif, 1966, p. 101). He believed that given two groups with

---

[1] See also the Behavior Interaction Model under development by Rabbie and his associates (Rabbie, J.M., 1986; Rabbie & Lodewijkx, 1987).

well-developed structures of roles, statuses, and norms, the existence of competing group goals (negative goal interdependence) will lead to intergroup hostility, while a common superordinate goal (positive goal interdependence) will lead to intergroup harmony. Stimulated by Sherif's ideas, Blake and Mouton (1961) designed training exercises that enabled participants to examine the conditions that either promote or prevent intergroup antagonism. Our own work on the minimal intergroup situation grew out of a number of experiences in working with the Blake–Mouton procedure that called into question elements of Sherif's theoretical formulations. First, we found that intergroup hostility was as readily aroused by competitive instructions to newly formed groups of strangers as to well-developed groups. Second, we found that intergroup hostility was also aroused by what we took to be cooperative or superordinate-goal instructions. These unanticipated results led us to design an experiment the aim of which was "to isolate the minimal conditions that are sufficient to generate discriminatory ingroup-outgroup attitudes" (Rabbie & Horwitz, 1969, p. 270).

The experiment employed several treatments that varied the forms of interdependence between the outcomes of two groups and compared these with a control condition in which there was minimal or near-zero interdependence between the groups. Doise (1988) has noted that the experiment designed by Tajfel et al. (1971) was modeled with some modifications on the control condition in our experiment. In the control, we randomly sorted strangers into Blue and Green groups for alleged "administrative reasons." Presenting the experiment as a study of first impressions, we asked subjects to stand up in turn, introduce themselves, and rate each other on a variety of personality traits scaled along a favorable–unfavorable dimension. In addition to the ratings of individual members, subjects also rated the traits of each group as a whole. These ratings, intended to measure ingroup–outgroup bias, were reactive in the sense that they introduced an element of outcome interdependence into the control condition. For subjects obviously desired favorable first-impression ratings for themselves and, possibly, for their respective groups; whether they received these desired outcomes depended on the ratings given them by the members of their ingroup and outgroup.

In the initial modification of our control condition by Tajfel et al. (1971), subjects were again sorted into groups for "administrative reasons." However, they were led to believe that they were divided according to similarities or differences in their individual characteristics, purportedly measured by tests of aesthetic preference (pro-Kandinski versus pro-Klee) or of estimation tendencies (overestimators versus underestimators). The dependent measures of bias were a series of matrices by means of which subjects could allocate money to and receive money from an anonymous member of each group. Tajfel's modifications thus had the effect, first, of transforming the experiment from one that manipulated intergroup interdependence as the sole independent variable to one that simultaneously manipulated two independent variables, intergroup interdependence and category differentiation. A second effect, as we shall show below, was to make explicit and strengthen subjects' perceptions of their differential interdependence with ingroup and outgroup members regarding their own money outcomes.

The results of both experiments showed that simply dividing subjects into two groups engendered weak, though significant, tendencies by subjects to favor own over other group members. Our 1969 experiment failed to detect a difference in the control condition, but with an increased N in a follow-up experiment, subjects were found to give more favorable ratings to the ingroup and its members than to the out-group and its members on social-emotional or relational traits. (Rabbie, 1972; Horwitz & Rabbie, 1982, p. 247-248). The experiment by Tajfel et al. (1971) found that subjects tended to allocate more money to ingroup than outgroup members, but that they did not depart too far from fairness, that is, from equal allocation.

Interpretative Issues in the Minimal Intergroup Paradigm

When Doise (1978) questioned subjects who had participated in a Tajfel experiment in Bristol, some of the young boys responded to his question by saying "you must be fair, but to give a little bit more to your own group is not unfair" (p. 163), suggesting that norms about proper ingroup–outgroup behavior within an intergroup system were at play in their allocations. Indeed, Tajfel et al. (1971) initially proposed the plausible interpretation that the bias might be due to the "functioning of a 'generic' social norm" (p. 176) that leads people to favor ingroup members and discriminate against outgroup members. It does not seem unlikely that, through socialization experiences in families, peer groups, and the like, the boys had come to define group membership as involving a general obligation for themselves and others to support the interests of ingroup members over outgroup members (Sherif, 1966, Chapter 2). A modified statement of the generic norm operative in intergroup encounters is that, all else equal, people expect that they *ought* to receive more consideration or weight for their own desires from ingroup than outgroup members and, in turn, that they *ought* to give more weight to the desires of ingroup than outgroup members.

In the same article, Tajfel et al. (1971) added a point that probably accounts for their later abandonment of the generic norm explanation. They asserted, gratuitously in our opinion, that the norm induces bias "even when such behavior has no utilitarian value to the individual or to his group" (p. 151). The statement appears to deny that subjects in the minimal intergroup situation perceived any interdependence among their outcomes.

The assertion that subjects' behavior in the allocation tasks had no utilitarian value to them as individuals is curious in view of the instruction to the subjects that "they would receive the amount of money that others had awarded them" (Tajfel et al., 1971, p. 155). It is especially curious in the light of Tajfel's report of subjects' spontaneous comments: "It may be worth mentioning that, in the interval between the two parts of the experimental session, several Ss talked to the E about the 'obvious thing to do'– to get as much money as possible out of the situation" (Tajfel et al., 1971, p. 172).

The assumption that there is no interdependence of interest among groups and their members in the minimal intergroup situation has been a central tenet in the development of social identity theory. The claim is repeatedly made that in the allocation task there is "neither . . . a conflict of interest . . . between the 'groups' nor is there any rational link between economic self-interest and the strategy of ingroup favoritism" (Tajfel & Turner, 1979, pp. 38–39). Again, insisting on the absence of goal interdependence, Turner (1981) asserts that "subjects discriminated against anonymous outgroup members . . . under conditions where they could not benefit from this strategy" (p. 22). It follows that if the cause of behavior cannot be found in the person's perceptions of the situation, they must be located within the person.

The intrapersonal cause proposed in the theory is the "need to maintain or enhance . . . self-esteem" (Tajfel & Turner, 1979, p. 40). The crucial first step in the chain of assumptions by which this need is deemed to produce "competitive intergroup processes" is that "social categorizations tend to be internalized to define the self" (Turner, 1981, p. 80). Intergroup competition is then said to flow from social comparison processes whereby one seeks superiority for oneself by aggrandizing one's own group or derogating the other group.

It is certainly true that social comparisons are present in the minimal intergroup situation. We have noted above that the measures of bias that have been used are reactive in that they may lead subjects to wonder about the amounts of money or the favorability of first-impression ratings that they receive in comparison to others. However, the first assumption in the chain of argument, namely, that subjects' classification into, say, Blues or Greens is internalized by them to define their selves, has not in our judgment been adequately tested (see the critique by Abrams & Hogg, 1988).

Experiment 1: Bias as a Function of Interdependence with Ingroup or Outgroup Members

The experiments reported next were designed as direct tests of the social-identity versus group-interdependence interpretations of the bias evoked in the minimal intergroup situation. An experiment by Rabbie, Schot, and Visser (1987) attempted to ascertain whether subjects using the Tajfel matrices perceived a "rational link between economic self-interest and the strategy of ingroup favoritism." The argument underlying the study was that in interdependent relationships between two or more parties, one's economic self-interest may often be best served by maximizing the others' gains. In a two-party Prisoner's Dilemma Game, each subject can maximize own outcomes over a series of trials by maximizing the other party's outcomes in the hope and expectation that the other will reciprocate and also adopt a cooperative strategy (Pruitt & Kimmel, 1977). Likewise in the Tajfel matrices, subjects would be expected to give most to others from whom they hope to receive financial rewards. If subjects believe that their own outcomes are dependent solely on allocations by an ingroup member, they should allocate most to an ingroup member; if they believe their outcomes are dependent solely on allocations by an outgroup member, they should allocate most to an outgroup member. In the usual Tajfel procedure, subjects are led to believe that their outcomes are dependent on both an ingroup and an outgroup member. Their allocations should then fall in between the conditions in which they are dependent on one or the other alone. If subjects' own allocations are influenced by self-interest, the pattern of their allocations to others should thus vary as a function of whom they perceive their potential benefactors to be.

The experiment designed to test this hypothesis employed three conditions of interdependence among ingroup and outgroup members. One condition replicated the standard Tajfel situation. Subjects, categorized as allegedly favoring one of two abstract artists, were informed that they would receive money from an anonymous person in their ingroup and in their outgroup. In the other two conditions, they were informed that they would receive money from someone in the ingroup alone or someone in the outgroup alone. The results showed that where subjects viewed their outcomes as dependent on the actions of both ingroup and outgroup members, they displayed the usual behavior of allocating slightly more money to ingroup than outgroup members. Where they viewed their outcomes as solely dependent on the actions of an ingroup member, they allocated much more money to ingroup than outgroup members. However, where they viewed their outcomes as solely dependent on the actions of an outgroup member, they allocated more money to *outgroup* members than ingroup members. The clear-cut evidence is that by altering the perceived interdependence of subjects' outcomes, one can obtain either ingroup or outgroup favoritism, holding category differentiation constant.

The results should not be taken to mean that subjects in the minimal intergroup situation act only to maximize their individual gains and are indifferent to the outcomes of others in their groups. Biases in favor of ingroup members remain evident in these data. In the condition in which subjects were dependent on both the ingroup and outgroup, they allocated as usual more money to ingroup than outgroup members. In the conditions in which subjects were solely dependent on either the ingroup or outgroup, they allocated significantly more money to ingroup members than to outgroup members. Their behavior could reflect the fact that they expected ingroup members to be more likely than outgroup members to cooperate with themselves (Hornstein, 1982). It could also reflect the other side of this "generic" norm, namely, that as group members they ought to give more consideration to the interests of the ingroup and its members than to the interests of the outgroup and its members. The results do cast doubt, however, on the interpretation that the biases exhibited in this experiment were due to subjects' incorporating into their self-concepts the experimenter's trivial and transitory classification of them as favoring one of two artists. On that interpretation, the subjects' self-concepts would have to be extraordinarily malleable. One would have to suppose that in the treatment in which subjects evidenced outgroup favoritism, their self-concepts were as easily dissolved and replaced as they were initially formed.

Experiment 2: Bias as a Function of the Salience of Individual or Group Outcomes

Given the ad hoc nature of the groups in the minimal intergroup situation, it is likely that subjects will attend more strongly to their individual outcomes than to group outcomes. An experiment by Rabbie and Schot (1989) compared subjects' allocation behavior in the usual Tajfel treatment and in treatments in which they were instructed either "to maximize their own individual economic profit" or "to maximize the economic profit of their group." Uninstructed subjects in the standard Tajfel treatment showed no difference from subjects instructed to maximize individual profit in the degree to which they favored ingroup members in their allocations. However, subjects who were instructed to maximize group profit showed significantly greater ingroup favoritism than in the other two treatments. The equivalence in allocation behavior between the uninstructed subjects and those instructed to maximize individual profit suggests that subjects in the usual Tajfel situation are mainly influenced by considerations of individual gain. The heightened ingroup favoritism displayed under group–profit instruction could be due to the subjects' belief that they would individually benefit by joining with others in their group in elevating their allocations to ingroup members. It could also be due to their identifying, as instructed, with the group goal of achieving maximum profit for the group as a whole.

Experiment 3: Bias as a Function of Identification with Group Goals

The process whereby one identifies with a group's outcomes as distinct from one's own is central to understanding the full network of interdependencies within and between groups. Heider (1958) treats one's positive or negative identification with another party's outcomes as a form of interdependence in which one is respectively satisfied or dissatisfied by the other party's good or bad outcomes, holding constant whatever other outcomes may accrue to oneself. In one-to-one relationships, Kelley (1979) has measured spouses' identification with each other by how much their satisfaction with own positive outcomes is reduced when their partner independently experiences negative outcomes (or how much their dissatisfaction with own negative outcomes is reduced when their partner independently experiences positive outcomes). In member–group relationships, Horwitz (1953) and Hornstein (1978) have shown how individual behavior can be motivated by group goals, as in rooting for a team or supporting a political party. Nor need one be a member of a group to identify with it. A Dutch woman, for example, may incur personal costs to aid the population undergoing mass starvation in Ethiopia, none of whose members she knows. If she perceives the Ethiopian government as responsible, she may also find satisfaction in its demise. She obviously shares no social identity with either group, but she identifies positively with the outcomes of one and negatively with the outcomes of the other. The example illustrates that forming group identifications and forming social identities are distinctive processes (Herman, 1978).

The Rabbie, Schot, and Visser (1987) experiment, previously described, revealed "hidden" outcome interdependencies that existed among individuals in the minimal intergroup situation. It left unexplained the subjects' allocating more money to ingroup than outgroup members when they were solely dependent on either one or the other. Similarly, the Rabbie–Schot experiment (1989) left open the possible explanations for increased favoritism toward ingroup members when subjects were instructed to maximize profit for the ingroup. The experiment reported next (Schot, Horwitz, Rabbie, & Visser, 1989) was designed to test the possibility that another form of interdependence was simultaneously implicated in the situation, namely, one in which the individual group members identify with the outcomes of their groups as such. The experiment was also designed to assess the degree to which placing the individuals in minimal groups may have triggered social-identity processes.

The first hypothesis of the study was that if subjects perceive groups as entities capable of receiving good or bad outcomes, they would view group membership as entailing an obligation to serve group interests. Hence, their mere assignment to an ad hoc group should automatically produce some degree of identification with group goals without producing concomitant changes in their self-concepts. The second hypothesis was that tendencies to incorporate a group into one's self-concept would increase as the degree of one's group identification intensified. Two treatments were used to vary the intensity of group identification. In a Minimal condition, subjects were, as usual, simply classified into Blues or Greens. In a Weak-Competition condition, they were explicitly designated as members of the Blue or Green group and the instruction was added that the experimenter was interested in which group "would come out best on a later task," utilizing the principle that intergroup competition will heighten members' identification with group goals (Sherif, 1966). The second hypothesis implied that if subjects' social identities were affected at all, the effect would be more likely to be evidenced in the Weak-Competition than in the Minimal condition.

To measure identification with group outcomes, a number of allocation matrices were constructed by means of which subjects could indicate how much they would be willing to forgo in gains of cents to themselves in order that the group not lose in symbolic points. To measure changes in social identity, we followed literally the lead provided by Turner's (1982) claim that "The first question determining group–belongingness is . . . 'who am I?'" (p. 16). Subjects were asked to respond to the open-ended query, "What is the first question that comes to your mind?" and then to a more focused "Who-Am-I" questionnaire (Kuhn & McPartland, 1954). The questionnaire consisted of twelve incomplete sentences, each beginning with the words, "I am . . . ".

The subjects were randomly assigned to all-male or all-female Blue and Green groups, half in the Minimal condition and half in the Weak-Competition condition. Immediately thereafter, subjects responded to the open-ended question about what first came to their minds and then to the incomplete sentences in the Who-Am-I questionnaire. They next indicated on the allocation matrices how much money they were personally willing to forgo in order that their group not lose points. The results were as follows: None of the 46 subjects mentioned wondering who I am in response to the open-ended question. None of the females ($N = 12$) or males ($N = 12$) in the Minimal condition described himself or herself as a Blue or a Green in the 288 possible responses to the Who-Am-I questionnaire. One of the twelve females and two of the ten males in the Weak-Competition condition did, however, use the term Blue or Green in describing themselves. The result suggests that identity processes may indeed be set in motion as identification with group goals increases or, in general, as increased interdependence renders group membership more consequential for subjects. The matrix measures showed that subjects in the Minimal condition were prepared to make modest monetary sacrifices in order to prevent their group's losing points, despite the uncertain value of these points to the group.

Subjects restricted themselves to an average gain of approximately four cents out of a possible gain of fifteen cents in order to limit their group's loss to approximately two points out of a possible loss of ten points. No main treatment effects were detected in the matrices, although the Weak-Competition treatment evoked somewhat greater tendencies to sacrifice own gains to prevent group losses than did the Minimal treatment among males, but not females, resulting in a near-significant interaction of sex by condition ($p < .08$).[2]

The results of this experiment have, in our view, a two-fold significance. First, they show that persons in the minimal intergroup situation perceive not only interdependencies of outcomes with other members (Rabbie et al., 1987), but also interdependencies of outcomes with their groups. Second, they show that peoples' perception of their social environment, containing group and intergroup systems, is antecedent to and not a consequence of their forming social identities. If so, the view that groups originate out of people's internal cognitive demands to place themselves and others into categories (Turner, 1982) cannot be correct, and the effort to treat intergroup dynamics as an expression of category differentiation (Doise, 1978) must be incomplete at best.

Interdependence in Large-Scale Groups

Prior to these experiments, Tajfel (1982, Chapter 16) had commented thoughtfully and at length on a paper in which we had urged the importance of distinguishing categories, as a collection of individuals who share certain attributes, from groups, as acting and reacting units in which individual members participate. He acknowledged: "There is no doubt that Horwitz and Rabbie are correct in stating that a 'social category' has often meant no more than a collection of individuals who share a common attribute or attributes distinguishing them from other such collections. In this sense, all people using a certain brand of toothpaste may be a category, although they are highly unlikely to become a 'group'" (p. 500). To his credit, he further acknowledged that he and his colleagues had employed a "confusing interchangeability of terms." He accounted for this as due to their wish to stress that they were "at least as much concerned with large-scale groupings as with face-to-face groups" (p. 501).

The sharp distinction that Tajfel drew here and elsewhere in his discussion between large groupings and face-to face groups — in Lewin's terms between a "loose mass" and a "compact unit" — reflects a mistaken view that the perception of interdependent relationships requires actual face-to-face interaction among members. Suppose, in Tajfel's example of the category of toothpaste users, that Brand X toothpaste was discovered to have toxic side effects. The previously abstract category

---

[2]The result is consistent with other findings that compare male and female intergroup behavior and that show that males tend to focus on group outcomes, while females tend to focus on intermember relationships (Horwitz & Rabbie, 1982; Rabbie, Visser, & van Oostrum, 1982; Horwitz, 1989).

could, and doubtlessly would, become perceived as a "loose" group capable of a class-action suit by the toothpaste company, as a potential marketing target by competing companies, and as a group suffering a disaster by individual victims or consumer advocates. What was formerly perceived as a category of individuals would become transformed into a group perceived as suffering a common fate, even before any interaction has occurred among its members. If the group moves from the passive state of having been acted upon to taking group action to improve its lot, some of its members, though not necessarily all, may engage in face-to-face interaction, developing in the process such group properties as norms, roles, communication structures, and the like, culminating in the formation of a "compact" or well-organized group.

Tajfel correctly stated that the "fundamental and *sine qua non* condition for the group process to be set into motion is to be found, according to Horwitz and Rabbie, in the group members' perception of their interdependence of fate" (p. 501). He agreed that this view "provides one possible (and highly plausible) view as to what 'switches on' the processes of social identification discussed by Turner" (p. 503), and later reiterated that "interdependence of fate is needed to establish the locus of origin for the development of social identity" (p. 505). Tajfel thereby dissociated himself from the extension of his original position made by Turner (1982) who, treating groups as equivalent to categories of similar individuals, views groups as coming into being as a consequence of individuals' social identities.

Traits of Groups Versus Traits of Individuals in Categories

Cognitive Processes in Trait Ascriptions

Two types of cognitive processes have been employed to account for persons' using trait-ascriptions to explain and predict behavior. One is that "the organization of social and other stimuli into categories constitutes the basis for imputing meaning to stimuli" (Stephan, 1985 p. 609). Studies of the processes of category formation are exemplified in the work of Bruner (1973), Tajfel and Wilkes (1963), and in studies of prototypes (Tversky, 1977; Rosch 1978; Cantor & Mischel, 1979). The second type of cognitive process is one whereby persons impute meaning to behavior by locating it within a "field," organized by means–ends relationships among perceived activity possibilities. Studies of such cognitive structures are exemplified by work on life spaces (Lewin, 1951), on causal schemata (Kelley, 1967) and on scripts (Schank & Abelson, 1977). Especially relevant for the present discussion is Heider's (1958) work on the genesis of trait-ascriptions in the person's perceptions of own and others' behavior.

Each of the two types of cognitive process deals with a different aspect of a person's generalizing about traits. Categorization theory begins with already-formed traits that are ascribed to some individuals and then generalized to other individuals who are placed in the same category. Heider's attribution theory deals with the initial formation of trait-ascriptions based on an actor's perceived behavior. The trait itself expresses a generalization about the class of actions that the actor has performed and will likely continue to perform, for example, a kind person will perform kindly acts, a democratic group will encourage diversity of opinion. Categorization theory involves a generalization of pre-existing traits across a range of individuals. Attribution theory involves a generalization, expressed as traits or dispositions, about a range of behaviors of an individual or a group.

There is no reason within categorization theory why the traits ascribed to individuals in a category should be positive, neutral, or negative. However, where groups interact with each other, negative trait-ascriptions appear to predominate over positive ones (Brewer, 1979a; Jaspers & Warnaen, 1982). These prejudicial attributions are often accompanied by strong emotions. As Pettigrew (1986) has noted, "affect is a central component of the phenomenon . . . of intergroup prejudice: an *antipathy against groups* . . ." (his italics, p. 181). We consider next how the phenomena of negative trait-ascriptions and antipathy toward others are handled in categorization theory versus attribution theory.

The Ascription of Negative Traits

To account for intergroup prejudice, categorization theorists have invoked motivational processes to supplement the cognitive ones. In the case of social-identity theory, the motivation is drawn from social-comparison theory, namely, that where people compare themselves with relevant others, they desire to be better, certainly not worse, than the others (Festinger, 1954; Ferguson & Kelley, 1964). However, social-comparison theory implies only that others will be less well evaluated than oneself, not negatively evaluated. As noted above, subjects in the minimal intergroup situation rated ingroup members more favorably than outgroup members only on social-emotional items. This effect could have been produced by subjects' assuming that common group membership involves the "generic" norm that one ought to give more consideration to the desires for favorable ratings on the part of ingroup members than outgroup members. It could also be due to subjects' wanting more favorable ratings for their own group as compared with the other. In treatments in which the comparison between group outcomes was strengthened (Rabbie & Horwitz, 1969; Rabbie, 1972, cited in Horwitz & Rabbie, 1982), the tendency to favor ingroups over outgroups spread to other dimensions of evaluation besides the social-emotional ones. To the extent that comparison processes were operating, however, they did not cause subjects to ascribe negative traits to outgroup members on the bipolar scales that were used (see also Brewer, 1979b). Indeed, if one were to assume that people generally elevate their self-esteem by ascribing negative traits to others with whom they compare themselves, they should all be misanthropes, perceiving those comparable to themselves to be unlikeable people.

The ascription of negative traits to an individual or a group as a behaving entity can be directly derived from the structure and dynamics of the cognitive processes by which persons make causal attributions about own and others' behavior (Heider, 1958). The great amount of attention given to the Jones–Nisbett (1971) formulation of the actor–observer effect has obscured the fact that Heider's original statement of the effect was much more qualified than theirs. He viewed the effect as limited to the condition in which people perceive themselves to be in disagreement or conflict with each other. In Heider's view, people tend to attribute their own actions and reactions to situational requirements, that is, to what they ought to do given the demands of objective reality or of suprapersonal values. They account for others' actions that deviate from what is situationally appropriate by attributing internal defects to them, generally speaking, disabilities or bad intentions. "The person tends to attribute his own reactions to the object world and those of another, *when they differ from his own*, to personal characteristics on O" (Heider, 1958, p. 157, italics added). Heider's theory is in essence a statement of how conflict between the parties leads each to ascribe negative, internal characteristics to the other.

As with individual actions, the action of a group that is perceived to violate the objective or moral requirements of a situation can be attributed to negative characteristics of the group, including its disabilities or bad intentions. For example, during periods of international tension, citizens in the United States commonly attribute the causes of the behavior of the Soviet government to its being dominated by a bureaucratized elite, to its expansionist goals, and its paranoidal reactions to the United States government's moves for self-defense. The mirror images by which Soviet citizens characterize the United States government (Bronfenbrenner, 1961) illustrate the principle that conflicts between groups, like conflicts between individuals, will engender negative characterizations by ingroup members about the internal deficiencies and inappropriate aims of the outgroup.

Intergroup Antipathy as a Function of Conflictual Interaction

The ascription of negative traits to a group can escalate into strong antipathies, flowing directly from the course of interaction between the parties. First, the negative characterizations of the outgroup arise out of conflicts about what is situationally appropriate behavior. The negative traits imply a generalization that these inappropriate behaviors, unless seen as passing aberrations, are likely to recur. Second, with both sides viewing the disagreement as caused by the other's negative characteristics, the groups may find themselves embroiled in what Kelley (1979) has called an attributional conflict. Each group sees the other's negative characterization of itself as evidence of prejudice and attributes this in turn to the other's ignorance or malice. Third, if each group views the other's desires as situationally inappropriate, each will give these desires less weight or consideration that the other feels entitled to, creating a relational conflict (Horwitz & Rabbie, 1982). An immediate effect of perceiving the outgroup as violating the rights of one's own group is to evoke anger and aggression (Rabbie & Horwitz, 1982; Rabbie & Lodewijkx, 1987). The relationship between the groups will deteriorate further if each group seeks to redress the wrong that it has experienced, but that the other does not believe it has inflicted. The attribution of negative characteristics to another group may initially arise out of a relatively manageable disagreement. However, it can set interactional processes in motion that will escalate into conflicts with high levels of emotional intensity.

Independence of Traits Ascribed to Groups and Categorized Individuals

The negative traits attributed to a group need not apply to its individual members, a phenomenon that is glossed over in equating groups with categories composed of similar individuals. The negative characterizations of the Soviet national system in the United States have often diverged from the positive characterizations of its private citizens as warm, friendly, and "not all that different from us." The absence of positive correlations between unfavorable attitudes toward a group and toward its individual members can be found in other settings of intergroup tension as well. Ben-Ari and Amir (1986) report the pre-*Intifada* findings of Levy and Guttmann (1976) and Zemach (1980) that the "interpersonal attitudes" of Israeli Jews toward Arabs were uncorrelated with their attitudes toward Arabs in "the political-national domains" (p. 56). Sears and Kinder (1971) found that favoring a white over a black mayoral candidate in Los Angeles was correlated, not with the negative attitudes of whites toward black individuals, but with negative attitudes toward the black group which was perceived, for example, as having gotten more than it deserved. Similarly, Sears and Allen (1984) found that white opposition to busing for school desegregation depended much less on whether one's own child would interact with individual blacks than on the view that "the civil rights movement was moving ahead too fast." In a series of laboratory and field experiments, Cook (1984) has shown, that although one can successfully promote respect and liking for individuals from disliked racial and ethnic groups, the favorable contact with individuals does not generalize "to positive attitudes toward the group from which the individual comes" (p. 163).

Effects of Contact Between Individuals Versus Groups

That a person can differentiate between the evaluation of a group and its individual members is not problematic if persons are viewed as capable of distinguishing between group action and individual action. It becomes problematic, however, if researchers do not make this distinction and view groups as equivalent to a category of similar individuals. The latter view is an unstated assumption in the equal-status contact hypothesis (Allport, 1954), according to which friendly attitudes toward individuals who are perceived to be typical of other individuals in a group should generalize to friendly attitudes toward the group as a whole. The empirical results fail to support the hypothesis that such "stimulus generalization" will occur (Amir, 1969), but the failure has not led to questioning whether groups and individuals are in fact perceived as similar entities, that is, similar stimuli. Thus, Pettigrew (1979) accounts for the failure of generalization by invoking intrapsychic processes whereby persons defend their stereotypes, treating the actions of a well-liked member of a disliked group as exceptions to the rule due, for example, to the individual's unusual effort or special circumstances. Hewstone and Brown (1986), on the other hand, argue that generalization fails where persons do in fact experience their cross-group contacts as exceptional rather than typical. They suggest that generalization would be expected to occur only where the person develops cordial relationships with an outgroup member who is perceived to have attributes that are representative of the attributes of others in the disliked social category. It is unclear, however, how the development of cordial relationships can be expected even to begin if each individual perceives the other to exemplify the negative traits that are characteristic of the other's social category. Neither Pettigrew nor Hewstone and Brown appear to consider the fact that persons can distinguish between the positive actions of individuals and the negative actions of their group.

We agree with Hewstone and Brown (1986) that friendly interaction between individuals across group lines will have little effect on their *intergroup* attitudes unless perceived by the parties as an "interaction between individuals qua group members or in ways that alter the structure of group relations" (quoting Brown and Turner, 1981, p. 34). However, in equating membership in a group with membership in a category of similar individuals, their view of harmonious intergroup relationships is limited to members' perceiving "a positively valued distinctiveness between the two groups" (p. 34). They thus fail to consider that persons can perceive groups as interacting with one another for group interests other than the enhancement of members' social identities. Consider the impact of Sadat's addressing the Israeli parliament in Jerusalem. It is unlikely that the enormous relief and exhilaration among Israelis grew out of the enhancement of their identities as Israelis or Jews vis-à-vis the Egyptians. Rather, Sadat's visit signified that the Egyptian government was willing to recognize the legitimacy of the Israeli government and was disposed to end the state of war between the two nations. Individual Israelis undoubtedly perceived a variety of likely benefits (and costs) to themselves as a result of this change. But in the first instance, Sadat's "intervention" had the effect of changing their previously held attributions about the menacing character of the Egyptian group. Likewise, the recent exchange of visits between Gorbachev and Reagan altered, not the identities of American and Soviet individuals, but their attributions about each government's behavior.

Interindividual and Intergroup Behavior: Personalization and Depersonalization

The main part of the title of this section is taken from Tajfel's (1978b) article of the same name. The distinction we have drawn between the traits of groups and the traits of individuals in categories raises the question about how the ascription of negative traits to a group affects one's perceptions of individual members of the group. Our answer to that question necessitates a modification of Tajfel's formulation about the difference between interindividual and intergroup behavior. It leads to a quite different understanding from his about why the interethnic and interreligious conflicts that wrack our world cause members of contending groups to dehumanize each other. The view to be presented is that depersonalization of others occurs to the degree that the others are perceived to act as agents or pawns of their group's interests. In illustration, we will compare our own and Tajfel's interpretations of

Nazi successes in gaining support for their campaign to exterminate Jews and others. The section concludes by considering, first, a number of principles that are applicable to improving relationships between individual members of antagonistic groups and, second, a promising line of inquiry for improving relationships between the groups themselves.

Attributions About Member Behavior

Tajfel developed his distinction between interindividual and intergroup behavior from Sherif's (1966) definition that intergroup behavior occurs "whenever individuals belonging to one group interact, collectively or individually, with another group or its members in terms of their group identification" (p. 12). Tajfel construed "group identification" to mean perceiving another as "similar to others in a category" rather than what Sherif intended, namely, perceiving another as "identifying with group interests." The contrast drawn by Tajfel was that in interindividual behavior one deals with others in terms of their individual characteristics; in intergroup behavior one deals with others in terms of their category's characteristics. Pettigrew (1986) has voiced his unease that this "demarcation is too firmly drawn" and causes us "to overlook the many important connections between the interpersonal and intergroup realms" (p. 185).

If "group identification" is treated as "identifying with group interests," interindividual and intergroup behavior can be ordered along a continuum. An interaction is wholly interindividual where one attributes the causes of others' actions to their individual interests rather than to their identifying with group interests. The interaction is wholly intergroup, where one attributes the causes of others' actions to their identifying with group interests rather than to their individual interests. Intermediate positions on the continuum are defined by the relative degree to which one perceives the other's behavior as shaped by individual versus group interests. In political life, for example, we may perceive the partisans of a group as fanatic extremists who so strongly identify with group interests as to sacrifice their own and others' individual interests (Campbell, 1965). We may also perceive gradations whereby the others are only moderately, weakly, or barely influenced by their group's desires or demands.

Depersonalization of Group Members

Personalizing others has been described as dealing with "other individuals in terms of their relationship to the self" (Brewer & Miller, 1984, p. 267). A key feature of others' relationship to the self is the degree to which they are prepared to take account of or to grant weight to our desires (Horwitz & Rabbie, 1982). The more that we perceive others to be bound by serving group interests, the less should we see them as free to accommodate to our individual desires, especially to those of our desires that run counter to the interests of their group. The effect is compounded in the case of intergroup conflict. As intergroup conflict intensifies, individuals in the outgroup tend to be seen as increasingly identified with their group (Sherif, 1966).

Moderates in the outgroup, for example, may become seen as captives of the group's most extreme elements. Outgroup members are therefore viewed as increasingly unwilling or unable to take our desires and feelings into account. They are "depersonalized," not only because they are perceived as unresponsive to our desires, but because their behavior is perceived as mechanically controlled by the desires or demands of their group.

As noted earlier, conflicts between groups lead to causal attributions about the negative properties and intentions of the outgroup. We may individuate outgroup members, differentiating them from one another on many dimensions, but the critical factor affecting our cross-group interaction with them is how strongly we believe they identify with the desires of the outgroup that we have negatively evaluated. Any number of underlying causes may be attributed to members' identifying with their groups (Horwitz & Berkowitz, 1975), including social pressure, brainwashing, fear of rejection, hatred of outgroups, socialization experiences, the desire for a "positive social identity," and more. But whatever the underlying cause, the degree to which we perceive their behavior as controlled by their group's desires or demands will determine the degree to which they are seen as "parts of" or mechanical extensions of their groups. When so viewed, we no longer perceive them as individuals who react to personal and private pains. We may then support the efforts of our own group to cope with the hostile outgroup by steps that can escalate from segregation of its members to intimidation, to banishment, to massacres, and finally to extermination, a process that is seen all too often in ethnic, religious, and political conflicts throughout the world (see D. Bar-Tal, Chapter 8).

Tajfel (1982) took strong exception to our view about the role of attributions about outgroups and their members "in such collective issues as the treatment of Jews in Nazi Germany" (p. 486). The Nazis, he argued, aimed to deprive Jews (and others) of their individuality by defining them as outside the category of human beings. The victims were marked off from their "definition of being human . . . . *No attributions needed to be made at all* (italics in the original), no more than attributions are made about insects subjected to a DDT treatment" (pp. 485–486).

The insect analogy highlights the inadequacy of what Tajfel called elsewhere in his chapter, a "categorial" analysis. Clearly, neither Nazis nor others are moved to kill living things simply because they are nonhuman – not even insects – unless they are perceived as harmful or threatening. Nazi propaganda portrayed not simply categories of nonhuman or subhuman individuals, but a world stage on which good and evil groups were contending (Bar-Tal, 1988a). The Jewish group was demonized as conducting a Communist or Capitalist, Internationalist or Zionist conspiracy which, in its drive for world domination, aimed to corrupt German racial purity and to undermine the "legitimate" claims of the German group as a master race. Thus, *Der Stürmer* of May 1, 1934 headlined what it described as a "Jewish murder programme against non-Jewish humanity" that had been going on for "thousands of years." The sub-headline read "The Jews are our downfall!" (Distel & Wakusch, 1978, p. 40). Given such group-centered attributions about the presumed evil qualities of the Jewish group, no attributions needed to be made at all about individuals in the group and could have led even otherwise "humane" Nazis to depersonalize or dehumanize Jewish individuals, ignoring the anguish of individual men, women, and children in the conviction that the eradication of the Jewish group was necessary for their own group's self-defense.[3] We may deplore peoples' overlooking individual differences within social categories, but it is important to recognize the social-psychological fact that people make group-level attributions that determine their behavior toward outgroups and their members.

In programs designed to improve intergroup relationships, it is important, as Ben-Ari and Amir (1986) have wisely urged, to specify which among a number of possible goals we aim to achieve. The goal of fostering harmonious interpersonal relationships among individuals who are members of conflicting groups involves different methods from that of improving relationships between the group themselves. The foregoing discussion suggests three general principles that may be used to facilitate cordial interpersonal interaction across antagonistic group lines. All have the intended effect of (a) minimizing the likelihood that the parties will perceive each other as group spokespersons whose behavior is dictated by their group's aims in the conflict and (b) increasing the likelihood that they will perceive each other as willing and able to take account of each other's individual desires in their interaction (see Amir & Ben-Ari, Chapter 12).

Principle 1: Reducing the Salience of Intergroup Conflict

The first principle, reminiscent of the old adage about not discussing religion or politics in mixed company, is that the intervention should avoid raising the divisive issues of intergroup conflict in the interaction between the parties. Thus, in the context of the Jewish–Arab conflict in Israel, Ben-Ari and Amir (1986) recommend that teachers bringing youth from both sides together should avoid reference to their national conflicts. Their argument, though couched in the language of social categories, is that introducing "the Arab–Jewish conflict confronts the participants in a way that defines them as two antagonistic entities, thereby strengthening the tendency to consider members of the outgroups as undifferentiated particles in a unified social category" (p. 56). Likewise, with regard to improving interpersonal relations among black and white students in the United States, Brewer and Miller (1984) conclude that "an emphasis on intergroup distinctions introduces dysfunctional social competition and outgroup rejection that interferes with ... interpersonal acceptance" (p. 287). The principle of downplaying intergroup conflicts does not imply that participants must efface or relinquish "valued group identities" as Hewstone and Brown (1986, p. 35) seem to think. The Cultural Assimilator technique (Triandis, 1976) aims to teach participants to understand how people from

---

[3]Similar group-level attributions appear in other instances of anti-Semitic behavior. Examples are the physical attacks on Russian Jews for allegedly killing Stalin following the so-called "doctor's plot" (Sharansky, 1988) and the recent allegation by a Black Muslim spokesman that the tragic rise in the incidence of AIDS among black infants is due to injections of the virus by Jewish doctors as part of a "Jewish conspiracy to rule the world" (*New York Times*, May 7, 1988) See also Bar-Tal, 1988b.

different cultural backgrounds view their own behavior. White subjects trained in this program were found to enjoy working with a black confederate more than did untrained whites, although as usual no change in interracial attitudes was obtained (Randolph, Landis, & Tzeng, 1977). An intensive training program designed by Birnbaum (1975) uses a method of "guided inquiry" with groups composed of individuals who are heterogeneous with regard to ethnicity, race, religion, social class, gender, age, and so forth, in order to examine the influences of these societal memberships on the social aspects of the participants' personal identities (Babad, Birnbaum, & Benne, 1983). Although the differences in their social identities are deliberately highlighted, participants appear to achieve a high degree of mutual understanding about how their own and others' group memberships have shaped each other's individual lives. The effect of thus focusing on differences in social identities seems to be increased tolerance for interpersonal differences, along with a sobering recognition of the difficulties inherent in resolving intergroup conflicts.

Principle 2: Use of Overlapping Group Memberships

The second principle is that cordial interpersonal relations will be fostered if the parties drawn from conflicting groups can be brought to view each other as common members of a third group. The principle is based on the assumption that overlapping group membership, like any group membership, entails a "generic" norm that people ought to give members' desires more consideration than they give those of nonmembers. The evidence for this principle in the case of race relations in the United States is quite compelling. Cook (1984) concludes from his numerous experiments on multiethnic groups that "task interdependence induces cooperative, friendly behavior and develops liking and respect for one's group-mates" (p. 183). The metanalysis of Johnson, Johnson, and Maruyama (1984) indicates that cooperative group experiences in classrooms promote liking and respect among members belonging to mutually disliked ethnic groups. An especially interesting finding, which bears on the assumption that common group membership enhances persons' willingness and ability to weight each other's desires, is that cooperative interdependence in the classroom increases the empathy of students across ethnic and racial divisions (Bridgeman, 1981).

Principle 3: Increasing the Salience of Superordinate Structures

A third principle, related to the foregoing, is that common group membership will enhance interpersonal relationships across the boundaries of conflicting groups, even when the participants view each other as representing the separate interests of their respective groups. Cooperative work on common tasks appears to decrease the perception that the outgroupers are simply "mechanical extensions" of their group and to increase the perception that they are willing and able to give due weight to one's own desires, at least for the duration of their direct interaction with oneself. This principle has been most extensively tested by organizational psychologists in field experiments with so-called "matrix organizations" (Galbraith, 1973). Lawrence and Lorsch (1967) have reported significant successes in using this method to develop productive interpersonal relationships across warring departments in industrial enterprises. It should be noted, however, that the departmental representatives held common membership in a superordinate structure, namely, the organization itself. Besides the positive effects of their working together in cross-departmental teams, the matrix procedure may also have heightened the participants' identification with the interests of the organization as a whole.

Improving Relationships Between Groups in Conflict

Much less can be said about principles for developing harmonious relationships between groups in conflict. The one case in which Cook (1984) succeeded in getting a "generalization of positive affect felt for other-ethnic friends to race-relations policies that would benefit them" (p. 183) was where he made it explicit that such policies would spare their new friends the experience of discrimination. On examination, his procedure appears to have changed, not attitudes toward the outgroup, but rather toward one's own ingroup which became perceived as responsible for discriminatory practices that harm a friend. The validity of Sherif's (1966) claim that superordinate goals will induce positive attitudes toward the outgroup is likewise suspect. In those instances in the camp studies (Sherif et al., 1961) in which the campers engaged in common goals, it is not clear whether their groups were dissolved or remained intact, whether, in short, the interventions had created superordinate structures as well as superordinate goals.

One promising line of research on changing attributions about antagonistic groups is provided by Flynn (1973). Each group embroiled in a conflict was given the task of describing how the outgroup viewed itself and of checking the correctness of its description with the outgroup. The activity, involving a form of mutual "intergroup listening," led each group to elevate its positive characterizations and lower its negative characterizations of the outgroup. The result was interpreted as due to each group's having given evidence that, as a group, it could understand and be responsive to the other group's own views. The study suggests that a useful direction for future research on intergroup conflict would be to develop methods for encouraging "disattribution" processes in order to overcome the pervasively negative attributions that groups in conflict make about each other's behavior.

Summary

This chapter began by pointing out that intergroup stereotyping and prejudice can have three different classes of targets: individuals categorized by their similarity, groups as goal-directed entities, and individuals as members of such groups. When Lippman (1922) introduced the concept, he viewed "stereotyping" as a means by which we impose order on the "blooming, buzzing confusion" (p. 95) presented by the diversity of individuals we encounter. The tradition persists today in the emphasis placed in social psychology on the cognitive processes by which diverse individuals are categorized as similar or different (Stephan, 1985). The emphasis on category processes has led, we believe, to overlooking the quite different attributional processes by which people ascribe characteristics to a group as a behaving entity and to its members who are perceived as interdependent with the group.

Even in the simplified situation of the minimal intergroup paradigm, the preoccupation with category processes has led researchers to ignore the effects on subjects' behavior of their perceiving differential interdependence with their ingroup and outgroup. The three experiments reported here show that given the forms of interdependence established in the minimal intergroup situation, subjects were influenced to act in the interest of maximizing their own and their groups' outcomes when displaying ingroup favoritism. The results render unnecessary the unlikely assumption fostered by category theorizing that subjects have incorporated the transitory and ad hoc group to which they were assigned into their self-identities (Tajfel & Turner, 1979). The results also render unnecessary the dubious effort to locate the origin of social groups in peoples' intrapsychic needs to join with similar individuals in order to establish their "positive distinctiveness" vis-à-vis other individuals (Turner, 1982, 1987). The failure to conceive of groups as behaving entities that can obtain good or bad outcomes has led to overlooking the important phenomenon of a person's positively identifying (Heider, 1958) with group interests as distinct from incorporating a group into the definition of one's identity. The "generic" norm that appears to underlie the differential interdependence with ingroups and outgroups in the minimal intergroup paradigm is that members of each group view themselves and others as expected to give more weight to the desired outcomes of the ingroup and its members than those of the outgroup and its members.

The emphasis on category processes has also drawn attention away from the attributional processes by which traits are ascribed to groups as active and reactive entities. Categorization processes are involved in the generalization of *already-formed* trait-ascriptions about some individuals to other individuals. Attributional processes are involved in the *formation* of trait-ascriptions, which represent generalizations about the causes of a group's perceived behaviors. The characterization of a group based on its behavior would thus be expected to differ—and does differ—from the characterizations of individuals based on their similarity to others. Under conditions of intergroup conflict, the behavior of outgroups will tend to be seen as at odds with what is objectively or morally required in the encounter. The causal attributions made about such "inappropriate" outgroup behavior account for the pervasive tendency for participants in intergroup conflict to ascribe negative traits to outgroups and to develop antipathy toward them. If attributions about groups are based on the perception of group behavior, it should be no surprise that antipathy toward a group will persist despite friendly one-to-one relationships that are developed in equal-status contacts with individuals who belong to the negatively evaluated group.

Finally, we discussed the conditions under which attribution about groups impinge on the attributions about its members. Sherif's (1966) definition of intergroup behavior implies that members of outgroups opposing our own group will tend to be depersonalized—in the extreme case, dehumanized—where their behavior is perceived to be entirely determined by the desires or demands of their group, that is, where the attributions are made that they are behaving as pawns or mechanical extensions of their group's "illegitimate" interests. Given that perception, they will be viewed as "uninfluenceable" by our own desires and conflicts with their group may be viewed as best resolved by taking measures to avoid, remove, or "liquidate" them. We reviewed the evidence that personalized relationships between members of opposing groups would be aided by interactions between them that demonstrated each other's readiness to weight the others' desires. Such interactions appear to be promoted by involving these members in overlapping or superordinate work-team structures, thereby invoking the "generic" norm that they owe special consideration to each other as interdependent members of a common group. By extension, we proposed that positive relationships between two opposing groups might be aided by activities within superordinate intergroup structures that enable each group to demonstrate its readiness to take account of the other group's desires.

Acknowledgments. The work of the second author was supported by a grant (560–27–012) from the Netherlands Organization for the Advancement of Research (NWO).

References

Abrams, D., & Hogg, M. (1988). *Social identifications: Social psychology of intergroup relations and group processes.* London: Routledge.

Allport, G.W. (1954). *The nature of prejudice.* Cambridge, MA: Addison-Wesley.

Amir, Y. (1969). Contact hypothesis in ethnic relations. *Psychological Bulletin, 71,* 319–342.

Babad, E.Y., Birnbaum, M., & Benne, K.D. (1983). *The social self: Group influences on personal identity.* Beverly Hills, CA: Sage Publications.

Bar-Tal, D. (1988a). *Group beliefs.* New York: Springer-Verlag.

Bar-Tal, D. (1988b). *Group beliefs of delegitimizing Jews in Germany 1933–1945.* Unpublished manuscript.

Ben-Ari, R. & Amir, Y., (1986). Contact between Arab and Jewish youth in Israel: Reality and potential. In M. Hewstone & R. Brown (Eds.), *Contact and conflict in intergroup encounters* (pp. 45–58). New York: Basil Blackwell.

Billig, M. (1976). *Social psychology and intergroup relations.* London: Academic Press.

Birnbaum, M. (1975). The clarification group. In K.D. Benne, L.P. Bradford, J.R. Gibb, & R.D. Lippitt (Eds.), *The laboratory method of changing and learning: Theory and application* (pp. 341–364). Palo Alto, CA: Science and Behavior Books.

Blake, R.R. & Mouton, J.S. (1961). Reactions to intergroup competition under win–lose conditions. *Management Science, 7,* 420–435.

Brewer, M.B. (1979a). The role of ethnocentrism in intergroup conflict. In W.G. Austin & S. Worchel (Eds.), *The social psychology of intergroup relations* (pp. 71–84). Monterey, CA: Brooks/Cole.

Brewer, M.B. (1979b). In-group bias in the minimal intergroup situation: A cognitive–motivational analysis. *Psychological Bulletin, 86,* 307–324.

Brewer, M.B. & Miller, M. (1984). Beyond the contact hypothesis: Theoretical perspectives on desegregation. In N. Miller & M.B. Brewer (Eds.), *Groups in contact: The psychology of desegregation* (pp. 169–195). Orlando, FL: Academic Press.

Bridgeman, D.L. (1981). Enhanced role taking through cooperative interdependence: A field study. *Child Development, 52,* 1231–1238.

Bronfenbrenner, U. (1961). The mirror image in Soviet-American relations: A social psychologist's report. *Journal of Social Issues, 17*, 45–47.

Brown, R. & Turner, J.C. (1981). Interpersonal and intergroup behavior. In J.Turner & H. Giles (Eds.), *Intergroup Behavior* (pp. 33–65). Oxford: Basil Blackwell.

Bruner, J.S. (1973). *Beyond the information given.* New York: Norton.

Campbell, D.T. (1958). Common fate, similarity and other indices of the status of aggregates of persons as social entities. *Behavioral Science, 3*, 14–25.

Campbell, D.T. (1965). Ethnocentrism and other altruistic motives. In D. Levine (Ed.), *Nebraska symposium on motivation* (pp. 283–311). Lincoln, NE: University of Nebraska Press.

Cantor, N., & Mischel, W. (1979). Prototypicality and personality: Effects on free recall and personality impressions. *Journal of Research in Personality, 13*, 187–205.

Cook, S.W. (1984). Cooperative interaction in multiethnic contexts. In N. Miller & M.B. Brewer (Eds.), *Groups in contact: The psychology of desegregation* (pp. 156–185). Orlando, FL: Academic Press.

Deutsch, M. (1982). Interdependence and psychological orientation. In V.J. Derlega & J. Grzelak (Eds.), *Cooperation and helping behavior* (pp. 15–42). New York: Academic Press.

Distel, B. & Wakusch R. (1978). *Catalogue concentration camp Dachau 1933–1945.* Munich: LippGmbH.

Doise, W. (1978). *Groups and individuals: Explanations in social psychology.* Cambridge, MA: Cambridge University Press.

Doise, W. (1988). Individual and social identities in intergroup relations. *European Journal of Social Psychology, 18*(2), 99–112.

Ferguson, C.K. & Kelley, H.H. (1964). Significant factors in overevaluation of own group's product. *Journal of Abnormal Social Psychology, 69*, 223–228.

Festinger, L. (1954). A theory of social comparison processes. *Human Relations, 7*, 117–140.

Flynn, L. (1973). *Reducing intergroup conflict through attributional changes.* Unpublished doctoral dissertation, Boston College.

Galbraith, J. (1973). *Designing complex organizations.* Reading, MA: Addison-Wesley.

Heider, F. (1958). *The psychology of interpersonal relations.* New York: Wiley.

Herman, S.N. (1978). *Jewish identity: A social psychological perspective.* London: Sage Publications.

Hewstone, M., & Brown, R. (1986). Contact is not enough: An intergroup perspective on the "contact hypothesis". In M. Hewstone & R. Brown (Eds.), *Contact and conflict in intergroup encounters* (pp. 1–44). Oxford, UK: Basil Blackwood.

Hornstein, H.A. (1978). Promotive tension and prosocial behavior: A Lewinian analysis. In L. Wispe (Ed.), *Altruism, sympathy and helping: Psychological and sociological principles.* New York: Academic Press.

Hornstein, H.A. (1982). Promotive tension: Theory and research. In V.J. Derlega & J. Grzelak (Eds.), *Cooperation and helping behavior* (pp. 231–248). New York: Academic Press.

Horwitz, M. (1953). The recall of interrupted group tasks: An experimental study of individual motivation in relation to group goals. *Human Relations, 7*, 3–38.

Horwitz, M. (1989). Gender differences in intergroup behavior, (in preparation).

Horwitz, M., & Berkowitz, N. (1975, August). *Attributional analysis of intergroup conflict.* Paper presented at the meeting of the American Psychological Association, Chicago, IL.

Horwitz, M., & Rabbie, J.M. (1982). Individuality and membership in the intergroup system. In H. Tajfel (Ed.), *Social identity and intergroup relations* (pp. 241–274). Cambridge/Paris: Cambridge University Press/Maison des Sciences de l'Homme.

Jaspers, J.M.F. & Warnaen, S. (1982). Intergroup relations, ethnic identity and self-evaluation in Indonesia. In H. Tajfel (Ed.), *Social identity and intergroup relations* (pp. 335–366). Cambridge/Paris: Cambridge University Press/Maison des Sciences de l'Homme.

Johnson, D.W., Johnson, R.T., and Maruyama, G. (1984). Goal interdependence and inter-personal attraction in heterogeneous classrooms: A metanalysis. In N. Miller & M.B. Brewer (Eds.), *Groups in contact* (pp. 187–212). New York: Academic Press.

Jones, E.E., & Nisbett, R.E. (1971). *The actor and the observer: Divergent perceptions of the causes of behavior.* Morristown, NJ: General Learning Press.

Kelley, H.H. (1967). Attribution theory in social psychology. In D. Levine (Ed.), *Nebraska symposium on motivation* (Vol. 15) (pp. 192–238). Lincoln, NE: University of Nebraska Press.

Kelley, H.H. (1979). *Personal relationships: Their structure and processes.* Hillsdale, NJ: Erlbaum.

Kelley, H.H., & Thibaut, J.W. (1978). *Interpersonal relations: A theory of interdependence.* New York: John Wiley & Sons.

Kuhn, M.H., & McPartland, T.S. (1954). An empirical investigation of self-attitudes. *American Sociological Review, 19,* 68–76.

Lawrence, P., & Lorsch, J. (1967). Differentiation and integration in complex organizations. *Administrative Science Quarterly, 12,* 1–47.

Levy, S., & Guttmann, L. (1976). *Values and attitudes of Israeli Youth.* Jerusalem: Institute of Applied Social Research.

Lewin, K. (1948). *Resolving social conflicts.* New York: Harper.

Lewin, K. (1951). *Field theory in social science.* New York: Harper.

Lippman, W. (1922). *Public opinion.* New York: Harcourt Brace.

Pettigrew, T.F. (1979). The ultimate attribution error: Extending Allport's cognitive analysis of prejudice. *Personal Social Psychology Bulletin, 5,* 461–476.

Pettigrew, T.F. (1986). The intergroup contact hypothesis reconsidered. In M. Hewstone & R. Brown (Eds.), *Contact and conflict in intergroup encounters* (pp. 169–195). Oxford, UK: Basil Blackwood.

Pruitt, D.G., & Kimmel, M.J. (1977). Twenty years of experimental gaming: Critique, synthesis, and suggestions for the future. *Annual Review of Psychology, 28,* 363–392.

Rabbie, J.M. (1972, July). *Experimental studies of intergroup relations.* Paper presented at the Conference on the Experimental Study of Intergroup Relations, Bristol, England.

Rabbie, J.M. (1986, August). Armed conflicts: Toward a behavioral interaction model. Paper presented at the Conference of European Psychologists for Peace, Helsinki.

Rabbie, J.M., & Horwitz, M. (1969). Arousal of ingroup-outgroup bias by a chance win or loss. *Journal of Personality and Social Psychology, 13,* 269–277.

Rabbie, J.M., & Horwitz, M. (1982). Conflict and aggression among individuals and groups. In H. Hiebsch, H. Brandstatter, H.H. Kelley (Eds.) *Social psychology* (pp. 99–106). Berlin, GDR: VEB Deutscher Verlag der Wissenschaften.

Rabbie, J.M., & Horwitz, M. (1988). Categories versus groups as explanatory concepts in intergroup relations. *European Journal of Social Psychology, 18*(2), 117–123.

Rabbie, J.B., & Lodewijkx, H. (1987). Individual and group aggression. *Current Research on Peace and Violence, 10,* 91–101.

Rabbie, J.M., & Schot, J.C. (1989). *Self-interest and identification with group goals in the minimal intergroup situation.* In preparation.

Rabbie, J.M., Schot, J., & Visser, L. (1987, July). *Instrumental intra-group cooperation and intergroup competition in the Minimal Group Paradigm.* Paper presented at the Conference on Social Identity at the University of Exeter, Great Britain.

Rabbie, J.M., Visser, L., & van Oostrum, J. (1982). Conflict behaviour of individuals, dyads, and triads in mixed-motive games. In J.M. Brandstatter, J.H. Davis, G. Stocker-Kreichgauer (Eds.), *Group decision making* (pp. 315–343). London: Academic Press.

Randolph, G., Landis, D., & Tzeng, O.C.S. (1977). The effects of time and practice upon culture assimilator training. *International Journal of Intercultural Relations, 1,* 105–119.

Rosch, E. (1978). Principles of categorization. In E. Rosch & B.B. Lloyd (Eds.), *Cognition and categorization* (pp. 28–49). Hillsdale, NJ: Erlbaum.

Schank, R., & Abelson, R. (1977). *Scripts, plans, goals and understanding: An inquiry into human knowledge structures*. Hillsdale, NJ: Erlbaum.

Schot, J.C., Horwitz, M., Rabbie, J.M., & Visser, L. (1989). Identification with group goals versus social identity in the minimal intergroup situation. In preparation.

Sears, D.O., & Allen, H.M. (1984). The trajectory of local desegregation controversies and whites' opposition to busing. In N. Miller & M.B. Brewer (Eds.), *Groups in contact: The psychology of desegregation*. (pp. 124–151). New York: Academic Press.

Sears, D.O., & Kinder, D.R. (1971). Racial tensions and voting in Los Angeles. In W.Z. Hirsch (Ed.), *Los Angeles: Viability and prospects for metropolitan leadership* (pp.51–88). New York: Praeger.

Sharansky, N. (1988). *Fear no evil*. New York: Random House.

Sherif, M. (1966). *In common predicament*. Boston, MA: Houghton Mifflin Co.

Sherif, M., Harvey, O.J., White, B.J., Hood, W.R., & Sherif, C.W. (1961). *Intergroup conflict and cooperation: The Robbers cave experiment*. Norman, OK: University of Oklahoma Book Exchange.

Stephan, W.A. (1985). Intergroup relations. In G. Lindzey and E. Aronson (Eds.), *The handbook of social psychology* (3rd ed.) Reading, MA: Addison–Wesley.

Tajfel, H. (Ed.) (1978a). *Differentiation between social groups*. London: Academic Press.

Tajfel, H. (1978b). Interindividual behaviour and intergroup behavior. In H. Tajfel (Ed.), *Differentiation between social groups* (pp. 27–60). London: Academic Press.

Tajfel, H. (1982). Instrumentality, identity, and social comparison. In H. Tajfel (Ed.), *Social identity and intergroup relations* (pp. 483–507). Cambridge/Paris: Cambridge University Press/Maison des Sciences de l'Homme.

Tajfel, H., Flament, C., Billig, K, & Bundy, R. (1971). Social categorization and intergroup behavior. *European Journal of Social Psychology, 1*, 149–175.

Tajfel, H., & Turner, J.C. (1979). An integrative theory of intergroup conflict. In W. Austin and S. Worchel (Eds.), *The social psychology of intergroup relations* (pp. 33–47). Monterey, CA: Brooks/Cole.

Tajfel, H., & Wilkes, A.L. (1963). Salience of attitudes and commitment to extreme judgment in the perception of people. *British Journal of Social and Clinical Psychology, 2*, 40–49.

Triandis, H.C., (Ed.). (1976). *Variations in black and white perceptions of the social environment*. Urbana, IL: University of Illinois Press.

Turner, J.C. (1981). The experimental social psychology of intergroup behavior. In J.C. Turner & H. Giles (Eds.), *Intergroup behavior*. (pp. 66–101). Oxford: Basil Blackwell.

Turner, J.C. (1982). Towards a cognitive redefinition of the social group. In H. Tajfel (Ed.), *Social identity and intergroup relations*. (pp. 15–40). Cambridge/Paris: Cambridge University Press/Maison des Sciences de l'Homme.

Turner, J.C. (1987). *Rediscovering the social group: A self-categorization theory*. New York: Blackwell.

Tversky, A. (1977). Features of similarity. *Psychological Review, 84*, 327–352.

van Leent, J.A.A. (1964). *Sociologie, psychologie, en social psychologie, hun opbouw, ontwickkeling en verhouding uit macro–micro oogpunt*. Arnhem/Zeist: W. de Haan van Loghum Slaterus.

Zemach, M. (1980). *Attitudes of the Jewish majority in Israel toward the Arab minority*. Jerusalem: The Van Leer Foundation.

Part III

Structure and Meaning of Stereotypes and Prejudice

Chapter 6

Stereotypes and Dispositional Judgment

Yaacov Trope

From a cognitive perspective, stereotypes are inevitable consequences of the limitations of human information processing capabilities and the complexity of social reality. As abstract representational structures, stereotypes help us simplify and organize the rich information we have about socially defined categories (Allport, 1954; Hamilton, 1979; Pettigrew, 1979). Moreover, they enable us to make diverse judgments on the basis of readily available and easily processed cues such as gender, age, race, and nationality. The price of these information processing advantages is bias in judgment of individual category members. The mere fact that the actor is a male rather than a female will lead people who hold sex stereotypes to infer more ambition, assertiveness, independence, and the like.

When judging strangers, category membership is the only information at our disposal. Under these circumstances, it would not be surprising if stereotypes bias our judgment. Frequently, however, we have a considerable amount of individuating information about another person in addition to his or her group membership (Ginossar & Trope, 1980, 1987; Bodenhausen & Lichtenstein, 1987; Hamilton, 1979; Higgins & Bargh, 1987; Locksley, Borgida, Brekke, & Hepburn, 1980; Trope & Burnstein, 1975). We may even be able to interact and directly observe how he or she behaves in concrete social situations (Amir, 1976). The observation of such behavioral episodes frequently invokes inferences regarding the other's *personality dispositions* (Heider, 1958; Jones, 1979; Ross, 1977; Winter & Uleman, 1983). These inferences, in turn, guide our reactions to that person across a broad range of circumstances.

An important question for stereotyping research, then, is whether stereotypes will continue to bias our attribution of personality dispositions to a specific group member when we can directly observe his or her *behavior* and the *situation* in which it occurs. If they do, they can produce enduring and profound biases in our reactions to others.

The present treatment of this issue is based on a two-stage model of dispositional judgment (Trope, 1986). In this model, dispositional judgment is conceptualized as an end-product of identification and inferential processing of prior and incoming stimulus information. The initial identification stage leads to the encoding of the input in terms of disposition-relevant categories. For example, the perceiver may categorize the *actor's move* as cooperative or competitive and the *situational norms* as prescribing cooperation or competition. These categorizations serve as input for the inferential stage wherein causal schemas guide the inference of personal dispositions. For example, at this stage the perceiver determines whether the actor's immediate cooperative or competitive behavior is indicative of true dispositional cooperativeness or competitiveness.

The present two-stage model specifies the perceptual and inferential processing of stereotypical and behavioral cues in dispositional judgment. The model leads to two main proposals regarding stereotyping: *First*, individuating behavioral episodes (i.e., the actor's behavior and the situation in which it occurs) does not necessarily attenuate stereotypical biases in dispositional judgment. In fact, individuating behavioral episodes frequently act to perpetuate stereotypical biases. *Second*, the processing of the incoming information at the perceptual stage frequently enables stereotypes to have a greater impact than behavioral episodes on dispositional judgment.

Below, I will first present the two-stage model and then outline its predictions regarding the effects of behavioral episodes and stereotypes on attribution. I will describe research bearing on these predictions and discuss the implications of the findings with respect to stereotyping in the attribution process.

A Two-Stage Model of Dispositional Judgment

The cognitive processes underlying dispositional judgment have attracted a great deal of attention in the attribution literature. Attribution theorists have been particularly interested in modeling people's inferential calculus for weighting and combining behavioral and situational information into judgment about dispositional qualities (Jones & Davis, 1965; Jones & McGillis, 1976; Kelley, 1967, 1972). Over the last two decades, this approach has generated a large amount of research on the inferential processing of behavioral and situational information (see reviews by Kelley & Michela, 1980; Ross & Fletcher, 1985).

Until quite recently (Higgins, Strauman, & Klein, 1985; Ross & Olson, 1981; Trope, 1986), attribution researchers have paid little attention to the encoding and retrieval processes that produce the input for the inferential process. The same has been true in research relating dispositional judgment to stereotypes (see review by Hamilton, 1979). This research has shown that stereotype-congruent behavior (e.g., failure by a woman) is attributed to internal causes, whereas stereotype-incongruent behavior (e.g., success by a women) is attributed to external factors (see Deaux, 1976; Deaux & Emswiller, 1976; Feldman-Summers & Kiesler, 1974; Regan, Strauss, & Fazio, 1974). However, there is little or no theoretical and empirical work on the contribution of perceptual processes to stereotyping. This problem motivated the distinction between perceptual and inferential processes in Trope's (1986) two-stage model. As will be shown below, the model specifies the manner with which perceptual and inferential processes interact to determine dispositional judgment.

The Identification Stage

Figure 6-1 presents a simplified version of the two-stage model. At the identification stage, the incoming stimulus information is identified in terms of disposition-relevant categories. First, behavioral cues are identified in terms of the disposition they overtly express. For example, before making inferences about the speaker's true attitude toward Israel, perceivers may first identify the content of the speech as pro- or anti-Israel. Second, situational cues are identified in terms of the disposition whose expression they elicit. In our example, perceivers may identify the audience addressed by the speaker as expecting a pro- or anti-Israeli speech.

Third, in addition to behavioral and situational cues, which constitute the immediate *behavioral episode*, the perceiver may have prior information about the actor. This information frequently includes group membership cues (stereotypical cues). At the identification stage, the stereotypical cues lead to the classification of the actor into a social group and to the invocation of the associated stereotypical categorizations. For example, an Arab accent or dress may invoke the Arab stereotype and the associated belief that the speaker is anti-Israeli.

As shown in Figure 6-1, behavioral, situational, and stereotypical categorizations depend, in part, on the information contained in the corresponding cues. However, like any stimulus categorization, behavioral and situational categorization may also depend on the *context* (Bruner, 1957; Higgins & King, 1981; Marcel, 1980; Zanna & Hamilton, 1977; Wyer & Srull, 1981). As each kind of cue acquires meaning, it may serve as a source of contextual expectancies regarding the categorization of the other incoming cues.

First, situational and stereotypical cues may serve as context affecting the categorization of behavioral cues. A speaker wearing Arab clothes (stereotypical cues) and addressing a group also wearing Arab clothes (situational cues) will be expected to take an anti-Israeli stand (behavioral categorization). Second, behavioral cues may serve as contextual information affecting the categorization of situational and stereotypical cues. For example, anti-Israeli statements (behavioral cues) will bias the perceiver in favor of identifying the audience as anti-Israeli (situational categorization) and in favor of identifying Arabs as anti-Israeli (stereotypical categorization).

It is assumed that the magnitude of these contextual effects depends on the ambiguity of the context, the ambiguity of the stimulus, the match between the context and the stimulus, and the order in which they are processed (Higgins & Stangor, 1988). An unambiguous context, one that is strongly associated with one and only one category, generates strong expectancies regarding the categorization of the stimulus. These expectancies will actually have an effect if (a) the context appears first, (b) the stimulus is ambiguous, that is, strongly associated with different categories, and (c) one of the stimulus alternative categorizations matches the contextually invoked category.

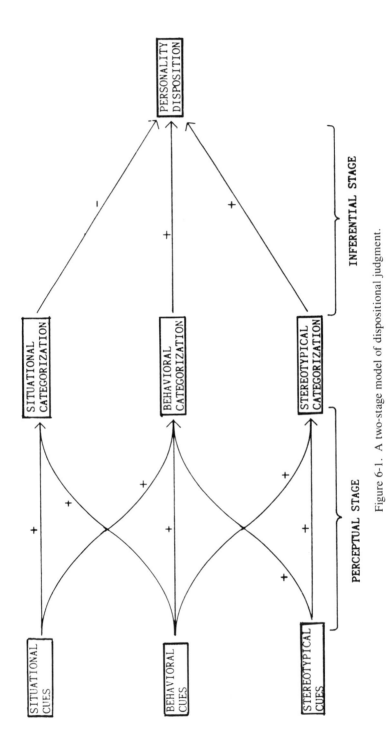

Figure 6-1. A two-stage model of dispositional judgment.

In the present case, stereotypical and situational cues will affect behavioral categorization to the extent that the behavioral cues are associated with more than one category and the stereotypical and situational cues unambiguously invoke one of these categories. For example, a smile will be perceived as a sympathetic reaction in the context of a friendly situation, but as a sarcastic reaction in the context of an unfriendly situation (Frijda, 1969). The same should hold true for the behavior's contextual effect on stereotypical and situational categorizations. That is, the behavior's contextual effects should be maximized when the behavioral cues are unambiguous and the situational and stereotypical cues are ambiguous.

Figure 6-1 assumes that stereotypical and situational cues do not produce contextual effects on each other. This is not to say that such contextual effects never occur. It is merely argued that these contextual effects are small in comparison to those relating situational and stereotypical cues, on one hand, and behavioral cues on the other hand. The assumption is that perceivers ordinarily expect the actor's behavior to be consistent with immediate situational demands and with the characteristics of the actor's social group. They presumably expect much less consistency between the immediate situation in which the actor happens to be and the characteristics of his or her social group.

For example, given a situational provocation or instruction to be aggressive, perceivers will expect the actor to respond aggressively, but *not* necessarily to belong to an aggressive group. Thus, the fact that a person with an American accent was provoked or instructed to be aggressive does not necessarily lead to the identification of Americans as aggressive. Neither does a stereotypical belief that the actor is aggressive lead to the identification of a given immediate situation as demanding aggressive behavior. Perceivers' stereotypical belief that an Arab person is aggressive will not necessarily lead them to identify the situation as provoking or justifying aggression. In sum, it seems reasonable to assume that the contextual effects relating stereotypes and situational inducements are small in comparison to the other contextual effects. For the sake of simplicity, Figure 6-1 makes the simplifying assumption that the stereotype–situation contextual effects are negligible.

The Inferential Stage

The model assumes that the results of the identification stage serve as input for the inferential stage. As shown in the right-hand side of Figure 6-1, the perceiver uses the behavioral, situational, and stereotypical categorizations to draw inferences regarding the actor's underlying dispositions. The inference is presumably guided by people's beliefs regarding the causes of behavior (Kelley, 1972). Specifically, given that both situational inducements and the actor's personal dispositions are believed to affect behavior, dispositional inference requires *subtraction* of the contribution of situational inducements from the disposition implied by the behavior itself.

By the subtractive rule, the actor will be attributed a given disposition to the extent that the actor is perceived to display the corresponding behavior and to the extent that the behavior is inhibited or at least not facilitated by situational inducements. For example, the actor will be attributed dispositional anger to the extent that he or she is perceived to react angrily and there is little or no provocation. Similarly, when congruent with group norms, cooperative behavior provides little information regarding the actor's dispositional cooperativeness, but when incongruent with group norms, the same cooperative behavior allows strong inferences regarding dispositional cooperativeness. In line with these assumptions, the right hand side of Figure 6-1 indicates that dispositional attribution is positively related to perception of the corresponding behavior and negatively related to the perceived contribution of situational inducements.

Note that the subtractive rule is used here to refer both to Kelley's (1972) *discounting* and *augmentation* principles. The subtraction of situational inducements that *facilitate* the observed behavior results in discounting, namely, the attenuation of behavior–correspondent dispositional attribution; in contrast, the subtraction of situational inducements that *inhibit* the observed behavior results in augmentation.

Finally, the model assumes that the immediate behavioral and situational categorizations are integrated with prior categorizations. Social judgment research suggests that when the immediate evidence is less than perfectly diagnostic, prior categorizations affect judgment about others' dispositional characteristics (Ajzen & Fishbein, 1975; Anderson, 1974; Darley & Fazio, 1980; Ginossar & Trope, 1980, 1987; Miller & Turnbull, 1986). The same inferential rule should apply to the utilization of prior stereotypical categorizations (see Figure 6-1). The perceiver is more likely to attribute the actor's behavior to any given ability, attitude, or personality trait to the extent that it is congruent with the actor's stereotypical categorization (see Deaux, 1976; Deaux & Emswiller, 1974; Hamilton, 1979; Jussim, 1986; Regan et al., 1974; Ruble & Stangor, 1987; Wyer & Martin, 1986).

The following three sections derive the model's predictions regarding the effect of situational, behavioral, and stereotypical cues on dispositional attribution. It will be shown that identification stage processes frequently attenuate the effect of situational and behavioral cues but magnify the effect of stereotypical cues.

The Effect of Situational Cues on Dispositional Attribution

Figure 6-1 suggests that the subtraction of situational inducements at the inferential stage is only one of the several determinants of the effect of situational cues on attribution. Processes operating at the identification stage may attenuate and even reverse subtraction. First, any ambiguity in the identification of situational cues will attenuate their subtractive effect. Second, and more important, Figure 6-1 suggests that situational inducements are used both to identify the disposition the actor expresses (behavior identification) and to infer the disposition he or she truly possesses (dispositional inference). At identification, the situation serves as context that biases the identification of behavior as expressing the very disposition from which the situation is subsequently subtracted. The reliance on this context-produced behavior identification *as if* it were independent evidence for the corresponding disposition counteracts subtractive effects of the situation. For example, the perceiver may be fully aware that the actor was provoked and may fully subtract the contribution of the provocation when inferring the actor's dispositional anger. However, a provocative situation (compared to a nonprovocative situation) can bias perceivers in favor of identifying the actor's reaction as angry, perhaps more angry than justified by the provocation. If provocation makes the actor appear extremely angry, he or she will be attributed no less and even more dispositional anger when provoked than when not provoked.

Relevant Research

In the two-stage model, then, weak subtractive effects and even additive effects of situational inducements are predictable outcomes of the joint operation of identification and inferential processes. Indeed, despite the apparent simplicity of the subtractive rule, empirical research has questioned its actual utilization by perceivers. Specifically, extensive research initiated by Jones and his colleagues has found that perceivers show little or no sensitivity to the magnitude of situational inducements and that they are willing to attribute behavior– correspondent dispositions to actors who are constrained by strong situational demands (Gilbert & Jones, 1986; Jones, 1979; Jones & Harris, 1967; Jones, Worchel, Goethals, & Grumet, 1971; Miller, 1976; Nisbett & Borgida, 1975; Quattrone, 1982; Snyder & Jones, 1974). Several studies even reported additive reversals of the subtractive rule, that is, stronger dispositional attributions for situationally congruent than for situationally incongruent behavior (Baldwin & Baldwin, 1970; Boggiano & Main, 1986; Costanzo, Grumet, & Brehm, 1974; Karniol & Ross, 1976, 1979; Kruglanski, 1970; Ross & Olson, 1981; Snyder, 1974; Snyder & Frankel, 1976).

These findings were interpreted as reflecting a "failure to discount" – a general inferential tendency to underutilize information about situational inducements when provided with behavioral evidence. It has been argued that perceivers pay little attention to situational inducements and give them little weight when drawing inferences from behavior (Jones, 1979). In contrast, the present two-stage model would suggest that even if fully subtracted at the inferential stage, situational inducements may have little or no effect on judgment because of identification stage processes. Behavioral cues are frequently ambiguous, and the resulting contextual effect of the situation may mask the situational subtraction in dispositional judgment.

A series of studies by Trope, Cohen, and Maoz (1988) directly tested the model's predictions regarding the effect of behavioral ambiguity on the situation's contextual and subtractive effects. The experiments presented an actor's ambiguous or unambiguous reactions to various unambiguous situational inducements. In one of the experiments, subjects first read "objective" information about a target person's likeability (situational cues) and then heard an actor make an evaluative report (behavioral cues) about the target person. After a short delay, we measured subjects' memory-based identifications of the meaning of the actor's report (behavior categorization) and their attribution of the report to the actor's dispositional severity or leniency toward people in general. The initial information about the target unambiguously indicated that the target is either a likeable or a unlikeable person and the actor's report was either unambiguous (either favorable or unfavorable) or ambiguous.

These manipulations were made possible by using information pertaining to cheerfulness–frivolty. Like other evaluatively different but descriptively similar trait pairs, cheerfulness and frivolty have opposite evaluative meanings but refer to various common behavioral characteristics (see Peabody, 1967). The common characteristics served as ambiguous information and the distinctive characteristics served as unambiguous information. Specifically, subjects heard an actor reporting either unambiguous cheerful characteristics, unambiguous frivolous characteristics, or ambiguous cheerful-frivolous characteristics (behavioral cues) about a target person who was initially described as having either unambiguous cheerful or unambiguous frivolous characteristics (situational cues).

Our identification data showed that the contextual effect of the target's likeability on the perception of the unambiguous favorable and unfavorable reports was negligible. The former report was seen as very positive (cheerful) and the latter as very negative (frivolous) regardless of the likeability of the target. In contrast, the likeability of the target strongly affected the identification of the ambiguous report. Subjects identified this report as positive or negative depending on whether the target was assumed to be likeable or unlikeable.

Thus, consistent with the model identification stage predictions, the data showed that the target person's likeability disambiguated the retrieved meaning of the actor's report to the extent that the report was initially ambiguous. Theoretically, this contextual effect of the target's likeability should counteract its subtraction at the inferential level. Indeed, our dispositional attribution data showed subtractive effects on the attribution of the unambiguous positive and negative reports, but not on the attribution of the ambiguous report. Specifically, the same unambiguous, positive, or negative report was attributed to greater dispositional leniency when it referred to a target person who was known to be unlikeable than when it referred to a target person who was known to be likeable. In contrast, the attribution of the ambiguous report was unaffected by the target's likeability: Subjects attributed to the actor the same amount of dispositional leniency regardless of whether the target person was known to be likeable or unlikeable.

Conclusions

The results of the Trope, Cohen, and Maoz et al.'s experiment suggest that identification stage processes act to attenuate the effect of situational inducements on dispositional attribution. Other studies (Trope, 1986; Trope, Cohen, & Giladi, 1989) used different behavioral cues (e.g., emotional verbal and nonverbal reactions) and different situational inducements (e.g., role requirements). The results of these studies led to the same conclusion: Perceivers use the situation to identify what the actor does. But then they use this identification as new evidence for the corresponding disposition. The contextual effect of the situation on the identification of ambiguous behavior thus undermines the situation's own effect on dispositional judgment. This conclusion has important implications for real-life situations. Since behavioral cues are rarely unambiguous, weak effects of the situation should be the rule rather than the exception.

Let us turn now to the predictions of the model regarding the effect of behavioral cues on dispositional judgment.

The Effect of Behavioral Cues on Dispositional Judgment

Figure 6-1 suggests that behavioral cues affect dispositional judgment through their own identification and indirectly through their contextual effects on situational and stereotypical categorization. Whereas through their own identification, behavioral cues have a positive effect on dispositional judgment, through their contextual effect on situational categorization, behavioral cues have a negative effect on dispositional judgment. Specifically, in context, situational cues will be identified as facilitating behavior. When subsequently subtracted at the inferential stage, this situation identification will attenuate dispositional judgment. For example, on one hand, a hug, compared to a mere handshake, is more likely to be identified as friendly behavior. On the other hand, the hug is more likely to bias the identification of the situation as one demanding friendliness. The subtraction of such situational demand, in turn, will attenuate judgment of dispositional friendliness. In general, if the perception of the situation covaries with the behavior, variation in the latter should have a diminished impact on dispositional judgment.

Whereas, through their contextual effect on situational categorization, behavioral cues have a negative effect on dispositional judgment, through their contextual effect on stereotypical categorization, behavioral cues have a positive effect on dispositional judgment. Specifically, the actor's immediate behavior may bias the identification of the actor's group membership and the activation of specific stereotypical beliefs. The stereotypical categorizations of the actor will thus shift in a behavior-congruent direction and add to the behavior's own effect on judgment.

Frequently, stereotypes are ambiguous with respect to specific dispositions. For example, policemen can be seen as dominant or submissive, actors as introverted or extroverted, and religious people as politically liberal or conservative. A policeman's immediate dominant behavior will activate the belief that policemen are generally dominant, whereas a submissive response will activate the belief that they are generally submissive. Such shifts in stereotypical categorization will augment the effect of the policeman's immediate submissive or dominant act on judgment of the correspondent dispositions.

In sum, one contextual effect of behavioral cues (on situational categorization) decreases their effect on dispositional judgment, whereas the other contextual effect of behavioral cues (on stereotypical categorization) increases their effect on dispositional judgment. Whether the net effect of these identification stage processes will be to increase or decrease the effect of behavioral cues on judgment primarily depend on the ambiguity of situational and stereotypical cues. Situational ambiguity will decrease the effect of behavioral cues on dispositional attribution, whereas stereotypical ambiguity will increase this effect of behavioral cues.

Relevant Research

I am not aware of any published research on the postulated contextual effect of
behavioral cues on stereotypical categorization. There is some indirectly relevant
research on the effect of behavioral cues on the identification of prior information.
Specifically, Ross and his colleagues have found that the recall of past behaviors and
attitudes are biased towards consistency with the immediate behavior (see Ross,
McFarland, Conway, & Zanna, 1983; Ross, McFarland, & Fletcher, 1981; Ross &
Shulman, 1973). Ajzen, Dalto, and Blyth's (1979) study related these contextual
effects to attribution. These authors found that the effect of an essay on attitude
attribution was greater when ambiguous biographical evidence about the essayist
was available than when such evidence was unavailable.

A recent study by Trope and Cohen (in press) tested the model's predictions
regarding the contextual effect of behavioral cues on situational identification and
on dispositional judgment. Subjects were presented with an actor's emotional reactions to emotion-eliciting situations. The reactions were always unambiguous, but
the emotions they conveyed and the ambiguity of the situation with respect to these
emotions were manipulated. For example, subjects read a description of an unambiguous happy reaction (e.g., "I smiled and felt good about myself") or an unambiguous angry reaction (e.g., "I felt I was heating up and losing my patience") to an
unambiguous happy situation (e.g., "The professor announced in class that my paper
was the best") or to an ambiguous happy/anger-provoking situation (e.g., "As in
many previous lessons, the biblical studies teacher asked me to read my answer
before starting the discussion of the question"). Based on this information, subjects
were asked either to identify the emotions the situation could elicit or to judge the
actor's emotional dispositions.

Consistent with the model, we found that the perception of the emotional meaning of the ambiguous situational cues was strongly affected by the actor's reactions.
The same situational cues were perceived as anger-provoking in the context of an
angry reaction and as happy in the context of a happy reaction. Although the perception of the unambiguous situations was also affected by the actor's reaction, the
effect was predictably much smaller: An anger-provoking situation was perceived as
such when the actor reacted angrily as well as when he or she reacted happily. These
results replicated across the different ambiguous and unambiguous situational cues
we used. In each case, situational ambiguity increased the contextual effect of the
actor's reactions on the perception of the situational cues.

According to the two-stage model, the results of the identification stage serve as
input for the inferential stage. This latter stage leads to the attribution of a disposition to the extent that the actor displays the corresponding behavior, and the
behavior is incongruent with situational inducements (Kelley, 1972). By this logic,
the attribution of emotional dispositions should be positively related to the actor's
reactions to any given situation. For example, greater dispositional happiness
should be attributed to an actor who expresses happiness than to an actor who
expresses unhappiness. However, if the perception of the emotion elicited by the
situational cues covaries with the reaction, the effect of the reactions on disposi-

tional attribution may be offset by the opposite subtractive effect of the situation (see Figure 6-1). Hence, by increasing the contextual effect of the reaction on the perception of the situational cues, situational ambiguity should attenuate the effect of the actor's reactions on dispositional attribution.

Our study confirmed this prediction with remarkable consistency. The actor's reactions to ambiguous situational cues always produced small effects on dispositional attribution. For example, learning about one's pregnancy was perceived as a happy situation when the pregnant woman reacted happily and as a frightening situation when she reacted fearfully. Consequently, the reactions had little effect on the attribution of dispositional happiness or fear. Neither the happy nor the fearful reaction was confidently attributed to the corresponding emotional dispositions.

In contrast, because the perception of the unambiguous situational cues was unaffected by the actor's reactions, the latter could produce stronger effects on dispositional attribution. For example, a request for directions in campus was perceived as a neutral situation regardless of whether the actor reacted with fear or with happiness. Consequently, both the fearful reaction and the happy reaction led to relatively strong corresponding dispositional attributions.

Conclusions

Trope and Cohen's (in press) findings show that identification stage processes may weaken the effect of immediate behavioral evidence on dispositional judgment. Together with the research evidence reviewed in the previous section, Trope and Cohen's data suggest that just as behavioral ambiguity weakens the effect of situational cues on dispositional judgment, so does situational ambiguity weaken the effect of behavioral cues on dispositional attribution. The important implication of these findings is that to the extent that behavioral cues affect the perception of situational cues, behavioral cues are unlikely to change our stereotypical beliefs about the actor.

The Perceptual and Inferential Effects of Stereotypes

We can now turn to the model's predictions regarding the role of stereotypical cues in dispositional judgment. Figure 6-1 indicates that stereotypical cues can affect dispositional judgment directly via their own categorization and indirectly via their contextual effect on behavior categorization. Perceivers presumably use their stereotypes to identify how the actor behaves, but then rely on these stereotype-produced identifications *as if* they constitute independent behavioral evidence for the corresponding disposition. As a result, the contextual effect of stereotypes may enhance stereotypical attributions.

The enhancement depends on the ambiguity of the stereotype, the ambiguity of the immediate behavior cues, the match between the two, and the order in which they are processed. The matching requirement is important. If the stereotype is irrelevant to the possible categorization of the behavior, the latter will be unaffected by the stereotype. For example, if the stereotype of university professors pertains to the intellectual sphere, it is unlikely to affect the categorization of a professor's emotional behavior.

Assuming that the stereotype and the behavior can match, the contextual effect of stereotypes is at its maximum if (1) the stereotype is unambiguous (2) it is presented first, and (3) the behavioral cues are ambiguous. Under these circumstances, stereotypes have the strongest impact on dispositional attribution. Not only will the stereotypes directly affect dispositional attribution, but they will bias perceivers in favor of identifying the available behavioral evidence as *independently* justifying such attribution.

For example, in his interaction with a Palestinian, an Israeli Jew may encounter frequent silences by the Palestinian. From the various meanings of such silences (e.g., shyness, unfamiliarity with the language, etc.), the Israeli may be biased in favor of one possibility, namely, the categorization of the silence as conveying hostility. The Israeli's contact with a particular Palestinian will thus only act to reinforce the Israeli's initial tendency to attribute hostility to the Palestinian. In general, the present two-stage model suggests that direct behavior observations may strengthen rather than weaken our initial stereotypic beliefs about the actor (see Duncan, 1976; Jussim, 1986; Lord et al, 1979; Bodenhausen & Lichtenstein, 1987).

Relevant Research

Darley and Gross (1983) provide the most direct evidence regarding the proposition that the opportunity to observe the actor's behavior tends to augment rather than to attenuate stereotyping in dispositional attribution. Darley and Gross presented their subjects with background socioeconomic information about fourth-grade children. The information indicated that the child was either from a low or from a high socioeconomic background. One group of subjects judged the child after seeing him perform on achievement test problems. The performance was designed to be ambiguous with respect to the child's ability. Another group of subjects judged the child without seeing his performance.

Darley and Gross found that in the absence of performance information, the child's socioeconomic background had little or no effect on the attribution of ability to the child. It was the group of subjects who observed the child that was biased by his/her socioeconomic status. These subjects attributed the same performance to a much higher level of ability when the child came from a high socioeconomic class than when he or she came from a low socioeconomic class.

This finding is consistent with the two-stage model. In the absence of immediate performance information, stereotypes could have only a direct effect on dispositional attribution (see Figure 6-1). When performance information was provided, its perception may have been biased by subjects' stereotypes regarding socioeconomic status, so that the performance of the high status children appeared superior to that of low status children. Such perceived performance differences may have added to subjects' initial stereotypic beliefs about the children and, thus, may have indirectly magnified the effect of the stereotypes on ability attribution.

However, Darley and Gross' (1983) study, like other studies relating stereotypes to dispositional attribution (Deaux, 1976; Deaux & Emswiller, 1976; Feldman-Summers & Kiesler, 1974; Regan, Strauss, & Fazio, 1974), has not assessed the separate and joint contribution of perceptual and inferential processes to stereotyping. This research does not tell whether and to what extent is the bias in dispositional attribution due to the effect of stereotypes on the perception of behavior, on the inference from behavior, or on both. What is needed is research that will trace the effect of stereotypes at the identification and inferential stages. For example, by manipulating the ambiguity of stereotype and behavioral cues, it should be possible to control the magnitude of the contextual effect of stereotypes. Measurement of behavior and stereotype categorizations and measurement of dispositional attribution would then allow assessment of the contribution of identification and inferential factors to stereotyping.

Conclusions

We started with the assumption that dispositional judgment obeys a logical inference rule. This rule requires the subtraction of the contribution of situational inducement from the disposition implied by the behavior itself and the integration of the result with one's prior knowledge about the individual, including his group membership. It is even possible that the weight of the immediate behavioral episode is no smaller or actually greater than the weight of group membership stereotypes.

Stereotyping may nevertheless dominate dispositional judgment because of identification-stage processes. Specifically, our research shows that the contextual effect of the situation on behavior categorization attenuates the situation's effect on dispositional judgment, just as the contextual effect of behavioral cues on situational categorization attenuates the effect of behavior on dispositional judgment (Trope, 1986; Trope & Cohen, in press; Trope, Cohen, & Maoz, 1988). In contrast, the contextual effect of stereotypes can only magnify their effect on dispositional judgment (see Darley & Gross, 1983; Duncan, 1976; Lord et al., 1979). Consequently, stereotypes may generally be more influential than the immediate behavior episode in determining dispositional attribution.

Moreover, as noted earlier, to the extent that the behavior evidence is ambiguous, its provision may augment rather than attenuate stereotyping. This may frequently hold for members of the outgroup. The relative unfamiliarity with the meaning of their behavior may render their behavior ambiguous and, therefore, susceptible to contextual effects of stereotypes.

The two-stage model assumption that it is the identification process that promotes stereotyping is important. Sometimes we may attempt to actively discount our stereotypic beliefs from our judgments about a particular actor. It is doubtful whether the inferential process is sufficiently flexible to allow such discounting (see Anderson, 1983; Ross, Lepper, & Hubbard, 1975; Fischhoff, 1975; Fischhoff & Beyth, 1982). However, even if successful at the inferential stage, discounting may fail at the identification stage. Specifically, if consciously disregarded, stereotypes may cease to directly affect attribution. However, because the identification process is largely unconscious and automatic, stereotypes may still bias behavior identification. The subsequent reliance on these identifications *as if* they were independent data guarantees that stereotypes will continue to bias attribution. Stereotyping may thus persist despite conscious endeavors to be impartial toward specific group members.

Acknowledgments. Preparation of this manuscript was supported by a Binational US-Israel Fund grant #84-00160.

References

Ajzen, Dalto, C.A., & Blyth, D.P. (1979). Consistency and bias in the attribution of attitudes. *Journal of Personality and Social Psychology, 37*, 1871–1876.

Ajzen, I., & Fishbein, M. (1975). A Bayesian analysis of the attribution process. *Psychological Bulletin, 82*, 267–277.

Allport, G.W. (1954). *The nature of prejudice.* Reading, MA: Addison-Wesley.

Amir, Y. (1976). The role of intergroup contact in change of prejudice and ethnic relations. In P.A. Katz (Ed.), *Toward the elimination of racism.* (pp. 125–152). New York: Pergamon Press.

Anderson, C.A. (1983). Abstract and concrete data in the perseverance of social theories: When weak data lead to unshakable beliefs. *Journal of Personality and Social Psychology, 19*, 93–108.

Anderson, N. (1974). Cognitive algebra: Integration theory applied to social attribution. In L. Berkowitz (Ed.), *Advances in Experimental Social Psychology* (Vol. 7) (pp. 2–102). New York: Academic Press.

Baldwin, C.P. & Baldwin, A.L. (1970). Children's judgments of kindness. *Child Development, 41*, 29–47.

Bodenhausen, G.V. & Lichtenstein, M. (1987). Social stereotypes and information–processing strategies: The impact of task complexity. *Journal of Personality & Social Psychology, 52*, 871–880.

Boggiano, A.K., & Main, D.S. (1986). Enhancing children's interest in activities used as rewards: The bonus effect. *Journal of Personality and Social Psychology, 51*, 1116–1126.

Bruner, J.S. (1957). On perceptual readiness. *Psychological Review, 64*, 123–152.

Costanzo, P.R., Grumet, J.G. & Brehm, S.S. (1974). The effects of choice and source of constraint on children's attributions of preference. *Journal of Experimental Social Psychology, 10*, 352–364.

Darley, J.M., & Fazio, R.H. (1980). Expectancy confirmation processes arising in the social interaction sequence. *American Psychologist, 35*, 867–881.

Darley, J.M., & Gross, P.H. (1983). A hypothesis-confirming bias in labeling effects. *Journal of Personality and Social Psychology, 44*, 20–33.

Deaux, K. (1976). Sex: A perspective on the attribution process. In J.H. Harvey, W.J. Ickes, & R.F. Kidd (Eds.), *New directions in attribution research* (Vol. 1) (pp. 335–352). Hillsdale, NJ: Erlbaum.

Deaux, K., & Emswiller, T. (1974). Explanations of successful performance on sex-linked tasks: What is skill for the male is luck for the female. *Journal of Personality and Social Psychology, 29*, 80–85.

Duncan, B.L. (1976). Differential social perception and attribution of intergroup violence: Testing the lower limits of stereotyping of blacks. *Journal of Personality and Social Psychology, 34*, 590–598.

Feldman-Summers, S., & Kiesler, S.B. (1974). Those who are number two try harder: The effect of sex on attribution of causality. *Journal of Personality and Social Psychology, 30*, 846–854.

Fischhoff, B. (1975). Hindsight ≠ foresight: The effect of outcome knowledge on judgment under uncertainty. *Journal of Experimental Psychology: Human Perception and Performance, 1*, 288–299.

Fischhoff, B., & Beyth, R. (1982). "I knew it would happen"– Remembering probabilities of once–future things. *Organizational Behavior and Human Performance, 13*, 1–13.

Frijda, N.H. (1969). Recognition of emotion. In L. Berkowitz (Ed.), *Advances in experimental social psychology*, (Vol. 4) (pp. 167–223). New York: Academic Press.

Gilbert, D.T., & Jones, E.E. (1986). Perceiver induced constraint: Interpretations of self-generated reality. *Journal of Personality and Social Psychology, 50*, 269–280.

Ginossar, Z., & Trope,Y. (1980) The effect of base-rates and individuating information on judgment about another person. *Journal of Experimental Social Psychology, 16*, 228–242.

Ginossar, Z., & Trope, Y. (1987). Problem solving in judgment under uncertainty. *Journal of Personality and Social Psychology, 52*, 464–476.

Hamilton, D.L. (1979). A cognitive-attributional analysis of stereotyping. In L. Berkowitz (Ed.), *Advances in experimental social psychology* (Vol. 12) (pp. 53–84). New York: Academic Press.

Heider, F. (1958). *The social psychology of interpersonal relations*. New York: Wiley.

Higgins, E.T., & Bargh, J.A. (1987). Social cognition and social perception. *Annual Review of Psychology, 38*, 369–425.

Higgins, E.T., & King, G. (1981). Accessibility of social constructs: Information-processing consequences of individual and contextual variability. In N. Cantor & J.F. Kihlstrom (Eds.), *Personality, cognition and social interaction* (pp. 69–121). Hillsdale, NJ: Erlbaum.

Higgins, E.T., Rholes, W.S., & Jones, C.R. (1977). Category accessibility and impression formation. *Journal of Experimental Social Psychology, 13*, 141–154.

Higgins, E.T., & Stangor, C. (1988). Context-driven social judgment and memory: When "behavior engulfs the field" in reconstructive memory. In D. Bar-Tal & A. Kruglanski (Eds.), *Social psychology of knowledge* (pp. 200–228). Cambridge, England: Cambridge University Press.

Higgins, E.T., Strauman, T., & Klein, R. (1985). Standards and the process of self-evaluation: Multiple affects from multiple stages. In R.M. Sorrentino & E.T. Higgins (Eds.), *Motivation and cognition: Foundations of social behavior* (pp. 83–105). New York: Guilford Press.

Jones, E.E. (1979). The rocky road from acts to dispositions. *American Psychologist, 34*, 107–117.

Jones, E.E., & Davis, K.E. (1965). From acts of dispositions: The attribution process in person perception. In L. Berkowitz (Ed.), *Advances in experimental social psychology* (Vol. 2) (pp. 220–265). New York: Academic Press.

Jones, E.E., & Harris, V.A. (1967). The attribution of attitudes. *Journal of Experimental Social Psychology, 3*, 1–24.

Jones, E.E., & McGillis, P. (1976). Correspondent inference and the attribution cube: A comparative appraisal. In J.W. Harvey, W.J. Ickes, & R.F. Kidd (Eds.), *New directions in attribution research* (Vol. 1) (pp. 389–420). Hillsdale, NJ: Erlbaum.

Jones, E.E., Worchel, S., Goethals, G.R., & Grumet, J.F. (1971). Prior expectancy and behavioral extremity as determinants of attitude attribution. *Journal of Experimental Psychology, 7*, 59–80.

Jussim, L. (1986). Self-fulfilling prophesies: A theoretical and integrative review. *Psychological Review, 93*, 429–445.

Karniol, R., & Ross, M. (1976). The development of causal attribution in social perception. *Journal of Personality and Social Psychology, 34*, 455–464.

Karniol, R., & Ross, M. (1979). Children's use of causal attribution schemas and the inferences of manipulative intent. *Child Development, 50*, 463–468.

Kelley, H.H. (1967). Attribution theory in social psychology. In D. Levine (Ed.), *Nebraska symposium of motivation* (Vol. 15) (pp. 192–241). Lincoln, NE: University of Nebraska Press.

Kelley, H.H. (1972). Causal schemata and the attribution process. In E.E. Jones, D.E. Kanouse, H.H. Kelley, R.E. Nisbett, S. Valins, & B. Weiner (Eds.), *Attribution: Perceiving the causes of behavior* (pp. 151–174). Morristown, NJ: General Learning Press.

Kelley, H.H., & Michela, J.L. (1980). Attribution theory and research. *Annual Review of Psychology, 31*, 457–501.

Kruglanski, A.W. (1970). Attributing trustworthiness in supervisors' worker relations. *Journal of Experimental Social Psychology, 6*, 214–232.

Locksley, A., Borgida, E., Brekke, N., & Hepburn, C. (1980). Sex stereotypes and social judgment. *Journal of Personality and Social Psychology, 39*, 821–831.

Lord, C.G., Ross, L., & Lepper, M.R. (1979). Biased assimilation and attitude polarization: The effect of prior theories on subsequently considered evidence. *Journal of Personality and Social Psychology, 37*, 2098–2109.

Marcel, I. (1980). Conscious and preconscious recognition of polysemous words: Locating the selective effects of prior verbal context. In R.S. Nickerson (Ed.), *Attention and performance*, (Vol. 8) (pp. 435–457). Hillsdale, NJ: Erlbaum.

Miller, A.G. (1976). Constraint and target effects in attribution of attitudes. *Journal of Experimental Social Psychology, 12*, 325–339.

Miller, D.T., & Turnbull, W. (1986). Expectancies and interpersonal processes. *Annual Review of Psychology, 37*, 233–256.

Nisbett, R.E., & Borgida, E. (1975). Attribution and the psychology of prediction. *Journal of Personality and Social Psychology, 32*, 932–943.

Peabody. (1967). Trait inferences: Evaluative and descriptive aspects. *Journal of Personality and Social Psychology Monographs, 7*(4, pt. 2).

Pettigrew, T.F. (1979). The ultimate attribution error. *Personality and Social Psychology Bulletin, 5*, 461–476.

Quattrone, G.A. (1982). Overattribution and unit formation: When behavior engulfs the person. *Journal of Personality and Social Psychology, 42*, 593–607.

Regan, D.T., Strauss, E., & Fazio, R. (1974). Liking and the attribution process. *Journal of Experimental Social Psychology, 10*, 385–397.

Ross, L. (1977). The intuitive psychologist and his shortcomings: Distortion in the attribution process. In L. Berkowitz (Ed.), *Advances in experimental social psychology*, (Vol. 10) (pp. 174–221). New York: Academic Press.

Ross, L., Lepper, M.R., & Hubbard, M. (1975). Perseverance in self-perception and social perception: Biased attribution processes in the debriefing paradigm. *Journal of Personality and Social Psychology, 32*, 880–892.

Ross, M., & Fletcher, G. (1985). Attribution and social perception. In G. Lindzey & E. Aronson (Eds.), *Handbook of social psychology* (3rd ed.). (pp. 73–122). Reading, MA: Addison-Wesley.

Ross, M., & McFarland, C., Conway, M., & Zanna, M.P. (1983). The reciprocal relation between attitudes and behavior recall: Committing people to newly formed attitudes. *Journal of Personality and Social Psychology, 45*, 257–267.

Ross, M., McFarland, C., & Fletcher, G. (1981). The effect of attitudes on the recall of personal histories. *Journal of Personality and Social Psychology, 40*, 627–634.

Ross, M., & Olson, J.M. (1981). An expectancy-attribution model of the effects of placebos. *Psychological Review, 88*, 408–437.

Ross, M., & Shulman, R.F.(1973). Increasing the salience of initial attitudes: Dissonance versus self-perception theory. *Journal of Personality and Social Psychology, 28*, 138–144.

Ruble, D.N., & Stangor, C. (1987). Stalking the illusive schema: Insights from developmental and social psychological analyses of gender schemas. *Social Cognition, 4*, 227–261.

Snyder, M.L. (1974). The field engulfing behavior: An investigation of the attributing emotional states and dispositions (Doctoral dissertation. Duke University, 1974). *Dissertational Abstracts International, 34*, 6259B–6260B.

Snyder, M.L., & Frankel, A. (1976). Observer bias: A stringent test of behavior engulfing the field. *Journal of Personality and Social Psychology, 34*, 857–864.

Snyder, M.I., & Jones, E.E. (1974). Attitude attribution when behavior is constrained. *Journal of Experimental Social Psychology, 10,* 585–600.

Trope, Y. (1986). Identification and inferential processes in dispositional attribution. *Psychological Review, 93,* 239–257.

Trope, Y., & Cohen, O. (in press). Perceptual and inferential determinants of behavior-correspondent dispositional judgment. *Journal of Experimental Social Psychology.*

Trope, Y., Cohen, O., & Giladi, O. (1989). *Perceptual and inferential mediators of order effects in dispositional judgment.* Unpublished manuscript. Hebrew University, Jerusalem, Israel.

Trope, Y., Cohen, O., & Maoz, I. (1988). The perceptual and inferential effects of situational inducements on dispositional attribution. *Journal of Personality and Social Psychology, 55,* 165–177.

Winter, L., & Uleman, J.S. (1983). When are social judgments made? Evidence for the spontaneousness of trait inferences. *Journal of Personality & Social Psychology, 49,* 904–917.

Wyer, R.S., & Martin, L.L. (1986). Person memory: The role of traits, group stereotypes and specific behaviors in the cognitive representation of persons. *Journal of Personality & Social Psychology, 50,* 661–675.

Wyer, R.S., & Srull, T.K. (1981). Category accessibility: Some theoretical and empirical issues concerning the processing of social stimulus information. In E.T. Higgins, C.P. Herman, M.P. Zanna (Eds.), *Social cognition: The Ontario symposium* (pp. 161–197). Hillsdale, NJ: Erlbaum.

Zanna, M.P., & Hamilton, D.L. (1977). Further evidence for meaning change in impression formation. *Journal of Experimental Social Psychology, 13,* 224–238.

Chapter 7

Values, Stereotypes, and Intergroup Antagonism

Shalom H. Schwartz and Naomi Struch

Introduction

How can apparently civilized individuals behave compassionately toward members of their own group but cruelly toward members of outgroups? Social psychological explanations suggest that antagonistic intergroup behavior is motivated by realistic intergroup conflict (Sherif & Sherif, 1953) and by gains for one's social identity (Tajfel, 1981). An important channel through which these motivations are held to work is by promoting the growth of stereotypes that denigrate outgroups.

Negative stereotypes foster antagonism by generating expectations of undesirable behavior from members of outgroups, by coloring perceptions and interpretations of their behavior, and by justifying actions that harm them (Hamilton, 1981). Consequently, programs designed to improve intergroup relations often focus on breaking down negative stereotypes, and evaluations of such programs use changes in stereotypes as one sign of success. Yet, the observed contents of many intergroup stereotypes (e.g., Karlins, Coffman, & Walters, 1969) are relatively inconsequential and not necessarily negative (musicality of blacks, passion of Italians, orderliness of Germans, sociability of Arabs). Often group stereotypes do not appear to contain elements sufficiently negative to explain the incidents of intergroup cruelty that the stereotypes presumably mediate.

In this chapter we will discuss problems in using stereotypes to understand intergroup behavior. We will then present a new approach to conceptualizing and measuring intergroup stereotypes that deals with these problems by focusing on beliefs about the basic values of group members. In order to link beliefs to intergroup behavior, we also develop the concept "perceived humanity of the outgroup." Stated most generally, we wish to generate hypotheses concerning the role that beliefs about the basic value hierarchy of an outgroup play in intergroup behavior. Since the approach is theoretically relevant to relations between members of any set of groups in conflict, these hypotheses could be tested in the context of relations between such groups as Arabs–Jews, blacks–whites, or Hindus–Tamils. The chapter concludes by briefly describing a preliminary study designed to examine the validity and usefulness of this approach.

Some Limitations of Traditional Research With Stereotypes

Research on stereotypes of groups commonly investigates traits ascribed to one group by another (lazy, friendly, dirty, and so on). These perceptions of group traits probably do reflect general attitudes toward groups and they may also underlie some antagonistic intergroup behavior (Amir, 1976). There are several reasons to suspect, however, that group level trait perceptions are not necessarily good indexes of what underlies the orientations that guide individuals in their everyday behavior toward outgroup members:

1. The specific traits that constitute a particular group stereotype (e.g., musicality, impulsiveness) may be irrelevant to most interaction among individuals. These traits may therefore rarely be activated cognitively during interaction and, hence, rarely influence perception and behavior. For example, the stereotype of Jews as industrious (Karlins et al., 1969) is unlikely to be activated in most daily interactions with them, because industriousness is of little relevance to most of the social contacts among people.

2. The traits that constitute a group stereotype may have little in common with the unique set of trait categories that each individual commonly uses in forming impressions of others (Dornbusch, Hastorf, Richardson, Muzzy, & Vreeland, 1965; Higgins, King, & Mavin, 1982). For example, few individuals commonly use the categories passionate and artistic that appear in the group stereotype of Italians (Karlins et al., 1969). As a result, such group stereotypes may have little influence on individual intergroup behavior.

3. Trait stereotypes do not reveal whether a person believes members of the outgroup are different from or similar to members of his own group. Yet it is the perception that members of the outgroup are different from ourselves, together with a negative evaluation of these differences, that probably influence us to treat them as unworthy of our concern (Rokeach, 1980). For example, stereotyping Germans as materialistic and ambitious is unlikely to promote antagonistic behavior toward them if one also tends to see one's fellow countrymen as characterized by these same traits.

These criticisms suggest that an approach to stereotypes useful for understanding intergroup behavior should meet three requirements. It should identify and focus on beliefs about others that are (1) relevant for guiding behavior in many interaction settings, (2) commonly used by most individuals when they form impressions, and (3) measurable in a way that reflects the degree of similarity or difference assumed to exist between own group and outgroup.

A Values Approach

Basic Values and Value Hierarchies

To meet the above requirements, we suggest studying stereotypes of basic personal values rather than stereotypes of traits or other qualities. Basic personal values refer to the central cultural and individual goals people hold and aspire to achieve (Kluck-hohn, 1951; Levy & Guttman, 1984; Rokeach, 1973; Schwartz & Bilsky, 1987; Scott, 1965; Smith, 1969; Williams, 1968). Values are the relatively stable criteria people use to evaluate their own and others' behavior across situations. People's values provide the valences they attach to the outcomes of specific behaviors. In this way, values underlie norms and attitudes (Rokeach, 1973). The values whose expression or attainment are affected by the outcomes of an action combine with the expectancies for those outcomes to determine whether people will choose that action (Feather, 1975).

The preferences people have among their values—their value hierarchies—reflect the cultural and individual ideals that motivate their behavior. People also express their distinctive humanity in the goals they strive most to achieve and in the behaviors they consider most and least desirable, that is, in their value hierarchies. As a result, beliefs about a group's value hierarchy reveal the per-ceiver's view of the fundamental human nature of the members of that group. Views about others' fundamental nature are relevant to virtually all significant interaction with them.

In order to understand intergroup behavior, therefore, we recommend investigat-ing the stereotyped beliefs people hold about the hierarchy of basic personal values that characterizes members of a particular group. In other words, we recommend studying beliefs people hold regarding the relative importance of different basic values as guiding principles in the life of members of a target group.

Let us comment on differences between value and trait stereotypes, since the same or similar terms may be used to refer to them both. For example, "indepen-dent" is a trait when used to describe a person's behavior, but it can be a value when referring to an ideal mode of behavior for that person; "wise" may describe a trait, and "wisdom," a value. As a result, trait stereotypes and value stereotypes might easily be confused.

Trait stereotypes are descriptions of the presumed characteristics of a group's members. In contrast, value stereotypes are presumed hierarchies of goals, reflec-tions of what is important to a group's members and, therefore, of what they—at their best—aspire to be and to do. Trait stereotypes reflect abilities, styles of behavior, and immediate motives a perceiver attributes to the group's members. But trait stereotypes do not necessarily reflect ideals that the perceiver assumes to be the group members' basic guiding principles. Hence, trait stereotypes are less likely than value stereotypes to reveal perceptions of a group's fundamental human nature.

Perceived Humanity of the Outgroup

A central assumption we make in order to relate stereotypes of value hierarchies to intergroup behavior is that the degree of humanity attributed to a group influences behavior toward its members. It is when people dehumanize others, viewing them as lacking the moral sensibilities that distinguish humankind, that they can ignore the internalized and social norms that enjoin compassion and oppose cruelty to others.

Virtually all groups subscribe to norms exhorting respect, concern, and even help for members of the ingroup, and decrying disregard, hostility, and aggression toward ingroup members (LeVine & Campbell, 1972; Sumner, 1906). Because they share our humanity, members of an ingroup with which we identify are usually seen as deserving the same humane treatment we want for ourselves. If only out of concern for protecting our own interests, it is to our advantage to regard the protection of the interests of ingroup members as desirable. Were it legitimate for us to disregard the basic interests of ingroup members, it would then be legitimate for others to disregard our interests too. Hence, out of identification or self-interest, most individuals abide by norms calling for protecting or promoting the welfare of ingroup members.

These considerations apply much less when relating to members of outgroups. They are usually assumed to share our humanity to a lesser degree. Their fate is, therefore, less relevant to our own, and their interests may be disregarded. We postulate that people's feelings of shared humanity with members of an outgroup are reflected in the similarity or dissimilarity people assume to exist between their own values (or those of their ingroup) and the values of the outgroup. The fundamental meaning of "shared humanity" is being similar to us in what makes us distinctively human — in our hopes, ideals, and aspirations. These are expressed in our value hierarchies, that is, in the priorities we give to attaining particular desirable goals rather than others.

The basic values of an outgroup may be perceived not merely as different but even as opposed to ours. For example, we might perceive members of our own group as ranking "freedom" and "equality" at the top and "obedience" and "social power" at the bottom of their value hierarchies, whereas outgroup members are seen as giving highest priority to the latter values and least priority to the former. When strong opposition is perceived between ingroup and outgroup value hierarchies, members of that outgroup may appear to us as virtually lacking in humanity. Interaction with them may appear threatening because their basic goals conflict with ours. Perceived opposition of basic values raises the prospect of goal-based realistic conflict with members of an outgroup. This, in turn, promotes the development of antagonistic social motivations toward them (Berkowitz, 1962; Sherif & Sherif, 1953). In addition, stereotyped conceptions of outgroups as lacking humanity justify action against them (cf. Tajfel, 1981; Wilder, 1986).

The above leads to the general hypothesis that the degree of assumed similarity between the basic value hierarchies of an outgroup and of self (or of the ingroup with which one identifies) should be one important determinant of the extent to which people treat members of that outgroup with dignity and respect or exploitatively and antagonistically. Of course, it is unlikely that all the values attributed to groups play an equal role in determining perceptions of assumed similarity and humanity of the outgroup. Those values perceivers place highest in their own hierarchies or see as most important to the outgroup are most likely to reflect the criteria of judgment they will apply in relating to members of that outgroup in different situations. Only if the values list studied is comprehensive, however, can empirical research uncover the most important values that guide respondents in relating to particular groups and across situations.

Comprehensiveness of the Values List

For the measurement of value hierarchy stereotypes to meet the two requirements of wide relevance across situations and common use in interpersonal perception, the basic values included should encompass the full range of important cultural and individual goals. A first approximation to an encompassing list for Western societies is Rokeach's (1973) list of 36 values. Theoretical analyses aimed at specifying a possible universal structure of human values (Schwartz & Bilsky, 1987; Schwartz, 1987) point to ten distinctive content domains of values (hedonism, achievement, social power, stimulation, self-direction, security, prosocial, restrictive conformity, maturity, tradition maintenance). Empirical analyses in seven societies (Australia, Finland, Germany, Hong Kong, Israel, Spain, United States; Schwartz & Bilsky, 1988) indicate that the 36 Rokeach values cover seven of these domains fairly adequately. A new list of 56 values, generated from the theory of the structure of values, covers all ten domains in a balanced manner. Thus, reasonably comprehensive values lists are available for research.

To sum up, stereotypes of value hierarchies based on a reasonably comprehensive list of values will meet the two requirements of including (1) those qualities relevant to behavior in most settings, and (2) those qualities commonly used by most perceivers to form impressions. Moreover, perceived ingroup/outgroup similarity is revealed by comparing the hierarchy of basic values respondents believe to characterize their own group with the hierarchy they ascribe to the outgroup. This meets the third requirement for an approach to intergroup stereotypes noted above.

Value Hallmarks of Humanity

Perceptions of the humanity of another group may be expressed in a second way in addition to beliefs about value similarity. Certain types of values may reflect the perceived humanity of a group directly, without regard for comparisons with own group rankings. These types of values may be seen as hallmarks of the degree to which people have transcended their basic animal nature and developed their human sensitivities and moral sensibilities. Two value domains identified in our research are of particular interest as potential hallmarks of degree of humanity: (1) "prosocial," including such values as *equality, helpful, forgiving*; (2) "hedonism," including such values as *pleasure* and *a comfortable life*.

These value domains are likely to indicate perceived humanity directly because the pursuit of prosocial values reflects a conscious desire to promote the welfare of others whereas the pursuit of hedonism values reflects selfish interests shared with infrahuman species. In analyses of samples from seven very diverse societies, these value domains were consistently opposed. That is, in each sample people who considered prosocial values relatively important tended to consider hedonism values relatively unimportant and vice versa (Schwartz & Bilsky, 1988). Whether our specification of prosocial and hedonism values as hallmarks of humanity applies universally or reflects a Western culture bias must be tested in broader cross-cultural research.

Related Approaches

Belief Congruence Theory

Our view that perceived value similarity between ingroup and outgroup influences intergroup behavior is closely related to Rokeach's (1960, 1968, 1980) "belief congruence" theory of intergroup prejudice. According to this theory, prejudice is based on the assumption that members of another group hold beliefs (attitudes and values) different from one's own. In empirical research generated by this theory, the congruence between own beliefs and beliefs ascribed to an outgroup stimulus person has predicted a multitude of prejudicial attitudes and social distance measures as well as a few behaviors (Rokeach, 1968; Rokeach & Mezei, 1966; Rokeach, Smith, & Evans, 1960; Insko, Nacoste, & Moe, 1983). There is also evidence that strongly prejudiced persons assume that their own beliefs are less similar to those of the outgroup than less prejudiced persons do (Byrne & Wong, 1962).

Since basic values are a type of belief (broad beliefs about desirable goals), these studies support the possibility that perceived value similarity is related to intergroup behavior. However, the belief congruence studies may shed little light on the ways value similarity affects intergroup antagonism. First, belief congruence studies may underestimate effects because they manipulate only one or a very few beliefs attributed to the other. Moreover, they manipulate beliefs about specific traits that target persons are said to possess; they do not manipulate the basic values target persons are said to consider important. These manipulations do not meet the requirements of comprehensiveness discussed above, and they may have little impact on the presumed humanity of the target.

Second, we find no studies that examine effects of belief congruence on overtly expressed antagonism. Belief congruence has been shown to influence prejudice, but impacts on prejudice are weak or even absent in just those conditions where antagonism might be expected—where people find themselves in close contact and must get along, where there is social pressure against positive relations, and where there is competition (Brown, 1984; Hyland, 1974; Insko et al., 1983; Moe, Nacoste, & Insko, 1981; Silverman & Cochrane, 1972).

Third, many of the studies may have inadvertently confounded the manipulation of belief congruence with a manipulation of perceived group membership. The typical manipulation to induce assumed belief incongruence referred to the target person as, for example, an "atheist" or "communist." This manipulation probably caused subjects to categorize the target person as a member of atheist or communist groups, groups they were known to dislike. Placing the target person in a disliked category, in turn, could induce prejudicial attitudes toward him/her. If even weak manipulations produced categorizing, this would explain why variations in amount of manipulated belief congruence often failed to influence the strength of effects (Insko et al., 1983).

To avoid confounding belief congruence with group categorizing requires a belief manipulation that implies no explicit group category. Because people do not identify particular groups as characterized by the way they rank sets of values, manipulating perceived hierarchies of basic values may vary perceived belief congruence without inducing group categorization. This would permit testing the effects of degree of belief congruence.

Finally, because the belief congruence research typically manipulates beliefs about the target rather than measuring them, it provides little evidence regarding the association between the existing degree of perceived belief similarity and prejudice. The one study that *measured* similarity and used a broad notion ("assumed cultural similarity") rather than the usual specific beliefs, obtained relatively strong effects (McKirnan, Smith, & Hamayan, 1983).

Social Identity Theory

Tajfel's (1981, 1982) social identity theory is the major relevant alternative to belief congruence that has inspired research on intergroup relations. This theory, which focuses on group categorization, holds that individuals are motivated to derive a positive social identity from their group membership. They do this by perceiving their own group as positively distinctive from other groups on salient, valued dimensions. The need to achieve positive group distinctiveness, in order to protect or enhance social identity, causes people to differentiate themselves from others and to be biased in favor of their own group, even in the absence of any conflict between groups.

Many of the studies relevant for testing social identity theory employ allocation tasks to measure intergroup behavior. These studies manipulate the presumed race, personality, aesthetic preferences, or attitudes of members of an outgroup, thereby varying degree of assumed similarity (Brewer, 1979). The studies reveal a positive bias favoring the ingroup, as predicted by social identity theory. The findings do not support belief congruence theory, however, because the degree of assumed similarity of traits or beliefs with the outgroup has little effect on the strength of this bias (Allen & Wilder, 1975; Billig & Tajfel, 1973; Brewer & Silver, 1978; Dion, 1973; Wilson & Kayatani, 1968), except in one study (Taylor & Guimond, 1978).

We do not conclude from these studies that degree of belief congruence and—by implication—degree of value similarity has no impact on intergroup bias. These studies may not have tested this relationship adequately for three reasons: (1) many of the dimensions of similarity used (e.g., skill in counting dots) were irrelevant to the task (allocating money); (2) many of the dimensions of similarity (e.g., aesthetic preferences) were unimportant as categories for impression formation; and (3) in studies that manipulated presumed race of the outgroup, subjects may have tempered their responses to avoid revealing obvious prejudice, as they are wont to do on direct measures (McConahay, Hardee, & Batts, 1981).

These three limitations on drawing inferences regarding the effects of belief similarity may be overcome by using perceived similarity of the *value hierarchy*. As explained above, the use of hierarchies of basic values would assure that the relevant and important dimensions of similarity are tapped. In addition, because respondents consider virtually all the values in the lists socially desirable, they are unlikely to view the task of describing a group's value hierarchy as a transparent way of measuring prejudice towards that group. Consequently, investigating perceived value hierarchies rather than trait stereotypes should help to forestall intentional concealment of bias.

Thus far, we have assumed that belief congruence and social identity theories are complementary. Indeed, Insko and colleagues (1983) derived a similarity-attraction prediction from social identity theory: discrimination against dissimilar groups and attraction to similar groups bolster one's sense of social worth. Tajfel (1982) himself, however, asserted that the two approaches generate opposite predictions. According to social identity theory, the greater the similarity to the outgroup, the greater the need for differentiation in order to affirm own group superiority and thereby enhance one's social identity. Hence, similarity to the outgroup should increase rather than decrease bias.

Brown (1984) limited this prediction to relationships of intergroup competition. In general, similarity, by increasing the number of dimensions on which comparisons can be made, points more strongly to a lack of uniqueness. This fosters rivalry when intergroup competition is high because it increases the need for group differentiation. Hostility results from impending loss of superiority in the competition. In the absence of competition, group similarity may be seen as grounds for more successful cooperation, so similarity increases attraction. Brown (1984) claims that most studies support this analysis of the effects of group similarity.

Brown's prediction that similarity increases bias against competing groups appears to contradict our predictions regarding the positive effects of perceived similarity of the basic value hierarchy. One must, however, note two important points: First, natural groups in long-term conflict (which parallels competition) are strongly differentiated in their own eyes; information about similarity is unlikely to threaten their sense of distinctiveness. Manipulations that assert so great a degree of similarity between natural groups that it might be threatening would more likely be disbelieved.

Second, in natural groups, in which similarity is measured rather than manipulated, respondents are free to modify the subjective degree of intergroup similarity they perceive in a manner that meets their own needs. They can therefore arrange to perceive sufficient intergroup dissimilarity to avert the threat to their unique identity. Consequently, we postulate that value similarity that is *measured* (not following manipulation) is positively associated with favorableness and negatively associated with antagonism toward the outgroup. This is the situation in everyday conditions even among competing groups.

Hypotheses Derived from the Basic Values Approach

The basic values approach is still largely untested. We will present a number of testable hypotheses derived from it in order to stimulate research and to demonstrate the potential fruitfulness of the approach. A first set of hypotheses concerns the associations between people's existing (not manipulated) perceptions of value similarity and their antagonism toward outgroups, taking into account the role of perceived humanity of the outgroup as a mediator.

1. Assumed dissimilarity of basic values with an outgroup is associated (a) with antagonism toward that group, and (b) with the belief that members of the outgroup are antagonistic toward one's own group.
2. These associations are stronger when value dissimilarity is based on the values perceived as highest in the hierarchy of own group or outgroup.
3. Perceptions of the humanity of the outgroup mediate associations between assumed value dissimilarity and intergroup antagonism.

The next two hypotheses concern value stereotypes.

4. Stereotyping an outgroup as attributing relatively little importance to prosocial morality values and/or great importance to hedonism values is associated with antagonism toward its members and expectations of antagonism from them.
5. Perceptions of the humanity of the outgroup mediate associations between stereotypes of the outgroup's prosocial morality and hedonism values and intergroup antagonism.

Empirical research may reveal that value stereotypes other than the two mentioned in hypotheses 4 and 5 are relevant in relations between particular groups, reflecting particular cultural concerns or historical experiences. For example, stereotyping of Germans as placing especially high priority on restrictive conformity values may also be associated with antagonism toward Germans. This would reflect the historically conditioned view that extreme obedience to authority in Germany contributed to the evils of World War II (Adorno, Frenkel-Brunswik, Levinson, & Sanford, 1950).

The following hypotheses are concerned with the effects of manipulating value similarity through providing information about outgroup members. They compare the effects of manipulating the perceived similarity of values versus specific beliefs or ethnic identity of outgroup members. These hypotheses challenge two claims in the belief congruence literature: (1) the particular contents of the beliefs manipulated are inconsequential; dissimilarity of all types fosters negative intergroup orientations. (2) belief congruence has little or no affect on readiness for intimate contacts with outgroup members.

6. Manipulating similarity of the basic value hierarchy more strongly influences the degree of antagonism expressed toward the outgroup than manipulating congruence of specific beliefs.[1] This does not hold, however, if the specific beliefs imply membership in strongly disliked groups.

---

[1] The direction of influence may not always fit the belief congruence prediction because, when similarity is increased by manipulation, too much similarity may threaten distinctiveness, as postulated in social identity theory.

7. Manipulating perceived value similarity more strongly influences willingness to engage in social contacts with outgroup members than manipulating perceived ethnic (or other group) identity. Value similarity effects on readiness for contact are weaker if people perceive strong social pressure against that contact (cf. Silverman & Cochrane, 1972).

   The basic values approach also has implications for everyday interaction and for intervention programs, as suggested in the following hypotheses:

8. The impacts that everyday cues of ethnicity and cultural level (e.g., speech style) have on prejudice toward outgroup members are mediated in part by perceived value similarity (McKirnan et al., 1983).

9. The positive impacts of intervention programs for reducing intergroup conflict and increasing tolerance are mediated in part by reductions in assumed intergroup value dissimilarity.

10. Cognitively oriented programs that engage participants in examining information about the real value hierarchies of own and outgroup will reduce intergroup antagonism to the extent that they reduce perceived dissimilarity of basic values without obliterating distinctiveness.

Measuring Value Similarity, Value Stereotypes, and Perceived Humanity

Value Similarity

To meet the requirements developed above (that values have wide relevance across situations and be used commonly by most individuals), values to be rated might best be sampled from the comprehensive list of 56 values in order to represent those value domains expected to be important in the societies under study. The Rokeach (1973) method of measuring value hierarchies can then be adapted. This method obtains from respondents a rank ordering of two lists of 18 values. Past research, using the 36 Rokeach values, included a list of end-state values and a list of values as modes of behavior that people aspire to attain or express in their daily lives. Each value is ranked according to its relative importance as a guiding principle in a person's life.

To measure value similarity, respondents provide both the value hierarchy they attribute to their ingroup and the value hierarchy they attribute to an outgroup. For each respondent, the correlation (Spearman rho) between the value hierarchy attributed to the ingroup and the value hierarchy attributed to the outgroup constitute the index of assumed value similarity.

For example, a sample of 119 Hebrew University undergraduates provided their perceptions of the personal value hierarchies of the typical Israeli education student (own group) and of the typical German education student (outgroup), using the Rokeach lists. Table 7–1 presents the hierarchies of composite ranks (1 – most to 18 – least important) for the two lists of values. The first column in each panel contains the value hierarchy Israeli students attributed to the typical Israeli education student, the second column the hierarchy attributed to the typical German education student.

Table 7-1. Value Hierarchies Perceived by Israeli Students (Composite Median Ranks)

Terminal values	Israeli $N=119$	German $N=119$	Instrumental values	Israeli $N=119$	German $N=119$
A comfortable life	14	1	Ambitious	8	3
An exciting life	15	6	Broadminded	1	7
A sense of accomplishment	4	3	Capable	3	6
A world at peace	5.5	5	Cheerful	13	16
A world of beauty	17	12	Clean	17	12
Equality	7	9.5	Courageous	14	13
Family security	3	15	Forgiving	15	18
Freedom	1	2	Helpful	7	15
Happiness	10	7	Honest	2	11
Inner harmony	12	9.5	Imaginative	11	17
Mature love	11	14	Independent	6	10
National security	13	17	Intellectual	5	1
Pleasure	16	13	Logical	10	4
Belief in God/salvation	18	18	Loving	12	14
Self-respect	5.5	4	Obedient	18	9
Social recognition	8.5	16	Polite	16	8
True friendship	8.5	16	Responsible	4	5
Wisdom	2	9.5	Self-controlled	9	2

The correlation between the two sets of ranks for the 18 terminal values is rho = .42; for the 18 instrumental values it is rho = .38. Thus, at the group level, Israeli students perceived the value hierarchies of Israeli and German education students as moderately similar. Note, however, the many large differences in the ranks of some values (e.g., a comfortable life, family security, wisdom, broadminded, honest, obedient). Individuals, of course, may differ substantially from one another in the degree of similarity they perceive between the values of their own group and of the outgroup. It is this individual variability that should be associated with intergroup behavior according to our theory. In the Israeli student sample, for example, the value similarity correlations (rhos) for individual respondents ranged from −.47 to +1.00, with a median of .28.

Value Domain Stereotypes

To compute scores for the respondents' stereotypes of how important particular value domains are to outgroup members, we use the value hierarchies respondents attribute to the members of the outgroup. Since each domain is represented by a specific set of values, stereotype scores are derived by averaging the importance ranks the respondent assigns to the single values that represent a domain. We are especially interested, of course, in the stereotypes held regarding the importance of the two value domains postulated to be hallmarks of degree of humanity—prosocial and hedonism.

The Israeli students, for example, perceived that prosocial values are ranked considerably less important by the German outgroup than by their own group (mean ranks 12.3 versus 8.1; averaging equality, world at peace, forgiving, helpful, honest, loving). In contrast, they perceived the German outgroup as ranking hedonism values (comfortable life, pleasure) more important (mean ranks 7.0 versus 15.0). Of course, it is the individual differences in perceived value stereotypes that are used to test hypotheses about the intergroup behavior of individuals.

When studying relations with a particular group, one may wish to investigate stereotypes of value domains thought to characterize that group in particular. Regarding Germans, as noted above, historically conditioned views direct our interest to the perceived importance to them of the restrictive conformity domain (obedient, clean, polite, self-controlled). Indeed, there is evidence in the Israeli student sample of this value stereotype. They perceive Germans as giving relatively high priority to restrictive conformity values when compared with Israelis (mean ranks 7.8 versus 15.0). One might hypothesize that the tendency to stereotype Germans as attributing relatively great importance to restrictive conformity values is associated with antagonism toward them.

Perceived Humanity

To measure perceptions of the humanity of a group, we ask respondents what proportion of the group's members they think perform each of 15 humane/inhumane behaviors (answer scale from /0/ none to /6/ all). Behaviors include caring for the handicapped, widowed, elderly, and poor, exploiting others, using deceit, acting strictly according to moral considerations, and so forth. A perceived humanity score is computed by averaging across items after reversing negative items (internal reliability $\alpha = .86$). By asking about the proportion of a group who perform each behavior, this instrument avoids respondents' frequently voiced objection that you can't characterize a group as a whole because group members differ from one another.

This instrument has been used to measure perceptions Jewish Israeli students have of the humanity of Israeli Jews and Arabs. Mean scores of 2.6 (Jews) and 2.5 (Arabs) indicate a perception that only a minority in both groups behaves humanely, with substantial variance across individuals ($\sigma = .65$ for Jews and .82 for Arabs). Individuals tended to use a similar part of the response scale, regardless of the group they rated. This probably reflects their assumptions about the goodness of human nature in general. To overcome this response tendency, we use the perceived humanity of own group as a control. Subtracting the perceived humanity of the outgroup from that of own group yields an index of the extent to which the outgroup is perceived as more or less humane than the respondent's own moral community. In a small sample of Jewish Israeli students (n = 11), this index of the perceived humanity of the Arab outgroup correlated substantially with perceived value similarity between the groups ($r = .41$).

A Preliminary Study

To illustrate the application of the values approach in studying intergroup behavior, we briefly describe part of a study that investigated associations of value similarity and value domain stereotypes with intergroup social motives (Schwartz, Struch, & Bilsky, 1987).[2] Social motives refer to individuals' preferences regarding the outcomes that people obtain in social interaction (Kelley & Thibaut, 1978; MacCrimmon & Messick, 1976). Social motives are expressed in the choices people make when allocating resources. Social motives may be arrayed on a continuum from altruistic to antagonistic. Choosing to maximize other's outcomes even at the expense of one's own, for example, expresses an altruistic social motive. Choosing to minimize the other's outcomes even at the expense of one's own expresses extreme antagonism.

In this study, social motives were measured by allocations of hypothetical resources in two matrixes adapted from Bornstein and colleagues (1983). Each matrix presented respondents with a choice among six allocation alternatives. The 119 Israeli students whose value perceptions were mentioned above gave their views of how the typical Israeli student would allocate resources (1) between himself and another Israeli student (ingroup to ingroup) and (2) between himself and a German student (ingroup to outgroup). They also indicated their views of how the typical German student would allocate resources (1) between himself and another German student (ingroup to ingroup) and (2) between himself and a typical Israeli student (outgroup to ingroup). In short, the study examined the effects of perceived value similarity and of value domain stereotypes on the views of Israeli students regarding the social motives that Israeli and German students express toward one another.

For purposes of analyzing the altruism/antagonism dimension of social motives, the different allocations were rated for altruism/antagonism by an independent sample of subjects. Based on these ratings, the allocations were ordered and scored from 1 (altruistic) to 6 (antagonistic). Scores for allocations on the two matrixes were averaged.

Value Similarity Hypotheses

As predicted by the basic values approach, assumed similarity of values with the German outgroup correlated negatively with antagonistic social motives toward that outgroup ($r = -.19$). Stated differently, the more similar Israeli students believed the values of Israelis and Germans to be, the less antagonistic they expected the social motives Israelis express toward Germans to be. Also as predicted, assumed similarity of values with the German outgroup correlated negatively with the belief that members of the outgroup express antagonistic social motives toward one's own group ($r = -.16$). That is, the more similar Israeli students believed the values of

---

[2]For a second application, see Struch and Schwartz (1989).

Israelis and Germans to be, the less antagonistic they expected the social motives Germans express toward Israelis to be. Because perceived humanity was not measured in this study, it could not be examined as a mediator.

Value Domain Stereotypes

As predicted, stereotyping the German outgroup as attributing relatively great importance to values in the prosocial domain correlated negatively with expecting Israelis to express antagonistic social motives toward Germans ($r = -.25$). Stereotyping the German outgroup as emphasizing prosocial values also correlated negatively with the belief that Germans express antagonistic social motives toward one's own Israeli group ($r = -.24$). In other words, the belief that Germans attribute relatively great importance to prosocial values was associated with expectations of less antagonism both from Israelis toward Germans and from Germans toward Israelis.

Stereotyping the German outgroup as attributing relatively great importance to values in the enjoyment domain was unrelated to antagonistic social motives toward a group. However, the enjoyment stereotype correlated positively, as predicted, with the belief that members of the outgroup express antagonistic social motives toward one's own group ($r = .21$). Stereotyping the German outgroup as attributing relatively great importance to values in the restrictive conformity domain was positively correlated with the expectation of antagonistic social motives toward Germans by Israelis, as predicted ($r = .24$). This stereotype was unrelated, however, to the belief that members of the German outgroup express antagonistic social motives toward one's own Israeli group.

This preliminary study demonstrates how research might be done with the basic values approach. The associations found are relatively weak, probably for reasons discussed elsewhere (Schwartz, Struch, & Bilsky, 1987). Hence, the study is more illustrative than conclusive in the support it offers for hypotheses derived from the values approach. More conclusive research investigating respondents' own antagonism and using stronger behavioral indexes is clearly the next order of business.

Summary

In order to explain intergroup antagonism, an approach to stereotypes should focus on beliefs about others that are relevant across many situations, commonly used by most persons when forming impressions, and measurable in terms of perceived own group/outgroup similarity. Stereotypes of the basic values of target groups meet these requirements better than trait stereotypes do. Basic values represent the central cultural and individual goals that people aspire to achieve. Beliefs about a group's hierarchy of basic values reflect the way a person perceives the humanity of the members of that group. Beliefs about the similarity between own group and outgroup values reflect one's sense of shared humanity with that group.

Stereotyping a group as having a value hierarchy dissimilar to one's own or as attributing little importance to prosocial but great importance to enjoyment values both suggest a perception of that group as relatively inhumane. Hypotheses relating basic value similarity and value stereotypes to intergroup antagonism are generated by assuming that people feel and more readily express antagonism toward groups perceived as inhumane. This approach is compared and contrasted with belief congruence (Rokeach, 1960, 1968, 1980) and with social identity (Tajfel, 1981, 1982) theories and findings. Finally, a preliminary study illustrating how to measure values variables and to test hypotheses from the basic values approach is presented.

Acknowledgments. Preparation of this chapter was supported in part by grants to the first author from the Office of Science and Development of the National Council for Research and Development (Israel) and from the Israel Foundations Trustees.

References

Adorno, T.W., Frenkel-Brunswik, E., Levinson, D.J., & Sanford, R.N. (1950). *The authoritarian personality.* New York: Harper.

Allen, V.L., & Wilder, D.A. (1975). Categorization, belief similarity, and group discrimination. *Journal of Personality and Social Psychology, 32,* 971–977.

Amir, Y. (1976). The role of intergroup contact in change of prejudice and ethnic relations. In P.A. Katz (Ed.), *Toward the elimination of racism* (pp. 245–308). New York: Pergamon.

Berkowitz, L. (1962). *Aggression: A social psychological analysis.* New York: McGraw-Hill.

Billig, M., & Tajfel, H. (1973). Social categorization and similarity in intergroup behavior. *European Journal of Social Psychology, 3,* 27–52.

Bornstein, G., Crum, L., Wittenbraker, J., Harring, K., Insko, C.A., & Thibaut, J. (1983). On the measurement of social orientations in the minimal group paradigm. *European Journal of Social Psychology, 13,* 321–350.

Brewer, M.B. (1979). Ingroup bias in the minimal intergroup situation: A cognitive-motivational analysis. *Psychological Bulletin, 86,* 307–324.

Brewer, M.B., & Kramer, R.M. (1985). The psychology of intergroup attitudes and behavior. *Annual Review of Psychology, 36,* 219–243.

Brewer, M.B., & Silver, M. (1978). Ingroup bias as a function of task characteristics. *European Journal of Social Psychology, 8,* 393–400.

Brown, R.J. (1984). The role of similarity in intergroup relations. In H. Tajfel (Ed.), *The social dimension* (Vol. 2) (pp. 603–623). Cambridge, England: Cambridge University Press.

Byrne, D., & Wong, T.J. (1962). Racial prejudice, interpersonal attraction, and assumed dissimilarity of attitudes. *Journal of Abnormal and Social Psychology, 65,* 246–253.

Dion, K.L. (1973). Cohesiveness as a determinant of ingroup–outgroup bias. *Journal of Personality and Social Psychology, 28,* 163–171.

Dornbusch, S., Hastorf, A.H., Richardson, S.A., Muzzy, R.E., & Vreeland, R.S. (1965). The perceiver and the perceived: Their relative influence on the categories of interpersonal cognition. *Journal of Personality and Social Psychology, 1,* 434–441.

Feather, N.T. (1975). *Values in education and society.* New York: Free Press.

Hamilton, D.L. (1981). *Cognitive processes in stereotyping and intergroup behavior.* Hillsdale, NJ: Erlbaum.

Higgins, E.T., King, G.A., & Mavin, G.H. (1982). Individual construct accessibility and subjective impressions and recall. *Journal of Personality and Social Psychology, 43,* 35–47.

Hyland, M. (1974). The anticipated belief difference theory of prejudice: Analyses and evaluation. *European Journal of Social Psychology, 4*, 179–200.

Insko, C.A., Nacoste, R.W., & Moe, J.L. (1983). Belief congruence and racial discrimination: Review of the evidence and critical evaluation. *European Journal of Social Psychology, 13*, 153–174.

Karlins, M., Coffman, T.L., & Walters, G. (1969). On the fading of social stereotypes: Studies on three generations of college students. *Journal of Personality and Social Psychology, 13*, 1–16.

Kelley, H.H., & Thibaut, J. (1978). *Intergroup relations: A theory of interdependence.* New York: Wiley.

Kluckhohn, C. (1951). Values and value orientations in the theory of action. In T. Parsons & E. Shils (Eds.), *Toward a general theory of action* (pp. 388–433). Cambridge, MA: Harvard University Press.

LeVine, R.A., & Campbell, D.T. (1972). *Ethnocentrism: Theories of conflict, ethnic attitudes, and group behavior.* New York: Wiley.

Levy, S., & Guttmann, L. (1984). A faceted cross-cultural analysis of some core social values. In D. Canter (Ed.), *Facet Theory: Approaches to social research* (pp. 205–221). New York: Springer-Verlag.

MacCrimmon, K., & Messick, D. (1976). Framework of social motives. *Behavioral Science, 21*, 86–100.

McConahay, J.B., Hardee, B.B., & Batts, V. (1981). Has racism declined in America? It depends on who is asking and what is asked. *Journal of Conflict Resolution, 25*, 563–579.

McKirnan, D.J., Smith, C.E., & Hamayan, E.V. (1983). A sociolinguistic approach to the belief-similarity model of racial attitudes. *Journal of Experimental Social Psychology, 19*, 434–447.

Moe, J.L., Nacoste, R.W., & Insko, C.A. (1981). Belief versus race as determinants of discrimination: A study of Southern adolescents in 1966 and 1979. *Journal of Personality and Social Psychology, 41*, 1031–1050.

Rokeach, M. (1960). *The open and closed mind.* New York: Basic Books.

Rokeach, M. (1968). *Beliefs, attitudes, and values.* San Francisco, CA: Jossey-Bass.

Rokeach, M. (1973). *The nature of human values.* New York: Free Press.

Rokeach, M. (1980). Some unresolved issues in theories of beliefs, attitudes and values. In M.M. Page (Ed.), *Nebraska symposium on motivation 1979* (Vol. 27) (pp. 261–304). Lincoln, NE: Nebraska University Press.

Rokeach, M., & Mezei, L. (1966). Race and shared belief as factors in social choice. *Science, 151*, 167–172.

Rokeach, M., Smith, P.W., & Evans, R.I. (1960). Two kinds of prejudice or one? In M. Rokeach, *The open and closed mind.* (pp. 132–168). New York: Basic Books.

Schwartz, S.H. (1987). *Invitation to collaborate on cross-cultural research on values.* Unpublished manuscript, Hebrew University, Jerusalem, Israel.

Schwartz, S.H., & Bilsky, W. (1987). Toward a universal psychological structure of human values. *Journal of Personality and Social Psychology, 53*, 550–562.

Schwartz, S.H., & Bilsky, W. (1988). *Toward a theory of the universal content and structure of values: Extensions and cross-cultural replications.* Unpublished manuscript, Hebrew University, Jerusalem, Israel.

Schwartz, S.H., Struch, N., & Bilsky, W. (1987). *Value similarity, value stereotypes and intergroup social motives.* Unpublished manuscript, Hebrew University, Jerusalem, Israel.

Scott, W.A. (1965). *Values and organizations.* Chicago: Rand McNally.

Sherif, M., & Sherif, C.W. (1953). *Groups in harmony and tension.* New York: Harper.

Silverman, B.I., & Cochrane, R. (1972). Effect of the social context on the principle of belief congruence. *Journal of Personality and Social Psychology, 22*, 259–268.

Smith, M.B. (1969). *Social psychology and human values.* Chicago: Aldine.

Struch, N., & Schwartz, S. H. (1989). Intergroup aggression: Its predictors and distinctness from in-group bias. *Journal of Personality and Social Psychology, 56*.

Sumner, W.G. (1906). *Folkways*. Boston: Ginn & Co.

Tajfel, H. (1981). *Human groups and social categories*: *Studies in social psychology*. Cambridge, England: Cambridge University Press.

Tajfel, H. (1982). Social psychology of intergroup relations. *Annual Review of Psychology, 33*, 1–39.

Taylor, D.M., & Guimond S. (1978). The belief theory of prejudice in an intergroup context. *Journal of Social Psychology, 105*, 11–25.

Wilder, D.A. (1986). Social categorization: Implications for creation and reduction of intergroup bias. In L. Berkowitz (Ed.), *Advances in experimental social psychology* (Vol. 19) (pp. 293–355). New York: Academic Press.

Williams, R.M. (1968). Values. In D.L. Sills (Ed.), *International encyclopedia of the social sciences* (Vol. 16) (pp. 283–287). New York: Macmillan.

Wilson, W. & Kayatani, M. (1968). Intergroup attitudes and strategies in games between opponents of the same or of a different race. *Journal of Personality and Social Psychology, 9*, 24–30.

Chapter 8

Delegitimization: The Extreme Case of Stereotyping and Prejudice

Daniel Bar-Tal

Social psychology has devoted much effort to the exploration of various social representations in the form of beliefs and attitudes, which serve to characterize social categories of individuals within the context of intergroup relations (Hamilton, 1981; Stephan, 1985). One outcome of this effort has been extensive study of two social representations—stereotypes and prejudice. Stereotypes are beliefs about another group in such terms as personality traits, attributions, or behavioral descriptions (Brewer & Kramer, 1985; Hamilton, 1981). Prejudice refers to negative attitudes toward another group that express negative affective or emotional reactions (Allport, 1954; Jones, 1972; Pettigrew, 1971; Stephan, 1985). Both categories, being loosely defined, are highly general concepts that lack explicit specifications regarding their outcomes in terms of the nature of intergroup relations. Thus, the contents of stereotypes are of a wide scope, ranging from descriptions with negative to positive connotations (e.g., lazy, superstitious, industrious, shrewd—see Katz & Braly, 1933). Likewise, although the conception of prejudice implies negative affective reaction, it does not specify the intensity of such reactions, and, therefore, may range from mildly to extremely negative. In addition, the two concepts focus mainly on cognitive and affective components of intergroup relations, and do not necessarily specify their role in guiding actual behavior towards the other group.

It is proposed that within the framework of the social psychological analysis of intergroup relations it is possible to suggest more specific group categorizations which have clearly defined cognitive, affective, and behavioral implications. The present chapter proposes such content category, named delegitimization.

Nature of Delegitimization

Consider the following excerpts:

> The 'enemy,' the self-proclaimed enemy is the relatively small fanatical Soviet Communist Party. Stalin is its leader and the Politburo is the principal source of the decisions which command the blind obedience of the hard core of loyal communist

party members everywhere in the world. These party members have despotic polit-ical power in Russia and elsewhere. They believe that it is their duty to extend that power to all the world. They believe it is right to use fraud, terrorism, and violence, and any other means that will promote their ends. They treat as enemies all who oppose their will (Dulles, 1950).

Since World War II, U.S. imperialism has stepped into the shoes of German, Japanese, and Italian fascism and has been trying to build a great American empire by dominating and enslaving the whole world. It is actively fostering Japanese and West German militarism as its chief accomplices in unleashing a world war. Like a vicious wolf, it is bullying and enslaving various peoples, plundering their wealth, encroaching upon their countries' sovereignty and in their affairs. It is the most rabid aggressor in human history and the most ferocious common enemy of the people of the world (Lin Piao in Fann and Hodges, 1971).

For hundreds of years Germany was good enough to receive these elements (Jews), although they possessed nothing except infectious political and physical diseases. What they possess today, they have by far the largest extent gained at the cost of the less astute German nation by the most reprehensible manipulations (Hitler, 1939, in Baynes, 1942).

The task which the State agents have had to accomplish in the Congo is noble and elevated. They have had to carry on the work of civilization in Equatorial Africa, guided by the principles set forth in the Berlin and Brussels resolutions. Face to face with primitive barbarity, struggling against dreadful customs, thousands of years old, their duty has been to modify gradually those customs . . . Civilised society attaches to human life a value unknown among savage peoples. When our guiding will is implanted among the latter, it must aim at overcoming all obstacles (Leopold II, King of the Belgians, 1897, in Snyder, 1962).

The above excerpts are examples of *delegitimization*. The present chapter will ana-lyze the nature of the concept delegitimization, suggest sources and conditions that influence its utilization, describe its functions, and outline several implications of the present conception.

Definition

Delegitimization is defined as categorization of groups into extreme negative social categories which are excluded from human groups that are considered as acting within the limits of acceptable norms and/or values. Delegitimization may be viewed as a denial of categorized group's humanity (suggested by S.H. Schwartz, personal communication, October 23, 1985).[1]

Since delegitimization, as a psychological process, is underlaid by a categoriza-tion, it is governed by all principles of group categorization as described by various social psychologists (see Cantor & Mischel, 1979; Eiser & Stroebe, 1972; Rosch, 1978; Tajfel, 1978; Tajfel & Turner, 1979; Taylor, 1981; Tessler, 1978). Also, as a content of knowledge, it is governed by the same cognitive and motivational processes as all the other constructs of knowledge (Kruglanski, in press). However,

---

[1]The present paper concerns delegitimization of groups, although delegitimization of individuals is possible as well. Goffman (1963) elaborated on the later subject.

delegitimization, in addition to being content specific, has several unique characteristics which differentiate it from other social representations such as stereotypes and prejudice.

1. The process of delegitimization is characterized by extremely negative, salient, and unique contents which serve as a basis for categorization. Typical examples of such content categories were presented above: despots, terrorists, imperialists, fascists, aggressors, enemies, carriers of infectious political and physical diseases, primitives, and savages.

2. Delegitimization implies inclusion of the delegitimized group in categories that are completely rejected by the norms and/or values of the delegitimizing group. While many groups are negatively stereotyped or experience prejudice, they may continue to be considered as part of the society (for example, Americans of Mexican origin in the United States, or Jews in France). Delegitimization, in contrast, indicates that the delegitimized group is outside the boundaries of the commonly accepted groups, and it is thus excluded from the society. The exclusion is often not temporary or conditional, but permanent and persistent.

3. Delegitimization is accompanied by intense negative emotions that derive from the extremely negative contents of delegitimizing categories. These emotions provide the direction and vigor for the delegitimizing beliefs. Individuals usually feel hatred, fear, aversion, anger, or disgust toward the delegitimized group.

4. Delegitimization is regulated by social norms that maintain and encourage this process. Delegitimization cannot easily flourish without institutionalized support. Indeed, delegitimization is sometimes enforced by political institutions or by legal code.

5. In addition to the unique cognitive and affective components, delegitimization also implies negative behaviors which the delegitimized group performs or can potentially enact. That is, delegitimization not only indicates that the characteristics of the delegitimized group, as may be reflected in the behaviors, values, traits, goals, or ideology, are extremely undesirable and absolutely unaccepted by the norms or values of the delegitimizing society, but, more importantly, that this group can potentially perform harmful behavior. Labels such as fascists, savages, or aggressors imply potential behavior, which may endanger the delegitimizing group, or even other groups.

6. Delegitimization also has behavioral implications for the delegitimizing group. It indicates that the delegitimized group does not deserve human treatment. A delegitimized group is positioned in a category of individuals or groups that should be treated negatively, even sometimes to the extreme—used as slaves or exterminated. These extreme actions are taken because the delegitimized group is considered a threat to the basic values, norms, or even the existence of the society itself and its structure. Thus, the delegitimizing group feels an obligation to avert the danger, in order to protect its existence.

It should be pointed out that the categories used for delegitimization are culture bound. That is, what is considered extremely negative and acceptable in one group does not necessarily apply to another one. For example, the category "communists" may be used as a delegitimizing category in the U.S., but not in the U.S.S.R., where it is considered a positive category. However, there are group categories that are likely to be considered as very negative and unacceptable by most groups in the world, if not by all of them. Examples of these group categories may be thieves, savages, aggressors, or parasites.

In this vein, one may note that the above definition of delegitimization complements Goffman's analysis of stigmatized persons (1963). Goffman, in his classic book, analyzed the psychology of stigmatized individuals who possess an attribute that discredits them and makes them different from others. More recently, Katz (1981) analyzed people's reactions to members of groups who are stigmatized. That is, "have attributes that do not accord with prevailing standards of the normal and good" (p.1). According to Katz, these reactions are a combination of hostility and rejection with sympathy and friendliness. However, the present work focuses on *attributed delegitimizing characteristics to groups*.

Ways of Delegitimization

This section describes several of the most commonly used means of delegitimization, although many more probably exist or can be created.

Dehumanization. This involves categorizing a group as inhuman either by using categories of subhuman creatures such as inferior race and animals, or by using categories of negatively evaluated superhuman creatures such as demons, monsters, and satans. Both categories involve characterizing the members of the delegitimized group as possessing inhuman traits, different from the human race. One example of delegitimization is the often used characterization of blacks by whites as an inferior race. In 1862, Robert Knox described Hottentots in South Africa:

> I have said that when the Dutch first landed at the Cape of Good Hope they met with the race called Hottentots, a simple feeble race of men, living in little groups, almost, indeed in families, tending their fat-tailed sheep and dreaming away their lives. Of a dirty yellow color, they slightly resembled the Chinese, but are clearly of a different blood. The face is set on like a baboon; cranium small but good; jaws very large, feet and hands small.... They differ as much from their fellowmen as the animals of Southern Africa do from those of South America (Knox, 1862, pp. 18–19).

Dehumanization has not been used only with blacks, but has been widely used, not infrequently, throughout the history of the human race towards various groups. It is still used today, as, for example, by Christians towards Jews, by Europeans towards Indians, or by Japanese towards Chinese.

Outcasting. The way of outcasting involves categorization into groups that are considered as violators of pivotal social norms. It includes such categories as murderers, thieves, psychopaths, or maniacs. These violators are usually excluded from society and often segregated in total institutions. Israeli Jews and Palestinians provide a recent example of mutual delegitimization by means of outcasting. The Israeli Jews have invested much effort in delegitimizing the members and sympathizers of the Palestinian Liberation Organization by labelling them as murderers and terrorists, while the Palestinians delegitimize Zionists as racists and terrorists (Bar-Tal, 1988).

Trait Characterization. This involves the attribution of personality traits that are evaluated as extremely negative and unacceptable to a given society. Use of labels such as aggressors, idiots, or parasites exemplifies this type of delegitimization. For instance, Dr. Robert Ritter, who was head of the Racial Hygiene and Population Biology Research Unit of the Ministry of Health in the Nazi regime of Germany, described the majority of Gypsies in 1941 as being "unbalanced, characterless, unreliable, untrustworthy and idle, or unsteady and hot-tempered. In short, work-shy and asocial" (Kendrick & Puxon, 1972).

Use of political labels. This type of delegitimization involves categorization into political groups which are considered totally unaccepted by the members of the delegitimizing society. The labels are mainly drawn from the repertoire of political goals, ideology, or values. Nazis, fascists, imperialists, colonialists, capitalists, and communists are examples of this type of delegitimization. Usually, these groups threaten the basic values of the delegitimizing society and are considered to endanger its well-being. The labelling of Americans as capitalists by the Russians and the labelling of Russians as communists by the Americans are examples of this type of delegitimization, and each case represents an evil which must be excluded from the society. Communism (to Americans) and capitalism (to Russians) are negative ideologies that are perceived as threatening the basic existence of their social, economical, and political systems (see White, 1984). Therefore, the adherents to these ideologies must be expelled from the society.

Group comparison. In this type of categorization, the label of the delegitimized group symbolizes the most undesirable group that serves as an example of evil in a given society. Use of such categories as Vandals or Huns is an example of this type of delegitimization. For example, during the First World War, Germans were labelled by Americans as Huns, and so a poster at the time read:

> German agents are everywhere, eager to gather scraps of news about our men, our ships and our munitions. . . . Do not become a tool of the Hun by passing on the malicious, disheartening rumors which he so eagerly sows.

Each society has in its cultural repertoire examples of other groups which serve as symbols of malice, evil, or wickedness.

Sources and Conditions of Delegitimization

Delegitimization can occur as a consequence of various antecedents. In most cases, it is derived from a will to elevate one's own group and to differentiate the other group, a will to exploit, or a conflict-ridden situation. These sources are not mutually exclusive, and sometimes are combined when a group delegitimized another group.

A group may delegitimize another group in order to "ideologically" maximize the distinction between the two groups (Bar-Tal, in press). At the same time, the aim of delegitimization is to devalue the delegitimized group and elevate the delegitimizing group. In this case, the will to feel superior and different is the most important cause for delegitimization. Groups may even base this type of delegitimization on ideology (see Billig, 1982). Indeed, Nazis based their delegitimization of Jews and Gypsies on the ideology of the German race purity, which advocated eliminating all the non-Aryan elements in the German society (see Bar-Tal, 1989; Dawidowicz, 1975; Kendrick & Puxon, 1972; Poliakov, 1974).

Delegitimization also serves in a simplistic way to rationalize exploitation. Human beings need an explanation and justification for exploitive behavior. The direct causes, such as a need for a cheap labor force, are not legitimate in most modern cultures. Delegitimization in this case provides the legitimization for exploitation. It usually derives from the claim that the other group is inferior or subhuman and, therefore, it is legitimate and moral to exploit it. Blacks in America as well as in Africa were delegitimized and exploited by whites who considered them an inferior race. Such categorization allowed the whites to enslave the blacks under inhumane conditions (e.g., Stamp, 1956; Takaki, 1971).

In times of conflict between groups, especially when the conflict gives rise to violent confrontations, the confronting groups often delegitimize each other in order to justify their negative attitudes, and especially their actions of killing and destruction. This source of delegitimization is most prevalent in human history. Groups in conflict often need delegitimization to explain the causes of conflict, to maintain it, and to prepare their members for the worst in the future. Delegitimization may precede an active conflict or may develop in the course of such a conflict. When an active conflict exists, the intensity of delegitimization provides an indication of its severity and strength. Delegitimization serves to maintain the vicious circle that underlies conflict perpetuation (see Bar-Tal's, 1988 analysis of the delegitimizing relations between the Israeli Jews and Palestinians). On the one hand, the enhanced use of delegitimization necessitates increasingly extreme actions, since more threat and danger are implied. On the other hand, the more negative actions are used, the more delegitimization is needed in order to justify them. Thus, delegitimization provides a conflict support mechanism, and it is very difficult to resolve a conflict as long as delegitimization continues. History has been replete with examples of delegitimization during conflicts, and especially during wars. The mutual delegitimization of Japanese and Americans during the Second World War, of Iranians and Iraqis in the Persian Gulf War, or of Chinese and Vietnamese in their border clashes are only a few examples from modern history.

In the following part, several hypotheses regarding the conditions that increase the possibility of delegitimization are offered. These conditions may also facilitate negative stereotyping and prejudice, but they are especially salient in the case of delegitimization. When the previously described sources exist, the proposed conditions may facilitate the development of delegitimization.

The more threatened a group, the more it will try to delegitimize the threatening group. A threat of a magnitude sufficient to disrupt the group's sense of security is likely to trigger the process of delegitimization which escalates as the threat intensifies. Under these conditions, delegitimization serves as a coping mechanism whereby the threat is reduced by providing: (1) an explanation for the threatening situation: and (2) a prediction of the delegitimized group's future behavior. Consequently, delegitimization psychologically prepares the delegitimizing group for future events. A number of experiments have shown that threat always and inevitably leads to reactions of hostility (e.g., Deutsch & Krauss, 1960; Krauss & Deutsch, 1966). Individuals or groups who experience threat, counter-react and display aggressive behavior, resistance, and anger. Also, another line of research shows that the more individuals attribute hostility and antagonism to another group, the more they feel prejudice towards members of this group (e.g., Groves & Rossi, 1958).

The more violent a conflict between groups, the more they will try to delegitimize each other. Situations of violent intergroup conflict promote attempts of delegitimization. In this case, delegitimization provides not only an explanation or prediction of the situation, but also a justification for the members of the delegitimizing group to perform acts which are otherwise not acceptable. Support for this hypothesis can be based on studies by Sherif and his associates about intergroup conflict (Sherif, 1966), which showed that as the intergroup rivalry and confrontations increased, members of the two groups in conflict displayed highly aggressive, antagonistic, and derogatory behaviors toward each other. Each group developed a negative attitude towards the other group and began to downgrade the other group as "playing dirty," being "cheaters," "unfair," or "cowards."

The greater the difference between groups, the easier it is to delegitimize. The more different the delegitimized group, the easier it is to establish a boundary and to deevaluate that group. Different physical appearance provides a visible and accessible basis for differentiation. Obviously, ethnicity, religion, socioeconomic status, or ideology may serve as a basis for differentiation (see Chapter 7 by Schwartz and Struch). When the delegitimizing group is different from the delegitimized group, it implies that the delegitimizing characteristics are possessed exclusively by the latter group and no negative implications are carried for the former one. It is, thus, not surprising that groups, for example, select scapegoats who are different from them (Allport, 1954).

The less a group values another group, the easier it is for this group to delegitimize the other group. This condition stresses the negation aspect of the delegitimized group which is central to the delegitimization process. Delegitimizing practices can be expected to be more easily carried out under conditions in which the other group is initially negatively evaluated. Negative evaluation facilitates the use of delegitimizing labels, since they do not require any dramatic change of perceptions, but only a polarization of previously held beliefs. In this line, experiments by Berkowitz and others (Berkowitz, 1962) indicate that members of groups for whom some dislike and devaluation already exists tend to be preferred substitute targets of frustration-induced hostility; further, the animosity was manifested both through overt aggression and the attribution of negative characteristics to the disliked and devalued person.

The less tolerant the group in its norms, the more prone it is to use delegitimization. Lack of tolerance indicates that the group tends to react negatively toward individuals or other groups who are perceived as different. Delegitimization will be utilized by groups that do not have a tradition of tolerance. A tradition of tolerance inhibits the group from using overgeneralized negative labels, particularly when such labels have behavioral implications, as in the case with delegitimization. On the individual level, several studies showed that people differ with regard to tolerance. Some people are characterized by more tolerance than others. The former display less prejudice than the latter (e.g., Allport & Kramer, 1946; Evans, 1952).

Functions of Delegitimization

Much has been written about the functions categorization fulfills for the individual (e.g., Cantor & Mischel, 1979; Eiser & Stroebe, 1972; Tajfel, 1981; Taylor, 1981; Tessler, 1978). Delegitimization, as a categorization of specific contents, serves several functions for individuals, as well as for groups. The personal functions refer to individuals' knowledge formation as a result of the categorization process. Organization of knowledge, evaluation of new information, and control over environment are personal functions discussed in the past by social psychologists (e.g., Cantor & Mischel, 1979; Eiser & Stroebe, 1972; Ostrom, Lingle, Pryor, & Geva, 1980; Rosch, 1978; Tajfel, 1978). Of special importance for the present analysis are those functions of delegitimization which serve groups. Although they may not be unique to delegitimization, their expressions and outcomes are especially salient in the case of delegitimization.

Justification for Extreme Negative Behavior

A particularly important function of delegitimization is to justify extremely negative behaviors toward the delegitimized group. This justification may appear following the extreme acts or it may lead to them. In the first case, delegitimization provides a solution for the cognitive need to explain and justify such extremely negative behaviors as indiscriminated killings of civilians, mass arrests, massive discrimination, or even genocide. This reflects the well-established psychological fact that people construct beliefs and attitudes following their behavior, in order to account for it (Bem, 1972; Zanna & Rempel, 1988). In the second case, the delegitimizing beliefs imply that the delegitimized group deserves extreme treatments. They provide the delegitimization to hurt the other group. Indeed, the most extreme attempts of genocide were carried out on the basis of a delegitimization process. Dr. Behrendt, a German scientist, wrote about Gypsies in 1939:

> They are criminal and asocial and it is impossible to educate them. All Gypsies should be treated as hereditarily sick. The only solution is elimination. The aim

should therefore be elimination without hesitation of this characteristically defective element of the population (Kendrick & Puxon, 1972).

Similarly, an American soldier in the Vietnam War expressed this function explicitly:

> When you go into basic training you are taught that the Vietnamese are not people. You are taught, they are gooks and all you hear is "gook, gook, gook, gook" . . . The Asian serviceman in Vietnam is the brunt of the same racism because the GIs over there do not distinguish one Asian from another . . . You are trained "gook, gook, gook," and once the military has got the idea implanted in your mind that these people are not humans, they are subhuman, it makes it a little bit easier to kill 'em (Boyle, 1972, p. 141).

Also, since the delegitimized group is often perceived as highly threatening, extreme measures against such a group are justified in order to avert the eventual danger. Members of the delegitimizing group feel that they can harm the delegitimized for self-defence.

Intergroup Differentiation

Each group strives to emphasize its boundaries of membership. This results from a need to differentiate one's own group from other groups (Tajfel & Turner, 1979). The greater the danger of opened boundaries as a consequence of geographical proximity, social mobility, political conditions, or cultural similarity, the stronger is the need to draw the differentiating boundaries. As elaborated above, delegitimization sharpens intergroup differences to an extreme, since it totally excludes the delegitimized group from commonly accepted groups. It indicates that the delegitimized group does not belong to groups which are evaluated positively by the norms and/or values of the delegitimizing group. Delegitimization allows for the placing of a definite boundary between one's own group and the delegitimized group. It indicates that there exists and should continue to exist a clear cut difference between the two groups. Individuals in the delegitimized group cannot be members of the delegitimizing group. In this respect, delegitimization provides a criterion for the discrimination between the two groups, since the delegitimized group serves as a negative group reference. Such differentiation often takes the form of legally forbidding marriages or other associations as happened in Germany during the Nazi regime with regard to non-Aryan groups, or in South Africa with regard to blacks. It can be argued that as long as clear-cut boundaries are maintained, delegitimization continues. Breaking down of social boundaries is a crucial condition for creating a reversal process, whereby delegitimization can be restrained.

Feelings of Superiority

For competitive societies, when a group maintains contact and/or relations with another group, each of them usually tries to achieve superiority over the other group. Groups compete among themselves, and through comparison, strive to view themselves as more successful, victorious, developed, or more moral and human. Delegitimization provides solid grounds for superiority in comparison to the delegitimized group, as it lowers the value of the latter group extremely. It indicates that the group has very negative characteristics to the extent that it should be excluded from the commonly accepted groups.

An illustration of the need for superiority can be found in a Khrushchev interview in *Pravda* on April 27, 1962. He said:

> We are convinced that communism will triumph because it provides better conditions for the development of the productive forces of society, provides conditions for the fullest and most harmonious development of society in general and for every individual in particular. . . . sooner or later communism will win everywhere in the world and, consequently, communism will bury capitalism (in Hanak, 1972, p. 79).

Group Uniformity

Each group strives to maintain some degree of unity reflected in uniformity which is one of the foundations for group existence. Members of an enduring group are likely to display at least some central beliefs of striking homogeneity. Lack of group uniformity and by definition, unity, may cause low cohesiveness and may even result in its disintegration. To avoid such processes, groups often apply pressures on their members to create uniformity of beliefs, attitudes, and behaviors. The pressure to maintain unity or specifically uniformity is particularly strong in situations of threat. Delegitimizing beliefs imply that the delegitimized group has characteristics that threaten the delegitimizing group. Labels such as murderers, imperialists, or Nazis indicate danger and threat. As a result, group members are called to unite behind the uniform beliefs and behaviors in order to avert the danger. In this respect, delegitimizing beliefs serve a function of maintaining uniformity.

In addition, the use of delegitimizing labels strengthens the agreement that the delegitimized group deserves negative attitudes and behaviors and weakens the possibility of considering alternative beliefs. The delegitimizing group applies pressure on its members to hold the delegitimizing beliefs, and sanctions against individuals who attempt to provide information inconsistent with the delegitimizing beliefs, or to consider alternative beliefs. Since members of the delegitimizing group seek to receive positive rewards and to avoid negative sanctions, they often conform to the group's pressure. The Nazi regime in Germany provides an example of how extreme pressures can be applied to keep group uniformity vis-à-vis various delegitimized groups. The Nazis delegitimized various ethnic, political, and social groups within the societal system and then used extreme means of terror to uphold the delegitimization and to unite the German into homogeneous society (Allen, 1965; Bracher, 1971).

Implications

In summary, delegitimization is a specific type of social categorization which is characterized by:

1. extremely negative and salient basis for categorization;

2. permanent exclusion of the delegitimized group from the society;
3. extremely intense negative effective component;
4. institutionalized norms supporting delegitimization;
5. implication of a threat from the delegitimized group; and
6. prescription for extremely negative behaviors towards the delegitimized groups.

Delegitimization may occur within any context of intergroup relations: international, interreligious, intercultural, or interideological. In most cases, the use of delegitimization points to intergroup conflict (i.e., incompatibility between the goals of the delegitimizing and delegitimized groups), although not all conflicts are necessarily accompanied by delegitimization (see Bar-Tal & Geva, 1985; Klar, Bar-Tal, & Kruglanski, 1988; Rapoport, 1960). Delegitimization develops when the relations between the delegitimizing and delegitimized groups are frozen at the extreme negative poles of the dimension describing the quality of intergroup relations. In cases of conflict, delegitimization implies intense and persistent conflict characterized by an absence of formal attempts and/or motivation to resolve it. In cases of exploitation, the exploiting group refuses to change the situation since the motives are satisfied and delegitimization stabilizes the exploiting relations on the part of the delegitimizing group.

On a personal level, once individuals form delegitimizing categories, they often freeze on them and become motivated to hold them as truth (see Kruglanski & Ajzen, 1983 for their analysis of freezing). In general, perceivers attempt to maintain formed group categories by seeking information that supports the differentiation on which the category is based (Hamilton, 1979; Tajfel, 1978). This tendency is accentuated in the case of delegitimization, which involves strong emotional reactions and serves vital social functions.

In spite of freezing, delegitimizing beliefs are not necessarily stable and unchangeable. Since they apply to the same principles of change as all the other contents of knowledge and knowledge is dynamic, delegitimizing beliefs can be changed. That is, delegitimizing categories can be replaced by other categories. Nevertheless, such change is especially difficult because of the emotional and behavioral implications that the delegitimizing labels carry. Among the important factors influencing such changes are the information that is available to the individuals, individuals' capacity to collect and process new information, and their motivation to maintain a given category (see Bar-Tal, Kruglanski, & Klar, in press for more extensive analysis).

Groups sometimes change the delegitimizing categories they use as objective changes in the existing situation take place – changes which promote cognitive availability of new information. Learning and education may reinforce the capacity to cognize various bits of evidence and to entertain alternative contents of knowledge (see Bar-Tal, 1988). Obviously, when a group is motivated, for various reasons, to perceive the delegitimized group in a different manner, the change is greatly facilitated.

Delegitimization is an extremely negative reaction which increases tension between groups, carries grave negative consequences such as discrimination, exploitation, hostile acts, and even genocide. In the present paper, the nature of delegitimization was analyzed to illuminate the consequences. Any group which delegitimizes another group must be aware of the implications of such an act.

Acknowledgments. The author would like to thank Steffen Fuller for helping to conceptualize portions of this paper and Marilynn Brewer, Ina Wiener, Shalom Schwartz, and Robert Holt for providing helpful comments on the earlier draft of this manuscript.

References

Allen, W.S. (1965). *The Nazi seizure of power.* Chicago: University of Chicago Press.

Allport, G.W. (1954). *The nature of prejudice.* Reading, MA: Addison-Wesley.

Allport, G.W., & Kramer, B.M. (1946). Some roots of prejudice. *Journal of Psychology, 22,* 9–39.

Bar-Tal, D. (1988). Delegitimizing relations between Israeli Jews and Palestinians: A social psychological analysis. In J. Hoffman & S. Mari (Eds.), *Arab-Jewish relations* (pp. 217–248). Bristol, IN: Wymdhamall Hall.

Bar-Tal, D. (1989). *Group beliefs of delegitimizing Jews in Germany: (1933–194)5).* Manuscript submitted for publication.

Bar-Tal, D. (in press). *Group beliefs.* New York: Springer-Verlag.

Bar-Tal, D., & Geva, N. (1985). A cognitive basis of international conflicts. In S. Worchel & W.G. Austin (Eds.), *The social psychology of intergroup relations* (2nd ed.) (pp. 118–133). Chicago: Nelson-Hall.

Bar-Tal, D., Kruglanski, A.W., & Klar, Y. (in press). Conflict termination: An epistemological analysis of international cases. *Political Psychology.*

Baynes, N.H. (Ed.). (1942). *The speeches of Adolf Hitler* (Vol. 1). Oxford: Oxford University Press.

Bem, D.J. (1972). Self-perception theory. In L. Berkowitz (Ed.), *Advances in experimental social psychology* (Vol 6) (pp. 1–62). New York: Academic Press.

Berkowitz, L. (1962). *Aggression: A social psychological approach.* New York: McGraw-Hill.

Billig, M. (1982). *Ideology and social psychology.* Oxford: Basil Blackwell.

Boyle, R. (1972). *The flower of the dragon: The breakdown of the U.S. Army in Vietnam.* San Francisco: Ramparts Press.

Bracher, K.D. (1971). *The German dictatorship.* London: Weidenfeld and Nicholson.

Brewer, M.B., & Kramer, R.M. (1985). The psychology of intergroup attitudes and behavior. *Annual Review of Psychology, 36,* 219–243.

Cantor, N., & Mischel, W. (1979). Prototypes in social cognition. In L. Berkowitz (Ed.), *Advance in experimental social psychology* (Vol. 12) (pp. 13–52). New York: Academic Press.

Dawidowicz, L.S. (1975). *The war against the Jews (1933–1945).* New York: Holt, Rinehart and Winston.

Deutsch, M., & Krauss, R.M. (1960). The effect of threat on interpersonal bargaining. *Journal of Abnormal and Social Psychology, 61,* 181–189.

Dulles, J.F. (1950). *War or peace.* New York: Macmillan.

Eiser, J.R., & Stroebe, W. (1972). *Categorization and social judgment.* London: Academic Press.

Evans, R.I. (1952). Personal values as factors in anti-Semitism. *Journal of Abnormal and Social Psychology, 47,* 749–756.

Goffman, E. (1963). *Stigma: Notes on the management of spoiled identity.* Englewood Cliffs, NJ: Prentice Hall.

Groves, W.E., & Rossi, P.H. (1958). Police perceptions of a hostile ghetto. *American Behavioral Scientist, 13*, 727–743.

Hamilton, D.L. (1979). A cognitive–attitudinal analysis of sterotyping. In L. Berkowitz (Ed.), *Advance in experimental social psychology* (Vol. 1) (pp. 53–84). New York: Academic Press.

Hamilton, D.L. (Ed.). (1981). *Cognitive process in stereotyping and intergroup behavior.* Hillsdale, NJ: Erlbaum.

Hanak, H. (1972). *Soviet foreign policy since the death of Stalin.* London: Routledge & Kegan Paul.

Jones, J.M. (1972). *Prejudice and racism.* Reading, MA: Addison-Wesley.

Katz, D., & Braly, K.W. (1933). Racial stereotypes of 100 college students. *Journal of Abnormal and Social Psychology, 28*, 280–290.

Katz, I. (1981). *Stigma: A social psychological analysis.* Hillsdale, NJ: Erlbaum.

Kendrick, D., & Puxon, G. (1972). *The destiny of Europe's Gypsies.* London: Sussex University Press.

Klar, Y., Bar-Tal, D., & Kruglanski, A.W. (1988). Conflict as a cognitive schema: An epistemological approach. In W. Stroebe, A.W. Kruglanski, D. Bar-Tal, & M. Hewstone (Eds.), *Social psychology of intergroup and international conflict* (pp. 73–85). New York: Springer-Verlag.

Knox, R. (1862). The races of man: A philosophical enquiry into the influence of race over the destinies of nations. In P.D. Curtin (Ed.), *Imperialism* (pp. 12–22). New York: Harper & Row.

Krauss, R.M., & Deutsch, M. (1966). Communication in interpersonal bargaining. *Journal of Personality and Social Psychology, 4*, 572–577.

Kruglanski, A.W. (in press). *Basic processes in social cognition: A theory of lay epistemology.* New York: Plenum.

Kruglanski, A.W., & Ajzen, I. (1983). Bias and error in human judgment. *European Journal of Social Psychology, 13*, 1–44.

Leopold II (1962). Leopold II defends his rule in the Congo, 1897. In L.L. Snyder (Ed.), *The imperialism reader* (pp. 236–238). Princeton, NJ: Van Nostrand.

Ostrom, T.M., Lingle, J.H., Pryor, J.B., & Geva, N. (1980). Cognitive organization of person impressions. In R. Hastie, T.M. Ostrom, E.B. Ebbesen, R.S. Wyer, D.L. Hamilton, & D.E. Carlston, (Eds.), *Person memory: The cognitive basis of social perception* (pp. 55–88). Hillsdale, NJ: Erlbaum.

Pettigrew, T.F. (1971). *Racially separate or together.* New York: McGraw-Hill.

Piao, L. (1971). Defeat U.S. imperialism by people's war. In K.T. Fann & P. Hodges (Eds.), *Readings in U.S. imperialism* (pp. 371–381). Boston: Porter Sargent.

Poliakov, L. (1974). *The Aryan myth: A history of racist and nationalist ideas in Europe.* London: Chatto-Heinemann.

Rapoport, A. (1960). *Fights, games, and debates.* Ann Arbor, MI: University of Michigan Press.

Rosch, E. (1978). Principles of categorization. In E. Rosch & B.B. Lloyd (Eds.), *Cognition and categorization* (pp. 27–48). Hillsdale, NJ: Erlbaum.

Sherif M. (1966). *Group conflict and cooperation.* London: Routledge & Kegan Paul.

Stamp, K.M. (1956). *The peculiar institution: Negro slavery in the American South.* New York: Knopf.

Stephan, W.G. (1985). Intergroup relations. In G. Lindzey & E. Aronson (Eds.), *Handbook of social psychology,* (3rd ed., Vol. 2) (pp. 599–658). New York: Random House.

Tajfel, H. (1978). *Differentiation between social groups.* London: Academic Press.

Tajfel, H. (1981). *Human groups and social categories.* Oxford: Blackwell.

Tajfel, H., & Turner, J. (1979). An integrative theory of intergroup conflict. In W.G. Austin & S. Worchel (Eds.), *The social psychology of intergroup relations* (pp. 33–47). Belmont, CA: Wadsworth.

Takaki, R.T. (1971). *A pro-slavery crusade.* New York: Free Press.

Taylor, S.E. (1981). A categorization approach to stereotyping. In D.L. Hamilton (Ed.), *Cognitive processes in stereotyping and intergroup behavior* (pp. 83–114). Hillsdale, NJ: Erlbaum.

Tessler, A. (1978). Self generated attitude change. In L. Berkowitz (Ed.), *Advances in experimental social psychology* (Vol. 11) (pp. 289–338). New York: Academic Press.

White, R.K. (1984). *Fearful warriors.* New York: Free Press.

Zanna, M., & Rempel, J.K. (1988). Attitudes: A new look. In D. Bar-Tal & A.W. Kruglanski (Eds.), *The social psychology of knowledge* (pp. 315–334). Cambridge, England: Cambridge University Press.

Chapter 9

Discriminatory Speech Acts: A Functional Approach

Carl Friedrich Graumann and Margret Wintermantel

Social Discrimination

The Concept of Social Discrimination

What does it mean when we say that we discriminate against others and that we often do so by means of language?

Discriminating in its broadest sense is one of the most elementary and pervasive processes of human activity. As the process by which we respond differently to different stimuli, it is practically synonymous with behavior (Stevens, 1939). In a more cognitive vein, we discriminate as we perceive or mark the distinguishing features of something. While this elementary differentiation is not our topic, it is the necessary prerequisite of what we mean when we speak of *social discrimination* or of *discriminating against others*. Here, to discriminate means to make a difference in treatment on a categorical basis, usually in disregard of individual properties or merits. Within the context of social-psychological research the practice of categorical discrimination means the according of differential treatment on the basis of (real or alleged) group or class membership. While such differential treatment comprises both acceptance and rejection (cf. Jaspars, 1983), the major interest of social scientists in discrimination has been in the various techniques and modalities of disadvantaging others, of denying or refusing some people access to outcomes or goals granted to others.

Hence, the concept of social discrimination is inextricably connected to notions of justice and equ(al)ity; the denial of equal treatment amounts to the denial of equal rights, as is easily seen from the favorite illustrations of social discrimination: Members of certain categories or groups are denied equality of employment, of pay, of housing, of political representation, or of the use of public facilities.

Beyond such conspicuous instances of the denial of equal rights as they are codified in national constitutions and international charters, there is a broad range of discriminatory behaviors by which members of one (e.g., majority) group deny members of another (e.g., minority) group equal treatment or standing, that is, the treatment or standing they "naturally" accord their own kind. In the words of a United Nations document cited by Allport (1954, p. 51): "Discrimination comes about only when we deny to individuals or groups of people equality of treatment which they may wish," but we prefer to qualify the denial by "on a categorical basis."

So members of a majority group may try to avoid close or personal contact with members of the minority, refuse to communicate with them directly or, if they have to deal with them, deny them equal standing and the right to reciprocate. Mainly this strategy of keeping others at a social distance or on a lower social stratum merely because of their group membership comprises a variety of discriminatory behaviors, many of which make use of the possibilities provided by language.

"Strategy" suggests intent which raises a familiar problem. It is true that in the context of the legal debate about minorities' rights to political representation the issue is whether discrimination is to be defined by discriminatory *effects* or by discriminatory *intent* (cf. Thernstrom, 1983). This debate resembles to a large extent the one waged about the psychological construct of aggression, and understandably so. If discrimination is intentional, it is a case of aggression. But many, maybe all, of the discriminatory effects may also be brought about by other than aggressive or discriminatory intentions or other causes.

For the purpose of this chapter we shall not take up and renew this debate, knowing too well that it would lead us into the dead end of interpreting unconscious intentions. We shall concentrate rather on the functions of social discrimination and those modes of speech which may be used to discriminate against others, that is, which are apt to deny others rights (in a nonlegal sense) or the equality of treatment to which they are entitled and may wish to get. Whether an individual discriminatory speech act (d-speech act) is uttered with or without (awareness of) intention shall be left to the empirical study of social discrimination. Our present concern is the relationship between language and social discrimination, in particular, the concept of discriminatory speech act within a social psychological framework. Social discrimination is conceived here as a form of social action. It implies an actor, whom we wish to name the discriminator, and a target person or group. Hence, social discrimination is a relative term. As all action, it may be actualized by either doing something or refraining from doing something. The same applies to discriminatory speech: Ignoring, that is, not mentioning someone may be as discriminating as explicitly referring to a person in a categorical manner.

The Functions of Social Discrimination

When, in the following, we list and discuss some facets of the functions of social discrimination, we neither imply that the list is exhaustive, nor do we understand these facets to be mutually exclusive. They should rather be considered as different aspects and purposes of social discrimination. Figure 9-1 is an attempt at visualizing the different functions.

1. *Discriminating as separating.* This is, as stated above, the basic operation of setting and keeping apart or differentiating A from Non-A, self from others,

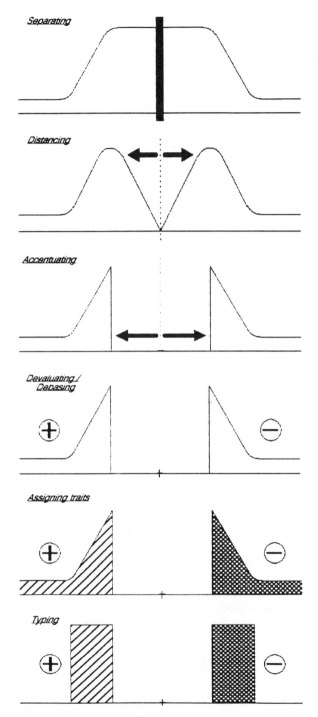

Figure 9-1. A graphic representation of the different functions of social discrimination. The left half always refer to the ingroup (or "own" category), the right to the outgroup (or "other" category).

ingroup from outgroup. The conceptual or cognitive means of separating is "drawing a line" by categorization or classification; the effect is structural order.

2. *Discriminating as distancing*. Drawing a dividing line between A and B is indifferent as to the (semantic or social) distance between A and B. But the best way to keep things or people apart is to place a distance between them, which makes order visible at a glance.

3. *Discriminating as accentuating*. When we differentiate by imposing classes and by placing distances between them, we mark dissimilarities rather than similarity, which tends to result in an accentuation of the difference between the categories in question. The cognitive effect of heterogeneity made salient is to be seen in the ease of perception and retention.

4. *Discriminating as evaluating*. Social discrimination tends to devaluate or debase the outgroup, hereby — at least implicitly — boosting the value of one's own group and one's own social identity (self-enhancement).

5. *Discriminating as fixating*. When we discriminate against somebody we do not treat him or her as an individual person with changing states and activities, but as a case or instance of a category or as a typical member of an outgroup. Treating someone generically, that is, interchangeably, is accomplished either by assigning (typical) traits to this person or by allocating him/her to a type (stereotype). In both cases the generic target is marked for good, that is, fixated. Hence, the discriminator will expect typical, that is, highly predictable behavior from the discriminated target. The psychological economy of the invariant over the variable, of the lasting over the fleeting, is evident: If someone (or something) is typed, we "know" who or what we have to deal with and how to behave whenever in the future we meet a typical "instance" of a category; Jews will be Jews, women are women, gays will be gays.

The Changing Face of Social Discrimination

The student of social discrimination is confronted with a problem that stems from the convergence of two social-psychological traditions, both of which leave much to be desired. The first tradition has firmly associated social discrimination with stereotypes and prejudice. This triad is still reflected in the way textbooks and research monographs deal with social discrimination. The underlying conception of the triad is that stereotypes form the cognitive basis or part of prejudice and that prejudice, in turn, is conducive to discrimination. The problem here is the same that we have in the relationship between attitude and behavior: Prevailing stereotypes and prejudice may be identified, but prejudiced individuals do not necessarily display observable discriminatory behavior.

On the other hand, people may, in effect, discriminate against others without (noticeable) prejudice, for example, when they refuse to sell or let their houses and apartments to members of a certain ethnic group "strictly for fear of what their neighbors will do" (Seeman, 1981, p. 380).

If there is (and we know there is) prejudice without discrimination and discrimination without prejudice, what has social psychology contributed to the issue of their relationship? What is the justification for the seemingly firm association of stereotype and prejudice with discrimination? Historically, there was a period of naiveté: If we know the attitude we can predict behavior; if we know the (antecedent) prejudice, we will be better able to fight the (consequent) discrimination. This simple model had to be abandoned for various theoretical and methodological reasons. Instead, we have now, in the era of a predominantly "cognitive" social psychology, a preoccupation with the cognitive aspects of prejudice and with the integration of the triad into the more general complex of "social cognition" (Hamilton, 1981).

In this situation the tradition of the problematic triad converges with a second trend, the neglect of (overt) behavior in social psychology. Leaving aside the era of behaviorism—which has not had much influence on social psychology—it is a fact that social behavior or interaction has, from the beginning of social psychology, fostered far less research interest than cognition and motivation as, for example, attitude and attitude change. Hence, whoever looks into the literature on stereotype, prejudice, and discrimination will find least about the latter topic and, language being none of social psychology's concerns, almost nothing about verbal behavior.

A recent literature review of unobtrusive studies on racism (Crosby, Bromley, & Saxe, 1980) deals with three categories of racist behavior: helping behavior, aggression, and *non*verbal, but not verbal behavior. To wit, there are studies where speech is recorded as a dependent variable (Bishop, 1976; Hendricks & Bortzin, 1976; Weitz, 1972), but its discriminatory character is measured in para- and extralinguistic features of speech, such as voice tone, loudness, seating distance, and length of speech. The reason for this focus on nonverbal variables becomes obvious when one regards the prejudiced speaker's dilemma, which is a notoriously, but not exclusively, "American dilemma" (Myrdal, 1944), viz., the conflict between the belief in the liberal and egalitarian ideals of a modern Western democracy, on the one hand, and individual or group interests, jealousies, anxieties, impulses, and prejudices with respect to one's own and one's own group's superiority, on the other hand. Since to utter the former is socially desirable, yet to pronounce one's prejudice is not, we may expect to find discrimination less in the outspokenness of verbal content, which is easily controlled by a speaker, than in what a speaker "gives off" unawares or in what can be read "between the lines." That is exactly where unobtrusive measures are required.

There is one other historical argument for this approach. As compared to the Forties, when Myrdal wrote his book, the intensity of the dilemma seems to have increased. At least students of racism in the United States are in agreement as to a change in discriminatory "style," due to the impact of the civil rights movement. The old-fashioned, blatant, "rednecked" racism has, approximately since the 1950s, given way to "modern racism" (McConahay, 1983, 1986), "symbolic racism" (McConahay & Hough, 1976), and "aversive" (Gaertner & Dovidio, 1986) and ambivalent forms of racism (Katz, 1981).

The ambivalence of this "modern" kind of racism and discrimination has its own peculiar rationale: Yes, racism is bad and gone; but it is a fact that blacks "are pushing too hard, too fast and into places where they are not wanted" (McConahay, 1986, p. 93). Accordingly, the "negative affect that aversive racists have for blacks is not hostility or hate. Instead, this negativity involves discomfort, uneasiness, disgust, and sometimes fear, which factors tend to motivate avoidance rather than intentionally destructive behaviors" (Gaertner & Dovidio, 1986, p. 63).

What we have here exemplified for racism also holds for sexism (cf. Spence, Deaux, & Helmreich, 1985) and other forms of "modern" discrimination: The fact that in many (or most?) Western countries straightforward ("old-fashioned") ethnic, religious, or other social prejudice has become socially undesirable, but nevertheless is virulent, leads to indirect and socially less objectionable forms of discrimination. Studying discrimination against *Gastarbeiter* (foreign workers) in West Germany, Wagner and Machleit (1986, p. 60) conclude in a similar vein:

> Most prejudiced people prefer to engage in those kinds of discrimination that can not be punished. One common type of discrimination that is largely tolerated is avoiding contact with members of ethnic minorities.

Hence, what we may take from the studies on "modern" discrimination for our own research interest is not to look for "blatant" discriminatory speech of an aggressive kind, but to examine speech samples for signs and symbols of such defensive, aversive, ambivalent attitudes; these are nevertheless signs of the major functions of discrimination: separating, distancing, accentuating differences, devaluating, and stereotyping – signs and symbols not necessarily recognized as discriminatory by everybody but signals "to whom it may concern."

Whom does discriminatory behavior concern? The target, of course, is the individual considered a member of a discriminated group. It is such categorized individuals who are refused equality of treatment. But, if we consider the avoidance hypothesis, the targets of social discrimination will, as a rule, not be the (face-to-face) addressees of discriminatory speech. The victims are the ones we talk *about* but avoid talking to. Herein lies a lesson to be learned from social-psychological research on "modern" discrimination.

Considering the use of the term "discrimination" in contemporary social psychology, one final conceptual clarification is required. In the studies on intergroup behavior, mainly in the Tajfel tradition, we very often find the terms of intergroup discrimination when intergroup differentiation would be the more adequate expression. Members of a group A may make a distinction between their own group and all others or a certain group B, and they may favor their ingroup, as has been demonstrated in many experiments (Tajfel, 1978). This, however, would not (yet) mean that A-group members per se deny other individuals equal treatment, which they may wish, on a categorical basis. "Ingroup favoritism" presupposes differentiation, not discrimination. But differentiation may grow into discrimination. Hence, Tajfel (1978, p. 51) has described at least one of the conditions for this change into a more antagonistic form of intergroup behavior as the "belief that the relevant social boundaries between the groups are sharply drawn and immutable, in the sense that, for whatever reasons, it is impossible or at least difficult for individuals to move from one group to the other."

This conception of ingroup–outgroup divisions reflects the functions of social discrimination as outlined above. It is certainly descriptive of everyday discriminating against minority groups when boundary lines are sharply drawn by refusing outgroup members equal rights, to housing, hiring, pay, promotion, or political representation. But these real-life discriminatory acts are, at best, examples, not topics of social psychological research. It is left to sociologists and political scientists to deal with them. Social psychology, with its preference for the experimental method, has to restrict discriminatory behavior to the dependent variables of differentially allocating (token) money or points in more or less "minimal" social settings (e.g., Tajfel, 1979, 1978; Turner, 1987) or of differentially evaluating in- and outgroups (e.g., Doise, 1972). The field-experimental exceptions to such lab-impoverished operationalizations of social discriminations were the hostile activities of the "Bull Dogs" and "Red Devils" in Sherif's camp studies (Sherif, 1967; Sherif & Sherif, 1953). The relative abstention of social psychologists from studying real-life discrimination may only partly be justifiable from a methodological viewpoint. Partly it is due to the traditional neglect of "verbal behavior" in social-psychological research. Since we propose to overcome this hesitance with respect to language, a large part of everyday social discrimination becomes accessible to psychological research, namely, verbal discrimination.

Language, Action, and Social Discrimination

The Functions of Social Discrimination in Language

Language is too universal, complex, and pervasive a phenomenon to be dealt with exhaustively from the perspective of one discipline. Since these authors believe that speaking and understanding language are fundamental constituents of social interaction and, hence, should be central topics of a social psychology (Graumann, 1987), they realize that the interest a social scientist takes in language has its own profile, different from that of other disciplines dealing with language. For the sociologist and social psychologist language is, primarily, the medium through and by which humans act and interact. While it is true that social psychology traditionally has been preoccupied with cognitions and the cognitive–affective components of behavior, it is equally true that cognitions (ideas, meanings, attitudes, etc.) "do not drift aimlessly through the social world, but circulate as utterances, as expressions, as words which are spoken or inscribed" (Thompson, 1987, p. 517). If we take this circulation of utterances as an object of social and psychological study this does not mean that we disregard language as a system of signs (cf. Bühler, 1965), but we concur with de Saussure (1966, p. 16) that we must study the life of signs within the context of social life or, in a more recent phrase, study the things we do with words (Austin, 1975) with respect to others.

One of the things we "do unto others" with words that conveys meaning is the establishment, the maintenance, and the reproduction or dissolution of social (interpersonal) relations. One aspect of the maintenance of social relations, that is of special interest for the study of social discrimination is the maintenance of *power relations* as, for instance, between ingroup and outgroup, majority and minority groups. If social discrimination as we understand it is the differential, that is, disadvantaging treatment of individuals, for instance as outgroup members, such treatment, whether verbal or nonverbal, is in the service of maintaining dominance. If language as we understand it is an essential means of maintaining social relations, the central question and topic of this contribution is to determine how speech acts may discriminate against others by sustaining relations of domination between a speaker's group and the group to which an addressee or an individual referent is assigned.

We will now exemplify some of the ways and means by which these purposes can be realized in words and speech acts.

Separating. A minimal but important form of drawing a dividing line between in- and outgroup is the systematic and persistent use of WE vs. THEY. These two words are the pronominal equivalent of "ingroup" and "outgroup." With the use of the first-person plural, speakers not only refer to the ingroup to which they belong; they also express their social identity; whereas with the use of the third-person-plural pronoun a social difference is indicated: With THEM we do not identify.

A convincing illustration of the social semantics of WE vs. THEY was given by Zavalloni (1973), who demonstrated that "WE and THEY may coexist as parameters of a single group membership" (p. 83). French and American respondents of (black or Jewish) minority or of majority groups "produced negative descriptions of their groups' memberships when THEY was used as a qualifier of the groups" (p. 85), while the use of WE was conducive to more favorable or, at least, neutral categories. The important finding is that the differentiating power of these personal pronouns is not restricted to preexisting groups but may draw dividing lines within one and the same group expressing the degree of a speaker's identification with the group.

Distancing. Sometimes, referring to THEM has the demonstrative quality of "that person (there)"; van Dijk (1984, p. 137) even speaks of "demonstratives of distance." The German equivalent of THEM is "die da" ("them there"). "Die" or "Them" are those we demonstratively point at, that is, from a social distance. Pointing at somebody, however, is a behavior which, in both its verbal and nonverbal form, is not considered good manners in our own group.

The semantics of social separation and distance is not restricted to the differential use of pronouns. What Mehrabian (1971) and Wiener (Wiener & Mehrabian, 1968), in their studies on "language within language," have termed forms of "nonimmediacy" are linguistic means to show less positive feelings toward persons or things by putting them at a distance in space or time, by avoiding to mention them at all, although the context suggests it, or by referring to them in ambiguous ways (Mehrabian, 1971, p. 92). A quite common way of avoiding immediacy is to replace direct reference to persons by reference to situations or even to abstract states of affairs in which the persons or groups in question are involved. Instead of stating explicitly that members of a group with which he sympathizes committed acts of violence against members of another (less likeable) group, a speaker merely states that in a state of tension "bullets began to fly." Without any shooting agents mentioned we may learn that some people "had" or suffered injuries or losses. Quite often the impersonal, abstract language of bureaucracy covers the human problem if, for instance, immigrants are referred to by "the rate of net inflow" (Sykes, 1985, p. 98). All of these means will be used when speakers try to distance or disassociate themselves from others in discriminatory speech acts.

Accentuating. Accentuating, or emphasizing differences, is usually accomplished by using disjunct categories rather than dimensional attributes regardless of the nature of the characteristic in question. While an elaborate psychological theory of accentuation (in social categorization and judgment) has been developed (cf. Eiser & Stroebe, 1972; for an overview see Lilli, 1975) with only marginal reference to the language of accentuation (cf. however Eiser & van der Pligt, 1984), we shall merely exemplify how intergroup differences and dissimilarities are suggested and accentuated by words while similarities are suppressed.

We take it for granted that the physical complexion of the human race has a wide dimensional (and certainly not unidimensional) range: from the darkest Negro to the palest Caucasian, from the deepest bronze of a North American aborigine to the complexion of a Chinese. Yet, we have never seen a "white" man nor a "black" woman nor a "red" skin, with the exception of actors and actresses wearing heavy makeup. While it would be correct to say that we all are colored, we tend to use this dimensional term for "nonwhites" only. This, in turn, would be justifiable if "white" people were really white. Moreover, the meaning of "colored" has changed over the years and may still be changing. Once a euphemism for "black" or Negro, it was replaced by "black" when this was no longer a pejorative word.

Another way of referring to human variety has been in terms of "races." Whatever the anthropological legitimacy of the construct "race" has been and will be, it was for purposes of social segregation that the largely fictitious category of the "Aryan" was used, mainly by the Nazis. One could have ignored or ridiculed the far-spread claim to be of Aryan descent (Poliakov, 1974) unless, in the ideology of anti-Semitism, the figure of the "non-Aryan" had not been invented, successfully introduced, and finally made an individual as well as collective target of racist hatred, persecution, and ultimately annihilation. The accentuation accomplished with this pernicious dichotomy was the sharp contrast between the superior (WE) race and the only negatively labeled racially inferior (THEY) "rest of the world." Here language has helped to prepare and to maintain a policy of segregation or apartheid, even of genocide.

Evaluating. Those who are kept at a distance and accentuated as very different are also, as a rule, devaluated by means of derogatory, "denigrating" words and phrases. The negativity of such discriminatory words can be attained by their privative construction, as with "non-Aryan" descent and "un-American" activities. It can be a word which is meant to convey the notion of a fundamental lack, for example, of culture, as in the Greeks' and Romans' "barbarians," or of true faith and proper worship, as in the Christians' "heathens."

Many ethnic groups have reserved the word for being human as the name for their own group, thus rendering the "rest of the world" less than or not human.

In our time and culture we may refer to certain outgroups in both a more neutral and a belittling and debasing language. We may, for example, refer to

Irish	or	harps
Jews	or	kikes
Gentiles	or	goyim
Germans	or	krauts/boches
Italians	or	wops
Negroes	or	niggers
Chinese	or	chinks, and so forth.

Allport (1954, p. 181), who lists some of these example, is right when he states that in the ethnic sphere even the plain nouns that are the first terms in each pair may have "emotional tone," but the second terms in each pair are their "higher key equivalents." With their usage a speaker "*intends* not only to characterize the person's membership, but also to disparage and reject him."

Fixating. What do we mean if we refer to another person as a Jew, a Belgian, or a Turk? There are only very few situations when the explicit reference to someone's nationality or country of origin is required and helpful; in most situations it is not. Why then do we still do it? When we refer to a person's group membership rather than to his or her personal identity ("He is a Belgian" or "She is Turkish") we usually offer this information as an explanation. But explaining individual behavior by reference to (alleged) group properties is stereotyping individuals and, hence, a case of deindividuation. Typing as the application of a group stereotype to an individual is the essence of social discrimination as we defined it: the (differential) treatment of individuals *as* group members or instances of a social category.

Sometimes, as in an experiment by Razran (1950), mere surnames, provided they are indicative of an ethnic group (like the "Jewish" Cohen, the "Irish" O'Brien and the "Italian" Valenti), will change an otherwise individual assessment of a person toward a fixed ethnic group prejudice, that is, upgrade or downgrade the evaluation of a personality.

It has often been stated about stereotypes, mainly of the national, ethnic, or racial kind, that they are relatively stable, even rigid. This permanence is at the core of the original concept of stereotype as introduced into social science by Lippman (1922). There are basically two ways to fixate others, that is, identify them permanently: We either assign traits or types of which the latter may be explicated as clusters of traits. The linguistic correspondence of these two ways of categorization has been called *labelling*. We assign traits by labelling others or ourselves with adjectives, while typing is usually accomplished by using nouns. Of these two cases of generic categorization, typing by nouns fixates the other person as a typical instance of a social category and reduces and perpetuates the perspective in which the person will be seen. "He is a neurotic" not only disregards the fact that the person referred to is married, a dentist, a piano player, a political liberal, and the like, but it also keeps him in this pigeonhole "for future reference." A person labelled a "Communist" or a "homosexual" may be many other things; in the narrower perspective of the substantive label he or she is "nothing but" or, at least, first of all, whatever we understand by and feel about "Communists" or "homosexuals." Nouns seem to form stronger labels than adjectives, at least in languages where the adjectival form differs from the noun: "He is a Jew" vs. "He is Jewish." The narrowness of the label-induced perspective is, on the other hand, easily widened when the labelling noun is qualified by another attribute; compare "a Negro" with "a Negro boxer," "a homosexual" with "a homosexual singer." The mere fact that the latter phrases draw attention to two attributes of a person seems to inhibit the "nothing but" character of the mono-label view and to loosen its rigidity (Allport, 1954, p. 181).

According to the voluminous, mainly clinical and criminological literature on labelling, we should expect that it is mainly affectively toned noun labels by which discriminated groups of "deviants" are meant to be stamped as inferior, for good.

Table 9-1 is a schematic summary of our functional conception of discriminatory speech as developed so far. We hypothesize (1) that the social functions of discriminating against others give meaning to the cognitive and emotional processes that are traditionally studied in the social psychology of stereotypes and prejudice, and (2) that these socially significant mental processes have linguistic manifestations for which, in the fourth column, we give a few examples. The validation of the proper relationships obtaining between the individual social functions as well as between these, their mental representations and linguistic manifestations, is a matter of future empirical research.[1]

Discriminating as Speech Acting

The above examples should demonstrate the kind of verbal devices that can be used in a discriminatory function. The question is: What are the prerequisites for the understanding of discriminating speech acts? To use language in interpersonal interaction requires agreement between the interaction partners with regard to different speech-related areas. One speech-related area is the semantics of the utterances and parts of utterances which are used. Normally, two persons who are speaking the same language understand each other with respect to the semantics of their language just because they know the language. This knowledge includes the possibilities afforded by the language for constructing meaning by choosing appropriate words and syntactic frames. The linguistic knowledge concerning the verbal means of referring to individual and to common experiences can be understood as a broad common ground (Clark, 1983; Clark & Carlson, 1982), enabling the interaction partners to communicate quite effectively. The second area in which agreement between the partners is required is the range of the pragmatic functions of what the speaker is saying in the communicative interaction. In this area there are specific meanings which refer to what is interactively being accomplished in the intercourse. This second kind of meaning can be called speaker meaning and has to be

---

[1]Central ideas of this paper have been incorporated into the conceptual part of a research proposal on "Verbal Discrimination" submitted to the *Deutsche Forschungsgemeinschaft.*

Table 9-1. Social, Mental, and Linguistic Features of Social Discrimination

Social function	Cognitive–emotional processes	Linguistic manifestation	Examples for explicit verbal discrimination
Separating	Differentiating	Differential naming	"We/they"
	Categorizing	Semantic categorization	"Black driver causes heavy accident"
Distancing	Dichotomizing	Non-immediacy, e.g.,	"We/them"
	Focus on differences	spatio-temporal distancing	"Those people"
		impersonal passive constructions	"Bullets began to fly"
		abstract nouns	"the rate of net inflow" (of immigrants) (Sykes, 1985)
		reification	
Accentuating	Exaggerating differences	Emphatic speech	"Foreign penetration of Switzerland"
	Polarizing	Contrasting	The world Jewish conspiracy
			"The international Jew" (Henry Ford)
Debasing/degrading	Categorical negative evaluation	Disparaging, pejorative speech	"Nigger"
	Affective responses to social category	Ridiculing	"Wop"
		Insinuating (doubts, fears)	Polish jokes
	("prejudice")	Calumniating	
Fixating	Stereotyping	Labeling	
Assigning traits	Categorical attribution of negative characteristics	Generic categorization by adjectives	"Lazy" "Moody" "Shifty"
Typing	Categorization as type or as typical	Generic categorization by nouns	"Fag," "dyke," "butch" "Pinko" "Woman driver"

differentiated from the linguistic meaning of the utterance. Speaker meaning refers to the purpose of the speaker, that is, whether he/she is going to request, to ask for, to persuade the listener. To conceptualize these two aspects of a single communicative utterance as separate acts that are carried out by the speaker goes back to speech-act theory. That is to say, Austin (1975) and Searle (1969) have shown that talking to another person means more than conveying a message; talking to the other always means performing an act. In being directed toward another, the speech act is essentially social. Examples of such kinds of communicative social acts performed by an utterance are commands, requests, assertions, promises, and so forth. Within speech-act theory, these acts are called illocutions. They have to be differentiated from the locution of the speech act. The locutionary component of the speech act refers to objects, states, and processes about which something is said in the communicative utterance. From a pragmatic point of view, the same proposition (as being the basic information of an utterance) can be seen as fulfilling different interpersonal functions depending upon the way it is uttered and upon certain contextual variables. An example of this is: By saying "It is cold outside," the speaker can perform different illocutionary acts, namely asking the other to close the door, warning the other, and advising him/her to take a warm coat, making sure that it would be nicer inside the house, and the like. The pure information is actually irrelevant for the illocutionary potential of the utterance. Another example for the fact that one can perform various social actions with the purpose of regulating interpersonal relationships may be a statement like "Peter kisses Gabi." Again, one can accomplish quite different things by saying this. One can, for example, let Hans know that he has no chance with Gabi, one can challenge Hans to kiss Ursula, one can intend this as a hint that the two of them should not be disturbed, and so forth. In short, one can pursue different social-interactive purposes with only one piece of information. Accordingly, the relation between the proposition on the one hand and the interactive function on the other is, in principle, a flexible one. This point is of special interest in discussing the verbal discrimination topic because it must be realized that not only those utterances can be ascribed discriminatory function that contain negative evaluations on a surface, easily recognizable level. There are not too many contexts in which people are allowed to discriminate in a direct manner, for example, by saying "This restaurant is closed for you because you are black and we don't want to have black people here" (cf. Crosby et al., 1980). As outlined above, it is rather the subtler forms of discrimination that seem to be used in our time. These subtle forms do not exhibit their discriminatory function immediately, but only on a deeper level of understanding between the participants. Discriminating through language refers primarily to the interactive-functional side of the utterance and to a lesser extent to the utterance meaning. Accordingly, it should be clear that only one part of verbal discriminations can be identified by the analysis of the literal meaning of the discriminatory utterance; the other part requires a closer examination of the speech situation, especially of the belief system relevant for the judgment of the discriminated social group. This belief system must be shared by speaker and hearer in order for discriminations of the subtle type to be successful.

Before we describe some of these hidden forms of discrimination achieved by verbal means, two other issues have to be mentioned. Besides the outlined view of discrimination as social action, there is a kind of discrimination that seems to be *inherent* in the semantics of a language and there is another sort of discrimination that is performed *because* of the way somebody speaks. We will briefly clarify what we mean by this distinction, and then we will come back to the illocutionary force of discriminatory speech acts.

Discrimination inherent in the language system. This special form of verbal discrimination is the only one that does not directly refer to individual use of language but to a more general relationship between language and social reality. This relationship can be conceptualized in different ways. The traditional view has been to see language as a tool, that, being totally neutral with regard to the social structure of a specific society/nation, can be used by all members of that society to express their communicative intentions. Accordingly, language is first of all seen as a system of verbal signs that exists independently from political, cultural, and societal states and (historical) changes. The function of the language system in this view is that it provides a means for symbolizing and representing experience (Langer, 1976). The other widely held view (especially in the social sciences) on the relationship between language and social reality goes back to the German philosopher, Humboldt. As early as 1835, Humboldt (1835/1985) tried to convince his listeners of his theory on the interdependence of language and social reality. Language structure, he argued, does influence the epistemology of the whole nation, including the individual, because the language contains certain views and perspective of/on reality and segments of reality. Accordingly, language gains power over the individual since one cannot escape the views represented in the "mother tongue," that is, one cannot choose another "neutral" language for his/her own communicative aims. (Even in poetry, one has to take into consideration the culturally shared and consensual meanings and meaning aspects of the single words and utterance units).

These Humboldtian ideas returned in modern socio- and pragmalinguistic approaches of a more data-based orientation. And they resurfaced in Berger and Luckmann's thesis of language being the vehicle for constructing reality (1967); especially the idea of language as reflecting what is going on in a society with respect to the power structures was taken over as a theoretical hypothesis which could be tested empirically. This kind of research was conducted by several authors, among others by Blakar (1975) who showed that the Norwegian language represents the perspectives and interests of, for example, urban people as opposed to rural people, of employers as opposed to employees, of adults as opposed to children, and so forth. Since Lakoff's analysis of "sexism in English" (1975) it is well-known that modern English, too, reflects power structures, at least with regard to male domination. For example, the pronoun "he" is normally used as a common gender word, even when it refers to women. There is one exception in the case of distinguishing social categories: If we refer to a person in a high-prestige position such as president, director, and so forth, then we are likely to use the pronoun "he." In contrast, if we refer to a low-prestige occupational role like nurse or secretary, then the pronoun is adjusted ("she"). The following quotation from Lakoff (1975, p. 57) goes even further: "Often a word that may be used of both men and women (and perhaps of things as well), when applied to women assumes a special meaning, that, by implication rather than outright assertion is derogatory to women as a group." Male dominance seems to be apparent in the contents of words and in language about women and men. In their report on language, gender, and society, Thorne and Henley (1975) showed that in English, at least, the male is associated with the universal, the general, the subsuming; the female is more often excluded or is the specific case:

"Words associated with males more often have positive connotations, they convey notions of power, prestige, and leadership. In contrast, female words are more often negative, conveying weakness, inferiority, immaturity, a sense of the trivial" (Thorne & Henley, 1975, p. 15). The inescapable use of these words may be seen as being a precondition of a lasting process of constructing inequality in a society. This inequality is based again on processes of accentuation (the difference between men and women), evaluation (e.g,. the strong vs. weak dimension), and fixation (the words as such are used in the same fixed meaning), which cannot be understood as being the product of individual, but of societal, discrimination processes. In these cases the discriminatory function is bound to the speech unit itself, and not to the language user, who may not have another choice. Gender, of course, is not the only dimension along which one divides the human world into unequal parts; there are other dimensions also, like age, class, race, and so forth. But it seems that no other distinction represented in our language is as resistant as that between male and female.

Discrimination because of the way other people speak.   Like all kinds of overt human behaviors, language behavior can be taken as a source of information about the person. The way a person uses language gives the judge important hints with regard to his/her social background, education, status, and the like. Moreover, this information is taken as a cue for judging personality characteristics like competence, personal integrity, including helpfulness and trustworthiness, social attractiveness, and so forth (Edwards, 1982). One distinction which proved to be important for social judgment is whether the person to be judged is speaking in the standard or nonstandard form of his/her language (Ryan & Giles, 1982; Ryan & Sebastian, 1980). For all languages there seems to be a consensus between speakers with regard to the differentiation between a standard variety and nonstandard varieties, the former being somehow better than the other speech varieties (Labov, 1972). Which variety is taken as a standard in a particular society seems to be dependent upon some non-linguistic factors. Primarily the politically and sociologically important structure of power relationships determines what the standard is. Accordingly, speakers who speak the standard form of their language are judged as being more competent and having a higher status than those who speak in a nonstandard way (Lambert, Hodgson, Gardner, & Fillenbaum, 1960). In our context of discrimination, it is important to realize the fact that it is the speaker who is judged and evaluated, not the speech style he/she is utilizing. It is, then, the speech style that marks a member of a particular social category. A social category defined by a special way of speaking can thus become a category of "the others" like any other social category. Some research has been done on the field of attitudes towards language and speech variation (Ryan & Giles, 1982), most of which does not directly concern the discrimination topic, but there are some instructive results showing the social judging process which may lead to discrimination. In a study about language variation and job suitability, Giles, Wilson, and Conway (1981) found that low-status jobs were seen as more suitable for individuals with a nonstandard accent (in English). Standard as opposed to nonstandard speakers were rated more suitable for positions of higher (clerical, executive, professional) status. In other studies, discrimination as negative evaluation against accented speakers was found (De la Zerda & Hopper, 1979; Kalin & Rayko, 1980). It must be seen, however, that the results are not as clear-cut as they seem to be, especially when interactions between speech variables and other personal parameters are considered. Hopper (1977) conducted a study on the effects of speech variables on the outcome of job interviews. As independent variables he chose the race of speaker, standard versus nonstandard accent, and qualifications; the dependent variable was judgments of employability for jobs involving supervision, sales, and technical positions. It was shown that two factors, competence to do a job and likability of the interviewee, were significant predictors of the hiring decisions. Interesting enough was the result that the black standard-variety speaker got very good judgments, that is, no negative discrimination was apparent. Street and Hopper (1982) explain this result by maintaining that perceived convergence towards the speech of a positive reference group might result in favorable evaluation. This seems to be an important process in the discrimination game: The separating and distancing function of discrimination can be reversed under certain situational constraints. If the discriminated group tries to accommodate to the favored group, will the frequency of discriminatory acts decrease as a consequence? Does a member of a discriminated group, if he/she acts in a nonstereotypical way, lose membership in the group? In speech, this "between" state of a person can be referred to, for example, by "strictly speaking, he is a conservative," meaning that he is no longer a real conservative. Some important empirical questions can be posed within this field of discrimination because of the way people speak.

Discriminatory Speech Acts

Phrases that serve the primary function of discriminating against groups or individuals occur frequently in everyday life. They appear as a constitutive part in political speech; they are always present in intergroup conflicts; and they can be heard in talks between friends, as well as in familial dialogues. In short, the number of communicative situations in which discriminatory phrases do occur seems to be unlimited. The pragmatic problem in studying verbal discrimination as a special form of social behavior seems to be that the discriminatory function can be recognized when the researcher takes into consideration not only the special situational circumstances, but also the belief systems held by discriminator and listener with regard to the social judgment of the discriminated group. When somebody tells a discriminating joke about another ethnic group, he/she is usually sure that the listener(s) not only know(s) the presuppositions of the joke, but that he/she also shares the basic judgments with regard to, for example, the well-known stupidity, dishonesty, muddiness, and the like, of the social group to be discriminated against. The laughter of the listener tells the speaker that his/her negative evaluations can be taken for granted, that is, have become a piece of common knowledge. Discrimination by means of language allows the discriminator not to appear "guilty" of having performed an aggressive act, because the discriminatory effect is not only dependent upon the utterance itself, but also upon the listener's understanding. "Typical woman" can be used both as an endearing remark and as a strong discrimination;

that is, both meanings are possible. However, which meaning is intended and/or correct as well as what is the understood meaning are questions which can be answered only after one has analyzed the preconditions of the special communicative situation. Among these preconditions are (1) the participants and their presupposed judgments with regard to the topic of the discrimination, (2) the interpersonal relationships between the participants, and (3) the way of realizing discrimination in actual speech. Discrimination can be understood both as a consequence and as an expression of prejudice. Speech in particular represents the main format in which prejudice may be expressed. At least it is this format which precedes all other, even inhuman and brutal, forms of discrimination. Moreover, acts of discrimination by more than one person seem to be bound to the verbal communication of the prejudice to which it refers.

There are many possible forms of prejudiced talk, and it is only recently that one has begun to study systematically the topics, the episode structures, and the rhetorics of prejudiced speech (van Dijk, 1984, 1987). In this research, the informal discourse in interpersonal interaction serves as data in which the deep patterns of prejudice represented in the knowledge of a social group may be exhibited. The manner in which people talk about members of certain outgroups and the way they understand each other provides a basis for the inference that ingroup members share a common set of propositions and negative attributions concerning a certain outgroup. As this knowledge transcends the level of the individual, it can be conceptualized as a special form of social representation (Moscovici, 1984). The patterns of prejudice underlying informal discourse and being socially represented are again but one aspect of the whole picture of discrimination, because d-speech not only "expresses" prejudiced thought, but is in itself a social act directed against another (group of) person(s).

Considering the concrete speech situation in which verbal discrimination is acted out, we distinguish two important kinds of "immediacy." First, we have to differentiate between *direct* and *nondirect* discrimination. Direct discrimination occurs when the discriminated person is the communication partner of the producer of the discriminatory speech act. In the case of nondirect discrimination, the d-speech act concerns a person who is not present; thus, it is a sort of ingroup "talk about others." In these ingroup interactions the two communicators understand each other quite well, and they normally share a common ground, at least with regard to the discriminated social group.

The second difference of relevance for the classification of discriminatory speech is the difference between *explicit* and *implicit* d-speech. In the explicit d-speech the proposition underlying the outspoken utterance attributes a negative predicate to somebody as a member of a social group or to an outgroup as a whole. That is, in the case of explicit verbal discrimination, the discriminatory function in most cases can be identified with the utterance taken out of the speech situation. In the implicit d-speech, however, the discriminatory function cannot be understood without knowing the conditions of the situation, the presuppositions and contextual implications of the utterance.

Both the direct and the nondirect discriminatory speech can be realized in explicit and in implicit ways. Moreover, the subfunctions or aspects of discrimination that were described above (separating, distancing, accentuating, evaluating, and fixating) may occur in either of the four conditions, the direct/explicit, the nondirect/explicit, the direct/implicit, and the nondirect/implicit d-speech. Thus, within this conceptual framework, we can differentiate 20 forms of discriminatory speech, some of which may be demonstrated by the following examples taken from ethnic, racist, or sexist discourse.

While nondirect d-speech is usually contained in the interviews with prejudiced majority group members (e.g., van Dijk, 1984), samples of direct d-speech, unless occasionally overheard, must be gleaned from the reports of victims. A few examples of *direct* d-speech:

> The dark-skinned immigrant at whom is shouted "Black bastard," the young black girl called "golliwog" or "wog" by white kids are illustrations of an explicit derogatory typing, with the distancing challenge, "Go back to your own country," added (Cashmore, 1987, p. 62).
> Without the chance to get to their own country, Jews in Nazi Germany found themselves barred from shops, baths, etc., by signs: "No Jews" or "Jews Unwanted" while the "Aryan" majority was told on banners and bills "Jews are our misfortune." The woman who is, more or less jokingly, reminded of the intrinsic shortcomings of her sex or gender type with the words "That's just women all over." Naming the type seems to be self-explanatory.
> The "guest worker" in West Germany who is told by his foreman in mock Pidgin German "Du nix kapier" ("you nix understand") is explicitly separated from and ridiculed by his "understanding" German superior.
> In a quasi-direct and quasi-implicit way a British racist who, when entering a pub and discovering back clients, asks rhetorically "Am I in the wrong pub?" is kind of separating and distancing himself from this colored social reality (Cashmore, 1987, p. 33).

There is much more evidence of the *nondirect* ingroup d-speech. The *distancing* function is commonest in the "demonstrative of distance" (van Dijk, 1984, p. 137) when racist discriminators refer to "those" and "such" people. The disparaging character is recognizable not only in "that," but also in "what" if they refer to the outgroup, as the following two examples show:

> A Dutch interviewee of van Dijk's (1984, p. 150) referring to people of other nationalities in his neighborhood: "I happen to live among *that*" (our emphasis).
> An English girl of 19, who is going with a dark Malaysian, about her father: " . . . if I brought a black guy home I think he'd be quiet, but he'd run off and complain to my mum. 'Have you seen *what* she's come with now?'" (Cashmore, 1987, p. 90–91 our emphasis).

Another way of keeping distance is a reversal of roles, when the prejudiced person states: "I think they are prejudiced against us, hanging around together and not really getting near us" (Cashmore, 1987, p. 99).

Accentuation comes in many forms of emphasizing and exaggerating differences. When a resident of a British community states about members of the ethnic minority: "They deliberately provoke people by walking round, looking different" (Cashmore, 1987, p. 22), we must conclude that "looking different" is in itself provoking. Other forms are the generalization or the exaggeration of threat as, for example, in "All foreigners carry a knife" or ". . . one could have a knife in one's back" (van Dijk, 1984, p. 139–140), or in the belief of an unemployed young Englishman " . . . there must be 30 million blacks over here now" (Cashmore, 1987, p. 84).

The strongest emphasis we frequently find in the *devaluating fixation* of traits or patterns of behavior: "I just don't like Pakis. They stink. Pakis really reek; you can tell one in the street a mile away. Blacks stink of sweat and a lot of them are pimps" (Cashmore, 1987, p. 86). The ultimate fixation by d-speech may be found in the quasi-religious statement of a white middle-class woman who is against mixed marriages: "God intended people to be a certain colour, not half and half" or, in a more intellectual vein: "A person may be 100 per cent black down to 12½ percent, but they're always black. *They never make the transition, the quantum jump to white*" (Cashmore, 1987, p. 84; our emphasis).

Conclusion and Outlook

These examples were, on the one hand, meant to illustrate the different functions or purposes of d-speech acts as contained in our functional model. On the other hand, if taken together, they are evidence for the thesis that an utterance per se is not yet a discriminatory speech act. What we need in order to identify an utterance as d-speech is knowledge of the situation in terms of both the preconditions of the given interaction and the presuppositions of the verbal interchange, such as the "common ground" of speaker and hearer (Clark, 1983). Considering the importance of ingroup talk about outgroups and outgroup members, information about the interpersonal or role relationship between speaker and hearer is vital. If it is true that discrimination has its own historicity (cf. Frederickson & Knobel, 1982) and that the blatant or cruder forms of discrimination are socially undesirable today, while prejudice is thought to prevail, the social psychologist interested in the latter will have to concentrate his research interest on what is communicated among insiders, that is, within the ingroup, rather than on ingroup–outgroup speech.

But the examples given should also remind us of the fact that speech is not merely reference to persons and things by means of signs, but in itself is *action*. Mainly for the social psychologist the question should be: What do we do if we utter d-speech acts? What do we do with respect to our own group or category; what do we intend with respect to the discriminated outgroup? The question opens a research field between language and social psychology.

The immediate interest of social psychologists should be obvious in two respects: First, we do not know under which conditions prejudice and stereotypes are (co)determinants of discriminatory behavior. But the analysis of d-speech is the proper basis from which to infer the kind of prejudice someone holds if we consider d-speech an "expression" of prejudice (cf. van Dijk, 1984, 1985). Second, we do not know under which conditions and to which degree d-speech is conducive to other discriminatory acts. But at least history has told us that, for example, anti-Semitic "antilocution" and "group libel" can be used as the mass-psychological preparation of the more extreme forms of social discrimination: segregation and extermination.

Acknowledgments. We wish to express our gratitude to our reviewers for their helpful critical comments on the first draft of this chapter, to Penny Pynes for her assistance as native speaker on the preparation of the final draft, and to W.D. Batz for the computer-graphic design of Figure 9-1.

References

Allport, C.W. (1954). *The nature of prejudice.* Cambridge, MA: Addison-Wesley.

Austin, J.L. (1975). *How to do things with words* (2nd ed.). Cambridge, MA: Harvard University Press.

Berger, P.L., & Luckmann, T. (1967). *The social construction of reality.* New York: Anchor Books, Doubleday.

Bishop, C.D. (1976). *The effects of perceived similarity on interracial attitudes and behaviors.* Unpublished doctoral dissertation. Yale University, New Haven, CT.

Blakar, R.M. (1975). How sex roles are represented, reflected and conserved in the Norwegian language. *Acta Sociologica, 18,* 162–173.

Cashmore, E.E. (1987). *The logic of racism.* London: Allen & Unwin.

Clark, H.H., (1983). Language use and language users. In G. Lindzey & E. Aronson (Eds.), *Handbook of social psychology* (Vol. 2) (pp. 179–231). Reading, MA: Addison-Wesley.

Clark, H.H. & Carlson, T.B. (1982). Speech acts and hearer's belief. In N.V. Smith (Ed.), *Mutual knowledge.* (pp. 1–37). London: Academic Press.

Crosby, F., Bromley, S., & Saxe, L. (1980). Recent unobtrusive studies of black and white discrimination and prejudice: A literature review. *Psychological Bulletin, 87,* 546–563.

De la Zerda, N., & Hopper, R. (1979). Employment interviewers' reactions to Mexican American speech. *Communication Monographs, 13,* 126–134.

de Saussure, F. (1966). *Course in general linguistics* (W. Baskin, Trans.). New York: McGraw-Hill.

Doise, W. (1972) Relations et représentations intergroupes. In S. Moscovici (Ed.), *Introduction à la psychologie sociale* (pp. 194–213). Paris: Larousse.

Edwards, J.R. (1982). Language attitudes and their implications among English speakers. In F.B. Ryan & H. Giles (Eds.), *Attitudes toward language variation* (pp. 28–33). London: Arnold.

Eiser, J.R. & Stroebe, W. (1972). *Categorization and social judgment.* London: Academic Press.

Eiser, J.R., & van der Pligt, J. (1984). Attitudes in a social context. In H. Tajfel (Ed.), *The social dimension* (Vol. 2) (pp. 363–378). Cambridge, England: Cambridge University Press. Paris: Maison des Sciences de l'Homme).

Frederickson, G.M., & Knobel, D.T. (1982). A history of discrimination. In T.F. Pettigrew, G.M. Frederickson, D.T. Knobel, N. Glazer, & R. Ueda (Eds.), *Prejudice* (pp. 30–87). Cambridge, MA: Harvard University Press.

Gaertner, S.L., & Dovidio, J.F. (1986). The aversive form of racism. In J.F. Dovidio & S.L. Gaertner (Eds.), *Prejudice, discrimination, and racism* (pp. 61–89). Orlando, FL: Academic Press.

Giles, H., Wilson, P., & Conway, T. (1981). Accent and lexical diversity as determinants of impression formation and employment selection. *Language Sciences, 3,* 92–103.

Graumann, C.F. (1987). Sprache als Medium sozialer Interaktion. In W. Maiers & M. Markard (Eds.), *Psychologie als Subjektwissenschaft* (pp. 57–65). Frankfurt: Campus.

Hamilton, D.L. (Ed.). (1981). *Cognitive processes in stereotyping and intergroup behavior.* Hillsdale, NJ: Erlbaum.

Hendricks, M., & Bortzin, R. (1976). Race and sex as stimuli for negative affect and physical avoidance. *Journal of Social Psychology, 98*, 111–120.

Hopper, R. (1977). Language attitudes in the job interview. *Communication Monographs, 44*, 346–351.

Humboldt, W. von (1835/1985). *Über die Sprache*. München: dtv.

Jaspars, J.M.F. (1983). Discrimination: Social psychology. In R. Harré & R. Lamb (Eds.), *The Encyclopedic Dictionary of Psychology* (p. 158). Oxford: Blackwell.

Kalin, R., & Rayko, D. (1980). The social significance of speech in the job interview. In R.N. St. Clair & H. Giles (Eds.), *The social and psychological contexts of language* (pp. 39–50). Hillsdale, NJ: Erlbaum.

Katz, I. (1981). *Stigma: A social psychological analysis*. Hillsdale, NJ: Erlbaum.

Labov, W. (1972). *Sociolinguistic patterns*. Philadelphia, PA: University of Pennsylvania Press.

Lakoff, R. (1975). *Language and woman's place*. New York: Harper & Row.

Lambert, W.E., Hodgson, R., Gardner, R.C., & Fillenbaum, S. (1960). Evaluational reactions to spoken language. *Journal of Abnormal and Social Psychology, 60*, 44–51.

Langer, S. (1976). *Philosophy in a new key: A study of the symbolism of reason, rite, and art*. Cambridge, MA: Harvard University Press.

Lilli, W. (1975). *Soziale Akzentuierung*. Stuttgart: Kohlhammer.

Lippman, W. (1922). *Public opinion*. New York: Harcourt Brace.

McConahay, J.B. (1983). Modern racism and modern discrimination: The effects of race, radical attitudes, and context on simulated hiring decisions. *Personality and Social Psychology Bulletin, 9*, 551–558.

McConahay, J.B. (1986). Modern racism, ambivalence, and the modern racism scale, In J.F. Dovidio & S.L. Gaertner (Eds.), *Prejudice, discrimination, and racism* (pp. 91–125). Orlando, FL: Academic Press.

McConahay, J.B., & Hough, J.C. (1976). Symbolic racism. *Journal of Social Issues, 32*, 23–45.

Mehrabian, A. (1971). *Silent messages*. Belmont, CA: Wadsworth.

Moscovici, S. (1984). The phenomenon of social representation. In R.M. Farr & S. Moscovici (Eds.), *Social representations* (pp. 3–70). Cambridge, England: Cambridge University Press.

Myrdal, G. (1944). *An American dilemma: The Negro problem and modern democracy*. New York: Harper.

Poliakov, L. (1974). *The Aryan myth*. London: Chatto/Heinemann.

Razran, G. (1950). Ethnic dislikes and stereotypes: A laboratory study. *Journal of Abnormal and Social Psychology, 45*, 7–27.

Ryan, E.B. & Giles, H. (1982). *Attitudes towards language variation*. London: Arnold.

Ryan, E.B., & Sebastian, R. (1980). The effects of speech style and social class background on social judgments of speakers. *British Journal of Social and Clinical Psychology, 19*, 229–233.

Searle, J.R. (1969). *Speech acts: An essay in the philosophy of language*. Cambridge, England: Cambridge University Press.

Seeman, M. (1981). Intergroup relations. In M. Rosenberg & R.T. Turner (Eds.), *Social psychology. Sociological perspectives* (pp. 378–410). New York: Basic Books.

Sherif, M. (1967). *Group conflict and cooperation: Their social psychology*. London: Routledge & Kegan Paul.

Sherif, M., & Sherif, C.W. (1953). *Groups in harmony and tension*. New York: Harper & Row.

Spence, I.T., Deaux, K., & Helmreich, R.L. (1985). Sex roles in contemporary American society. In G. Lindzey & E. Aronson (Eds.), *Handbook of social psychology* (3rd ed., Vol. 2) (pp. 149–178). New York: Random House.

Stevens, S.S. (1939). Psychology and the science of science. *Psychological Bulletin, 36*, 221–263.

Street, R., & Hopper, R. (1982). A model of speech style evaluation. In E.B. Ryan & H. Giles (Eds.), *Attitudes towards language variation* (pp. 175–188). London: Arnold.

Sykes, M. (1985). Discrimination in discourse. in T. van Dijk (Ed.), *Handbook of discourse analysis* (Vol. 4) (pp. 83–101). London: Academic Press.

Tajfel, H. (1970) Experiments in intergroup discrimination. *Scientific American, 223* (5), 96–102.

Tajfel, H. (Ed.). (1978). *Differentiation between social groups*. New York: Academic Press.

Thernstrom, A.M. (1983). The right of ethnic minorities to political representation. In C. Fried (Ed.), *Minorities: Community and identity* (pp. 329–339). Berlin: Springer.

Thompson, J.B. (1987). Language and ideology: A framework for analysis. *The Sociological Review, 35*, 516–536.

Thorne, B., & Henley, N. (1975). Difference and dominance: An overview of language, gender, and society. In B. Thorne & N. Henley (Eds.), *Language and sex: Difference and dominance* (pp. 5–42). Rowley: Newbury House.

Turner, J.C. (1987). *Rediscovering the social group. A self-categorization theory*. Oxford: Blackwell.

van Dijk, T.A. (1984). *Prejudice in discourse*. Amsterdam: Benjamins.

van Dijk, T.A. (1985). Cognitive situation models in discourse production: The expression of ethnic situations in prejudiced discourse. In J.P. Forgas (Ed.), *Language and social situations* (pp. 61–79). New York: Springer-Verlag.

van Dijk, T.A. (1987). *Communicating racism: Ethnic prejudice in thought and talk*. Beverly Hills, CA: Sage.

Wagner, U., & Machleit, U. (1986). "Gastarbeiter" in the Federal Republic of Germany: Contact between Germans and migrant populations. In M. Hewstone & R. Brown (Eds.), *Contact and conflict in intergroup encounters* (pp. 59–78). Oxford: Blackwell.

Weitz, S. (1972). Attitude, voice and behavior: A repressed affect model of interracial interaction. *Journal of Personality and Social Psychology, 24*, 14–21.

Wiener, M. & Mehrabian, A. (1968). *Language within language: Immediacy, a channel in verbal communication*. New York: Appleton-Century-Crofts.

Zavalloni, M. (1973). Social identity: Perspectives and prospects. *Social Science Information, 12*, 65–91.

Part IV

Change of Stereotypes and Prejudice

Chapter 10

Changing Stereotypes with Disconfirming Information

Miles Hewstone

Introduction

Some of the most powerful bases of intergroup stereotyping are rooted in the social and economic structure of society itself. Whether we are talking about blacks and whites in the U.K. or the U.S., Germans and Turks in the Federal Republic of Germany, or Catholics and Protestants in Northern Ireland, it should be acknowledged at the outset that such groups are often characterized by different living conditions, different occupational positions, and so on (see Hewstone & Brown, 1986a). These structural factors notwithstanding, social psychologists can arguably best analyze stereotypes in terms of their psychological bases and consequences. This chapter deals with how stereotypes can be changed by providing information that disconfirms existing, predominantly negative images of the outgroup.

The importance of social psychological processes is evident from the key role Stephan (1985) assigns to assimilation and contrast. The categorization of objects (including social groups) is based on similarities within and differences between categories; assimilation and contrast effects refer respectively to the accentuation of these basic processes. By downplaying or assimilating within-group differences, within-group similarity is perceived to be greater than it actually is; by emphasizing or contrasting between-group differences, the differences between groups are seen as greater than they in fact are (see Eiser & Stroebe, 1972; Tajfel, 1969). As Stephan notes, these two processes lead to a variety of distortions in the processing of information about social groups: the formation of stereotypes and negative attitudes between groups; the generation of negative expectancies about the outgroup; the obstruction of attempts to change stereotypes; and the avoidance of intergroup contact. Interventions are therefore required to break this negative spiral, and they might include propaganda or public information campaigns, new legislation, and planned intergroup contact.

This chapter selectively reviews our knowledge about one specific kind of intervention: whether outgroup stereotypes change in response to information that disconfirms the existing view of an outgroup. The approach is primarily cognitive, examining the processes such as attention, memory, and causal attribution which may impede the revision of stereotypic beliefs. This cognitive approach is then extended in two ways. First, the neglected content of traits is reviewed; traits are shown to vary both in their implications for behavior, and in their potential disconfirmability. Second, some of the relevant motivational and affective influences on stereotype–disconfirmation are considered, particularly as they interact with cognitive processing of outgroup information.

Models of Belief Change

Weber and Crocker (1983) have compared three models of how beliefs such as stereotypes change in response to disconfirming information. The "bookkeeping" model (Rothbart, 1981) views stereotype change as a gradual process in which each new instance of stereotype-discrepant information modifies the existing stereotype. Any single piece of disconfirming evidence elicits only a minor change; substantial changes occur incrementally with the accumulation of evidence that disconfirms the stereotype. The "conversion" model (Rothbart, 1981) is more dramatic, allowing for a single, salient, incongruent instance to bring about schema change. According to this second model, schema change is all-or-none and is not brought about by minor disconfirmations. The third model, "subtyping," argues that when all the disconfirming information is concentrated within a few individuals, those individuals will be subtyped (seen as a separate subcategory). This model predicts more change when incongruent information is dispersed across individuals than when it is concentrated in a few (cf. Gurwitz & Dodge, 1977).

Weber and Crocker's (1983) four studies provide partial support for two of the models. The bookkeeping model may describe how stereotypes change when incongruent information is dispersed across multiple outgroup members (because in this condition individuals could not easily be subtyped, and the stereotype changed with each new piece of incongruent information). The subtyping model may be the best description of stereotype change when incongruent information is concentrated in a few outgroup members (the small number of individuals in whom information is concentrated are easily subtyped). Finally, although unsupported in this research, the conversion model might apply when a perceiver is unsure of a stereotype, and thus easily swayed by available information.

The problem of subtyping, a mechanism that protects stereotypic beliefs from disconfirming information by dividing a category into distinct components, has occupied a number of scholars. It has been variously labeled "compartmentalization" (Freud, 1961 ed.), "re-fencing" (Allport, 1954), "differentiation" (Abelson, 1959), and "exemption" (Williams, 1964). Yet, how serious a problem is it? It could be argued that subtyping is a process that will gradually break up a negative stereotype, by increasing the number of positive subgroup stereotypes (Pettigrew, 1981). Alternatively, there is the danger pointed out by Taylor (1981), that as the number of subtypes increases, any behavior performed by a member of the group can still be fitted into at least one stereotypical conception. The problem of subtyping undoubtedly helps to explain why generalization (of positive judgments from outgroup targets to the outgroup in general) has been a critical problem for interventions such as the "contact hypothesis" (see Hewstone & Brown, 1986b). And yet, given that outgroups tend to be viewed as more homogeneous than ingroups, generalization from target to group should at least be easier for outgroups than ingroups (Quattrone & Jones, 1980).

How, then, can subtyping be overcome? With regard to the contact hypothesis, Hewstone and Brown (1986b) argued that if positive intergroup interaction (during which we assume that disconfirming information is encountered) takes place on an intergroup basis, then there is a chance that any positive change in attitude will be seen as applying not just to those present, but to others in the same category. The intergroup level of contact refers here to behavior between individuals that is determined by their identity as group representatives, rather than by their individual characteristics and personal relationships (Brown & Turner, 1981).

Although Rothbart and John (1985) have criticized Brown and Turner's use of the interpersonal/intergroup distinction, the distinction agrees with Rothbart and John's "prototype view." Both emphasize the importance of an outgroup member's typicality as a determinant of whether disconfirming information will generalize to the outgroup as a whole. Wilder (1984) systematically varied the prototypicality of the outgroup member in a contact situation (actually no contact took place) and found, as predicted, that there was a significant improvement in the evaluation of the outgroup only after a pleasant encounter with a typical outgroup member. Interestingly, there was no comparable change in stereotypes, but as Wilder noted, stereotypes based on multiple confirming examples may be unlikely to change in response to minor disconfirmation (Rothbart, 1981). However, such change should be greater with a stronger association between outgroup exemplars and the outgroup in general, and perhaps with disconfirming information based on multiple outgroup members, as long as they are (1) prototypical and (2) seen as independent of one another (Wilder, 1986). Of importance to the present argument, Wilder (1984, Experiment 3) provided support for the idea that typicality works by making it easier for subjects to generalize from the behavior of a target to the behavior of other outgroup members. This is consistent with Weber and Crocker's (1983) above-mentioned finding, that people's stereotypes about occupational groups changed most when they were presented with counter-stereotypic information about representative members of those groups.

An apparently alternative view to these intergroup/prototypical approaches has been put forward by Brewer and Miller (1984). They argued in favor of contact between group members that was based on increased differentiation and personalization. By differentiation they mean that individual outgroup members are seen as distinct from one another, but that subgroups formed in this way are still seen as parts of the larger social category. Personalization denotes that outgroup individuals are responded to in terms of their relationships to the ingroup individual's self, such that self–other interpersonal comparisons are made across category boundaries. This sounds like an interpersonal, rather than intergroup, approach, but the supporting studies (Miller, Brewer & Edwards, 1985) convey a different picture. When the experimental conditions made category membership most salient and when focus of attention was directed away from personal attributes of individuals, there was stronger bias against the outgroup. However, it should be noted that Miller and colleagues did *not* attempt to individuate group members, and that they maintained the presence of categories throughout the experiment. Thus, presumably, the perceived typicality of outgroup members—what Hewstone and Brown see as crucial—was maintained. Given that category memberships were always evident, then manipulations such as "category-based team assignment" may have had their detrimental effects by augmenting categorization, rather than simply ensuring that categories were not dissolved.

Overall, there is little evidence for the impact of stereotype-disconfirming information based on atypical outgroup exemplars, although some temporary effects may be observed (see Hamill, Wilson, & Nisbett, 1980). Thus typicality is seen as crucial. Because ingroup–outgroup bias may be heightened by the presence of multiple members of both groups (e.g., Dustin & Davis, 1970), the most effective strategy is to link disconfirming information explicitly to (proto)typical outgroup exemplars and to disperse that information across multiple outgroup members.

While Weber and Crocker's models of belief change offer a systematic approach to stereotype disconfirmation, they can be added to by a more detailed analysis of the cognitive processes involved.

Cognitive Processes in the Revision of Stereotypic Beliefs

The social cognitive approach to intergroup relations is essentially concerned with the role of mental representations—or cognitive schemata—in processing information about persons or social events (e.g., Brewer & Kramer, 1985; Hamilton, 1981; Stephan, 1985). It includes interdependent processes such as attention, encoding, and retrieval (Hastie, 1981). This section deals with three particular cognitive processes that clearly have been shown to influence the processing of stereotype-disconfirming or incongruent information.

Attention

Variables affecting the perceiver's focus of attention include both external variables, such as salience (see Taylor & Fiske, 1978), and internal factors such as expectations or existing schemata (Stephan, 1985). Focusing on the latter factors, it has been claimed that expectancies and schemata bias selection of information to be processed (Snyder & Swann, 1978). There is a bias in favor of collecting expectancy-confirming evidence (Snyder & Cantor, 1979; for a critical discussion, see Higgins & Bargh, 1987) and in selectively attending to expectancy-confirming information during social interaction (Snyder & Frankel, 1976). These are, of course, biases that influence whether any stereotype-*dis*confirming information will actually be processed. Furthermore, category-based expectancies may lead perceivers to believe that *non*presented (but related) information has been perceived (Cantor

& Mischel, 1977), and to expect and then perceive behavior that is associated with the category, even if it has not been observed (Hamilton & Rose, 1980; Rothbart, Evans, & Fulero, 1979).

Given all this evidence for attention to schema-congruent or expected information, Stephan (1985) refers to a "perplexing issue" (p. 606)—when do expectancies bias attention in the direction of perceiving confirming evidence, and when is attention dominated by unexpected or novel information? Some relevant dimensions noted by Stephan are: how explicit the expectancy is, and how strong its association with a particular group is (McArthur, 1982); the degree of discrepancy between the expectancy and the actual behavior (there is a higher probability of attention to unexpected behavior with a greater degree of discrepancy); and the costs and rewards to the perceiver of expected and unexpected behaviors.

Clearly, the tendencies towards the perception of and attendance to confirming evidence have implications for the present chapter. They represent barriers to the processing of stereotype-disconfirming information. We now turn to what seems logically the next question: *if* attended to, is stereotype-disconfirming information retained in memory?

Memory

If stereotypes operate like cognitive schemata—influencing attention and encoding processes—then they should also provide an organized structure within which that information can be stored and represented in memory (Hamilton, 1979; Hamilton & Trolier, 1986). A question that has aroused considerable interest is the one posed by Hastie (1981): "To what extent does the creation or selection of a (group) schema determine memory for specific information relevant to that schema?" (p. 63). The answer is quite complex.

On the one hand, there is substantial evidence that both recall and recognition of information provided about individual category members are influenced by stereotypes; stereotype-relevant traits or behaviors are more likely to be correctly remembered than are stereotype-irrelevant characteristics (Brewer, Dull, & Lui, 1981; Cohen, 1981; Rothbart, Evans, & Fulero, 1979). For example, Rothbart and colleagues led subjects to expect that members of a hypothetical group would be either intellectual or friendly. Members of the group were then described as performing a number of behaviors. On a later memory task, subjects recalled more behaviors congruent with their expectancy if the expectancy had been induced prior to (but not after) the presentation of the behaviors. Although there are some qualifications to this finding (see Hastie, 1981), overall the results do provide evidence of good recall for schema-confirming or congruent information.

On the other hand, there is some evidence for what is apparently the opposite effect—superior memory for information that clearly disconfirms a schema. The results of several studies indicate that schema-inconsistent items are more likely to be retained than schema-consistent items (e.g., Hastie & Kumar, 1979; Srull, 1981). The central study here is that by Hastie and Kumar. Subjects read sentences describing a series of behaviors attributed to a single, fictional character, along with a brief personality-trait sketch. The behavior descriptions were selected to be congruent or incongruent with respect to the personality sketch, and the analysis centered on comparing the relative recall of congruent and incongruent behaviors. Experiment 1 revealed superior recall for incongruent versus congruent or neutral behaviors, but this result was qualified by set size (the numbers of congruent and incongruent items in the list). When incongruent items were relatively uncommon, they were likely to be recalled, but when the set sizes were equal, recall was very similar. Two further experiments included conditions in which lists were comprised of equal numbers of congruent and incongruent behavior descriptions. Interestingly, the fewer incongruent items in a list, the higher the probability of recalling any particular item. The overall picture from these studies was that schema-incongruent events were better remembered than congruent ones, while irrelevant events were the worst remembered.

At first glance, Hastie and Kumar's results might seem to imply better memorability of, and thus greater impact of, stereotype-disconfirming information. However, irrespective of how they are explained (cf. Hamilton & Trolier, 1986; Higgins & Bargh, 1987; Taylor & Crocker, 1981), these results may have only minor implications for stereotype research. First, as Higgins and Bargh point out, Hastie and Kumar's paradigm was not studying how people test already-formed impressions or beliefs (e.g., stereotypes), but rather how people form such beliefs in the first place. Higgins and Bargh emphasize, in particular, that the findings should not be interpreted as showing that information inconsistent with a well-formed prior belief is better recalled. Second, other studies have shown that the "inconsistency effect" can be eliminated, for example, by loading the subject's attentional capacity while he or she is reading the behaviors (Bargh & Thein, 1985; Srull, 1981, Experiment 4). Arguably, the types of real-life intergroup contact in which individuals are typically exposed to stereotype-disconfirming information will often be situations where they are overexposed to new information; thus they fall back on simplifying strategies (see Hewstone & Brown, 1986b; Rothbart & John, 1985). Third, in many situations ingroup members might discount or "explain away" behaviors that disconfirm the outgroup stereotype (Hewstone, 1988; Pettigrew, 1979). It is not clear from Hastie and Kumar's (1979) method section whether the impression–formation instructions encouraged use of all available information, but Hastie's (1984) research certainly requires subjects to integrate all available information, and not to discount some of it. Attributions for stereotype-disconfirming behavior are dealt with below, but the relationship between attributions and memory for disconfirming information is relevant here. Crocker, Hannah, and Weber (1983, Experiment 1) provided subjects with either a situational or a dispositional attribution for an inconsistent behavior. The unexpected act was more likely to be recalled only if it was accompanied by a dispositional attribution to the target.

In sum, the evidence seems to support better recall of schema-consistent information, when research uses well-formed beliefs, such as stereotypes. Thus memory biases constitute a second cognitive process that attenuates the potential impact of stereotype-disconfirming information.

Causal Attribution

A number of studies have pointed to the fact that behavior in line with expectations is attributed to internal causes, whereas behavior discrepant with expectations is attributed to situational factors (e.g., Regan, Straus, & Fazio, 1974). It appears that, in explaining expectancy-confirming or schema-consistent behavior, perceivers may simply rely on dispositions implied by a stereotype, not even bothering to consider additional factors (Pyszczynski & Greenberg, 1981). If one adopts Posner and Snyder's (1975) criteria of automatic cognitive processes—they occur without intention, without giving rise to awareness, and without interfering with other ongoing mental activity—then expectancy-confirming attributions may be automatic social judgments (see Winter, Uleman, & Cunniff, 1985).

Using the Bayesian notion of the diagnostic ratio, Stephan (1985) has proposed an interesting model of how perceivers combine information about group membership and particular behaviors to form an explanation of stereotypical behavior. Stephan suggests, following Ajzen and Fishbein (1975), that a set of hypotheses may be generated, each with its respective diagnostic ratio (i.e., the subjective probability of an explanation being used to explain *a* given behavior, divided by the probability of that explanation being used to explain *any* behavior). A fairly simple rule for the selection of one hypothesis of explanation would be to "map" the set of hypotheses (e.g., "lack of ability," "task difficulty," and "bad luck" as explanations for failure) onto the set of stereotypical traits (e.g., "aggressive," "stupid," "rude," etc). Overlapping items, in this case lack of ability/stupid, would be obvious causal candidates. This kind of model receives some support from Hewstone, Jaspars, and Lalljee's (1982) study of intergroup attributions for success and failure, which identified clear correspondence between shared beliefs about groups and intergroup attributions.

In contrast, more detailed attributional processing may follow the disconfirmation of expectancies (Hastie, 1984; Pyszczynski & Greenberg, 1981; Weiner, 1985). Thus Pettigrew (1979) has detailed a variety of explanations for positive behavior by a member of a disliked outgroup—"the special case," "luck or special advantage," "high motivation and effort," and "manipulated situational context." By explaining away disconfirming behaviors in this way, perceivers preserve their negative outgroup stereotypes (Hamilton, 1979).

Stephan (1985) contends that expectancy–confirmation effects can account for the finding that observers make internal attributions for other ingroup members performing socially desirable acts, and external attributions for undesirable acts (and vice versa for outgroup members; Taylor & Jaggi, 1974; cf. Hewstone & Ward, 1985). However, we should not perpetuate the error of assuming that positive outgroup behavior will always be externally attributed. Of Pettigrew's (1979) four main attributions noted above, two are external (luck or special advantage and situation); but two are clearly internal (the special case and high motivation or effort). One lesson of the research on intergroup attribution (see Hewstone & Jaspars, 1984) is that, just like interpersonal attributions, explanations for ingroup and outgroup behavior reveal a fascinating richness and imaginativeness (cf. Darley & Goethals,

1980). This is most evident when open-ended explanations are elicited. For example, in a recent study of explanations for success and failure by ingroup and outgroup members, Hewstone, Gale, and Purkhardt (1988) reported that boys from a private school explained ingroup success mainly in terms of ability, but explained outgroup success primarily in terms of ability and effort. This result could be interpreted in terms of a Multiple Necessary Cause schema (Kelley, 1972) for outgroup success, because this outcome is unexpected.

While social perceivers are skilled at explaining away disconfirming outgroup behavior, their attributions have a further important consequence for belief perseverance. Anderson, Lepper, and Ross (1980) led their subjects to believe that there was, and then asked them to explain, either a positive or negative relationship between a trainee's preference for risky versus conservative choices, and his subsequent success as a firefighter. Although minimal evidence was provided to subjects, compared with the information we sometimes hold about social groups, their experimentally induced beliefs persisted after they were told that no such relationship actually existed. Anderson and colleagues (1980) reported a highly significant correlation between the presence or absence of general explanatory principles in subjects' explanations and the degree of belief perseverance following debriefing. This finding was followed up by Anderson (1983, Experiment 2), who reported that subjects engaged in causal thinking even when not explicitly asked to do so. Kulik (1983) has provided a complementary demonstration of the role played by causal attributions in belief perseverance. He found that substantial situational pressures had almost no influence on attributions for confirming behaviors, while subjects were very sensitive to potential situational causes for behavior that disconfirmed their prior beliefs. Regarding stereotypes, these studies imply that beliefs, once formed, are hard to alter; and that behaviors encoded as disconfriming expectancies can be explained in ways that make the behavior appear consistent (see also Miller & Turnbull, 1986; Strenta & Kleck, 1984).

Notwithstanding the force of these attributional arguments, a cautionary note is in order. Trope (1986; see also Trope, Chapter 6) has advanced a two-stage model that decomposes the attribution of personal dispositions into identification processes and dispositional inference processes. While it is not clear that the model is applicable to *causal*, as opposed to trait, attributions (cf. Smith & Miller, 1983), Trope correctly points out that studies such as Taylor and Jaggi's (1974) have not assessed the separate and joint contribution of perceptual and inferential processes to stereotyping. We do not know whether stereotypes influence the perception of behavior (e.g., Hastorf & Cantril, 1954) and/or the inference from behavior. Trope suggests that since the identification process is largely automatic, stereotypes may still affect the categorization of behavior (and, in turn, dispositional attribution), even when the perceiver consciously strives to make unbiased inferences.

In sum, causal attributions appear to play a key role in the evidential impact of stereotype confirming versus disconfirming information. Together with other cognitive processes such as attention and memory they can lead to more detailed cognitive models of belief change. Attention to cognitive processes, however, should not lead to the neglect of the *content* of stereotypic beliefs.

Varieties of Stereotypical Traits

Thus far, it has been implicitly assumed that a cognitive approach can account for change in all stereotypical traits in a similar manner. The content of the trait or attribute on which an expectancy is based, however, is a factor that merits closer attention. This section considers, first, the behavioral implications that can be derived from different traits, and then the extent to which traits vary in their potential disconfirmability. Once again the argument focuses on the importance of these ideas for an analysis of stereotype–disconfirmation.

Reeder and Brewer (1979) have put forward a "schematic model of dispositional attribution" that starts from the following premise: the rules of inference for dispositional attribution may vary depending on the nature of the attribute to be inferred. They outline three main types of "implicational schemata," which refer to the perceiver's prior assumptions about the range of behavior believed likely to occur, given different levels of a disposition (e.g, very friendly, quite friendly, very unfriendly).

The "partially restrictive schema" conveys the idea that persons with an extreme disposition at one end of a trait dimension are not expected to behave in ways typical of the opposite end of the dimension. For example, if we are given information about the extremely friendly behavior of an outgroup member, then if this trait follows the partially restrictive schema, that same individual would not be expected to manifest extremely unfriendly behavior. Moderate behaviors, in contrast, are less informative about the actor's disposition, because people with a variety of dispositional states might behave in this manner. This schema leads to the conclusion that disconfirming information should consist of extreme examples of positive behavior, because moderately positive disconfirming behaviors may fall within the range of behavior implied by negative stereotypes.

The "hierarchically restrictive schema," in contrast, suggests that the range of behavior at the upper extreme of a dimension is not restricted, while at the lower extreme it is. According to Reeder and Brewer (1979), this schema is exemplified by dispositional attributions involving skill or ability—very able individuals may experience a range of outcomes, depending on motivation and task demands, while people at lower ability levels are not expected to perform at a level above that of their aptitude. This schema helps us to understand why, for example, information concerning ingroup failure does not disconfirm the attribution of ability ("even clever people fail sometimes"), and why evidence of outgroup success may be discounted.

The third type of schema, the "fully restrictive schema," implies a fairly inflexible link between dispositional level and range of possible behavior. It refers to traits on which some individuals are judged to have stable levels, while others are not. Reeder and Brewer suggest that dispositions such as preferences, values and personal styles may be conceived in terms of this schema. Thus, for example, "neat" people are expected to be invariably tidy.

Reeder and Brewer put forward these implicational schemata to explain inconsistencies in the attributional literature, but they can also be applied to stereotyping. As implied by the examples chosen, these schemata help to explain why it is so difficult to change some traits—because they are related to schemata that allow a wide range of behavior—and, by extension, why some traits are rarely attributed—because they allow only a narrow range of behavior. An interesting issue, worthy of future research, is whether the same traits may be associated with different implicational schemata for ingroup and outgroup members. In short, in order to predict whether disconfirming information will alter outgroup stereotypes, we need to know the "theory" behind the relevant trait. Implicational schemata may seem to imply complex processes on the part of perceivers. However, even if we take them simply as *as if* models of trait attribution (cf. Kelley, 1972), they suggest a closer analysis of the content of stereotypical traits. This line of research has been further extended by the work of Rothbart and colleagues.

Rothbart and Park (1986; see also Rothbart & John, 1985) have suggested three factors that might influence how easy or difficult it is, (1) to confirm a given trait, and (2) to disconfirm it, once established. The first factor, "occasions," refers to the frequency with which occasions arise that would permit behavior confirming or disconfirming a given trait. To take Rothbart and Park's example, there are fewer occasions in everyday life to engage in *devious* versus *messy* behavior. This fact restricts the opportunities for outgroup members to disconfirm the trait of deviousness. Further, this "occasions" factor was found to be related to the favorability of traits. Rothbart and Park reported a low but significant positive correlation between the favorability of a trait and the number of occasions available for disconfirming it. This relationship suggests that more occasions are available for disconfirming favorable than unfavorable traits, which in turn implies that it is especially difficult to disconfirm unfavorable traits (which, or course, often characterize outgroup stereotypes).

Rothbart and Park's second factor, "instances," refers to the number of instances required before an inference is made. Again using their example, we may decide that someone (especially a member of a disliked outgroup) is devious on the basis of just a few instances of behavior, whereas relatively more instances of behavior are required before we decide that someone is messy. Once we have decided that someone is devious, it will take a large number of nondevious behaviors to disconfirm this view, because a devious person can still engage in both devious and nondevious behavior. Rothbart and Park relate this factor to implicational schemata. A trait such as deviousness seems to be characterized by a hierarchically restrictive schema—a devious, or dishonest, person is capable of a range of behavior from dishonest to honest, while the behavior of an honest (nondevious) person is restricted to honest behaviors. A trait such as messy, on the other hand, seems to be characterized by the partially restrictive schema, allowing both messy and tidy people a range of behaviors at both ends of the trait dimension. This factor also interacts with trait favorability. Rothbart and Park reported strong correlations between the favorability of a trait and the number of instances required for it to be confirmed ($r = +.71$) and disconfirmed ($r = -.70$). Thus favorable traits seem to be difficult to acquire, but easy to lose, whereas unfavorable traits are easy to acquire, but difficult to lose.

The third factor identified by Rothbart and Park, "imaginability," refers to the fact that trait concepts vary in the degree to which they are defined by clear and specific behavioral referents. Although there is no evidence linking this factor to stereotype change, Rothbart and Park note that it is intuitively easier to specify behaviors that confirm or disconfirm a trait such as messy, compared with devious. The example of devious, as they note, is particularly interesting, because it (or some similar trait, such as sly or shrewd) is often ascribed to minority outgroups (cf. the Jews — Karlins, Coffman, & Walters, 1969; the ethnic Chinese in Southeast Asia — Hewstone & Ward, 1985).

Taken together, the work discussed in this section shows that the content of stereotypical traits must be included in any complete discussion of stereotype disconfirmation. Such an analysis is rendered yet more complex when one acknowledges that in real life, situations vary too, in terms of the traits that they allow to be expressed (Rothbart & John, 1985). Consider Gordon's (1977) characterization of black–white interaction in a Namibian mine compound, discussed by Foster and Finchilescu (1986): "Interaction is framed by rigid rules of conduct — mining etiquette — which require blacks to be anonymous (many are known only by their number), humble, deferential, circumspect and yet accepting of their lot. If a black calls a white 'mister,' he is censured for 'acting white,' and if he asks too many questions he is branded an 'agitator'" (p. 126). Under such circumstances, how can a black worker disconfirm negative stereotypes?

This use of content to extend a purely cognitive approach is supplemented in the following section by briefly considering some relevant motivational and affective influences on stereotype-disconfirmation.

Motivational and Affective Influences

Social cognitive research has been criticized for overemphasizing the more passive, less flexible ways in which prior knowledge contributes to the processing and interpretation of social information. Showers and Cantor (1985) have argued that more attention should be paid to the interface between motivation (including goals, mood, and expertise) and social cognition. With special reference to intergroup contact — a key area for investigating the impact of stereotype-disconfirming information — Pettigrew (1986) has also argued that the neglect of affect is a serious limitation in purely cognitive approaches: "To treat intergroup contact as if it were dealing with cold cognition is to slight what makes the entire area of intergroup conflict problematic — *heat*" (p. 181).

Personal involvement is one motivational variable that may limit some of the cognitive effects noted in this chapter (e.g., attention, memory, and attribution for expectancy-confirming information). Borgida and Howard-Pitney (1983) used personal involvement manipulations to explore the robustness of perceptual salience effects (e.g,. Taylor & Fiske, 1978) and did not support the generalizability of such effects to conditions of high personal involvement. They found (Borgida & Howard-Pitney, 1983, Experiment 1) salience effects for low-involvement subjects (subjects listening to a discussion about changes in course requirement that did not concern them personally), but not for high-involvement subjects. They suggested that high personal involvement may motivate subjects to engage in more "systematic" (Chaiken, 1980) or "central" (Petty & Cacioppo, 1981) processing. Low involvement subjects, in contrast, may engage in less detailed processing, called variously "heuristic" (Chaiken, 1980) or "peripheral" (Petty & Cacioppo, 1981), and thereby be susceptible to the kind of salience effects Taylor and Fiske (1978) called "top-of-the-head" phenomena. With reference to processing of stereotype-disconfirming information, it would obviously be interesting to investigate whether perceivers' processing of such information is influenced by their personal involvement.

Outcome dependency is another motivational factor that can influence whether perceivers will attend to inconsistent information. Erber and Fiske (1984; see also Fiske & Neuberg, Chapter 4) manipulated outcome dependency by having subjects judged interdependently with a partner on a joint task, to determine whether they would receive a monetary prize. They found (Experiment 1) that subjects attended more to inconsistent information (as measured by attention/ gaze duration) when their outcomes were dependent on it. Further evidence of more detailed processing was reported in Experiment 2, which provided a detailed analysis of subjects' "concurrent protocols." Outcome dependent subjects were more likely to comment in dispositional terms about the fit of the inconsistent information to the other person's dispositions. Contrasted with the above-cited studies showing situational attribution for inconsistency (Crocker et al., 1983; Kulik, 1983), this finding suggests that outcome-dependent subjects may engage in a more detailed causal attribution process than the presumably non-outcome-dependent subjects in these earlier studies.

Moving from motivational to more affective concerns, it should first be emphasized that a cognitive or schematic approach to stereotypes does not by definition imply neglect of affect. However, as Fiske (1982) has stated, the social cognition literature on stereotyping has barely addressed affect. Fiske proposes a schema-based model of affect in relation to stereotypes. Affect is stored with a schema and is available immediately upon categorization, so that evaluations and affect are cued by categorization. In this view, a perceiver first comprehends an input (e.g., a description of an outgroup target person) by assimilating it to an existing knowledge structure, and then evaluates the target on the basis of the affect linked to the schema.

This model leads to the prediction that schematic match determines affective responses, for which Fiske cites experimental evidence. Such a model raises a number of, as yet unanswered, issues: does this mean that stereotype-disconfirming exemplars evoke different affect from stereotype-confirming exemplars (there is evidence that people who confirm perceivers' expectancies are more liked than those who disconfirm them—Costrich, Feinstein, Kidder, Maracek, & Pascale, 1975; Gergen & Jones, 1963; Taylor & Gardner, 1969). And, if so, what implications does this have for generalization from target to outgroup? More research is clearly needed on the relation between affect and cognition with respect to stereotyping and intergroup relations. Some of the gains of such an integration are evident in the following example.

Stephan and Stephan (1985) have provided a striking demonstration of the importance of affect in stereotyping and intergroup relations by detailing the concept of "intergroup anxiety." This anxiety, grounded in anticipated negative consequences, may be especially important in intergroup contact. Feared consequences include psychological (e.g., embarrassment, threat to group identity) and behavioral (e.g., fear of being exploited or dominated) consequences, as well as anxieties about how one will be evaluated by members of both outgroup (e.g., with scorn, or ridicule) and ingroup (e.g., with disapproval). Concentrating here on only its cognitive consequences, Stephan and Stephan propose that anxiety will increase schematic processing and simplify information processing in general. People may seek out and attend to information confirming their (negative) expectations about outgroup members, while failing to notice or remember small inconsistencies. In fact, because the focus of attention is narrowed when anxiety is high (Easterbrook, 1959), the kind of simplified cognitive strategies noted earlier in this chapter may be expected to accentuate intergroup perceptions. As Stephan and Stephan (1985) note: "The occurrence of such processing biases implies that few positive changes in outgroup schemata are likely to take place under conditions of high anxiety. The operation of these biases provides further insight into the reasons why so many preconditions must be met for contact to reduce prejudice. The inertia of our cognitive structures and processing biases is enormous" (p. 168).

It should be clear from this treatment of intergroup anxiety that attention to motivational and affective influences is complementary to a cognitive approach to intergroup relations. As Hamilton and Trolier (1986) have persuasively argued, to a large extent affective and motivational factors exert an influence on stereotyping via their effects on information–processing. Cognitive processes both mediate and are mediated by motivational-affective effects. For this reason, a systematic analysis of the impact of stereotype-disconfirming information cannot afford to exclude any of these factors.

Conclusion

It was noted at the outset of this chapter, that stereotypes have social-structural as well as psychological bases. Without wishing to play down the importance of the former factors, or the extensive social support sometimes enjoyed by negative outgroup stereotypes (see Pettigrew, 1981), I have argued for more careful study of the factors that govern whether disconfirming information will lead to a change in stereotypes. The contribution of such an approach can be shown by asking, and answering, the question "When will beliefs change?" Higgins and Bargh (1987) have noted the variety of reasons why people's beliefs, including stereotypical beliefs, tend to be maintained. These include *passive* outcomes of cognitive processes (e.g., attention to belief-confirming data), as well as more *active* belief-preserving mechanisms (e.g., the creation of subtypes). In view of the many relevant influences identified in this chapter, it should perhaps surprise no one that stereotypes are so difficult to change. However, considerable progress has been made with a primarily cognitive analysis, supplemented by attention to motivation and affect. Planned interventions, of experimental and other sorts, must attempt to cut off the cognitive "escape routes" (inattention, poor memory, discounting, explaining away) which attenuate the impact of stereotype-disconfirming information. In conclusion, it is suggested that stereotype-disconfirming information be: (1) linked to typical out-group exemplars; (2) presented to highly motivated perceivers; and (3) provided under conditions that do not induce intergroup anxiety. Further research fulfilling these criteria might show that, after all, stereotypes *can* be changed by the presentation of disconfirming information.

Acknowledgments. This chapter was written while the author was a Fellow at the Center for Advanced Study in the Behavioral sciences, Stanford; the financial support of the National Science Foundation (BNS-8700864) and the John D. and Catherine T. MacArthur Foundation is gratefully acknowledged.

References

Abelson, R.P. (1959). Modes of resolution of belief dilemmas. *Journal of Conflict Resolution, 3*, 343–352.

Ajzen, I., & Fishbein, M. (1985). A Bayesian analysis of attribution processes. *Psychological Bulletin, 82*, 261–277.

Allport, G.W. (1954). *The nature of prejudice*. Reading, MA: Addison-Wesley.

Anderson, C.A. (1983). Abstract and concrete data in the perseverance of social theories: When weak data lead to unshakable beliefs. *Journal of Experimental Social Psychology, 19*, 93–108.

Anderson, C.A., Lepper, M.R., & Ross, L. (1980). Perseverance of social theories: The role of explanation in the persistence of discredited information. *Journal of Personality and Social Psychology, 39*, 1037–1049.

Bargh, J.A., & Thein, R.D. (1985). Individual construct accessibility, person memory, and the recall-judgment link: The case of information overload. *Journal of Personality and Social Psychology, 49*, 1129–1146.

Borgida, E., & Howard-Pitney, B. (1983). Personal involvement and the robustness of perceptual salience effects. *Journal of Personality and Social Psychology, 45*, 560–570.

Brewer, M.B., Dull, V., & Lui, L. (1981). Perceptions of the elderly: Stereotypes as prototypes. *Journal of Personality and Social Psychology, 41*, 656–670.

Brewer, M.B., & Kramer, R.M. (1985). The psychology of intergroup attitudes and behavior. *Annual Review of Psychology, 36*, 219–243.

Brewer, M.B., & Miller, N. (1984). Beyond the contact hypothesis: Theoretical perspectives on desegregation. In N. Miller & M.B. Brewer (Eds.), *Groups in contact: The psychology of desegregation* (pp. 281–302). New York: Academic Press.

Brown, R.J., & Turner, J.C. (1981). Interpersonal and intergroup behavior. In J.C. Turner & H. Giles (Eds.), *Intergroup behavior* (pp. 33–65). Oxford: Blackwell.

Cantor, N., & Mischel, W. (1977). Traits as prototypes: Effects on recognition memory. *Journal of Personality and Social Psychology, 35*, 38–48.

Chaiken, S. (1980). Heuristic versus systematic information processing and the use of source versus message cues in persuasion. *Journal of Personality and Social Psychology, 39*, 752–766.

Cohen, C.E. (1981). Person categories and social perception: Testing some boundaries of the processing effects of prior knowledge. *Journal of Personality and Social Psychology, 40*, 441–452.

Costrich, N., Feinstein, J., Kidder, L., Maracek, J., & Pascale, L. (1975). When stereotypes hurt: Three studies of penalties for sex-role reversals. *Journal of Experimental Social Psychology, 11*, 520–530.

Crocker, J., Hannah, D.B., & Weber, R. (1983). Person memory and causal attributions. *Journal of Personality and Social Psychology, 44*, 55–66.

Darley, J.M., and Goethals, G.R. (1980). People's analyses of the causes of ability-linked performances. In L. Berkowitz (Ed.), *Advances in experimental social psychology* (Vol. 13) (pp. 1–37). New York: Academic Press.

Dustin, D.W., & Davis, H.P. (1970). Evaluative bias in group and individual competition. *Journal of Social Psychology, 80,* 103–108.

Easterbrook, J.A. (1959). The effect of emotion on cue utilization and the organization of behavior. *Psychological Review, 66,* 183–201.

Eiser, J.R., & Stroebe, W. (1972). *Categorization and social judgement.* London: Academic Press.

Erber, R., & Fiske, S.T. (1984). Outcome dependency and attention to inconsistent information. *Journal of Personality and Social Psychology, 47,* 709–726.

Fiske, S.T. (1982). Schema-triggered affect: Applications to social perception. In M.S. Clark & S.T. Fiske (Eds.), *Affect and cognition: The 17th Annual Carnegie Symposium* (pp. 55–77). Hillsdale, NJ: Erlbaum.

Foster, D., & Finchilescu, G. (1986). Contact in a 'non-contact' society: The case of South Africa. In M. Hewstone & R.J. Brown (Eds.), *Contact and conflict in intergroup encounters* (pp. 119–136). Oxford: Blackwell.

Freud, S. (1961 ed.) *The interpretation of dreams.* New York: Science Editions.

Gergen, K.J., & Jones, E.E. (1963). Mental illness, predictability, and affective consequences as stimulus factors in person perception. *Journal of Abnormal and Social Psychology, 6,* 95–104.

Gordon, R.J. (1977). *Mines and migrants.* Johannesburg: Ravan.

Gurwitz, S.B., & Dodge, K.A. (1977). Effects of confirmations and disconfirmations on stereotype-based attributions. *Journal of Personality and Social Psychology, 35,* 495–500.

Hamill, R., Wilson, T.D., & Nisbett, R.E. (1980). Insensitivity to sample bias: Generalizing from atypical cases. *Journal of Personality and Social Psychology, 39,* 578–589.

Hamilton, D.L. (1979). A cognitive-attributional analysis of stereotyping. In L. Berkowitz (Ed.), *Advances in experimental social psychology* (Vol. 12) (pp. 53–84). New York: Academic.

Hamilton, D.L. (Ed.). (1981). *Cognitive processes in stereotyping and intergroup behavior.* Hillsdale, NJ: Erlbaum.

Hamilton, D.L., & Rose, T. (1980). Illusory correlation and the maintenance of stereotypic beliefs. *Journal of Personality and Social Psychology, 39,* 832–845.

Hamilton, D.L., & Trolier, T.K. (1986). Stereotypes and stereotyping: An overview of the cognitive approach. In J.F. Dovidio & S.L. Gaertner (Eds.), *Prejudice, discrimination and racism* (pp. 127–163). Orlando, FL: Academic Press.

Hastie, R. (1981). Schematic principles in human memory. In E.T. Higgins, C.P. Herman, & M.P. Zanna (Eds.). *Social cognition: The Ontario Symposium.* (Vol. 1) (pp. 39–88). Hillsdale, NJ: Erlbaum.

Hastie, R. (1984). Causes and effects of causal attribution. *Journal of Personality and Social Psychology, 46,* 44–56.

Hastie, R., & Kumar, P.A. (1979). Person memory: Personality traits as organizing principles in memory for behaviors. *Journal of Personality and Social Psychology, 37,* 25–38.

Hastorf, A.H., & Cantril, H. (1954). They saw a game: A case study. *Journal of Personality and Social Psychology, 49,* 129–134.

Hewstone, M. (1988). Attributional bases of intergroup conflict. In W. Stroebe, A.W. Kruglanski, D. Bar-Tal, & M. Hewstone (Eds.), *The social psychology of intergroup conflict: Theory, research and applications* (pp. 47–71). New York: Springer.

Hewstone, M., & Brown, R.J. (Eds.). (1986a). *Contact and conflict in intergroup encounters.* Oxford: Blackwell.

Hewstone, M., & Brown, R.J. (1986b). Contact is not enough: an intergroup perspective on the "contact hypothesis." In M. Hewstone & R.J. Brown (Eds.), *Contact and conflict in intergroup encounters* (pp. 1–44). Oxford: Blackwell.

Hewstone, M., Gale, L., & Purkhardt, N. (1988). *Intergroup attributions for success and failure: Group-serving bias and group-serving causal schemata.* Unpublished manuscript, University of Bristol.

Hewstone, M., & Jaspars, J. (1984). Social dimensions of attribution. In H. Tajfel (Ed.), *The social dimension: European developments in social psychology* (pp. 379–404). Cambridge/Paris: Cambridge University Press/Maison des Sciences de l'Homme.

Hewstone, M., Jaspars, J., & Lalljee, M. (1982). Social representations, social attribution and social identity: The intergroup images of "public" and "comprehensive" schoolboys. *European Journal of Social Psychology, 12,* 241–269.

Hewstone, M., & Ward, C. (1985). Ethnocentrism and causal attribution in Southeast Asia. *Journal of Personality and Social Psychology, 48,* 614–623.

Higgins, E.T., & Bargh, J.A. (1987). Social cognition and perception. *Annual Review of Psychology, 38,* 369–425.

Karlins, M., Coffman, T.L., & Walters, G. (1969). Fading of stereotypes in three generations of college students. *Journal of Personality and Social Psychology, 13,* 1–16.

Kelley, H.H. (1972). Causal schemata and the attribution process. In E.E. Jones, D.E. Kanouse, H.H. Kelley, R.E. Nisbett, S. Valins, & B. Weiner, *Attribution: Perceiving the causes of behavior* (pp.151–174). Morristown, NJ: General Learning Press.

Kulik, J.A. (1983). Confirmatory attribution and the perpetuation of social beliefs. *Journal of Personality and Social Psychology, 44,* 1171–1181.

McArthur, L.Z. (1982). Judging a book by its cover. A cognitive analysis of the relationship between physical appearance and stereotyping. In A. Hastorf & A. Isen (Eds.), *Cognitive social psychology* (pp. 149–211). New York: Elsevier North-Holland.

Miller, D.T., & Turnbull, W. (1986). Expectancies and interpersonal processes. *Annual Review of Psychology, 37,* 233–256.

Miller, N., Brewer, M.B., & Edwards, K. (1985). Cooperative interaction in desegregated settings: A laboratory analogue. *Journal of Social Issues, 41,* 63–79.

Pettigrew, T.F. (1979). The ultimate attribution error: Extending Allport's cognitive analysis of prejudice. *Personality and Social Psychology Bulletin, 5,* 461–476.

Pettigrew, T.F. (1981). Extending the stereotype concept. In D.L. Hamilton (Ed.), *Cognitive processes in stereotyping and intergroup behavior* (pp. 303–331). Hillsdale, NJ: Erlbaum.

Pettigrew, T.F. (1986). The intergroup contact hypothesis reconsidered. In M. Hewstone & R.J. Brown (Eds.), *Contact and conflict in intergroup encounters* (pp. 169–195). Oxford: Blackwell.

Petty, R.E., & Cacioppo, J.T. (1981). *Attitudes and persuasion: Classic and contemporary approaches.* Dubuque, IA: W.C. Brown.

Posner, M.T., & Snyder, C.R.R. (1975). Attention and cognitive control. In R.L. Solso (Ed.), *Information processing and cognition: The Loyola Symposium* (pp. 55–86). Hillsdale, NJ: Erlbaum.

Pyszczynski, T.A., & Greenberg, J. (1981). Role of disconfirmed expectancies in the instigation of attributional processing. *Journal of Personality and Social Psychology, 45,* 323–334.

Quattrone, G.A., & Jones, E.E. (1980). The perception of variability within in-groups and out-groups: Implications for the law of small numbers. *Journal of Personality and Social Psychology, 38,* 141–152.

Reeder, G.D., & Brewer, M.B. (1979). A schematic model of dispositional attribution in interpersonal perception. *Psychological Review, 86,* 61–79.

Regan, D.T., Straus, E., & Fazio, R. (1974). Liking and the attribution process. *Journal of Experimental Social Psychology, 10,* 385–397.

Rothbart, M. (1981). Memory processes and social beliefs. In D.L. Hamilton (Ed.), *Cognitive processes in stereotyping and intergroup behavior* (pp. 145–181). Hillsdale, NJ: Erlbaum.

Rothbart, M. Evans, M., & Fulero, S. (1979). Recall for confirming events: Memory processes and maintenance of social stereotypes. *Journal of Experimental Social Psychology, 15,* 343–355.

Rothbart, M., & John, O.P. (1985). Social categorization and behavioral episodes: A cognitive analysis of the effects of intergroup contact. *Journal of Social Issues, 41,* 81-104.

Rothbart, M., & Park, B. (1986). On the confirmability and disconfirmability of trait concepts. *Journal of Personality and Social Psychology, 50,* 131-142.

Showers, C., & Cantor, N. (1985). Social cognition: A look at motivated strategies. *Annual Review of Psychology, 36,* 275-305.

Smith, E.R., & Miller, F.D. (1983). Mediation among attributional inferences and comprehension processes: Initial findings and a general method. *Journal of Personality and Social Psychology, 44,* 492-505.

Snyder, M., & Cantor, N. (1979). Testing hypotheses about other people: The use of historical knowledge. *Journal of Personality and Social Psychology, 15,* 330-342.

Snyder, M.L., & Frankel, A. (1976). Observer bias: A stringent test of behavior engulfing the field. *Journal of Personality and Social Psychology, 34,* 857-864.

Snyder, M., & Swann, W.B. (1978). Hypothesis-testing processes in social interaction. *Journal of Personality and Social Psychology, 36,* 1202-1212.

Srull, T.K. (1981). Person memory: Some tests of associative storage and retrieval models. *Journal of Experimental Psychology, 7,* 440-462.

Stephan, W.G. (1985). Intergroup relations. In G. Lindzey & E. Aronson (Eds.), *Handbook of social psychology* (Vol. 2) (pp. 599-658). New York: Random House.

Stephan, W.G., & Stephan, C.W. (1985). Intergroup anxiety. *Journal of Social Issues, 41,* 157-175.

Strenta, A.C., & Kleck, R.E. (1984). Physical disability and the perception of social interaction: It's not what you look at but how you look at it. *Personality and Social Psychology Bulletin, 10,* 279-288.

Tajfel, H. (1969). Cognitive aspects of prejudice. *Journal of Social Issues, 25,* 79-97.

Taylor, D.M., & Gardner, R.C. (1969). Ethnic stereotypes: Their effects on the perception of communications of varying credibility. *Canadian Journal of Psychology, 23,* 161-173.

Taylor, D.M., & Jaggi, V. (1974). Ethnocentrism and causal attribution in a South Indian context. *Journal of Cross-Cultural Psychology, 5,* 162-171.

Taylor, S.E. (1981). A categorization approach to stereotyping. In D.L. Hamilton (Ed.), *Cognitive processes in stereotyping and intergroup behavior* (pp. 83-114). Hillsdale, NJ: Erlbaum.

Taylor, S.E., & Crocker, J. (1981). Schematic bases of social information processing. In E.T. Higgins, C.P. Herman, & M.P. Zanna (Eds.), *Social cognition: The Ontario symposium on personality and social psychology* (pp. 89-134). Hillsdale, NJ: Erlbaum.

Taylor, S.E., & Fiske, S.T. (1978). Salience, attention and attribution: Top of the head phenomena. In L. Berkowitz (Eds.), *Advances in experimental social psychology* (Vol. 11) (pp. 249-288). New York: Academic.

Trope, Y. (1986). Identification and inferential processes in dispositional attribution. *Psychological Review, 93,* 239-257.

Weber, R., & Crocker, J. (1983). Cognitive processes in the revision of stereotypic beliefs. *Journal of Personality and Social Psychology, 45,* 961-977.

Weiner, B. (1985). "Spontaneous" causal thinking. *Psychological Bulletin, 97,* 74-84.

Wilder, D.A. (1984). Intergroup contact: The typical member and the exception to the rule. *Journal of Personality and Social Psychology, 20,* 177-194.

Wilder, D.A. (1986). Cognitive factors affecting the success of intergroup contact. In S. Worchel & W.A. Austin (Eds.), *Psychology of intergroup relations* (pp. 49-66). Chicago: Nelson Hall.

Williams, R.M. (1964). *Strangers next door: Ethnic relations in American communities.* Englewood Cliffs, NJ: Prentice-Hall.

Winter, L., Uleman, J.S., & Cunniff, C. (1985). How automatic are social judgments? *Journal of Personality and Social Psychology, 49,* 904-917.

Chapter 11

Can Leaders Change Followers' Stereotypes?

Yoram Bar-Tal

Although a review of the social psychology literature reveals that stereotyping is considered a group-level phenomenon (e.g., Ashmore & Del Boca, 1981; Brigham, 1971; Wilder, 1981, 1986), most attempts to deal with stereotype change have focused on *intrapersonal* processes. Relatively few attempts have been made to study the effects of *intragroup* processes, such as leaders' influence on followers, on stereotype change. More importantly, even in those cases in which the effect of leadership on ingroup members' stereotypical thinking has been examined (e.g. Pettigrew, 1961; Weigel & Howes, 1985), the conditions under which such interventions succeed have not been defined.

This chapter examines how and to what extent leaders can help to change group members' stereotypes. Since there is not research available on this topic, the chapter will raise various hypotheses regarding leaders' influence on stereotype change and discuss possible avenues for future research and practice. The chapter first examines the structure and process of stereotype formation. The leadership phenomenon is then analyzed and its facilitating and inhibiting components discussed terms of their relevance to the problem of stereotype change. Finally, this chapter examines several methods that leaders can use in changing their group members' stereotypes.

Stereotypes and Stereotypical Thinking

Recent developments in the study of stereotypes have shifted the focus of attention from an emphasis on the negative content of stereotypes to an attempt to understand the cognitive processes and structures that underlie the formation of stereotypes, considered as a specific category of knowledge (e.g., Hamilton, 1981a; McCauley, Stitt, & Segal, 1980). On the assumption that the principles that govern the formation and use of stereotypes do not differ from those that govern the formation and use of other social knowledge, they can be studied in the same way. Present-day cognitive social psychology is primarily interested in seeing how far it can successfully push a purely cognitive analysis, with little regard for motivational factors. Within this framework, the study of stereotypes has tended to disregard the influence of motivations on stereotype formation and use. The theory of lay epistemology proposed by Kruglanski (e.g., 1980; in press), which emphasizes both cognitive *and* motivational factors in the process of knowledge acquisition, thus offers a new and important framework for furthering our understanding of stereotypes and stereotypical thinking.

Theory of Lay Epistemology

Lay epistemology theory is concerned with the process through which individuals form knowledge, including stereotypes. The theory suggests two distinct phases in the process of knowledge acquisition: first, a cognitive generation stage, in which the contents of knowledge come into existence in our mind; and second, a cognitive validation stage, in which the degree of validity attributed to the generated contents is assessed and the degree of confidence with which the knowledge is held is determined (cf. Kruglanski, 1980; Kruglanski & Ajzen, 1983). The validation of the contents is conducted in accordance with the principle of logical consistency: the individual deduces from the hypothesis under consideration some of its implications and tests them against appropriate evidence. As the individual continues to collect information and makes these comparisons, his or her epistemological activity can be characterized as "open." But if testing shows that the hypothesis is consistent with the evidence, and it is accepted, the individual "closes" on the knowledge. It is important to note that the acceptance of any hypothesis is potentially revokable. An individual can always become aware of plausible alternative hypotheses that are inconsistent with the one originally accepted. This "openness" could undermine the individual's faith in the original hypothesis and possibly lead to its renouncement as erroneous. Often, however, an individual's epistemological activity can be characterized by "closure" to inconsistent information, that is, by disregard of any information which is inconsistent with the generated knowledge. The "openness" and "closure" tendencies were termed by Kruglanski (in press) as "unfreezing" and "freezing," respectively.

Lay epistemology theory identifies classes of external and internal factors that influence the freezing-unfreezing tendencies. External factors include, for example, the availability and saliency of information, the existence of epistemic authority, time pressure, and group pressure. Internal factors may include such variables as the individual's capacity to produce various alternative hypotheses on a given topic (e.g., past knowledge, intelligence, creativity) and his or her epistemic motivation. The theory suggest three types of epistemic motivations: (1) the need for ambiguity; (2) the need for nonspecific structure; and (3) the need for specific structure.

The need for ambiguity can be engendered either by the desire for valid knowledge or by the fear of arriving at invalid conclusions. Under this motivation, individuals are predisposed to unfreeze the generation of alternative hypotheses and to test as many implications of their hypothesis as possible, so as to insure that they are holding valid knowledge.

The need for nonspecific structure is based on the desire for certainty. This epistemic motivation predisposes individuals to freeze the generation of alternative hypotheses in order to have structure and to hold firm knowledge. Such a motivation is apparent, for example, in cases where the individual is under time pressure to decide on a course of action. In such circumstances, any hesitation or rethinking frustrate the individual's ability to perform quickly.

The need for specific structure is engendered by the desire to confirm that certain beliefs the individual is holding are correct. In this case, individuals are predisposed to seek only the information that is consistent with their desired content and to avoid information that will weaken their certainty in its validity. Such biased thinking is directly related to some individualistic need. That is, the preference for a given conclusion over another is explained by the desire of the individual to fulfill a wish or to avoid a fear.

Stereotypes as Frozen Contents

In lay epistemology terms, it is possible to characterize stereotypes as frozen contents of knowledge. The implications of such a definition correspond with two conceptual features of stereotypes, that: (1) stereotypes are the result of a categorization process that uses specific social categories and can be called "stereotypical thinking" (see, Fiske & Neuberg, Chapter 4); and (2) stereotypes persist and resist alteration.

These characteristics reflect the influence of the epistemic motivations of need for nonspecific or specific structure. Under the first motivation, a person has a desire to form a quick social category—stereotypical thinking. This desire may arise, for example, when a person experiences either a lack of sufficient information or too much information regarding the target individual. In this situation the person tends to use schematic rather than piecemeal processes (cf. Kruglanski & Freund, 1983). Under the second motivation, the specific stereotypical content serves the person's need(s). In this situation, a person exhibits a preference for information consistent with the preconceived content and rejection of inconsistent information.

That stereotypical content is based on social categories implies that it consists of beliefs with evaluative dimension that generalize about a group of people. In spite of disagreement in the literature as to whether the concept of stereotyping should include an evaluative component (e.g., Ashmore & Del Boca, 1981; McCauley, Stitt, & Segal, 1980), recent findings regarding intergroup biases point out not only that the evaluative component is important, but that when attempts are made to change stereotypes, it is because of the problematic nature of negative evaluation (e.g., Turner, 1985; Wilder, 1981, 1986). Thus, although the evaluative contents of stereotypes may be of a negative or positive nature, the present chapter will focus on attempts to change negative stereotypes.

Stereotype Change

Contents of stereotypes can be changed in numerous ways and the literature of attitude change focuses on many techniques which facilitate such change (see for review, Himmelfarb & Eagly, 1974; McGuire, 1985). Lay epistemology theory implies that the study of stereotype change can focus on the direct change of evaluative content and/or on change in the motivations that underlie the formation of the stereotype. In either case, such change requires unfreezing of the original contents. According to lay epistemology theory, epistemic unfreezing can be achieved through manipulation of available *information* and/or through manipulation of *epistemic motivation* (e.g., Klar, Bar-Tal, & Kruglanski, 1988).

Most of the literature that deals with stereotype change suggests that it can be achieved through various methods of altering information about the stereotype's target (see Hewstone, Chapter 10). One example of this can be found in a proposed method that emphasizes the unique characteristics of each outgroup member rather than those that are perceived as common to the group as a whole (e.g., Taylor, 1981; Wilder, 1978, 1981, 1986). Since stereotypes are the outcome of a generalization process, providing information about a specific individual in order to show his or her uniqueness can thus achieve less stereotypical thinking toward outgroup members. This method is called the individualization technique. The strategy is especially successful when the individuation information is inconsistent with the stereotyping information.

Another example of change through information is found in work on the contact hypothesis. The idea behind the contact hypothesis (e.g., Allport, 1954; Amir, 1969) is that information absorbed as a result of face-to-face interaction may lead to learning about the other group's members and thus result in a change of the stereotypical beliefs. An analysis of the conditions under which interaction between groups promotes stereotype change (e.g., Allport, 1954; Amir, 1969, 1976) provides a hint regarding the importance of motivational changes. Recommendations that the interaction between groups be of a cooperative nature, the parties be on an equal basis, the task have a high probability of success and low social threat, and the situation be without tension, frustration, or conflict, indicate that the function of contact between groups is not merely to provide information. Rather, it is implied that information can be effective in altering stereotypes when it is accompanied by specific motivations.

Although is has been recognized that stereotyping may involve motivational processes (Allport, 1954; Pettigrew, 1979; Stephan & Stephan, 1985), change of motivation has not yet been adapted as a technique for altering stereotypes. In the example mentioned above, motivation is recognized as a factor that may heighten the impact of information, but not as a factor that by itself can change stereotypes or the tendency to use them. Lay epistemology theory, however, suggests that changes in epistemic motivation may play a major role in changing both stereotypes and stereotypical thinking.

An analysis of the need for specific structure reveals that the persistence of belief in the content of a stereotype, even in the face of contradictory information, is based on an individual's struggle to satisfy a particular need. Stereotype change may thus be achieved when the individual is convinced that the need in question can be satisfied more efficiently by altering than by maintaining a belief in the content of the stereotype. An alternative method is to convince the individual that a change of the stereotypical belief may achieve a more basic need than the one that underlies the stereotypical thinking. A similar effect can be achieved if the individual is convinced that the need underlying the stereotype is less central or important than the alternative needs which are being blocked by the stereotyping thinking.

It should be pointed out that the described techniques do not necessarily solve the problem of stereotyping. Unfreezing of the need for nonspecific structure, for example, may not bring lasting change in the stereotype's content. It is possible that the unfreezing may affect a specific behavior toward the stereotype's target in a particular situation, without a change in the evaluative content of the stereotype. That is, the behavior may be guided by piecemeal rather than stereotypical thinking in a given situation only. Similarly, a change in specific stereotype content does not necessarily lead in principle to a less stereotypical mode of thinking. On the contrary, adherence to one specific content may be replaced by adherence to another.

To recapitulate, it has been suggested that stereotypes can be conceptualized as manifestations of two epistemic motivations: the need for nonspecific structure and the need for specific structure; and that stereotype change can be achieved by two means: changing the evaluative content of the stereotypes and/or changing the epistemic motivations that underlie the stereotypical thinking. The following pages will examine the extent to which the role of leader allows manipulation of information available to followers and/or manipulation of their epistemic motivation.

Leadership and Stereotype Change

In order to discuss the leader's influence in changing followers' stereotypes, it is first necessary to explain the principles of this influence.

Leaders, Followers, and the Process of Influence

The realization that leaders' influence on their followers' behavior is mediated and determined by many factors precipitated a shift from a search for an answer to the general question of the extent of leaders' influence to an examination of the specific conditions under which leaders can achieve maximum impact on their followers' behavior. Even the interest in moderators of leader behavior—follower reaction studied within the various contingency models (for review, see Hunt, 1984; Hunt & Larson, 1974; Yukl, 1981) did not generate research that discovered meaningful patterns of covariation between leader-behavior and follower-response (e.g., Bar-Tal, 1985; Griffin, Skivington, & Moorhead, 1987; McCall & Lombardo, 1978). One explanation for this lack of significant findings is that the effect of specific contingent variables is dependent upon the effect of other specific variables (cf. Y. Bar-Tal, in press). This realization has led to the development of interactive process models that are characterized by bi-directional transactions of influence and phenomenology-based psychological concepts (Y. Bar-Tal, in press; Griffin et al., 1987; Pfeffer, 1981). In line with this trend, the present chapter utilizes Lewin's (1951) field theory to examine the leader–follower interaction and gain an understanding of how and when leaders can affect their followers' stereotypes by either presenting new information and/or changing their epistemic motivation.

On the basis of Lewin's propositions suggesting that a person's behavior (B) is a function of his or her goals (P), which he or she strives to achieve by "locomotion," and the person's perception of the characteristics of the situation (E) that may facilitate, inhibit, or even alter the person's goals, it is necessary to analyze separately the leader's and followers' behavior. Application of this framework with the leader's behavior as the center of analysis can explain the tendency and, to a certain degree, the success of leader's attempts to change followers' stereotypes. The goal of changing followers' stereotypes does not always exist, and it is not always possible to explain why one leader would set such a goal and another would not. It is possible, however, to hypothesize that it depends upon whether the leader perceives that the advancement of his or her higher hierarchy goals or the goals of the group require a change of followers' stereotypes. When such a goal does exist, the leader's perception of the reaction of the group may mediate his or her attempts at change. Finally, the leader's accurate assessment of the followers' salient needs as well as their perception of the leader may influence his or her choice of tactics.

When the follower's behavior is the focus of the analysis, the environmental factor (E) includes his or her perception of the leader's and the other followers' behavior, in addition to a perception of the external and internal immediate situation of the group. In this framework, the assumption is that *any element of the environment may affect the follower's behavior to the extent that it is perceived by the follower as relevant to his or her goals or process of locomotion. Therefore, if a leader is trying to change the follower's stereotypes, the leader's behavior may affect the follower's behavior only to the extent that it is perceived as relevant to the follower's goals in the situation.*

This process is partially mediated by the effect the follower's motivations and expectations have on his or her perception and interpretation of the leader's behavior. If the leader presents new or alternative information consistent with the follower's goals and the follower is epistemologically motivated by a need for ambiguity, there is likely to be a change in the stereotype. If the information is inconsistent with the follower's goals and he or she is motivated by a need for specific or even nonspecific structure, there may be little or no change in the stereotype.

Lay epistemology theory suggests further that the extent to which leaders' information is utilized depends on the type and strength of the epistemic motivation as well as the saliency of the information. If an advocated change in the content of a stereotype threatens the follower's positive social identity, for example, usually a strongly held goal reflecting a need for specific content, salient information may be rejected. On the other hand, particularly salient information may override or even influence a change in the epistemic motivation.

In order to demonstrate the utility of the present framework for understanding how leaders can change their followers' stereotypes, it is necessary to be familiar with the variables that may arise from both the followers' needs and goals (P) and their perception of the leader's behavior (E). It is, of course, not possible to suggest a final list of all the specific variables of followers' P and E and the patterns of interaction between them, but leadership as well as stereotype research suggest certain factors, which may be related to the P and E of group members and which may influence their readiness for a change in stereotype content. In the following pages some of these factors, as well as the possible interactions among them, are presented. First the analysis will focus on aspects of the followers' environment (i.e., the leader's behavior) and then on the followers' needs and goals.

The Interaction of Follower's Personal and Environmental Variables

Leaders characteristics. It was suggested earlier that characteristics of the leader may comprise part of the followers E. This framework allows incorporation of such characteristics as the leader's idiosyncrasy credits or his or her bases of power into the follower's E.

The "idiosyncrasy credit" (Hollander, 1958, 1964) is a concept that best demonstrates the reciprocal nature of influence between the leader and group members. It explains the apparent paradox that leaders are likely to be influential in bringing about innovations, such as a change in stereotypes, even when they appear to be conforming to the group's norms (and thus to the original stereotypical content). Idiosyncrasy credits can be accumulated by the leader through the advancement of the group's goals as perceived by the group's members. The goals may involve changes and innovations in the group's function, but they also include maintenance of the group's norms. Hollander suggested that leaders earn idiosyncrasy credits in the initial stage of their leadership by contributing to the group's primary task and by loyalty to the group's norms. Only with sufficient credits can the leader exercise influence directed toward change. Since stereotype change may involve deviation from norms or goals, leaders perceived idiosyncrasy credits may help facilitate the achievement of change.

But it should be remembered that, although idiosyncrasy credits are usually used to characterize the leader and the result of the leader's behavior, it is the interaction between the followers' needs and their perception of the leader that is important. While acknowledging that different leaders may need different amounts of effort to earn these credits, and that some of them, due to their charisma, may be required to do very little, idiosyncrasy credits can best be conceptualized as a characteristic attitude of group members that determines their a priori tendency to accept the changes in stereotypes suggested by the leader, whether or not the changes are perceived as advancing their needs. As such, idiosyncrasy credits demonstrate the potential as well as the shortcomings of a leader's ability to change his or her follower's stereotypes. Without them, followers may resist stereotype change that is perceived as contradicting their goals.

Another characteristic of the leader which may be useful in achieving stereotype change is his or her power position. French and Raven (1959) suggested a typology of five bases of power the leader may have over the followers: referent power (liking), expert power, reward power, coercive power, and legitimate power. When a leader commands reward power or coercive power, it means that he or she is perceived by a follower as able to provide incentives the follower is interested in or impose painful sanctions contingent upon the follower's ability to alter his or her stereotypical content or stereotypical thinking. However, the follower's compliance is not a function of the leader's power but of the interaction between the needs of the follower to receive the rewards or avoid the punishments and the ability of the leader to provide them (Bass, 1967; Kerr & Jermier, 1978).

With regard to expert power, the ability of the leader to convey information and convince is of great importance to any change in followers' stereotypes and the perception of the leader as an expert may be of special significance. The expert can be characterized as the person who is seen as possessing information that is needed by group members. Kruglanski termed such a person an "epistemic authority." Epistemic authority exerts determinative influence on the acceptance of information as valid (cf. Kruglanski & Jaffe, 1988). The degree to which a person is perceived as an epistemic authority determines the extent to which the perceiver accepts information attributed to the source as valid, even when it is inconsistent with his or her knowledge. In terms of lay epistemology theory, a person does not usually entertain and/or generate rival alternative hypotheses to those suggested by an epistemic authority. A leader who is perceived by the group members as an epistemic authority can change both the content of the stereotype and the motivations that affect epistemic freezing. The leader may contradict the negative content of the stereotype, on one hand, or may convince the group members to open themselves to all available information (to be under motivation for validity), on the other.

The ability of the leader as an epistemic authority to change the stereotypes of his or her followers is based on the assumption that the follower's acceptance of information from the leader is consistent with the follower's goals and needs in the situation. Two types of goals relevant to the follower's tendency to seek information from the leader can be identified. The first is common to all group members and relates to the role of the leader. The second may be characteristic of a specific follower. The following sections contain examples of goals belonging to each type and an analysis of the ways they may interact with a leader's attempts to change stereotypes.

Group members' collective goals. It has been suggested that group members are motivated by the need to reduce uncertainty regarding their activities and their inter- and intragroup relationships (e.g., Kagan, 1972; Staw, 1977). Kagan, for example, argued that resolving uncertainty is a primary motive, while other motives are considered to be secondary and idiosyncratic. Since ingroup members are an important source of one's information (e.g., Abrams, 1987; Festinger, 1954; Heider, 1958; Moscovici, 1976; Tajfel, 1972; Turner, 1985), individuals rely on their group members to facilitate their comprehension of the world around them and thus may be heavily influenced by them. However, more than any other single member of the group, the leader's role is to provide meaning to the group's activities in relation to its internal and external environment (e.g., Pfeffer, 1981). In this vein, Griffin et al. (1987) suggested that:

> The relationship between leader and subordinate is one of developing a mutual and shared meaning for the activities. Leaders infuse activities with symbols which,

when vested with a shared consensus of meaning, become legitimate interpretations. Symbols in the form of stories, myths, rituals, and words are mechanisms for
framing an understanding. (p. 207)

The followers' need for shared meaning and understanding can be conceptualized in
lay epistemology terms as a need for nonspecific structure. Thus, to the extent that
the leader's activity is perceived by group members as providing cognitive structure,
it allows them to accept and freeze on new contents suggested by the leader. This
may allow the leader to infuse ingroup members' stereotypes with positive evaluative contents toward outgroup members.

   If the contents suggested by the leader imply the unfreezing of beliefs that fulfill
an important role in the group life, group members may, nevertheless, resist the
change. The categorization of individuals according to their belonging in the
ingroup or outgroup, for instance, helps to distinguish between members and nonmembers of the group (Wilder, 1986). Although an extensive literature indicates
that mere categorization of persons into an ingroup and outgroup is sufficient to
foster stereotyping (Brewer, 1979; Dion, 1973) and that the blurring of boundaries
between groups or a lack of cohesion within the group lessen stereotyping (Allen &
Wilder, 1975; Commins & Lockwood, 1978; Wilder & Tompson, 1980), the
dichotomy is critical for group life. Groups have very little utility if they are without
boundaries. The categorization helps the group members develop esteem ("we are
much better than the outgroup members"), strengthens the identification of group
members with the group, and enhances the cohesion of the group (Wilder, 1986).
An attempt by the leader to change stereotypical beliefs by presenting information
that threatens to erase group boundaries may therefore be perceived as an attack on
this very important function of group life, and group members may strongly resist it.

Goal characteristics of individual group members. While recognizing the common
need of all group members for information that helps them to structure their social
environment, individual differences in the need for cognitive structure should not
be overlooked. Individual differences in the need for nonspecific structure have long
been a center of attention (e.g., Budner, 1962; Cacioppo & Petty, 1984; Cohen,
Stotland & Wolfe, 1955; Frenkel-Brunswik, 1949; MacDonald, 1970; Rydell &
Rosen, 1966). Over the years different names have been given to the trait, such as
tolerance for ambiguity, need for structure and need for cognition; different theoretical definitions have been suggested and different operationalizations deployed.
Frenkel-Brunswik, for example, suggested that intolerance for ambiguity is a preference for familiarity, symmetry, definiteness, and regularity. It also implies a tendency toward black-white solutions, over-simplified dichotomizing, and premature
and unqualified either/or solutions. Rosen (1964) suggested that need–cognition
relates to aspects such as orientation to the process of acquiring knowledge, orientation to the possession of knowledge, need to know facts, and need to comprehend
relations among ideas. The common denominator of all of these characterizations is
that they describe traits that can be placed on the dimension of cognitive freezing–unfreezing.

As suggested earlier, this dimension plays and important role in the tendency to form and use stereotypes. Thus, individuals who are high in the need for nonspecific structure may tend to resist more forcefully attempts to unfreeze their beliefs. The picture may be different, however, when the source of change is the individual who is also perceived as a source of structure. Indeed, it is possible to hypothesize that the ability of leaders to alter group members' stereotypes is of special significance when one considers the fact that there are strong relationships between the tendency of group members to use stereotypical thinking and their tendency to obey and conform to authority figures (cf. Adorno, Frenkel-Brunswik, Levinson, & Sanford, 1950; Rokeach, 1954; Sorrentino, Short, & Raynor, 1984). In this line, Weigel and Howes (1985) suggest that since racial prejudice is embedded in a network of beliefs and values that reflect deference to established authority and preoccupation with conventionally acceptable standards of conduct, the contemporary racist may be particularly responsive to the forceful invocation of normative standards by persons in authoritative roles. On a more general level, Rokeach (1954) asserted that an increase in dogmatism is related to more admiration or glorification of those perceived to be in a position of positive authority. That is, the authoritative leader especially can change the stereotypes of those group members who under other circumstances tend to resist the alteration of social stereotypes. It is not surprising, then, that authoritative national leaders manage to change the attitudes and stereotypic perceptions of their followers. DeGaulle and Ben-Gurion, for example, started a process of stereotype change toward the Germans, Begin toward the Egyptians, Sadat toward the Israelis, MacArthur toward the Japanese, and Nixon toward the Chinese.

Another example of individual differences among group members is the need for personal control. This need has been discussed mainly in terms of a general disposition inherent in all people (e.g., Adler, 1930; Brehm, 1966; DeCharms, 1968; Kelley, 1971; White, 1959). Clearly, however, not all individuals react identically to issues of personal control. Burger and his colleagues (e.g., Burger, 1986,1987); Burger & Arkin, 1980; Burger & Cooper, 1979) found that those high in the desire for control can be described as assertive, decisive, and active, and are motivated to act in ways that help maintain a sense of personal control. They are more likely than their counterparts to have a strong affective response to situations in which they perceive an attempt to usurp their personal control and to react to such situations with increased efforts to reassert control over events. They are also more likely to react to social pressure by intentionally resisting the impact of this pressure on their judgments and behavior. Thus, an individual group member who perceives his or her personal control threatened by the drive of the leader to change his or her stereotypes may exhibit a lack of compliance. Moreover, the stronger the pressure the leader exercises, the more these group members will be threatened by it.

On the basis of the foregoing analysis it can be hypothesized that leaders, in changing their group members' stereotypes, must do so in a way that will correspond with group members' needs rather than fight against them. Even then, introduction of such changes to the group requires that the leader establish credibility in the group as an epistemic authority, command various power resources, and have enough idiosyncrasy credits to introduce changes of norms. Not every leader in every situation will have these qualifications, but it seems that for group members, the leader is the person who is most likely to be able to exert the kind of influence that can lead to stereotype change. The next section of this chapter will focus on specific techniques leaders can use in their attempts to change stereotypes.

How Leaders Can Change Their Followers' Stereotypes

It has been argued that changes or reductions in the use of stereotypes require changes in either the content of the information held about the target group and/or the epistemic motivation underlying the creation of the stereotype. This last section of the chapter draws on the theory and research described above to suggest several specific techniques leaders can use to engender stereotype change in their followers.

Information Change as a Means of Altering Group Members' Stereotypes

It is possible to point to numerous methods by which leaders can achieve stereotype change among group members via a change in information. Among them are the reduction of the accessibility and centrality of the ingroup–outgroup categorization, the creation of positive expectations, and a change in the group norms.

Reducing the centrality and accessibility of the ingroup–outgroup categorization. A leader may reduce the centrality and accessibility of the ingroup–outgroup dichotomy and as a result this categorization may lose its power to stimulate stereotypic perception. Stereotypic categories need not be a stable fixture in a person's phenomenology. Rather they may depend on other categories which are in turn primed by contexts or events (cf. Higgins & Stangor, 1988). The leader can achieve reduction of centrality and accessibility of the specific category label assigned to outgroup members by providing information that will stimulate evaluation of the outgroup members in terms of other categories as well (cf. Linville & Jones, 1980; Taylor, 1981). As indicated by Hamilton (1981b):

> To the extent that one makes meaningful differentiations among subgroups within a larger class of persons, then one's statements about members of a subtype will constitute less sweeping characterizations. For example, to say that career women are characterized by attributes, A,B, and C, whereas housewives are X,Y, and Z still constitutes stereotyping, and such descriptions are still over-generalizations (in that, for example, not all housewives are Xish), but the number and diversity of individuals assumed [to have] a certain trait is greatly reduced in comparison to more traditional assumptions that all members of the subordinate category (i.e, women) are the same. (p. 341).

Thus, when group members evaluate the members of the outgroup, a leader can focus their attention to additional attributes by indicating various new or alternative categories to which the outgroup members may also belong. This can be done before a contact or an occasion when outgroup members are likely to be evaluated so that the ingroup is primed for considering an expanded selection of possible category labels. The shift in accessibility and centrality of the ingroup–outgroup category can also be achieved by modeling. That is, the leader, by constantly referring to the different and varied categories labels that can be applied to outgroup members, may produce change in the ingroup members' practice. Finally, the leader may point out that it is possible to gain more knowledge about the outgroup members by examining them on many dimensions rather than on one dimension only. The advantage of reducing the centrality or accessibility of the ingroup–outgroup categorization is that the leader does not have to attack the stereotype directly and does not need to use coercive or reward sources of power. Instead, this technique calls upon referent power and the ingroup members' perceptions of the leader as an epistemic authority.

Creating positive expectations. A leader can create positive expectations among ingroup members regarding the nature and outcome of future interaction with outgroup members. Rather than letting the expectations formed by stereotypical beliefs guide and regulate their interactions with outgroup members (for review see Rothbart, 1981; Snyder, 1981), the leader can provide the group members with information that creates positive expectations and overrides the effect of stereotypical beliefs. This technique is especially effective when group members do not have much personal contact with outgroup members. On the one hand, the information provided by the leader may reduce the ingroup members' reliance on the stereotype (e.g., Anderson, 1983; Gregory, Cialdini, & Carpenter 1982), and, on the other, prevent them from constructing the interaction in such a way that it will confirm their stereotypical beliefs (e.g., Slusher & Anderson, 1987). The leader's ability to provide information that will shape positive expectations is clearly related to group member's perceptions of the leader as an epistemic authority in the domains related to the interaction. This technique, when successful, may not only change the nature of the specific interaction but, in the long run, may break the vicious cycle of self-fulfilling prophecy and transform the contents of the stereotype itself.

Changing the norms of the group. A leader may establish new ingroup norms directed against the overt manifestation of biases against outgroup members. In order for the group members to accept such norms, the leader must exercise coercive or reward powers or draw on idiosyncrasy credits. Such a change may reduce the legitimacy of overt expressions of biases against outgroup members. It does not, however, necessarily produce a change in the content of the stereotype. Moreover, people are not always aware of the fact that they are using stereotypes against outgroup members. Even if members of the ingroup accept the new norm, it may not eliminate biasing practices against the members of the outgroup. Nevertheless, this technique, if successful, may have long term consequences. J.F. Kennedy's attempt to enforce civil rights for blacks in the South is one example of this method. Similarly, it is possible to point to the laws against anti-Semitism in Poland after the Second World War as another example. In both cases, the establishment of new norms was based on leaders' coercive and reward powers.

Harnessing Epistemic Motivation for Stereotype Change

It has been argued that the resistance of group members to stereotype change is often due to the fact that the stereotypical beliefs fulfill group members' important needs (cf. D. Bar-Tal, in press). The change of group members' stereotypes therefore requires an intervention that impacts on the needs that underlie and contribute to the freezing of knowledge acquisition. Rather than providing information that relates specifically to the stereotype's contents, the leader can provide information that aims at convincing group members that the need in question can be satisfied more efficiently via different (more positive) categorizations of outgroup members, or that other needs which underlie different contents are more important or more basic.

Fulfillment of needs via alteration of stereotypes' contents. A leader can indicate to group members that their needs would be better satisfied by contents that contradict their stereotypic perceptions. A specific example of this technique can be derived from the theory of social identity (e.g., Tajfel & Turner, 1979). On the assumption that group members try to maintain their unique identity by treating the outgroup members as a social category rather than as individuals, it is possible to convince them that the practice of individualizing outgroup members makes the ingroup even more unique. That is, the practice of individualizing outgroup members can be a distinct characteristic which may differentiate the ingroup from the outgroup. To use this tactic, the leader first has to convince the ingroup that deindividuation of outgroup members is a common practice among members of many groups, and if group members want to differentiate themselves from the others, they have to do something different. In the same vein, it is possible to indicate to the group members that other groups tend to emphasize the negative nature of outgroup members. A positive perception of outgroup members may also differentiate them from other groups. This can lead to the establishment of a norm that will encourage the ingroup members to be aware of and sensitive to positive characteristics of outgroup members. Such a norm is adopted when it serves group members' needs. An example are the norms that are established among various religious groups when morality is an important dimension along which the group members characterize themselves (e.g., Quakers).

Categorization and stereotyping are used to fulfill individual as well as group needs. It should be remembered that stereotyping fulfills an important informative function. It generates expectations about the characteristics of the stereotype's target. These expectations in turn guide behavior toward the target (cf. Wilder, 1981). A leader may harness this need for information by demonstrating to group members to group members that individuating information has more informative value than mere categorization. That is, by using or actively seeking individuating information, the group members may be able to react to the situation in more efficient ways and thus better master their world. Such a technique is especially effective when group members realize that individuating information about an outgroup member may lead them to different conclusions than those that are based on attributions stemming solely from that person's membership in the outgroup (see Fiske & Pavelchak, 1986).

Making salient the inconsistency between stereotypic contents and important needs.
A leader may achieve unfreezing of the group members' stereotypical beliefs by convincing them that, in doing so, they may fulfill an even more basic need than the one that underlies their stereotypical thinking. This can be achieved, for example, by manipulating the epistemic need for ambiguity. Kruglanski and Freund (1983) have demonstrated that the manipulation of the need for ambiguity left subjects less affected by ethnic stereotypes. The need for ambiguity may be induced by convincing group members that the price of committing oneself to a mistake may be high. In group research, the classic study of Sherif, Harvey, White, Hood, & Sherif (1961) demonstrates that when a more central need becomes salient, the practice of ingroup–outgroup categorization becomes less salient. In the case of Sherif and colleagues, the existence of superordinate goals common to two groups lead to the individuation of the other group's members.

Finally, in cases where minority of the group holds stereotypic categories, it is possible to use the group itself as a referent for a change. The leader may encourage specific group members to compare themselves to the group. Given the normative and informative influence the group has over its individual members, the leader may mobilize the group to put pressure on the dissenting members to make changes in their stereotypes. Alternatively, they may realize that, in order to fulfill the important need of being identified with the group, they may have to give up the overt expression of the specific stereotype.

Summary

The present chapter examines the processes and techniques by which leaders may change their follower's stereotypes. Basic questions regarding the construction and maintenance of stereotypical beliefs as well as the facilitating and limiting aspects of leader's influence over group members were examined. The analysis leads to the conclusion that although leaders are in a better position to generate changes in stereotypic content or epistemic motivations underlying the construction of stereotypes than other members of the group, it is not an easy task. Because of the important functions that stereotypical thinking and categorization fulfill for the group members as a collective and as individuals, it is likely that they will resist attempts to alter their stereotypes. Nevertheless, there are a number of specific techniques that may be used by leaders who want to change the stereotypic perceptions of their followers.

References

Abrams, D. (1987, May). *Referent informational influence, norm formation and conformity: Social categorization in the Sherif and Ash paradigms.* Paper presented at the 7th General Meeting of the European Association of Experimental Social Psychology, Varna.

Adler, A. (1930). Individual psychology. In C. Murchinson (Ed.), *Psychologies of 1930* (pp. 395–405). Worcester, MA: Clark University Press.

Adorno, I.W., Frenkel-Brunswik, E., Levinson, D.J. & Sanford, R.N. (1950). *The authoritarian personality*. New York: Harper & Row.

Allen, V.L., & Wilder, D.A. (1975). Categorization, belief similarity, and intergroup discrimination. *Journal of Personality and Social Psychology, 32*, 971–977.

Allport, G.W. (1954). *The nature of prejudice*. Reading, MA: Addison-Wesley.

Amir, Y. (1969). Contact hypothesis in ethnic relations. *Psychological Bulletin, 71*, 319–342.

Amir, Y. (1976). The role of intergroup contact in change of prejudice and ethnic relations. In P.A. Katz (Ed.), *Towards the elimination of racism* (pp. 245–308). New York: Pergamon.

Anderson, C.A. (1983). Imagination and expectation: The effect of imagining behavioral scripts on personal intentions. *Journal of Personality and Social Psychology, 45*, 293–305.

Ashmore, R.D., & Del Boca, F.K. (1981). Conceptual approaches to stereotypes and stereotyping. In D. Hamilton (Ed.), *Cognitive processes in stereotyping and intergroup behavior* (pp. 1–35). Hillsdale, NJ: Erlbaum.

Bar-Tal, D. (in press). *Group beliefs*. New York: Springer-Verlag.

Bar-Tal, Y. (1985). *Viewing leadership from the followers' perspective: A comparison with contingency models*. Unpublished doctoral dissertation, Boston University.

Bar-Tal, Y. (in press). What can we learn from Fiedler's contingency model? *Journal for Theory of Social Behavior*.

Bass, B.M. (1967). Social behavior and the orientation inventory. *Psychological Bulletin, 68*, 260–292.

Brehm, J.W. (1966). *A theory of psychological reactance*. New York: Wiley.

Brewer, M.B. (1979). In-group bias in the minimal intergroup situation: A cognitive-motivational analysis. *Psychological Bulletin, 86*, 307–324.

Brigham, J.C. (1971). Ethnic stereotypes. *Psychological Bulletin, 76*, 15–33.

Budner, S. (1962). Intolerance of ambiguity as a personality variable. *Journal of Personality, 30*, 29–51.

Burger, J.M. (1986). Desire for control and the illusion of control: The effects of familiarity and the sequence of outcomes *Journal of Research in Personality, 20*, 66–76.

Burger, J.M. (1987). Desire for control and conformity to a perceived norm. *Journal of Personality and Social Psychology, 53*, 355–360.

Burger, J.M. & Arkin, R.M. (1980). Prediction, control. and learned helplessness. *Journal of Personality and Social Psychology, 38*, 482–491.

Burger, J.M., & Cooper, H.M. (1979). The desirability of control. *Motivation and Emotion, 3*, 381–393.

Cacioppo, J.T., & Petty, R. (1984). The need for cognition: Relationship to attitudinal processes. In R.P. McGlynn, J.E. Maddux, C.D. Stoltenberg, & J.H. Harvey (Eds.), *Interfaces in psychology* (pp. 113–139). Lubbock, TX: Texas Tech Press.

Cohen, A., Stotland, E., & Wolfe, D.M. (1955). An experimental investigation of need for cognition. *Journal of Abnormal Social Psychology, 51*, ,291–297.

Commins, B., & Lockwood, J. (1978). The effects of intergroup relations of mixing Roman Catholics and Protestants: An experimental investigation. *European Journal of Social Psychology, 8*, 383–386.

DeCharms, R. (1968). *Personal causation*. New York: Academic Press.

Dion, K.L. (1973). Cohesiveness as a determinant of ingroup–outgroup bias. *Journal of Personality and Social Psychology, 28*, 163–171.

Festinger, L. (1954). A theory of social comparison processes. *Human Relations, 7*, 117–140.

Fiske, S.T., & Pavelchak, M.A. (1986). Category-based versus piecemeal-based affective responses: Developments in schema-triggered affect. In R.M. Sorrentino & T. E. Higgins (Eds.), *Handbook of motivation and cognition: Foundations of social behavior* (pp. 167–203). New York: Guilford Press.

French, J.R.P. & Raven, B.H. (1959). The bases of social power. In D. Catwright (Ed.), *Studies in social power* (pp. 118–149). Ann Arbor, MI: University of Michigan Press.

Frenkel-Brunswik, E. (1949). Intolerance of ambiguity as an emotional and perceptual personality variable. *Journal of Personality, 18,* 108–143.

Gregory, W.L., Cialdini, R.B., & Carpenter, K.M. (1982). Self-relevant scenarios as mediators of likelihood estimates and compliance: Does imagining make it so? *Journal of Personality and Social Psychology, 43,* 89–99.

Griffin, R. W., Skivington, K.D., & Moorhead, G. (1987). Symbolic and interactional perspective on leadership: An integrative framework. *Human relations, 40,* 199–218.

Hamilton, D.L. (Ed.) (1981). *Cognitive processes in stereotyping and intergroup behavior.* Hillsdale, NJ: Erlbaum.

Hamilton, D.L. (1981b). Stereotyping and intergroup behavior: some thoughts on the cognitive approach. In D. Hamilton (Ed.), *Cognitive processes in stereotyping and intergroup behavior* (pp. 333–353). Hillsdale, NJ: Erlbaum.

Heider, F. (1958). *The psychology of interpersonal relations.* New York: Wiley.

Higgins, E.T., & Stangor, C. (1988). Context-driven social judgement and memory: When "behavior angulf the field" in reconstructive memory. In D. Bar-Tal & A.W. Kruglanski (Eds.), *The social psychology of knowledge (pp. 262–298).* Cambridge, England: Cambridge University Press.

Himmerlfarb, S., & Eagly, A.H. (Eds.) (1974). *Readings in attitude change.* New York: Wiley.

Hollander, E.P. (1958). Conformity, status, and idiosyncrasy credit. *Psychological Review, 65,* 117–127.

Hollander, E.P. (1964). *Leaders, groups and influences.* New York: Oxford University Press.

Hunt, J.G. (1984). Organizational Leadership: The contingency paradigm and its challenges. In B. Kellerman (Ed.), *Leadership multidisciplinary perspectives,* (pp. 113–138). Englewood Cliffs, NJ: Prentice- Hall.

Hunt, J.G., & Larson, L. (Eds.) (1974). *Contingency approaches to leadership.* Carbondale, IL: Southern Illinois University Press.

Kagan, J. (1972). Motives and development. *Journal of Personality and Social Psychology, 22,* 51–66.

Kelley, H.H. (1971). *Attribution in social interaction.* New York: General Learning Press.

Kerr, S., & Jermier, J.M. (1978). Substitutes for leadership: Their meaning and measurement. *Organizational Behavior and Human Performance, 22,* 375–403.

Klar, Y., Bar-Tal, D., & Kruglanski, A.W. (1988). Conflict as a cognitive schema. In W. Stroebe, A. Kruglanski, D. Bar-Tal, & M. Hewstone (Eds.), *The social psychology of intergroup conflict.* (pp. 79–85). New York: Springer-Verlag.

Kruglanski, A.W. (1980). Lay epistemo-logic process and contents. *Psychological Review, 87,* 70–87.

Kruglanski, A.W. (in press). *Basic processes in social cognition: A theory of lay epistemology.* New York: Plenum.

Kruglanski, A.W., & Ajzen, I. (1983). Bias and error in human judgment. *European Journal of Social Psychology, 13,* 1–44.

Kruglanski, A.W., & Freund, T. (1983). The freezing and unfreezing of lay inferences: Effects on impressional primacy, ethnic stereotyping, and numerical anchoring. *Journal of Experimental Social Psychology, 19,* 448–468.

Kruglanski, A.W., & Jaffe, Y. (1988). Lay epistemology: A theory for cognitive therapy. In L.Y. Abramson (Ed.), *An attributional perspective in clinical psychology.* New York: Guilford Press.

Lewin, K. (1951). *Field theory in social science.* New York: Harper and Row.

Linville, P.W., & Jones, E.E. (1980). Polarized appraisal of out-group members. *Journal of Personality and Social Psychology, 38,* 689–703.

MacDonald, A.P. (1970). Revised scale for ambiguity tolerance: Reliability and validity. *Psychological Reports, 26,* 791–798.

McCall, M.W. & Lombardo, M.M. (1978). *Leadership: Where else can we go?* Durham, NC: Duke University Press.

McCauley, C., Stitt, C.L., & Segal, M. (1980). Stereotyping: From prejudice to prediction. *Psychological Bulletin, 87*, 195–208.

McGuire, W.J. (1985). Attitude and attitude change. In G. Lindzey & E. Aronson (Eds.), *Handbook of social psychology* (Vol. 2) (pp. 233–346). New York: Random House.

Moscovici, S. (1976). *Social influence and social change.* London: Academic Press.

Pettigrew, T.F. (1961). Social psychology and desegregation research. *American Psychologist, 16*, 105–112.

Pettigrew, T.F. (1979). The ultimate attribution error: Extending Allport's cognitive analysis of prejudice. *Personality and Social Psychology Bulletin, 5*, 461–476.

Pfeffer, J. (1981). Management as symbolic action: The creation and maintenance of organizational paradigms. In L.L. Cummings & B. Staw (Eds.), *Research in organizational behavior* (Vol. 3) (pp. 1–52). Greenwich, CT: JAI Press.

Rokeach, M. (1954). The nature and meaning of dogmatism. *Psychological Review, 61*, 194–204.

Rosen, E. (1964). A factor analysis of the need for cognition. *Psychological Report, 15*, 619–625.

Rothbart, M. (1981). Memory processes and social beliefs. In D. Hamilton (Ed.), *Cognitive processes in stereotyping and intergroup behavior* (pp. 145–181). Hillsdale, NJ: Erlbaum.

Rydell, S.T. & Rosen,E. (1966). Measurement and some correlates of need-cognition. *Psychological Reports, 19*, 139–165.

Sherif, M., Harvey, O.J., White, B.J., Hood, W.R., & Sherif, C.W. (1961). *Intergroup conflict and cooperation: The robber's cave experiment.* Norman: University of Oklahoma Books Exchange.

Slusher, M.P., & Anderson, C.A. (1987). When reality monitoring fails: The role of imagination in stereotype maintenance. *Journal of Personality and Social Psychology, 52*, 653–662.

Snyder, M. (1981). On the self-perpetuating nature of social stereotypes. In D. Hamilton (Ed.), *Cognitive processes in stereotyping and intergroup behavior* (pp. 183–212). Hillsdale, NJ: Erlbaum.

Sorrentino, R.M., Short, J.C., & Raynor, J.O. (1984). Uncertainty orientation: Implications for affective and cognitive view of achievement behavior. *Journal of Personality and Social Psychology, 46*, 189–206.

Staw, B.M. (1977). Motivation from the bottom up. In B.M. Staw (Ed.), *Psychological foundations of organizational behavior* (pp. 311–321). Santa Monica, CA: Goodyear.

Stephan, W.G., & Stephan, C.W. (1985). Intergroup anxiety. *Journal of Social Issuers, 41*, 157–175.

Tajfel, H. (1972). La categorization sociale. In S. Moscovici (Ed.), *Introduction a la psychologie sociale* (Vol. 1) (pp. 272–302). Paris: Larousse.

Tajfel, H., & Turner J.C. (1979). An integrative theory of intergroup conflict. In W.G. Austin & S. Worchel (Eds.), *The social psychology of intergroup relations* (pp. 33–47). Monterey, CA: Brooks-Cole.

Taylor, S.E. (1981). Categorization approach to stereotyping. In D. Hamilton (Ed.), *Cognitive processes in stereotyping and intergroup behavior* (pp. 83–114). Hillsdale, NJ: Erlbaum.

Turner, J.C. (1985). Social categorization and the self concept: A special cognitive theory of group behavior. In E.J. Lawler (Ed.), *Advances in group processes: Theory and research* (Vol. 2) (pp. 77–121). Greenwich, CT: JAI Press.

Weigel, R.H. & Howes, P.W. (1985). Conceptions of racial prejudice: Symbolic racism reconsidered. *Journal of Social Issues, 41*, 117–138.

White, R. (1959). Motivation reconsidered: The concept of competence. *Psychological Review, 66*, 297–333.

Wilder, D.A. (1978).Reduction of intergroup discrimination through individuation of the outgroup. *Journal of Personality and Social Psychology, 36*, 1361–1374.

Wilder, D.A. (1981). Perceiving persons as a group: Categorization and intergroup relations. In D. Hamilton (Ed.), *Cognitive processes in stereotyping and intergroup behavior* (pp. 213–257). Hillsdale, NJ: Erlbaum.

Wilder, D.A. (1986). Social categorization: Implications for creation and reduction of intergroup bias. In L. Berkowitz (Ed.), *Advances in Experimental Social Psychology* (Vol. 19) (pp. 291–355). New York: Academic Press.

Wilder, D.A., & Thompson, J. (1980). Intergroup contact with independent manipulation of in-group and out-group interaction. *Journal of Personality and Social Psychology, 38,* 589–603.

Yukl, G.A. (1981). *Leadership in organizations.* Englewood Cliffs, NJ: Prentice-Hall.

Chapter 12

Enhancing Intergroup Relations in Israel: A Differential Approach

Yehuda Amir and Rachel Ben-Ari

Introduction

Accelerated democratization has fostered greater interaction between heterogeneous groups in many spheres of life, strengthening in many cases intergroup conflict and tension, prejudice, and negative relations.

The purpose of this chapter is to discuss the application of knowledge about intergroup relations to deal differentially with intergroup conflict, thereby producing better intergroup understanding and perceptions. At first, three models that deal with change in intergroup relations will be presented: the contact model, the information model, and the psychodynamic model. Following that, the three major intergroup conflict situations in Israel will be analyzed, and the application of the above three models will be discussed for each situation. These three conflict situations are between Arabs and Jews, Western and Middle-Eastern Jews, and religious and secular Jews. Consequently, some general considerations will be presented which should be taken into account when dealing with intergroup change programs. Finally, an evaluation will be made emphasizing the stages of development of these conflict situations in Israel with some perspectives for the future.

The existing ways of dealing with change in intergroup relations stem from three major models: the contact model, the information model, and the psychodynamic model. The *contact model* is based on the belief that intergroup contact will lead to a change in mutual attitudes and relations of the interacting members. Underlying this belief is the assumption that contact among individuals from diverse groups creates an opportunity for mutual acquaintance, enhances understanding and acceptance among the interacting group members, and consequently reduces intergroup prejudice, conflict, and tension (Allport, 1954).

The underlying rationale for the contact model is that during contact, members of one group may discover new positive information about the members of the other group.

In order to achieve these positive ends, prerequisite conditions should be maintained during contact (Amir, 1969, 1976), such as: equal status between the members of the interacting groups, intergroup cooperation in the pursuit of common goals, contact of an intimate rather than a casual nature, and a social climate supporting the intergroup contact.

The *information model* focuses on the information available to members of one group about the other one (Brislin, 1986; Triandis, 1975). The main assumption of this model is that ignorance and lack of information comprise the basis for the development of prejudice, stereotypes, and the consequent tension between groups. Therefore, members of one group must understand the cultural characteristics of the other group before being able to understand and positively evaluate individual members of this group. An obvious way to achieve these goals is to recruit the means of mass communication and/or the educational system for the dissemination of the new information about the target culture.

Controversy exists as to the necessary focus of the information. One approach stresses an emphasis on group similarities in teaching the history of the different groups in the society, highlighting their achievements and contributions. Concentrating on the similarities should enhance intergroup attraction and understanding (Stephan & Stephan, 1984).

The second approach focuses on group differences. Misperceptions and dissimilarities are assumed to be the basis of conflict. Accordingly, the focus should be on explaining and legitimizing the differences between the groups rather than ignoring them (Triandis, 1975).

Both approaches share the underlying assumption that members of one group lack important information about the other group, and this disrupts their possible understanding and positively perceiving the latter group.

The *psychodynamic model* assumes that the negative reactions of the individual toward members of the other group stem from problems in the individual's psychodynamic process and not necessarily with the target group itself. Therefore, only the treatment of the individual's personal problems or conflicts will lead to a positive change in his or her reaction toward the other group. The implementation of this model involves programs that may help participants to understand themselves and their own mental set-up, such as personal treatment, T-groups, or "new culture groups" (Gudykunst, Hammer, & Wiseman, 1977).

Though the amount of work produced on the basis of these three models during the last 20 years is impressive (Bennett, 1986; Landis & Brislin, 1983; Peled & Bar-Gal, 1983), its quality and scientific sophistication are far from satisfying. Many "change" programs have been produced, but most have not clearly defined their objectives or theoretical basis. (There are exceptions to this rule, such as the work done by Triandis and his co-workers; see Triandis, 1975.) Implementation usually takes one of two forms. In the first, training utilizes *one* specific approach or technique which, even when theoretically well conceived and technically excellent, is not necessarily geared towards solving the major intergroup problem at hand. The second form involves workshops or training programs that employ pieces and parts of different approaches and techniques. The idea is that if one approach does not attain the desired change, another one will do the trick. This is a "cookbook" approach, mixing many ingredients in different shapes and quantities. As we have already pointed out, the quality of the final product is often questionable.

It seems obvious that a major consideration in constructing ways and techniques for changing ethnic relations concerns *what* it is one wants to change; only later can one address *how* to change it. One must specify whether program goals focus on learning about the other culture, changing the readiness for social acceptance, developing a more positive emotional orientation, changing attitudes or perceptions, and so forth. Goal delineation is crucial because different goals require different methods for their attainment. Moreover, the relevance of specific goals and the probability of their attainment may not be the same for different cultural and ethnic groups.

These issues can be illustrated by examples from intergroup relations in Israel — between Israeli Arabs and Jews, between Middle-Eastern and Western Jews, and between religious and secular Jews. Special emphasis will be given to the possibilities for producing intergroup change among youth or in the schools.

One may ask, why choose youth for achieving intergroup change within the society? The literature suggests that experiencing cross-ethnic relations, particularly in early childhood and in the schools, may be critical in children's social development. Positive relations in early childhood prepare children to live in a multiethnic society and to maintain social attitudes and behavior relatively free of prejudice toward members of other subgroups (Crain & Mahard, 1978; Inbar & Adler, 1977). There are data showing that under suitable conditions, early exposure to members of other groups reduces the likelihood that children will grow up with negative attitudes toward these groups (Amir, 1976; Hochschild, 1984; Johnson, Johnson, & Maruyama, 1984; St. John, 1975).

Undoubtedly, promoting positive intergroup relations on a national level could be promoted more effectively if institutions other than the school would also carry out such a policy. However, schools are one of the very few public institutions that encompass a cross-section of the entire population at a certain age level, and where the law empowers the government to dictate matters of policy. Moreover, interventions in schools promise to have a more long-term effect than in other social institutions since schools influence the youngest, most attainable members of society. In addition, it seems reasonable to assume that if a society prefers ethnic integration of its adults, the earlier in life this process is initiated, the easier it is for its youth to adjust to it, accept it, and form its norms and attitudes accordingly.

In the following pages, the three Israeli intergroup situations will be separately analyzed.

Arab–Jewish Relations

Historical Background

The intergroup situation of the Jewish majority and the Arab minority in Israel can be typified as two groups living side by side as distinct entities. Their relations are characterized by an almost total separation in most areas of life and by some pronounced negative feelings and attitudes towards each other. These conditions of separatism among adults are accentuated among youth. Although the adult Jews and Arabs have some contact in various work settings, no such opportunity for contact exists among youth who reside in different localities and attend separate educational institutions.

Jews are generally oblivious to the realities of the Arab sector and do not exhibit much interest in Arabs and their culture. The Jewish educational system also exhibits conspicuous neglect of the Arab issue. Among Israeli Arabs, there is a strong feeling of minority discrimination and a heightened sensitivity to their being ignored by the Jewish majority.

This state of affairs, unchanged since the establishment of the State of Israel, has been sustained and intensified by the continuous conflict and tension between Israel and its Arab neighbors. The acceptance of Arab–Jewish separation has been fostered, in part, by the shared view that this intergroup situation is temporary. The Arabs have believed that sooner or later the Jewish state would cease to exist, relieving them of a minority status. The Jews have believed that the problem of Arab presence in Israel would be solved either by Arab emigration from Israel or by massive Jewish immigration that would reduce the Arabs to an insignificant minority. Thus, neither side has attempted to change the existing status quo.

Lately, after more than 40 years of Israel's independence, and probably as a consequence of the peace treaty between Israel and Egypt, some change in the attitudes of both sides appears to have taken place. Both Jews and Arabs have gradually come to realize that they will have to continue to live together in one country. Consequently, some readiness can be detected to act towards changing the existing status quo in intergroup relations (Peled & Bar-Gal, 1983).

Goals and Techniques of Change

It is conceivable that some of the goals to be achieved are identical for both Arabs and Jews, while others may be unique to each group. Among the common goals for both Jews and Arabs in Israel one could suggest the change in negative attitudes and stereotypes, and an increased readiness to get to know, accept, and tolerate each other. As for distinctive goals, it may be worthwhile for Arabs to learn to function effectively in the Jewish society. The Israeli Arab lives in a country with a Jewish orientation, and must constantly interact with Jewish institutions and authorities. In order to function effectively, he or she must get acquainted with the Israeli *Jewish* society, its orientations, customs, and needs. We should also take into account that neither side is interested in attaining social and cultural integration, or in promoting interpersonal relations of an intimate nature, nor even liking each other too much. On the contrary, both sides favor strict cultural pluralism, and each group prefers to retain its cultural and national uniqueness, social and physical separation, as well as a distinct group identity.

In dealing with Arab and Jewish youth in Israel, we have to recognize that their separate educational systems are usually geographically distinct. In this context, it appears worthwhile to consider one of the well-accepted directions, namely, the informational one. This approach focuses on providing essential information and changing misconceptions about the other group. The attainment of the goals may be facilitated by relating first to the cognitive aspects of the problem, that is, to supplying relevant and accurate information on the issue at hand. According to theory, the factual content regarding the other culture is critical for modifying perceptions that have been based on the absence of correct information or on misinformation. Theories maintain that stereotypes stem from negative associations formed about the other group, and any positive associative content would be expected to promote the establishment of more positive attitudes and perceptions. It stands to reason that the choice of the specific learning material should be accommodated to the span of interest and the level of maturation of the child.

It seems that the informational approach may be acceptable in the schools because it is directly applicable to the general orientation of these institutions. The success of the informational approach may be increased by supplementing it with the contact approach. The latter exposes the individual to *in vivo* information about the other group. Such information may be more difficult to deny, repress, or disregard than nonexperiential information.

Some major difficulties may hinder an extensive implementation of the contact approach. As was mentioned earlier, the Arab and Jewish populations in Israel live in geographically separated communities, creating an objective barrier in establishing contact between them. In addition, close relations between the groups, especially on a bisexual basis, may be considered by both national groups as highly undesirable and even threatening. Thus, although the direct contact may be potentially powerful as a vehicle for promoting better intergroup perceptions, attitudes, and relations, its applicability to our case is limited, maybe even negligible.

The psychodynamic approach does not seem relevant to the present case. Developing self-insight and sharing of feelings is difficult to implement on large populations, since it is basically an individualistic approach and is carried out in small groups. Since our aim is to work with large student populations, this approach is not promising. Moreover, it is questionable whether this approach is at all applicable to young people who may not be mature enough to profit from interactions involving self-evaluation and sharing of feelings.

On the basis of the above considerations, it seems that the optimal orientation for the development of educational programs aiming to promote intergroup understanding and relations between the Arab and Jewish youth should be based upon the informational approach, that is, learning about the other group and its culture, possibly combined with a minimal number of intergroup meetings. We should, however, be aware of the limitations of any, even an optimal personal or interpersonal approach: Without a solution of this intergroup conflict at the macro-political level, the effects of micro-interventions will be highly limited.

Relations Between Western and Middle-Eastern Jews

Historical Background

The intergroup dynamics between Jews from Western and Middle-Eastern origin differ from those arising between Arabs and Jews. When the State of Israel was founded, Israel's society comprised about 600,000 Jews, 77 percent of them from

Western origin. In its first decade, Israel absorbed approximately one million Jews, about 60 percent of them of Western origin. Since the mid-60s, each group has comprised about half the Jewish population. The basically modern Western cultural patterns of Israeli society were easier for the Western immigrants, but these patterns made adjustment of Middle-Easterners more difficult. The latter had been educated in a conservative tradition; Western cultural patterns were strange and even at times objectionable (Eisenstadt, 1973).

Differences in cultural background and considerable differences in educational and occupational level have resulted in a high correspondence between ethnic background and social class. Westerners acquired solid social positions, while most Middle-Easterners populated the bottom of the social ladder (Smooha & Peres, 1974). In addition, the encounter was accompanied by prejudice, stereotypes, social distance, and tension.

In spite of this social–cultural cleavage, members of both groups identify themselves as members of a common Jewish people and show a basic sense of identification with the land and people of Israel. This fundamental historical, national, and religious identification with a common past is one of the bedrocks of the State of Israel. Ethnic interaction and integration constitute a national extension of the desire of all Jewish subgroups for reconstituting the social and political unity of the Jewish people, and thereby express a positive social striving which is generally accepted as a national norm in Israel. As such, there is broad acceptance of the goal of ethnic mixing at least on the level of public proclamations. No institution or group opposes this policy in principle.

A range of findings illustrates the national consensus for heightened intergroup understanding and interaction and the reduction of tension between Western and Middle-Eastern Jews. Peres (1976) found that more than two-thirds of Jewish high school students supported the blurring of ethnic differences. Along with this aspiration, both Western and Middle-Eastern students wished to attain a way of life that favored Western cultural values. Chen, Lewy, and Adler (1978) reported a different expression for the same wish: Most parents with children enrolled in integrated junior high schools favor integration, and only a minority (15 percent) oppose it. The position of ethnic acceptance implied by the findings of studies recently carried out in integrated Jewish schools is that interpersonal acceptance is predominantly determined by scholastic standing, while ethnic background is of secondary importance (Amir, Sharan, Bizman, Ribner, & Ben-Ari, 1978; Hadad & Shapira, 1977; Schwarzwald & Cohen, 1982). Another down-to-earth expression of the tendency towards interethnic mingling is the percentage of "mixed" marriages, which rose from 9 percent in 1952 to 21 percent in 1984.

It is important to note that the percentage of Middle-Easterners belonging to and regarding themselves as part of Israel's middle-class society increases from year to year. This trend contributes strongly to a de-emphasis of ethnic origin, especially among children and youth. The latter represent native Israelis, two or three generations distanced from the ethnic origin.

Goals and Techniques of Change

What seems to be the major problem to be overcome through interventions with these two ethnic groups? It is the cognitive aspect, such as the two groups not knowing each other and consequently distorting perceptions about each other? Is the root of the problem emotional-personal, such as a low self-esteem of the "minority" group? Or could it be based on prejudice or hatred—because of historical, economic, or ideological reasons?

All the above may have played some role in the past. At present, however, when we are already dealing with second- and third-generation Israelis, these features do not seem to represent the major social problem needed to be solved. The main aspects that still divide these two ethnic groups seem to be: (1) the *status* difference between the groups and (2) some *social* rejection of Middle-Easterners by Westerners.

Even with regard to status and social relations, much has changed for the better during the last two decades. Many of the Middle-Easterners previously labeled "low-class" moved economically into the middle-class and were accepted as equals by the Western group. At the same time, a change in the orientation of the Israeli society has been taking place during the last 25 years, namely, from an ethnic- to a class-conscious society. Thus, when class differences between the ethnic groups narrowed, the salience of ethnicity decreased. Still, social acceptance of Middle-Easterners by Westerners, especially when the former are from low social strata, is as yet a problem. This phenomenon seems to keep alive the social-psychological aspect of this intergroup conflict.

The practical solution to this problem that has emerged is, therefore, two-fold: (1) to narrow the status (i.e., primarily economic) gap between certain segments of the Middle-Eastern group and other strata of the Israeli society and (2) to further the social acceptance of the Middle-Eastern subgroup by the other part of the Israeli society. To achieve these goals, the focus of national effort to promote intergroup relations has, for the last 15 years, been in the area of ethnic integration in the schools.

The view developed here attributes a dual role to ethnic interaction in Israel's schools. The social-integrative dimension is concerned with increasing the cohesiveness of Israel's multiethnic Jewish population. There is also a preventive dimension to integration directed at precluding frustration among the lower status groups, who may feel that they are denied equal access to public resources. These feelings can lead to the eruption of social discord and unrest. Both factors are crucial considerations in shaping the policy of ethnic integration in Israeli society at large, as well as in the schools.

In light of this background, the question arises as to the most effective approach for reducing tension and promoting understanding and acceptance between Jewish youth from different ethnic origins. Clearly, the optimal solution in the case of Jewish and Arab groups—*learning* about the other group—does not seem to address the main difficulties of the Jewish groups. The perceived differences between these latter groups are not very marked to begin with, and both groups know each other quite well.

The approach that seems worthy of consideration is that of interaction. As already stated, this approach is generally accepted to be promising when dealing with social acceptance and attitude change regarding social-emotional aspects. Social psychological research has clearly shown that these goals can effectively be achieved through cross-ethnic interactions, while other approaches seem to have only limited effect (e.g., Amir, 1969, 1976). This is especially important because the main need and ultimate goal of promoting intergroup relations between Jewish youth from Western and Middle-Eastern backgrounds lies, as already stated earlier, in the sphere of social acceptance.

The psychodynamic approach would not be appropriate in this case because of the same reasons mentioned with regard to the Arab–Jewish conflict.

Relations Between Religious and Secular Jews

Historical Background

Since the start of modern immigration movement of Jews to Israel at the turn of this century, relations between religious (sometimes called Orthodox) and secular Jews were strained. This problem has gained momentum since the formal establishment of the State of Israel 40 years ago. During the last decade these relationships have even become, at times, extremely tense and violent.

The exact numerical ratio of these groups is hard to determine, because it depends on how one defines what constitutes being religious or secular. Still, about 50 percent of the Israeli population would define themselves as secular, about 30 percent as "traditional," and 20 percent as religious. Most research findings indicate that the traditional group feels "nearer" in numerous respects to the secular group rather than to the religious one. Thus, there is a general consensus that the secular group comprises a majority, while the religious are in the minority.

The severity of the conflict between these groups stems from its ideological basis. The two groups are divided on major aspects of daily life: What should or should not a citizen be allowed to do? What code of ethics and law should be adopted – religious or civil? These codes do determine the everyday way of life of each citizen and, therefore, major importance is attributed to it. The difficulty is that these two ways of life have many unbridgeable components, each of which founded on some ideological or religious basis on which there is naturally no agreement between the groups. The peculiarity of the relations between these two groups is that, while the majority group is willing to accept the minority group's way of life as an acceptable code of behavior for the latter, the minority group feels that its way of life, at least in its public aspects, should become the law of the country and the behavioral norm for the total population.

From a social-psychological point of view, most members of the two groups live separately, physically as well as mentally. In general, the two groups live in different communities or neighborhoods, their children go to different kindergartens and schools. Some institutions for higher education are attended primarily by one group or the other. Even in the army some units are made up exclusively of one group or the other. The religious avail themselves of religious courts, whereas the secular take advantage of secular ones.

In terms of attitudes and feelings towards different aspects of life, the two populations are extremely apart from each other. It is as if they were living on different social-psychological as well as physical planets (Barnea & Amir, 1981). Prejudice, intergroup rejection and alienation, as well as hatred and occasional violence are a natural consequence of such a social situation.

What makes things even more difficult is that lately a trend can be observed in both groups towards extremism. This is especially noticeable among religious youth, where the direction is toward religious fundamentalism. The radicalism is generally supported by the major social institutions of the religious sector. Concurrently, tendencies in the opposite direction can be detected among secular groups, which are expressed by violent acts against religious people and institutions.

Goals and Techniques of Change

What goals should be achieved through social interventions? It seems that these groups are so far apart that *any* goal of bringing the groups closer would be worthwhile considering. Yet, is there any change at all to achieve any meaningful goal through interventions at the micro-level?

Change in the cognitive or evaluative components of the attitudes towards each other is questionable. It stands to reason that these attitudes are based on highly significant differences in the mental and moral structure of the individuals involved (e.g., religious-ideological orientations and their behavioral consequences). Thus, even where these attitudes involve stereotypic thinking and have some prejudicial basis, there seems little realistic opportunity for change. The efficacy of treating the affective or behavioral components of the attitude also seems questionable. Each group actually questions the legitimacy of the other. There seems little chance for change in spheres such as interpersonal liking or social acceptance when another group's very existence threatens one's own social and ideological well-being and daily functioning.

In social situations like this, it may be difficult to set up goals for intergroup change that may be achieved through social-psychological techniques and manipulations. It may be more reasonable to assume that a real change will only come as a consequence of some events at the macro-level, such as major political or general ideological developments. These might include the attainment of a shared code of conduct by the leadership of both groups or the presence of a major outside danger threatening the physical existence of both groups. In the absence of change at the macro-level, social-psychological interventions at the individual or small-group level may be ineffective.

If the present evaluation is correct, efforts for change should be geared to the macro- rather than the micro-level. As a matter of fact, a number of years ago, the situation regarding Arab–Jewish relations was similar to the one between religious and secular. Subsequently, the peace process between Egypt and Israel in the late

'70s produced a major stimulus for positive intergroup relations between Arabs and Jews. This change provided the groundwork for possibly effective interventions regarding social-emotional change at the micro-level of individuals.

General Considerations

After having described the three intergroup conflict areas in Israel, we would like to point to some aspects that have been neglected or were dealt with rather superficially in research and theory construction in intergroup relations, as well as in the application for producing change programs and interventions in this field. We shall try to tie this up with the Israeli situation which involves a number of unique characteristics that must be taken into consideration when designing a cross-cultural training program.

Micro- Versus Macro-Level Considerations

Most cross-cultural studies and training programs have been directed at the micro-level, without necessarily taking into consideration the situation at the macro-level, namely, the relationship between the two societies. In many cases, this approach is adequate. Yet, as the analysis of intergroup relations in Israel points out, this is not always the case. In the case of the Arab/Jewish and the religious/secular conflict, macro-level considerations must be taken into account. In these two situations, the groups are involved in a major cultural conflict, in addition to a political (regarding the Jewish secular-religious case) or a national (regarding the Arab-Jewish case) one. In such a situation, achievable goals at the micro-level may be quite restricted, if not absent without prior solutions at the macro-level.

One-Group Versus Two Group Orientation

Projects on intergroup relations, especially with regard to ethnic attitudes and their change, generally concentrate on only *one* group (as, for instance, in regard to anti-Semitism or black–white relations, which generally deals with whites *or* blacks, gentiles, but not Jewish reaction, etc.). This approach may prove to be completely misleading because in ethnic relations there are at least two parties involved. The attitudes, feelings, and behavior of the group studied with regard to the other group may very well be contingent on the latter group's outlook on the former. Studying one side of the coin without taking into account the other one seems to be a major obstacle in fully understanding the complex mosaic of ethnic relations between different groups.

Cross-cultural programs also tend to focus on training representatives from *one* group in order to enable their acceptance of others, their acceptance by others, or their functioning and adjustment in another society. Little account is taken of the reaction of the other group. Moreover, the goals of the cross-cultural training and, consequently, the methods chosen to implement these goals may not be the same for both groups.

When referring to the possibilities to produce changes in the three intergroup situations, it is imperative to consider both groups which are involved in each of the conflicts. For each group, possible goals should be defined, and consequently, optional ways of achieving them should be outlined. The analysis of the three intergroup situations showed that the intergroup aims for each of the dyadic groups may be different from each other. Furthermore, different aims may require different techniques, which in turn could necessitate separate programs for each group. This may be the case for Arabs and Jews, as well as for secular and religious Jews. On the other hand, in the Jewish interethnic situation, the optional intervention seems to be the same for both groups (contact and integration) though the aims for each group may be somewhat different.

In principle, when trying to produce a positive ethnic change, both groups involved should be dealt with, in one way or another. Still, if a clear status differential between the groups is evident, special emphasis should be given to treatment of the majority or the high-status group, because in such a situation change in intergroup relations may first of all require some new orientation of the latter group toward the minority or low-status group. For our examples, this would be relevant for the Jewish-Arab and the Jewish Western/Middle-Eastern situations, where the burden of initial change lies in these cases in the hands of the former groups. Paradoxically, in the secular-religious conflict, the religious minority group tries to prescribe the rules. Thus, the initiative for intergroup change and interventions lies in this group's hands.

Multidimensional Approach

Applied work as well as some of the theoretical approaches in ethnic relations tend to lead to oversimplifications, which may consequently be misleading and even produce invalid conclusions. Thus, for instance, numerous studies in Israel found negative attitudes of Western toward Middle-Eastern Jews (e.g., Amir, Sharan, & Ben-Ari, 1984, 1985). A possible generalization and recommendation which has actually been drawn from this line of research would be to suggest the improvement of *mutual* relationships and attitudes between the two groups. However, more sophisticated research has shown that the attitudes of the Middle-Easterners toward the Westerners are not negative (e.g., Amir et al., 1978). If there is at all a problem for the Middle-Eastern group, it is their self-acceptance as an ethnic group rather than their acceptance of the other one.

Furthermore, many times intergroup relations and ethnic attitudes are multidimensional. It may be completely misleading to ignore this diversity by considering the intergroup relations as unidimensional, generally as reflected on a single positive–negative dimension. Additional dimensions seem to be ignored, including possible dimensions of intensity of feelings, involvement, and so forth. For instance, research findings clearly indicate that attitudes of Jewish Israelis toward Arabs are generally negative on an intellectual competence component, while quite positive on social-human relation aspects (e.g., Amir & Ben-Ari, 1985; Ben-Ari & Amir, 1986; Bizman & Amir, 1982). Any change program should take this into consideration; otherwise it may concentrate on a trivial rather than on important intergroup aspects.

Conflict History

Any project that aims to change the existing state between two antagonistic groups must consider the fact that its recipients may bear a history of negative feelings against each other. It seems advisable that the planned cross-cultural training start with a process of cross-cultural *un*learning in order to prepare the ground for successful change. This aspect is ignored in many change programs and should undoubtedly be taken into consideration.

All three intergroup situations in Israel have an extensive history, during which negative feelings, perceptions, and behavior patterns have developed. The depth of these negative aspects varies from one case to the other. The Jewish interethnic situation seems to be the easiest, while the other ones are much more severe.

Motivation

Motivation must also be addressed. Underlying any attempt at fostering learning are assumptions regarding the positive motivation of the learner. Under such conditions the design of a training project must search for ways to cope with this problem.

As the Israeli situation illustrates, this condition is not always there. If one can talk at all about positive motivation in regard to the Israeli intergroup situations, this may be found in the minority or low-status groups, which have probably something to gain from a change. This refers to the Middle-Eastern group in the Jewish intergroup conflict and to the Arab group in the Arab–Jewish situation. The motivation of the weaker group to produce a change is obviously stronger than for the stronger group. A possible motivation for the stronger group to promote or to accept change may stem from fear of negative reactions from the weaker group if no change takes place. As for the religious–secular conflict, there seems to be a hesitancy among members of both groups to initiate change. This in turn reduces the motivation for action and social intervention and may even strengthen negative motivation, specifically in the direction of intergroup avoidance and severing of interpersonal ties.

Intergroup Relations in Israel—Where To?

This chapter tried to emphasize the importance of evaluating and defining the socially relevant goals for intergroup change before launching on an intervention program in this area. Only after the goals that should and could be achieved are clearly defined should programs relevant to these goals be set up to achieve them.

This argument was exemplified by the three main intergroup conflicts presently prevailing in Israel. Comparing these three situations, it becomes apparent that each of them is at a different stage of development: The Jewish interethnic situation is at the most advanced stage, the Jewish secular-religious situation is at the least advanced, and the Jewish-Arab situation falls somewhere between the other two. These stages of development can be characterized and ranked (from least to most advanced) as follows. *First stage*: Agreement between the groups on the principle of coexistence; *Second stage*: Agreement between the groups regarding the objectives to be achieved in the context of coexistence; *Third (most advanced) stage*: Finding ways and means of achieving these objectives.

The relations between the Jewish ethnic groups can be located at the third stage. As stated above, all parties agree on the need for coexistence in Israel and on the necessity of integration of different ethnic groups. Moreover, there is complete agreement on the various objectives which must be achieved in the context of integration. (All agree, for example, upon the need for integration in education, as outlined above.) At present, we are at the stage of developing ways and techniques for the achievement of these objectives and investigating their effectiveness. The third stage of intergroup relations is characterized by a relatively calm dialogue, and agreement can be reached via objective investigation and evaluation of techniques, in contrast to the subjective nature of the conflicts characterizing the first two stages.

The relations between Arabs and Jews can be located at the second stage of development. Parallel to the previous case, there is a basic agreement on the need for coexistence. In the context of Arab-Jewish relations, however, unlike that of Jewish interethnic relations, this principle was not taken for granted. For many years, each side hoped to claim the country as its own homeland. Still, over time and in view of the circumstances, both sides despaired of realizing this dream. They came to accept the principle of coexistence, thus entering the second stage of defining objectives within the framework of coexistence.

It is true that in addition to mutually accepted aims, each party has objectives not accepted by the other. These can be divided into aims on the "micro" and on the "macro" levels. Still, it would appear that there is more agreement on the former, such that a move to the third stage, of discussion of objectives and of the optimal means of achieving them, is possible and has indeed taken place. However, the resolution of macro-level contested aims has yet to advance beyond the second stage, and changes at the macro-level are necessary before further progress can be made. Clearly, the involvement of political forces and national interests on "macro" issues makes a positive change at this level extremely difficult.

The relationship between religious and secular Jews is the least advanced of the three intergroup conflicts in Israel. This conflict is still at the first stage of development, not yet agreeing on the principle of coexistence. As described above, the relationship between the Jewish religious groups is characterized by tension due to attempts on the part of each faction to worsen the conditions in which the other lives.

Thus, it seems that the religious and secular Jews are still far from the stage of formulating common aims. At this point they negate the possibility of any sort of cooperation. The difficulty of achieving any sort of change in this conflict area is aggravated by the fact that it is based upon an ideological conflict involving major "macro" forces (e.g., political powers).

To what extent can the reasons for the differential development of these three sets of intergroup relationships be understood? While a definitive explanation of this issue is beyond our reach today, we may attempt an evaluation of the forces, either aiding or retarding the advancement of these relationships.

As stated above, the Jewish interethnic situation is characterized by general agreement on the ideal of coexistence. The salient ideology among Jews in Israel of "ingathering of the exiles" and of complete social integration supports intergroup coexistence, which simultaneously constitutes both a reason and a necessary condition for the existence of the Israeli society in Israel. These phenomena may support the achievement of harmonious coexistence in the face of numerous difficulties and obstacles.

In contrast to this situation, the agreement on the principle of coexistence between Arabs and Jews can be characterized as "making the best of a bad deal." Since the other group cannot be done away with, there is no choice but to accept the fact of coexistence and to minimize the conflict and friction engendered by it.

The relationship between the secular and religious Jews differs from both Arab–Jewish and Jewish ethnic relations. In this case, neither side has despaired of "defeating" the other and forcing the "loser" to submit to the rules of the "victor." Thus, neither side sees any reason to compromise on coexistence which, by its nature, entails the acceptance of the other, and the making of concessions by both sides. Furthermore, coexistence of secular and religious Jews implies better acquaintanceship, increased intimacy, and even integration between the two. All of these options pose a very real threat to the continued existence of each of the groups. This threat can only be defused by total separation between them and rejection of the other group.

In sum, an attempt was made in this chapter to show that with regard to one of these conflicts—between Israeli Arabs and Jews—an informational approach would be the optimal to produce change for the pertinent goals. For the conflict between the different Jewish ethnic groups, the contact–interaction approach seems preferable. Finally, to improve relations between religious and secular Jews, solutions should be sought at the macro-level rather than concentrating on micro-level interventions.

Acknowledgments. The authors would like to thank Dr. Michael Hoffman for his thoughtful suggestions on a previous version of this chapter.

References

Allport, G.W. (1954). *The nature of prejudice.* Cambridge, MA: Addison-Wesley.

Amir, Y. (1969). Contact hypothesis in ethnic relations. *Psychological Bulletin, 71,* 319–342.

Amir, Y. (1976). The role of intergroup contact in change of prejudice and ethnic relations. In P.A. Katz (Ed.), *Towards the elimination of racism* (pp. 245–308). New York: Pergamon Press.

Amir, Y., & Ben-Ari, R. (1985). International tourism, ethnic contact and attitude change. *Journal of Social Issues, 41*(3), 105–115.

Amir, Y., Sharan, S., & Ben-Ari, R. (Eds.) (1984). *School desegregation: Cross-cultural perspectives.* Hillsdale, NJ: Erlbaum.

Amir, Y., Sharan, S., & Ben-Ari, R. (Eds.) (1985). *Integration in education.* Tel-Aviv: Am-Oved. (In Hebrew).

Amir, Y., Sharan, S., Bizman, A., Ribner, M., & Ben-Ari, R. (1978). Attitude change in desegregated Israel high schools. *Journal of Educational Psychology, 70,* 63–70.

Barnea, M., & Amir, Y. (1981). Mutual attitudes and attitude change following intergroup contact of religious and nonreligious students. *Journal of Social Psychology, 115,* 65–71.

Ben-Ari, R., & Amir Y. (1986). Cultural information, intergroup contact and change in ethnic attitudes and relations. In W. Stroebe, A. Kruglanski, D. Bar-Tal, & M. Hewstone (Eds.), *The social psychology of intergroup and international conflict: Theory, research and application* (pp. 151–165). New York: Springer.

Bennett, J.M. (1986). Modes of cross-cultural training. *International Journal of Intercultural Relations, 10,* 117–134.

Bizman, A., & Amir, Y. (1982). Mutual perceptions of Arabs and Jews in Israel. *Journal of Cross-Cultural Psychology, 13,* 461–469.

Brislin, R.W. (1986). A culture general assimilator. *International Journal of Intercultural Relations, 10,* 215–234.

Chen, M., Lewy, A., & Adler, C. (1978). *The junior high school research project: Process and outcome.* Unpublished manuscript, Tel-Aviv University. (In Hebrew.)

Crain, R.L., & Mahard, R.E. (1978). Desegregation and black achievement: A review of the research. *Law and Contemporary Problems, 42*(3), 17–56.

Eisenstadt, S.N. (1973). *The Israeli society: Background, development and problems* (2nd ed.). Jerusalem: Magnes Press. (In Hebrew.)

Gudykunst, W.B., Hammer, M.R., & Wiseman, R.L. (1977). An analysis of an integrated approach to cross-cultural training. *International Journal of Intercultural Relations, 1,* 99–110.

Hadad, M., & Shapira, R. (1977). Commanding resources and social integration. *Megamot, 23,* 161–173. (In Hebrew.)

Hochschild, J. (1984). *The new American dilemma.* New Haven, CT: Yale University Press.

Inbar, M., & Adler, C. (1977). *Ethnic integration in Israel: A comparative case study of Moroccan brothers who settled in France and in Israel.* New Brunswick, NJ: Transaction.

Johnson, D., Johnson, R., & Maruyama, G. (1984). Goal interdependence and interpersonal attraction in heterogeneous classrooms: A metanalysis. In N. Miller & M.B. Brewer (Eds.), *Groups in contact: The psychology of desegregation* (pp. 187–212). Orlando, FL: Academic Press.

Landis, D., & Brislin, R.W. (Eds.) (1983). *Handbook of intercultural training* (Vol. 2). New York: Pergamon.

Peled, T., & Bar-Gal, D. (1983). *Intervention activities in Arab-Jewish relations: Conceptualization, classification and evaluation.* Jersulam: The Israel Institute for Applied Social Research.

Peres, Y. (1976). *Ethnic relations in Israel.* Tel-Aviv: Sifriat Poalim. (In Hebrew.)

Schwarzwald, J., & Cohen, S. (1982). The relationship between academic tracking and the degree of interethnic acceptance. *Journal of Educational Psychology, 74,* 588–597.

Smooha, S., & Peres, Y. (1974). Ethnic inequality in Israel. *Megamot, 20,* 5–42. (In Hebrew.)

Stephan, W.G., & Stephan, C.W. (1984). The role of ignorance in intergroup relations. In N. Miller & N.B. Brewer (Eds.), *Groups in contact: The psychology of desegregation* (pp. 229–255). Orlando, FL: Academic Press.

St. John, N.H. (1975). *School desegregation outcomes for children.* New York: Wiley.

Triandis, H.C. (1975). Culture training, cognitive complexity, and interpersonal attitudes. In R. Brislin, S. Bochner & W. Lonner (Eds.), *Cross-cultural perspectives on learning* (pp. 39–77). Beverly Hills, CA: Sage and Wiley/Halstead.

Author Index

Subject Index

Springer Series in Social Psychology
Recent Titles

Entrapment in Escalating Conflicts: A Social Psychological Analysis
Joel Brockner/Jeffrey Z. Rubin

The Attribution of Blame:
Causality, Responsibility, and Blameworthiness
Kelly G. Shaver

Language and Social Situations
Joseph P. Forgas (Editor)

Power, Dominance, and Nonverbal Behavior
Steve L. Ellyson/John F. Dovidio (Editors)

Changing Conceptions of Crowd Mind and Behavior
Carl F. Graumann/Serge Moscovici (Editors)

Changing Conceptions of Leadership
Carl F. Graumann/Serge Moscovici (Editors)

Friendship and Social Interaction
Valerian J. Derlega/Barbara A. Winstead (Editors)

An Attributional Theory of Motivation and Emotion
Bernard Weiner

Public Self and Private Self
Roy F. Baumeister (Editor)

Social Psychology and Dysfunctional Behavior:
Origins, Diagnosis, and Treatment
Mark R. Leary/Rowland S. Miller

Communication and Persuasion:
Central and Peripheral Routes to Attitude Change
Richard E. Petty/John T. Cacioppo

Theories of Group Behavior
Brian Mullen/George R. Goethals (Editors)

Changing Conceptions of Conspiracy
Carl F. Graumann/Serge Moscovici (Editors)

Controversial Issues in Social Research Methods
Jerald Greenberg/Robert G. Folger

The Social Psychology of Intergroup Conflict
*Wolfgang Stroebe/Arie W. Kruglanski/Daniel Bar-Tal/Miles Hewstone
(Editors)*

The Social Psychology of Facial Appearance
Ray Bull/Nichola Rumsey

Attitudes and Behavioral Decisions
Arnold Upmeyer (Editor)

Springer Series in Social Psychology
Recent Titles